THE OPEN PHILOSOPHY
AND THE OPEN SOCIETY

THE OPEN PHILOSOPHY
AND THE OPEN SOCIETY

a Reply to Dr. Karl Popper's Refutations of Marxism

By MAURICE CORNFORTH

INTERNATIONAL PUBLISHERS
NEW YORK

Copyright © Maurice Cornforth 1968

Library of Congress Catalogue Card Number: 68-27395
Printed in the United States of America

FOREWORD

The object of this book is to discuss fundamental ideas of Marxist philosophy and their implications for social theory and socialist policy. My premise is to accept Marxism as essentially a scientific outlook which seeks to work out and test ideas and policies, in all spheres, in accordance with the canons of rational scientific discussion and in no other way.

I have chosen the method of constructing this book as a reasoned reply to criticisms of Marxism. And of all the critics, I have picked on a single one, Dr. Karl Popper, as the one to answer. I have done this because Dr. Popper's whole case against Marxism rests on his contention that it is nothing but a system of dogmas, so that his arguments against Marxism provide a ready-made and accommodating peg on which to hang the argument that Marxism is, on the contrary, a rational scientific discipline.

There is the more reason for a Marxist to tackle the case put against Marxism by Dr. Popper because not only is he perhaps the most eminent of our contemporary critics, and not only does he present his case with great ability and force, but because, so far as I can judge, the points he makes against Marxism include practically all the main points against it which carry most weight in contemporary debate. Of course, some of his arguments (for example, those he directs against Marx's *Capital*, or again, against the theory and practice of socialist economic planning) are borrowed from arguments originally put forward in greater detail by other critics. However, I have preferred to stick throughout to tackling the case as put by Dr. Popper rather than encumber the discussion with references to the writings of others who have put the same case before or since. Dr. Popper's arguments against Marxism are extremely comprehensive, and it is high time someone tried to answer him in detail.

Dr. Popper himself occupies an unchallengeable position in modern letters as an exponent of principles of scientific method. His contributions in this sphere, first in his famous book *Logik der Forschung* (published in English under the title *Logic of Scientific Discovery*) and then in numerous articles in English and American journals, have had and continue to have a great and beneficial influence on modern thought. I would like to emphasise that I do not seek to attack or refute all that Dr. Popper has to say about science or about society. On the contrary, I accept and agree with a good deal of it. This book is not a polemic against Dr. Popper, but an answer to his polemic against Marxism. I am seeking only to answer his charges and (as the sequel will show, this is often the right word) smears against Marxism, so as to make as clear as I can what Marxism really stands for, and to show that a rational and scientific approach to social problems (which Dr. Popper professes to demand) lends support to Marxism.

Dr. Popper has popularised in sociology and politics the use of the word "open". In the title of this book, and in the discussions it contains, I have ventured to borrow it from him. A society is "open" when there is nothing to stop individuals, if they choose, from developing their abilities and personalities to the fullest extent, and when social institutions are so ordered that they can be changed and developed, by decision of the members of society, in any way that will assist individuals to live more fully and more freely. On the other hand, it is "closed" when the members of society are bound by rules and regulations, conventions and prejudices, strictly enforced, which restrict their choices and impose on them a pattern of life rigidly limited by institutions which may not be changed.

The open society and progress towards the open society demand (so Dr. Popper declares, and I agree with him) an open way of thinking, characterised by rationality as opposed to blind belief in dogmas. For the open society we need an outlook which rejects dogmas and judges things only on the basis of evidence, always ready to think again when experience falsifies earlier conclusions. This I have ventured to call an "open philosophy".

Dr. Popper's objection to Marxism is that he imagines it to be a closed philosophy, a system of dogmas, what he calls "a reinforced dogmatism". And inevitably, so he maintains, the Marxist dogmas enjoin a corresponding closed attitude in social life—the imposition on society of rules, regulations, tyrannies of custom, enforced by political tyranny, which effectively close for individuals, and for society as a whole, all the avenues of free development.

But, one may ask, is a society really "open" when social production is tied to ensuring the accumulation of capital from surplus value, and the enjoyment of benefits and privileges by some depends on exploiting the labour of others? And can one's mind be really "open" so long as one is unable to see that such is the case with contemporary capitalist society, or to see the possibilities of advance which could be opened up for mankind if only the exploitation of man by man were done away with? So far from Marxism being a system of dogmas to close our minds and discourage the unfettered exercise of reason to work out how best to promote freedom and the brotherhood of men, it systematises a way of thinking to open our minds to the appreciation of things as they are and the practical possibilities of changing them for the better.

The open way of thinking is the way of thinking which bases itself on demonstrable rules for finding out how things are, and which strives to appreciate, therefore, the actual conditions of our material existence and the necessary conditions for changing them—which therefore closes the mind to misrepresentations and dogmas, and opens the mind to the real possibilities of human life. That is why I have called the philosophy of Marxism "the open philosophy" and the communist society towards which Marxism directs our sights "the open society".

A good deal of this book is controversial—not only because I engage in a controversy with opponents of Marxism but because there is controversy within Marxism itself. Inevitably, to answer the objections of opponents, especially the kind of objections Dr. Popper makes about Marxism being a dogma and the policies it advocates policies of dictatorship and tyranny, involves discussions which are controversial as among friends. In this connection I cannot but conclude this Foreword by acknowledging a particular debt of gratitude to R. Palme Dutt, who read through most of this book in the form in which I first drafted it. I alone am responsible for the point of view I express and for such unclarities and fallacies as may be found in it. But by his critical observations he helped me on several points to make it more clear and, I hope, more cogent than it would otherwise have been.

M. C.

London, October 1967

NOTE

Dr. Popper's anti-Marxist writings are contained in three of his books, from which I have quoted extensively. For this purpose I have adopted the following abbreviations in references to them:

The Open Society and its Enemies, Vol. 1		1–OS
	Vol. 2	2–OS
The Poverty of Historicism		PH
Conjectures and Refutations		CR

Page references refer to the fourth (revised) paperback edition of *The Open Society and its Enemies*, 1962; to the paperback edition of *The Poverty of Historicism*, 1961; and to the original edition of *Conjectures and Refutations*, 1963.

CONTENTS

PART ONE

TOWARDS AN OPEN PHILOSOPHY

THE SCIENTIFIC CHARACTER OF MARXISM

I. MARXISM IN WONDERLAND

"You should say what you mean," the March Hare told Alice at the Mad Tea Party. "I do," Alice replied. "At least, I mean what I say— that's the same thing you know." "Not the same thing a bit!" said the Hatter.

The rather lengthy expositions and refutations of Marxism by Dr. K. R. Popper place Marxists in the same predicament as the Hatter placed Alice. Regardless of what we may say, he undertakes to say what we mean—and then to show that it is both absurd and obnoxious.

Dr. Popper regards Marxism as a "reinforced dogmatism". To deal with it, he has himself devised a method of reinforced refutation. He says what Marxism means, and shows how wrong it is. If any Marxist objects, "But that is not what we Marxists say!" he replies, "It is what Marxism means." How can one answer such a refutation? As Dr. Popper says in his preface to the second edition of *The Open Society and its Enemies*, "my criticism was devastating".

His exposition, explanation and refutation of Marxism is based on the assumption that Marxism is essentially unscientific. How unscientific it is he shows in *The Open Society and its Enemies*, where he expounds and exposes first Plato and then Hegel, and then warns the reader— Marxism is like *them*! After such an introduction the reader's prejudices are thoroughly aroused, and he is well prepared to assist at the final exposure and dissolution of Marxist dogmas.

What Marx did, however, was not to follow blindly in the footsteps of Plato and Hegel, but to work out the foundations of the scientific theory of man and society. That is what he said he tried to do, and that is what he did. Marxism is scientific. Marx's achievement was to apply the standard methods of science to the study of society and the solution of social problems. By so doing he performed a signal service for the working-class movement, for his scientific theory (*a*) demonstrated the character and consequences of the exploitation of labour in modern society, (*b*) formulated a practical aim of ending that exploitation and its consequences, and (*c*) supplied principles on which to decide the practical policies necessary for realising the aim. Only the application and continued application of scientific method could produce that kind of practical understanding and purpose of which Marx and Marxists consider the working-class movement to stand in need.

Marxism stands or falls entirely by whether it can or cannot justify its scientific claims. But if it is, as is claimed, scientific, then it must be allowed to share the generally recognised character of scientific theories and views—namely, that it stakes no claim to finality or completeness but keeps on adding to, modifying, reformulating and rearranging its generalisations and recommendations as new experiences and new problems are presented. A Marxist is, presumably, a follower of Marx; and Marxism is the *continuation* of Marx's work in developing the scientific theory of the working-class movement and of socialism. Yet when Marxists try to press forward the scientific development of Marxism—and that includes not only expansion and elaboration but correction—our critics tell us: Stop! Marxism is unscientific and is not allowed to develop like that.

Dr. Popper has himself written a good deal about scientific method, notably in his book *The Logic of Scientific Discovery* and in the papers collected in the volume *Conjectures and Refutations*. His contributions to the subject are important and enlightening; and if I shall venture to suggest that he has not said the last word (and he himself, I suppose, would hardly claim that) it is not intended to belittle in the least the value, importance and originality of what he has said. While answering his refutations of Marxism I am well aware of how much we stand in his debt. We are indebted to him in two ways. First, the points he has made about "the logic of scientific discovery" are of great assistance in formulating and explaining the actual scientific procedures of Marxism. Second, his efforts to say what we mean are of great assistance at least in making clear what we do not mean. So far as we are concerned, we say what we mean and also (which Dr. Popper, like the March Hare and the Mad Hatter, seems to find it hard to appreciate) we mean what we say. We say that Marxism is based on scientific procedures and can only continue on that basis. And we mean it!

2.   IS MARXISM FALSIFIABLE?

In his writings on scientific method Dr. Popper dealt with the question of the criterion of demarcation between scientific theories, on the one hand, and non-scientific (pseudo-scientific or metaphysical) theories on the other. It is generally agreed that a theory is scientific only if it is capable of being *tested* by experience. He pointed out that to be capable of being tested is to be capable of being *falsified*. Thus it is not enough to be able to describe types of instances which would *confirm* a theory; it is necessary to be able to describe what sort of instance would *falsify* it. "The criterion of the scientific status of a theory is its falsifiability" (CR. 37).

This point, a valid and important one, can be appreciated by reflecting that to test anything it is essential to have a criterion of *failure*. If there is only a vague idea of what is required to pass the test, but no clear idea of what will bring failure, then it is possible to wangle almost anything past the test and the test is as good as worthless. Or if the test is so devised that anything will pass it, then it is no test at all. This, Dr. Popper insists, goes for scientific theories. "It is easy to obtain confirmations for nearly every theory—if we look for confirmations. Every genuine test of a theory is an attempt to falsify it, or refute it. Testability is falsifiability" (CR. 36).

It is quite possible, as he and others have pointed out, for certain ingenious theories to masquerade under the title of science when they are in fact non-scientific—since they have been so constructed as to be incapable of falsification. They are so constructed that *whatever* happens fits in with the theory, and *nothing*, therefore, can falsify it.

It has been suggested that certain Freudian theories may be of this sort. Freud said that every man wishes to kill his father and marry his mother. If a man objects that he does not in fact wish to do such things, Freud replies that of course he is not aware of so wishing because the wish has been repressed. And in general, *whatever* a man consciously wishes and does, it can *always* be made out to be linked with and not incompatible with his unconscious oedipus-complex. But this puts the Freudian theory outside the bounds of science. It is not a scientific but a pseudo-scientific theory. It is a "reinforced dogmatism", so built up or reinforced as to be unfalsifiable or irrefutable.

These considerations suggested to Dr. Popper the happy idea of contriving a final refutation of Marxism. People had long been trying in vain to cite facts which would refute Marx's social theories. No wonder they did not succeed, for these theories are so devised as to be irrefutable—and that refutes them!

If Marxist social theories *were* irrefutable in this sense, then they would indeed be unscientific. But the fact that a theory has not been falsified does not imply that it is unscientific because unfalsifiable. For example, the law of the conservation of energy (the first law of thermodynamics) is generally regarded as a genuine and well-tested scientific law; but it has not been falsified. We can quite well say what sort of things could happen if the law of the conservation of energy did not hold; the point is, it does hold and they do not happen. Similarly, we can quite well say what sort of things could happen if the basic laws formulated by Marx as governing social development did not hold; the point is, they do hold, and these things do not happen. Unhappily for the refutation, Marxism is *not* irrefutable. Its basic laws, like those of thermodynamics, correspond with how things in fact go. What they forbid to happen never does happen.

Dr. Popper says, with truth, that "every 'good' scientific theory is a prohibition: it forbids certain things to happen" (CR. 36). Thus a "good" or "genuine" scientific law, as distinct from a pseudo-scientific one, can always be expressed in the form: "So and so cannot happen." For example, the first law of thermodynamics tells us "You cannot build perpetual motion machines", and the second law tells us "You cannot build machines that are one hundred per cent efficient". This way of expressing laws brings out very well their practical value. Thus the laws of thermodynamics instruct machine-technologists about the limits of practical possibility within which they can operate (indeed, it was in connection with the construction of steam engines that these laws were first discovered). An engine cannot run without fuel, and the task of the designer is to construct an engine in which the energy of the fuel will be most efficiently converted into work. That allows a very large but not unlimited range of possibility for the construction of engines. But, of course, if someone did contrive an engine which ran without fuel, or which was one hundred per cent efficient (it would be a kind of fairy-tale engine), that would falsify the laws of thermodynamics—and technologists would have to undertake some new and very fundamental rethinking of their concepts. No one expects this to happen, but it is imaginable (i.e. it can be described in fairy tales). The laws of thermodynamics are thus falsifiable but not falsified. That is, no doubt, why they are considered to be such very "good" laws.

The fundamental laws which Marx formulated as governing social development similarly "forbid certain things to happen". They say that there must always be a certain kind of correspondence between forces of production and relations of production. This allows all manner of things to be done within the bounds of such correspondence, but denies the possibility of going outside those bounds. From the point of view, therefore, of social action—or what Dr. Popper calls "social engineering"—it says what is possible and what is not possible. For example, to use all the resources of modern technology for human welfare is possible, but not without reconstituting property relations in correspondence with the social character of production—it is not possible to combine such use of resources with capitalist ownership and capitalist profit. What Marxism "forbids to happen" can be *imagined* as happening—indeed, in many democratic countries the principal political parties make a parade of such imaginings at every general election; but it never happens. If uninterrupted economic development were to be combined with capitalist enterprise and capitalist profit, then Marx's theory would be falsified—just as if a perpetual motion machine were built the laws of thermodynamics would be falsified.

The "social engineering" which treats Marxism as reinforced dogmatism is thus just about on a level with ordinary engineering which treats the laws of thermodynamics as reinforced dogmatism. Dr. Popper maintains that the true scientist, always eager to test his theories in every conceivable way, devotes his main energies to trying to contrive falsifications. This view of scientific work overlooks the fact that a scientific attitude also demands the guidance of practical undertakings in accordance with scientific discovery. Dr. Popper seems to think that a scientific attitude towards the social discoveries claimed by Marx would enjoin continually trying all manner of means to go against the laws which Marx formulated, in the hopes of falsifying them. The scientifically-minded person must try to preserve capitalism so as to see whether Marx's laws cannot be falsified. The Marxist who, accepting the laws, advises the abolition of capitalism, is a mere dogmatist and lacks any conception of the ways of science. This is like saying that chemists should practise alchemy, in the hopes of falsifying the laws of chemistry; and that engineers should devote all their ingenuity to constructing perpetual motion machines.

But Dr. Popper formulates his objection to Marxism also along the following lines. Marxism forbids certain things to happen, but nevertheless *some* things which it forbids *do* happen. In that case the Marxists admit to having made a mistake, but say that, all the same, "the fundamentals" of the theory have not been falsified. That shows, says Dr. Popper, that the theory is nothing but a reinforced dogmatism.

It has formulated its "fundamentals" in such a way that they cannot be falsified. It is not a scientific theory, which submits itself to tests, but an unscientific theory which evades every test.

The Russian Revolution has been alleged, by Dr. Popper and others, to provide a case in point. Marx certainly said at one time that the socialist revolution would begin in the most advanced industrial countries. He "forbade" it to begin anywhere else—but in fact it began in Russia. But when this falsification of an earlier prediction (or prohibition, for every prediction is a prohibition) took place, Marxists simply said that certain specific features of social development in particular countries had been underestimated; the revolution began in Russia because "the chain breaks at its weakest link".

Does a candid examination of this example really support the allegation that Marxism is reinforced dogmatism? On the contrary, Marxism remains falsifiable. Marxists can, it is true, readily account for the socialist revolution starting in Russia. But if it had started, say, in the Far East or Central Africa, or if it had never started at all, that could not have been accounted for, and really would have falsified Marxism. But it did start, and started where Marxism permitted it to start. In point of fact Marx himself, in his later correspondence, wrote that his observations were leading him to the conclusion that revolution was unlikely after all to start in the industrial countries. Things were happening in these countries to postpone the revolution he had earlier expected, but in Russia to accelerate it. His approach to questions was the normal one of a scientific thinker who is continually ready to revise former estimates in the light of new evidence, but does not find it necessary to scrap the whole fundamental theory of his science every time such a revision is indicated.

Similarly the fact that after the Second World War there was for many years full employment in Britain, in contradiction to Marx's statements about capitalism always creating "a reserve" of unemployment, does not lead British Marxists to conclude that the whole Marxist theory of capitalism and socialism has been falsified, but only that certain special conditions had temporarily come into existence in Britain.

Scientists generally agree that if predictions made in the light of a general theory are falsified, and it is then proposed to "save" the theory by adding "supplementary hypotheses", the theory must none the less be scrapped if the *only* evidence offered for the supplementary hypotheses is that they save the theory. Thus, for example, the old

Ptolemaic theory that the planets move in circular orbits round the earth failed to accord with observations, but was "saved" by postulating irregularities, or epicycles, in the motions of the planets. However, because the only evidence offered for these epicycles was that they saved the theory, scientists now generally agree that observation has falsified the Ptolemaic theory.

It has been suggested that this is how Marxism is "saved" whenever what happens deviates from a prediction. But in fact the Marxist procedure has never been to invent supplementary hypotheses. For example, to account for full employment in Britain we do not invent a supplementary hypothesis—a kind of economic epicycle. We simply examine what has actually happened, which has by no means exceeded the bounds of possibility allowed by the general theory of Marxism, and find that it has led to consequences predictable and accountable within the theory. And similarly with the Russian Revolution.

The rescue of Marxism in such cases is interestingly paralleled by a second example from the theory of planetary motions. After the Ptolemaic theory had been supplanted by Kepler's laws, certain irregularities were observed in the motion of the planet Uranus which did not accord with the predictions made by the laws. So it was suggested that there was in fact another planet, whose existence had previously passed unnoticed, the influence of which would account for the irregularities. Sure enough, this other planet (now named Neptune) was observed when telescopes were directed in the right direction—so Kepler's laws were "saved", since they did not "forbid" there being another planet but allowed for its existence. It is just the same with Marxism, when social "irregularities" (such as the Russian Revolution or full employment in Britain) take place—we look for and find the causes of these "irregularities".

3.   FUNDAMENTALS OF MARXIST SOCIAL THEORY

Is there really anything wrong with saying, as Marxists say, that the "fundamentals" of Marxist social theory are not refuted even when certain particular expectations of events are falsified? Is it really a defect of a theory when its fundamentals are so framed that a rather wide range of possible happenings can be fitted into it? If so, then not only Marxism but a number of other theories too, generally regarded as scientific, must be relegated into the category of pseudo-science. Scientists are for ever being faced with failures of prediction, which they manage nevertheless to fit into the framework of their theories; and that is how the theories generally develop.

To deal with the question of whether Marxism is science or pseudo-science it is advisable to begin by asking what the fundamental propositions of Marxist social theory actually say, and how Marx arrived at them.

Before Marx formulated these scientific propositions, social events were generally accounted for in terms of people's intentions and motives, and the structure and institutions of society in terms of the prevailing ideas. This way of accounting for social phenomena really does suffer from the defect of being able to account for anything. People always have intentions, and whatever may happen it can always be accounted for by saying that certain people acted with certain intentions—if what happens is what they intended, well and good; if not, then that is because they made a miscalculation, or because other people with other intentions interfered with them. Moreover, because it is practically impossible ever to discover with certainty what people's intentions really were, it is always possible to attribute to them intentions fitting in with what took place, and so to account for what took place by the attributed intentions. Similarly, whatever the structure and institutions of society, it can always be said that they came to exist because certain people thought that was the best way of arranging social affairs, or else because some people's good intentions were frustrated by other people. This type of theory (described by Marx as "idealist", because it makes intentions and ideas the primary motive force in society) can therefore be judged unscientific precisely on the criteria proposed by Dr. Popper for distinguishing unscientific from scientific theories. Its obvious short-coming is that it leaves one still asking—what accounts for people's different intentions and ideas, and for some being more successfully realised than others?

Marx's formulation of fundamental propositions for social science disposed of such previously unscientific ways of interpreting and accounting for events in very much the same way that, in other branches of inquiry, previously unscientific theories were disposed of when certain fundamental propositions for the respective sciences were formulated. For example, the old type of physics, derived from Aristotle, accounted for physical motion on the principle that every body seeks its natural place and changes according to the potentialities of change inherent in it. As Galileo, Newton and others effectively

THE SCIENTIFIC CHARACTER OF MARXISM 25

showed, such theories accounted for nothing because they could account for anything. Again, the theory of the original creation of biological species accounted for nothing because it could account for anything—whatever forms of life were observed could be accounted for by including them in the original plan of the Creator.

Dr. Popper has pointed out that scientific theories are not arrived at by so-called "induction" from numerous observations but rather by posing *questions* and answers to them—answers that can then be observationally tested in all manner of ways. He did not, however, conclude (as he could have done) that the establishment of fundamental theory, or guiding principles, for any field of inquiry has always depended on someone asking the right questions. Yet the genius of the great innovators in science has consisted in their formulating the right questions: once that is done, the answers are generally rather obvious. Marx's theory originates from his asking a question about society.

What is the key question from which Marx's social theory proceeds? The theory is not understood unless the question is understood—and this is why so many people (Dr. Popper included) fail to understand it, and so say it means what it does not mean.

Faced with all the multitudinous phenomena of social life (both contemporary and as recorded by history) and seeking to embrace them all within a theory, Marx did *not* ask "What will account for all these phenomena?" Indeed, a question of the form "What accounts for all the phenomena?" is *never* the key question for establishing fundamental scientific theory. The phenomena in detail are to be accounted for by detailed investigations guided by scientific theory, which is quite another thing from the theory laying down in advance just what accounts for them all. So far from being a key question for science, the question "What accounts for everything?" is the very question which commonly leads to pseudo-science—something is posited which can so readily account for anything that it accounts for nothing. Marx is often alleged to have posed against the pseudo-scientific theory that ideas account for everything the rival pseudo-scientific theory that economic interest accounts for everything. This he did not do, and he and Engels denied it frequently and emphatically.

The key question Marx asked was the simple and searching one: *What is the condition for social life of any kind to take place?* Once he asked this question the answer was obvious. The condition for any kind of social life is that people should associate together to produce their material means of life. The proposition that *to engage in any form of social activity people must first associate to produce their means of subsistence*, was the fundamental proposition on which Marx based the science of society.

Having arrived at this proposition, Marx was then able to formulate the *fundamental concepts* in terms of which the social mode of production may be defined. These are the concepts of *forces of production* and *relations of production*. In order socially to produce their means of subsistence men must fashion tools and implements and acquire the skill and knowledge for their use—and these are their forces of production. And in using those forces of production they must enter into social relations of production. Men "produce only by co-operating in a certain way and mutually exchanging their activities", wrote Marx in *Wage-Labour and Capital*. "In order to produce they enter into relations with one another, and only within these relations does production take place." The relations of production are therefore the multiple relations between individual people as "they exchange their activities and take part in the whole action of production". They include the property relations which people enter into in owning means of production and in appropriating and distributing the products, and define the economic structure of society and the division of society into classes.

Having thus concluded that the condition for social life is that men should engage in a mode of production, consisting of their entering into definite relations of production for the utilisation of definite forces of production, Marx proceeded to frame *a general hypothesis* about the way social life develops—it may be called the general law of all social development. This said that *people must always adapt their relations of production to their forces of production, and work out ideas and organise themselves in institutions to enable them to do so.*

This theory (often known as "historical materialism", and here stated only in its barest and simplest terms) served Marx (as he put it in the Preface to *The Critique of Political Economy*) "as a guiding thread for my studies". That is to say, in the study of any particular phase of social development, past or present, he proceeded to consider what the forces of production were, what the relations of production were, and how people's arguments about ideas and conduct of institutions enabled them to adapt their relations of production to their forces of production. This procedure served at one and the same time to account for the principal currents of social activity and their interplay, and to define and delimit the actual possibilities and possible directions of social change.

Such study, evidently, has to be empirical, like any scientific study— it is always necessary to ascertain the facts, they cannot be deduced from general theory. The general theory, like any "good" scientific theory, guides the inquirer by telling him *what to look for*; it does not tell him in advance exactly what he will find. And obviously, on the one hand, it is possible for the inquirer to make all sorts of errors (for example, to overlook certain things that are happening, or to mistake one kind of happening for another) without such errors falsifying the general theory. On the contrary, the reapplication of the general theory will assist him to rectify such errors. And on the other hand, the general theory is sufficiently general, and sufficiently "flexible", to allow a very wide margin of possible variations of development to occur without its being thereby falsified. On the contrary, in a given situation the theory permits many different alternative things to happen and, whichever does happen, is still capable of finding out how to account for it and to follow its development.

The general guiding theory of Marxism is tested in its application to inquiries about particular events or sequences of events. And so far it has not been falsified but confirmed. As I pointed out before, this does not make it unfalsifiable. Certain things would assuredly falsify it, only they do not happen—for example, a Stone Age community managing its affairs by parliamentary government and conducting controversies about the rights of man, or a successfully managed capitalism.

The methodology by which Marx arrived at his theory of social development is exactly the same as that employed by Darwin in establishing the theory of evolution of species by natural selection. Engels in fact remarked on this in his speech at Marx's funeral, when he said: "Just as Darwin discovered the law of development of organic nature, so Marx discovered the law of development of human history." It is remarkable that Marx and Darwin both published their basic conclusions within a few years of each other, each having worked independently in applying the same scientific methodology in their respective spheres of inquiry.

Darwin's theory rests on the fundamental premise that every living organism lives by adaptation to an environment from which it assimilates its requirements of life. This, he realised, is the universal condition for the existence of living species—just as Marx realised that social production is the universal condition for the existence of human societies. Marx's point about the human species—that men live in society by the social production of their means of life—was in fact a special application to men of the more general proposition about all living organisms propounded by Darwin. What distinguishes men from other animals, Marx explained, is the way they obtain their requirements by social production: from this comes the human peculiarity of speech, and the whole social and intellectual life by which men separate themselves from the rest of living nature. Human evolution then becomes not biological but social. Men do not acquire and satisfy new needs by any alteration of the organs of their bodies, but by acquiring new forces of production; and they change their social life and their own individual habits in so doing.

Having propounded his fundamental proposition, Darwin proceeded to formulate the general hypothesis of natural selection. In exactly the same way, having propounded his fundamental proposition, Marx proceeded to formulate the general hypothesis about adapting relations of production to forces of production. Darwin, in his work, collected and sifted an enormous mass of data, demonstrating in detail how his hypothesis worked out—and he was able to fit all manner of apparent anomalies into the general theory. Marx in his work did the same. The scientific methodology employed was identical; and if historical materialism is to be rejected as pseudo-science, so must the theory of the evolution of species by natural selection.

This account of the parallel in scientific methodology between the evolutionary theories of Marx and Darwin does not, incidentally, invalidate the criticisms that Marx himself made of certain supplementary aspects of Darwin's original theory. To the general hypothesis of natural selection Darwin added a supplementary concept—which he borrowed from Malthus—about "the struggle for existence" and "the survival of the fittest". Marx criticised these supplementary formulations of Darwin. It is now pretty generally agreed that those formulations were defective, and so the Darwinian theory does not survive in the exact form which Darwin himself originally gave it. But the "fundamental" Darwinian theory of evolution by natural selection survives.

Marx's theory, of course, lacks the "exactness" characteristic of those sciences which deal with physical and chemical phenomena. For the generalisations and laws stated in the theory are not formulated in quantitative terms. This is alleged to produce in Marx's theory an unscientific vagueness. Once again, if this objection makes Marx's theory unscientific, it makes Darwin's theory equally unscientific. Yet surely no one in his senses would expect all generalisations about social and biological evolution to be given the quantitative form of the laws of mechanics or thermodynamics.

It is worth noting, however, that despite these differences we may discern in the "exact" sciences, too, the self-same procedure for establishing fundamental theory as is exemplified in the social and biological theories of Marx and Darwin. For example, in establishing the fundamental theory of mechanics the idea was adopted that the condition for the existence of any body in motion relative to other bodies is that it has a certain motion of its own and is acted on by external forces. Having once hit on this fundamental idea, there were then formulated the fundamental concepts of mass, force, inertia, energy, and so on, in terms of which the laws of mechanics were formulated—corresponding to the fundamental (but in this case non-quantitative) concepts of relations of production and forces of production formulated by Marx.

The scrutiny of Marx's fundamental ideas about society reveals, then, their scientific character. Dr. Popper's failure to grasp this fact illustrates his failure, in his published work on scientific method, to grasp more than one single aspect of scientific procedures. He says that science proceeds by making "conjectures" which are "falsifiable", and then devising all manner of ways of trying to falsify them. So far as it goes, that is true enough. But yet the body of scientific theory consists of more than just a collection of falsifiable conjectures which are variously revised or replaced by other conjectures as falsification actually overtakes them. Every well-developed science rests on its fundamental theory, and is guided by it in its inquiries. This is a feature of science which Dr. Popper never examines—possibly because he distrusts such expressions as "fundamental theory", which he thinks redolent of pseudo-scientific metaphysics.

This shortcoming is evidenced when, after saying that "every 'good' scientific theory . . . forbids certain things to happen", he adds: "The more a theory forbids, the better it is" (CR. 36).

In making this pronouncement about how to judge how "good" a scientific theory is, Dr. Popper had, perhaps, in mind examples like the zoological statement: "eagles do not catch flies". This statement is true, and well-authenticated—but its scientific value, as an item of zoological science, is slight. It simply "forbids" eagles to catch flies, and permits them to do anything else. But a "good" scientic account of eagles must be much more exacting in what it forbids and permits these birds to do. However, what undoubtedly applies to items of scientific theory about particular phenomena, does not apply to those very general theories and very general laws which, by virtue of their great generality, serve as the fundamentals for all scientific theory dealing with a whole class of phenomena (biological, physical, chemical, social, and so on). For example, the first and second laws of thermo-dynamics simply "forbid" energy not to be conserved and entropy not to increase; they allow anything to happen within these pro-hibitions. Again, the Darwinian theory simply forbids species or varieties to survive for long unless adapted to their environments (a very liberal prohibition); and similarly, the Marxist theory simply forbids societies to develop without adapting relations of production to forces of production. These laws and theories would not be "better" if they forbade more. On the contrary, they would not be much good if they forbade too much.

What Dr. Popper seems to have overlooked in his pronouncements about prohibitions and falsifications is the work of *abstraction* and *generalisation* in scientific theory. The task of "fundamental" theory is to abstract the necessary or universal condition of existence of the phenomena studied, and to put forward corresponding generalisations. Such fundamental theory, very abstract and very general, does not, should not and cannot satisfy Dr. Popper's principle that "the more a theory forbids the better it is". It is, indeed, difficult to imagine why on earth Dr. Popper should ever have enunciated such a principle— except that it gives him a stick to beat Marxism with. But it is not a "good" stick, and in wielding it Dr. Popper joins the very numerous and very distinguished company of those who have allowed anti-communism to cloud their judgment.

In short, in making out that Marx's theory about society is rein-forced dogmatism, Dr. Popper has totally neglected to consider Marx's actual methodology. Marx in fact laid the foundations of his theory of society in just the same way as others have laid the founda-tions of other sciences. And this is plainly evidenced in what Marx said. As we shall see, having ignored Marx's actual methodology, Dr. Popper proceeds to explain that Marx's theory really means all kinds of pseudo-scientific things (summed up in such denigratory epithets as "historicism" and "essentialism") which, however, could not have been products of Marx's scientific method, and which Marx did not say.

Instead of examining Marx's scientific method, Dr. Popper deals at some length with the "origins" of Marx's theory in the philosophy of Hegel. Hegel was a philosopher who accepted the idealist view of human affairs, that ideas are what accounts for everything; but in contrast to those who said, and continue to say, that there is no accounting for ideas and that therefore there is no discernible "law of development" in human history, Hegel *did* see a law of historical development, namely the logical law of the working out of ideas. Marx, it is true, was greatly impressed by Hegel's conception of a discoverable law of development—but not by Hegel's account of what this law of development was. He totally rejected Hegel's idealism, and sought instead to arrive at the formulation of a law of development by the well-tried methods of empirical science. He called this "putting Hegel on his feet". The result was the theory of historical materialism.

Dr. Popper, on the other hand, concludes that because Marx admired and was stimulated by Hegel, therefore his theory originated from Hegel, and therefore it must be as foreign to science as Hegel's theory was. He concludes that the Marxist theory is *essentially* unscientific on the grounds that it *originated* from Hegel. This kind of exposition comes, incidentally, very strangely from one who has also devoted much space to exposing the fallacy of deducing what a thing is, its "essence", by theorising about its "origins".

4. DOES MARXISM ALLOW LOGICAL CONTRADICTIONS?

Dr. Popper further maintains that what makes Marxism into "a reinforced dogmatism" is its use of "dialectics"—which he sees as totally opposed to science. He does not object so much to Marx's "materialism" as to "dialectics". "Although I should not describe myself as a materialist, my criticism is not directed against materialism", he says. "The materialist element in this theory could be comparatively easily reformulated in such a way that no serious objection to it could be made" (CR. 331–2). But "thanks to dialectics . . . Marxism has established itself as a dogmatism which is elastic enough, by using its dialectic method, to evade any further attack. It has thus become what I have called a reinforced dogmatism" (CR. 334).

True to his own method of reinforced refutation, Dr. Popper proceeds to say what "dialectics" means—and makes it mean something remarkably stupid.

"Dialectics . . . is a theory which maintains that something—more especially human thought—develops in a way characterised by what is called the dialectic triad: thesis, antithesis and synthesis" (CR. 313).

As against this, it is worth recalling what Lenin said about dialectics in his very famous book *What the Friends of the People are and how they fight the Social-Democrats.* "Anyone who reads the definition and description of the dialectical method given by Engels will see that the Hegelian triads are not even mentioned, and that it all amounts to regarding social evolution as a natural-historical process of development. . . . What Marx and Engels called the dialectical method is nothing more nor less than the scientific method in sociology, which consists in regarding society as a living organism in a constant state of development, the study of which requires an objective analysis of the relations of production which constitute the given social formation and an investigation of its laws of functioning and development."

Quite in accord with this, Lenin also said that "the most essential thing in Marxism is the concrete analysis of concrete conditions", and that "genuine dialectics" consists of "a thorough detailed analysis of a process".

Dr. Popper has, of course, read Marx and Engels (though possibly not Lenin). However, having read them, he concludes that they did not mean what they said, so he has undertaken to say it for them. Having foisted on to them the rather incoherent "theory" that "something, more especially human thought" always develops through "thesis, antithesis and synthesis", he proceeds to foist on them a logical conclusion even more absurd than the alleged theory.

According to the "dialectical" theory of "triads", the thesis and antithesis are "contradictory". Therefore, says Dr. Popper, dialecticians "assert that contradictions cannot be avoided, since they occur everywhere in the world. Such an assertion", he continues, "amounts to an attack upon the so-called 'law of contradiction' (or, more fully, upon the 'law of the exclusion of contradictions') of traditional logic, a law which asserts that two contradictory statements can never be true together, or that a statement consisting of the conjunction of two contradictory statements must always be rejected as false on purely logical grounds" (CR. 316). Hence, he concludes, dialectics rests on the absurdity of asserting that logically self-contradictory statements are true.

This is, indeed, an absurdity. But Marx was never responsible for enunciating it—he never said anything of the kind. On the contrary, he frequently (like any other scientific inquirer) concluded that certain generalisations were false because certain verified statements of fact contradicted them; and he would hardly have done that if he had thought that the logical "law of the exclusion of contradictions" could be dispensed with. If two logically contradictory statements could both be true, then a generalisation could still be true even though facts contradicted it. One could then say whatever one liked, there could be no test of truth or falsehood, and, as Dr. Popper correctly remarks, "one would have to give up any kind of scientific activity: it would mean a complete breakdown of science" (CR. 317).

Dr. Popper's foisting on to Marxism the absurd view that logical contradictions are allowable in true statement depends on making a play with the use of the word "contradiction" quite in the style of the characters Alice met in Wonderland.

If, in describing a certain person, one says that "he is a mass of contradictions", no one but the Mad Hatter, the March Hare, or Dr. Popper, would conclude that one means that a true statement of his character is logically self-contradictory. Similarly, Marx wrote about "the contradictions of capitalism", indicating that in the development of capitalism the combination of "socialised production" with "private appropriation" produces certain strains and instabilities. But to state that capitalism combines socialised production and private appropriation, between which there exists a relationship of a type which may, without misuse of language, be termed "contradictory", is not a logically self-contradictory or inconsistent statement, but a perfectly consistent general factual statement, of the kind which may be verified or falsified. There is not a sentence in the "concrete analysis of concrete conditions" or "thorough detailed analysis of a process", undertaken by Marx, Engels, Lenin, or any responsible Marxist practising the dialectical method, by which they sort out and display the "contradictions" exemplified in conditions and processes, which contains even a hint at a logical contradiction.

Having concluded that Marxism means to say that logical contradictions are allowable, Dr. Popper triumphantly produces his final demonstration that Marxism is "reinforced dogmatism". "For if we are prepared to put up with contradictions, pointing out contradictions in our theories could no longer induce us to change them. In other words, all criticism (which consists in pointing out contradictions) would lose its force. Criticism would be answered by 'And why not?' or perhaps even by an enthusiastic 'There you are!'; that is, by welcoming the contradictions which have been pointed out to us" (CR. 317). So you cannot falsify Marxism, because Marxism maintains that falsification or contradiction does not falsify. This account of Marx's "reinforced dogmatism" does not, of course, quite accord with other accounts which Dr. Popper gives of how Marxism evades falsification. But never mind that! His reinforced refutations can never fail, because, whatever Marx or Marxists may say, he will always find a way of saying what we mean which renders it utterly absurd.

Outside of Wonderland, it is a commonplace that the Marxist "dialectic" is concerned with understanding things "in their changes and interconnections", and formulating "laws" about how real changes and interconnections go.

As Engels said in the introduction to *Anti-Duhring*, it is a mistake if "in considering individual things" one "loses sight of their interconnections", or if "in contemplating their existence" one "forgets their coming into being and passing away". And if one makes such a mistake, he continued, one ends by being involved in contradictions. Thus "for everyday purposes we know, for example, and can say with certainty whether an animal is alive or not; but when we look more closely we find that this is often an extremely complex question . . . it is impossible to determine the moment of death, for physiology has established that death is not a sudden instantaneous event but a very protracted process. In the same way every organic being is at each moment the same and not the same; at each moment it is assimilating matter drawn from without, and excreting other matter; at each moment the cells of its body are dying and new ones are being formed; in fact within a longer or shorter period the matter of its body is completely renewed . . . so that every organic being is at all times itself and yet something other than itself". Hence if you overlook the way things come into being and cease to be, the way they disintegrate and are renewed, and the way they exist only in complex interrelations with other things, and try to say of each thing what its state is at each moment regardless of its changes and relationships, you will be led to make contradictory statements—"it is . . ." and " it is not . . .".

What does this imply? It certainly does not imply that we should be "prepared to put up with (logical) contradictions". On the contrary, the occurrence of logical contradictions is a sign that the categories employed in describing things in abstraction from "their interconnections" and "coming into being and passing away" are inadequate to the "concrete analysis of concrete conditions". When, in accordance with principles of dialectics, one substitutes for such abstract and inadequate accounts of things the "thorough detailed analysis of a process", the logical contradictions vanish.

To describe, for example, how an organic body renews its cells in the course of its interaction with its environment, and to describe the "contradictory" relationship of the processes of decay and renewal which make up its life, does not involve making logically contradictory statements. On the contrary, the whole analysis is done in strict conformity with the principles of consistency, or non-contradiction, laid down by formal logic. Dialectics does not encourage us in inconsistency, but, on the contrary, accepts the most rigid demands of formal logical consistency of statement. To say "A thing is the same and not the same" is a logical contradiction which no scientifically-minded person can be "prepared to put up with". To say "At every moment it is assimilating new matter and excreting old matter" is to give a more adequate account of it, and contains no logical contradiction whatsoever. Dialectics does not permit logical contradictions, but gets rid of them.

The truth is that if one says "It is the same and yet not the same", the question immediately raised by such an enigmatic statement is the question: "In what respect is it the same, and in what respect not the same?" For (as Aristotle pointed out when he originally formulated the logical law of non-contradiction) to say that something is in all respects the same and in all respects not the same is a logical contradiction which cannot be allowed. To explain, then, "At every moment it is assimilating new matter and excreting old matter" is to answer the question about the respects in which the thing changes while otherwise remaining the same. By supplying information about the processes going on in the thing, it explains that while the thing remains the same in respect of its external form it ceases to be the same in respect of the matter composing it. From that one might then further conclude that in all probability the external characteristics will sooner or later undergo change as well and become different as a result of internal changes.

When one thus undertakes, in accordance with dialectics, "a thorough detailed analysis of a process", which exhibits its contradictory sides and how the character and mode of change of the whole is determined by the relationship of these contradictory sides, the result is something which, far from being logically self-contradictory, completely satisfies all the logical criteria for scientific statement. We get statements which can be verified or falsified, and which are relevant to the drawing of probable conclusions about the further development of a process.

This point can, incidentally, be put in a formalised way, in complete accordance with the principles of formal logic. Let P be a process, which contains contradictory sides or aspects A and B. If one then considers A by itself, apart from its relationship with B, one can infer a conclusion about P which may be written "A(P)"; and similarly, considering B by itself, one infers the conclusion "B(P)". These conclusions are then incompatible or inconsistent with each other. If, however, one makes a correct analysis of P, as containing the contradictory sides A and B, one reaches the conclusion "AB(P)". This conclusion is a statement of the mode of relationship and interaction of the contradictory sides of P; and from it one may infer the probable course of development of P.

The Marxist dialectic does not, as alleged, allow logical contradictions. Nor is it designed, as alleged, for producing statements which cannot be tested, but for precisely the opposite end—producing scientific statements which *can* be tested. As for Dr. Popper, all he has done is to derive logical absurdities from a pseudo-scientific theory about "triads", and then solemnly to inform his readers: This is what Marxism means! One is tempted to ask which he thinks the stupider— the Marxists, or the readers to whom he presents such nonsense.

5. DIALECTICAL MATERIALISM AND SCIENTIFIC METHOD

If dialectical materialism is not the nonsense Dr. Popper makes it out to be, what exactly does it say? What is its content and aim, as a philosophy?

One thing should be made clear at the outset, and that is that Marx and Engels never and nowhere worked out a fully systematic statement of dialectical materialism. All they did was to argue against other views in philosophy and lay down certain guiding principles for the development of their own. So the scientific philosophical principles need more working out, and Marxism in this sphere means working them out—on the basis of following up the indications afforded by Marx and Engels, and following them up, moreover, in a way that does not involve groundless dogmas, or logical absurdities, but accords with the advances of logical and scientific knowledge, and social technology, achieved to date. These have gone considerably past the point reached in Marx's day. Although Dr. Popper seems to think that a *bona fide* Marxist is by definition ignorant of progress in logical and mathematical analysis, scientific discovery and technological achievement, the job of Marxists is, on the contrary, to take account of these matters and formulate the Marxist position accordingly. Marxism, as I have said, is the continuation of Marx's work. In this Marxists inevitably become involved in controversies with one another, as well as with opponents of Marxism. That, of course, is how the thing develops, how it continues.

The practitioner of reinforced refutation may fancy he detects here a loophole for the insinuation of reinforced dogmatism. If Marxism is permitted such rational and scientific development (he will ask), cannot *any* statement found valid be then labelled "Marxist", while any discredited statement, even if made by a Marxist, will by definition be excluded from "Marxism"? This is obviously a quibble. The development of Marxism continues so long as it continues to follow the original guiding principles. If these are refuted then Marxism is destroyed, and if what is then propounded is still called "Marxism" it is a mere impersonation. In the same way, we regard the man as the same person as the boy; but if at a certain point he were knocked on the head, laid out and buried, and someone else assumed his name, we would regard that person as an impersonator. These sorts of consideration apply to anything that grows, including scientific theories.

I fully agree with Dr. Popper that *all* views should be subject to continuous test, and modified or, if need be, scrapped, in the light of it. But if I nevertheless remain a Marxist it is not because I except Marxism from this critical principle, but because I do not interpret a "critical" attitude as entailing readiness to fall over backwards in deference to every "critic". For my part, I am a Marxist because I have not yet found any logical or scientific argument that refutes Marxism, though there are plenty that contribute to its development, whereas I have always found that arguments which claim to refute Marxism are neither logical nor scientific.

To arrive at a general idea of what dialectical materialism, as the basic philosophical outlook exemplified or applied in Marxist social theory, says and means in contemporary terms, it is advisable to start by taking into account, first, what sort of *question* it seeks to answer, and second, to what sort of answer it is *opposed*. Generally speaking, these are two considerations of paramount importance for the exposition and explanation of views. A sure way of misunderstanding or misrepresenting what people mean is to suppose them to be trying to answer some other question than the one that actually interests them, and opposing other views than those they are actually concerned to oppose.

I begin, then, by remarking on a question which dialectical materialism is sometimes supposed to answer, but which is *not* the question that it begins by posing. Dialectical materialism does *not* set out to answer the question: "What is the nature of the universe?" It does *not*, therefore, consist of any set of statements about "the totality of things", or about "everything", or about "the world as a whole", or about "the ultimate substance of things" or "the ultimate structure of reality". If it is supposed that dialectical materialism is the sort of "metaphysical system" which proposes an answer to those sorts of questions, then it is misunderstood and misrepresented from the outset. As modern studies of logic and scientific method have quite conclusively shown, those are all badly formulated questions and any answers proposed to them are worthless because incapable of any sort of test. And as Engels, anticipating these studies, emphatically stated in his *Ludwig Feuerbach*: "One leaves 'absolute truth' alone . . . instead, one pursues attainable, relative truths along the path of the positive sciences"; and in the introduction to *Anti-Duhring*: "Modern materialism . . . no longer needs any philosophy standing above the other sciences. . . . What still independently survives of all former philosophy is the science of thought and its laws—formal logic and dialectics. Everything else is merged in the positive science of nature and history."

Marxism and dialectical materialist philosophy emphatically teach that well-grounded and reliable theory about ourselves and the universe around us can be obtained only be the methodical investigation of particular phenomena open to observation, and is always subject to the tests of experience. To ask, therefore, about the structure of the universe as a whole, or about what kinds of things exist and what are their properties and relations, in advance of investigation, and to propound any theory which on general philosophical grounds answers "it must be like this", is as contrary to Marxism as it is contrary to the accepted precepts of logic and scientific method. What is sensible is rather to ask about the nature, constitution, structure or laws of operation of observable objects or processes—and to seek the answer by the methods of science, and test it in experience. Such knowledge as we can get about "the totality of things" can be got only by piecing together items of knowledge about particular things— hence it necessarily remains always incomplete and provisional. Moreover, Marxism is practical—it seeks to develop theory to inform practice and to be tested in practice. Grandiose theories about "the universe as a whole" do not inform practice, but only befuddle it, and cannot be submitted to any practical test. To inform practice we want testable theories about what concerns us in practice (just as Dr. Popper himself maintains).

The question to which dialectical materialism proposes an answer concerns rather the *approach* or *method* to be adopted in making and developing reliable theory to inform practice and to be tested in practice. Thus it rejects the invitation "Please invent a theory about the nature of the universe", but accepts the invitation "Please state the principles to be adopted in making theories". When we speak about "materialism" and about "dialectics", separately or together, we are not propounding a philosophical theory about "everything" in contrast to or supplementing scientific theories about particular things, but we are propounding the approach or guiding principles recommended for making theories.

We shall see later that dialectical materialism, as an answer to the question "Please state the principles to be adopted in making theories", does nevertheless in a sense also supply an answer to the question "What is the nature of the universe?" For to answer the question of the approach to be adopted in making theories cannot but lead to conclusions about the form of statements corresponding to accessible reality. For example, any statement that can inform practice must deal with things detectable by the senses and which exist only in their interconnections with other things in processes of change. This shows that the world we live in and get to know is a world of material change; and that, of course, is a very general conclusion about "the nature of the world". The point is, first, that a question about "the nature of the universe" cannot be answered directly, but only derivatively via questions about approach and method; and second, that the job of reliably informing ourselves about the world we inhabit requires the investigation of particular things and not of "the nature of the world as a whole".

Dr. Popper mentions with some scorn the contention that Marxism

is not "a theory" but "a method". It is, he insists, "a theory". So it is—
it is a theory employing a method. Marxism is a theory about human
affairs employing the method of dialectical materialism. But dialectical
materialism is not a theory about "everything" added to theories
about particular matters of concern. Marxism does not have a theory
about human affairs plus the theory of dialectical materialism, but its
theory is dialectical materialist. And the same principles for making
theory which are exemplified and applied in Marxist theory about
man are found implicit also in all scientific theory about nature.
Dialectical materialism is "fundamental" in Marxism, not in the
sense of its being a dogma about the universe into which everything
must somehow or other be made to fit, regardless of the facts, but in
the sense of its being a generalised statement of the principles of
approach or method to be adopted in studying facts in such a way as
to arrive at "the concrete analysis of concrete conditions", or the
"thorough detailed analysis of a process".

But that, it may be objected, abolishes the peculiar character of
dialectical materialism as "the philosophy of Marxism" and merely
equates it with "scientific method'. In the broadest sense, it is true,
materialist dialectics can claim to be "nothing but scientific method".
This is just what Lenin said: it is "nothing more nor less than the
scientific method . . .". The distinguishing feature of Marxism is
not that it invents and uses some new-fangled method of its own,
quite different from the method evolved, used and approved in the
normal conduct of the sciences, but that it develops and applies
scientific method *universally*, and that includes drawing conclusions
about men, human society and human affairs. Marxism seeks to apply
scientific ways of understanding to *everything* that comes within
human ken, including humanity itself. It is therefore critical of and
opposed to traditional ways of understanding *ourselves*, which are by
no means scientific—and *this* is what primarily distinguishes Marxism
as a philosophy or outlook opposed to what is still generally current.

Of course, scientific understanding of ourselves relies on already
achieved scientific understanding of nature, for man becomes what he
is and lives by his intercourse with nature. At the same time (and this
is a point our English Marxist Christopher Caudwell emphasised in
The Crisis in Physics), by understanding the relation of men with
nature it enhances and corrects the concept of nature, which is to
some extent distorted so long as men's intercourse with nature is
misconceived.

But while materialist dialectics is in truth "nothing more nor less than scientific method", that does not by any means reduce the field of inquiry of Marxist philosophy to the problems commonly debated by non-Marxists under the heading of "scientific method". If we were to take Dr. Popper as our guide, these would be simply problems about the formal criteria of differentiation between "scientific" and "non-scientific" theories (the scientific ones are "falsifiable"), plus some problems about probability, induction (so-called), and the special techniques required for special investigations. I do not wish to suggest that these are not genuine problems, or that Dr. Popper and other contemporary writers on "scientific method" and "the logic of scientific discovery" have not dealt with them usefully. But it would not be true to suggest that the field of inquiry of dialectical materialism is reduced to "nothing more nor less" than *these* problems —because while these problems *do* fall within it, it comprises a great deal *more*.

Dialectical materialism is primarily concerned with something which these more limited inquiries about scientific method neglect, namely, the *way of thinking*, the *principles of working with and assembling concepts*, requisite for scientific understanding in general. As Engels put it in the Preface of *Anti-Duhring*, the results of scientific work are summarised in concepts "but the art of working with concepts is not inborn and is not given with ordinary everyday consciousness, but requires real thought"; and consequently to master facts by theory we should be "equipped with the consciousness of the laws of dialectical thought". Science, he added, "can no longer escape the dialectical synthesis". But "to make this process easier for itself", it must not only rid itself of so-called "philosophy standing apart from it, outside it and above it", but also of its own traditional "limited method of thought".

This brings me to the question of the sort of approaches to which dialectical materialism is *opposed*. Marx and Engels said over and over again that it is opposed to "idealism" and to "metaphysics". Its opposition to "idealism" is expressed by the word "materialism", and to "metaphysics" by the word "dialectics". These words, expressive of opposition—"materialism" against "idealism", and dialectics" against "metaphysics"—are here used in rather specialised senses (different from those in which the same words are sometimes used in other contexts) which must now be explained.

2

THE MATERIALIST APPROACH

I. MATERIALISM VERSUS IDEALISM

"The great basic question of all philosophy," wrote Engels (*Ludwig Feuerbach*, Chapter 2) concerns "the relation of thinking and being. . . . The answers which the philosophers gave to this question split them into two great camps. Those who asserted the primacy of spirit to nature . . . comprised the camp of *idealism*. The others, who regarded nature as primary, belong to the various schools of *materialism*."

Alice was reproached by the March Hare and the Mad Hatter with obscurity of utterance. Whatever could she mean? Similarly, many Wonderland philosophers profess themselves baffled by the obscurity of Engels' statements. But like his younger contemporary, he simply meant what he said.

In the above statement Engels opposed "thinking" to "being", and "spirit" to "nature", and said that "the great basic question of all philosophy" concerned which side of this opposition was "prior" to the other. Evidently, the opposition is that of the "material" on the one side, and the "non-material" (or "ideal") on the other. He classed "being" and "nature" as "material", and "thinking" and "spirit" as "non-material". This is the sort of terminology regarded as so very obscure by many philosophers nowadays—but it is merely expressive of distinctions which are perfectly familiar to everyone, and which receive perfectly precise expression in the things people ordinarily say, however much some philosphers may try to confuse them.

The "material", as people ordinarily understand it (and we need not credit Engels with intending to give ordinary words any extra-ordinary meaning), is the sort of thing which affects the senses—which we can see, hear, smell, touch or taste. The non-material, on the other hand, is not accessible to the senses. Thus, for example, a tree or a mountain is material, whereas the idea of a tree or of a mountain is non-material. In ordinary language we would say that we see or touch a material thing, whereas we think or understand an idea. It would be as nonsensical to say that "we think a tree" as that "we see a thought". Again, a person's body is material, but his thoughts, desires, and other operations of his mind or "spirit" are non-material. Hence the opposition which Engels posed, between the material and non-material, or between "being" and "thinking", or "nature" and "spirit", is both familiar and obvious.

From this opposition there ensues the opposition between materialism and idealism in theory, depending on the answer to the question "which is prior", the material or the non-material. To be an *idealist* is to approach questions of the analysis and explanation of phenomena on the basis that there are ideas, intentions and purposes (whether of God or man), and that what is or happens is made what it is or made to happen by them, i.e. that the non-material is prior to the material. To be a *materialist*, on the other hand, is to approach such questions on the basis that there are material things and happenings, and that ideas about them, and intentions and purposes relating to them, result from the material circumstances in which such ideas, intentions and purposes are engendered, i.e. that the material is prior to the non-material.

Thus to say that thunderstorms, for example, are manifestations of the anger of the gods exhibits an idealist approach, whereas to say that they are electrical disturbances exhibits a materialist approach. Again, to say that a social event (for instance, the French Revolution) is the expression of some idea (such as the idea of liberty) exhibits an idealist approach; whereas to say that it results from class struggles rooted in the relations of production (from which also arise the characteristic ideas motivating the event) exhibits a materialist approach. Again, to say (as certain modern philosophers have said) that material objects are logical constructions out of the data of sense exhibits an idealist approach; whereas to say that the data of sense are the means whereby we become aware of material objects exhibits a materialist approach.

All theories exhibit an idealist or a materialist approach (or in many cases a muddled and inconsistent mixture of the two), and "the great basic question of philosophy" is the question of which is the right approach to make.

Marxism recommends and adopts a consistently materialist approach to all questions; and it propounds and bases itself upon a materialist philosophy in as much as it investigates and formulates the guiding principles of a consistently materialist approach, in opposition to idealism. What are these principles?

The first principle of materialism, as presented by the Marxist materialist philosophy, is that material processes certainly take place, and material things certainly exist, independent of any ideas about them.

To explain this we need to enter a little further into the meaning of such words as "material" and "matter", and the implications of their use. The use of the adjective "material" derives its meaning, of course, only from its opposition to "ideal", "mental" or "spiritual". Thus we speak of "matter" and "material processes" in contrast to "mind", "spirit" and "ideas". Thus if, for example, one says that a dining-room table is "material" one is not specifying some property of it, as one is when one says it is "made of wood" or "has a plastic top". One is simply contrasting and distinguishing it from one's idea of a table, emphasising that it is there in the dining-room independently of one's idea of it.

Materialism asserts the *independence*, the independent *existence*, of whatever is material. The use of the word "material", in the Marxist statement of the fundamental standpoint of materialism, emphasises the *existence* of the material world *independent* of the ideas and perceptions by which we become aware of it, and of any other ideas, or ideal or spiritual entities, which may be imagined to exist.

Thus in his work *Materialism and Empirio-Criticism* Lenin carefully explained that to speak of "material" things and processes, and in general of "matter" and of "the material world", does not imply any particular theory of the constitution of material things (not, for instance, that they are made of "matter", as distinct from being made of something else, such as "energy"; nor that they consist of "solid particles" as opposed, say, to "wave motions"). It implies their objective existence, independent of our own or any other consciousness of them or ideas about them. As to the constitution of material things—what they are made of, what their structure is, what properties they have—that has to be found out by investigating them, and much of the product of such investigation must remain at the level of conjecture.

Lenin's exposition of the use of the terms "matter" and "material" in the statement of the fundamental standpoint of materialism was made in answer to those idealists who claimed that the discoveries of physics had demonstrated that "matter does not exist" and that "materialism is out of date". True, the older materialist philosophies (derived from ancient speculations in Greece, China and India) were associated with a definite theory about the constitution of matter, namely, that the material world consists of solid indivisible particles, or "atoms", moving about in empty space. In the seventeenth century Descartes regarded matter in another way, as "extended substance" filling space, and invented a theory of "vortices" in matter to account for various observed phenomena. Maxwell later elaborated the same type of idea when he postulated the "ether" which fills the whole of space and in which electro-magnetic waves occur. The old atomic theory of matter was discredited by subsequent investigations of the atom, and the theory of the ether was discredited by investigations of electro-magnetic phenomena and replaced by the theory of relativity. But that does not mean that physics has shown that there is no such thing as matter, or material process. The idealists who said it had were simply confusing materialism in general with relics of pre-scientific materialist speculation. Modern physics has replaced pre-scientific speculation by scientific investigation. That does not make materialism out of date, but only out-dates certain speculative materialist hypotheses.

Does this, then, reduce materialism to nothing but the bare abstract assertion that there is an objective reality independent of ideas? No, for material things and processes are *known* to us through our sensations and perceptions. As Lenin put it: "Matter is that which, acting upon our sense-organs, produces sensation; matter is the objective reality given to us in sensation." Materialism does not consist in the merely empty assertion that something or other exists independent of ideas, but asserts that objective reality—the material world—has the fundamental characteristics of being *knowable through the senses*, that is, of *causal process in space and time*.

The first principle of materialism can therefore be put like this: that causal process in space and time, given to us in sensation, exists or continues *independently* of any mind or spirit, consciousness or idea. The second principle is the complement of this, and *denies* the *independent* existence of anything non-material. Perceptions, ideas, intentions, feelings, purposes, ideals, consciousness and mind only exist as products of particular kinds of material processes. They are the perceptions, ideas and so on of material organisms, products of the functioning of specific organs of their bodies, formed in the conditions of their material mode of life.

For materialism, then, there is nothing *outside* the material world. There is no separate or independent spiritual world, no mind or spirit separate from matter. There is one world, the material world; and, as Engels put it in *Anti-Duhring*, " the unity of the world consists in its materiality". "Space and time," he wrote, are "the basic forms of all being". There is nothing apart from what is comprised in causal process in space and time; and all those phenomena which we call mental or spiritual take place *within* the material world, as products of particular forms of material motion at particular times and places.

Thirdly, then, materialism propounds the principles for a theory of man; a general account of ourselves. We ourselves are material organisms. And as such we become aware of ourselves and of our environment through the sensations which we obtain in the course of our material interactions, and through the processes of thought which we develop from our sensations. Although our senses may often deceive us and our ideas often prove illusory, nevertheless the material world which is given to us in our sensations, and which supplies all the data for our thought, objectively exists as the arena of all our action and the object of all our consciousness and knowledge. We get to know it and to know ourselves, and to master material processes for our own purposes and learn how to satisfy our needs, by active investigation, in which theory is first drawn from practical experience and then tested in it.

Such, then, are the basic philosophical principles of materialism, as presented by Marxist philosophy in opposition to idealism.

Dr. Popper, as we saw, has kindly said that there can be "no serious objection" to materialism, provided it is "reformulated" in some unspecified but nevertheless "comparatively easy" way. But he adds: "I should not describe myself as a materialist." This addition bears witness, at least, to his honesty. For his part, he simply emphasises that theories should be susceptible to experiential test, and so be falsifiable; and he presumably finds no objection to materialism in so far, and only in so far, as it advocates that theories should be testable in experience. But he would not call himself a materialist because he regards the best of the theories as no more than conjectures, which one makes in order then to engage in the scientific pursuit of trying to falsify them—whereas *materialism* would generally be understood to imply (and Marx's materialism certainly does imply) something more. However conjectural and subject to correction particular theories about particular things may be, *materialism* means claiming that there are principles to be adopted in formulating theories which are not conjectures at all, but are certainly true.

Dr. Popper's exclusive emphasis on the *conjectural* character of scientific theories comes from his exclusive preoccupation with the way those theories are made subject to *experiential test*. Well of course, scientific theories *are* made subject to experiental test—otherwise they would not be scientific; and consequently they always *do* have a conjectural or provisional character. But what is the point of such theories? Why should it be considered so vitally important to place our whole trust in conjectures which are subject to experiential test and may therefore be falsified? Why prefer the hazard of reliance on conjectural and falsifiable theories to the assurance and satisfaction of reliance on unfalsifiable ones? Dr. Popper accuses Marxism of propagating a reinforced dogmatism which is incapable of falsification and can provide a ready-made answer to any question. Marxism does at least answer the above questions, which is more than he can do. And in answering them we may now accuse him in return of inclining to a one-sided account of scientific theory, which is totally incapable of answering pertinent questions about science.

We do not *conjecture* the existence of the material processes of which we ourselves are part and on which our very being, our whole conscious existence depends. We get to know them, and in knowing them learn in some degree to master them for our own purposes. That is what we do through science, and that is why scientific theories, made subject to experiential test, are so important for us.

2. THE CASE AGAINST IDEALISM

Engels had no doubt at all that materialism is the right approach, and idealism wrong—and the reasons for his confidence on this point are pretty clear. He was not a dogmatist who believed himself the prophet of some revelation "that matter is prior". He was simply a scientific thinker, distinguished by a capacity for generalising the principles of his thinking, who realised that the idealist approach could never be productive of anything but what he called "fancies"—that is, theories which could not be tested, or which would be, as Dr. Popper now expresses it, "unfalsifiable"; whereas the materialist approach is the only one to produce testable theories. Thus in Chapter 4 of *Ludwig Feuerbach* he proceeded to justify the decision always to adopt the materialist approach, as follows: "It was resolved to comprehend the real world—nature and history—just as it presents itself to everyone who approaches it free from preconceived idealist fancies. It was decided relentlessly to sacrifice every idealist fancy which could not be brought into harmony with the facts conceived in their own and not in a fantastic connection. Materialism means nothing more than this."

Evidently, then, it cannot be claimed that a theory is true because it is materialist—the truth of a theory can be substantiated only by testing and retesting it in experience. On the other hand, there can be no scientifically valid grounds for adopting any theory *unless* it is materialist. Particular idealist theories may be rejected because they make assertions 'which do not accord with experience—but *every* idealist theory may be rejected, not because experience shows it to be false (for whatever the experience, some idealist fancy or other can always be thought up to account for it), but because it is a mere "preconceived fancy" which no experience can substantiate. However much particular materialist theories may be falsified by events, we can remain sure that the right explanation is along materialist lines; and however well particular idealist theories may evade falsification, we can remain sure that they are nevertheless mere fancies. That is why Marxism rejects every idealist theory about human affairs. But it does not adopt its own materialist theory because it claims to be able to deduce it from "first principles of materialist philosophy". It adopts it because the investigation of human affairs leads to it; and Marxists continue to stand by it and develop it because it continues to ring true as a guide to practice unfalsified by the event.

If we want to inform our practice, we cannot but follow the paths of materialism. If we want to find out what we are and what we can do, what our real needs are and how we can satisfy them, the materialist approach must be our guide.

What is the fundamental error in idealism, as a way of thinking?

To say, for example, that there are disembodied spirits, or first causes, or eternal forms (as different schools of idealism have said) is a quite different *kind* of error from saying that there are unicorns or phoenixes or (as Aristotle said in his treatise on zoology) sabre-toothed tigers. Similarly, it is a different *kind* of error to say that thunderstorms are caused by gods getting angry than it is to say (as certain early materialist speculations erroneously suggested) that they are caused by heavy particles in clouds banging against each other. Again, it is a different *kind* of error to say that one gets from Golders Green Crematorium to Heaven via the ministrations of the Church of England than it is to say that one gets from London to Birmingham via Crewe.

The latter sorts of error consist in wrongly describing and relating material things, and can be exposed and corrected in the course of practice, by observation and experiment. The former sorts of error are different, since spirits, first causes, eternal forms, gods and the way to Heaven are not observable, so that statements about them cannot be checked in the same practical empirical way. When one theologian says that only one angel can stand on the point of a needle while another says it will accommodate more, the way to enforce the one view against the other is to convene a church council and get the one party excommunicated, since it is impossible to devise any instrument for measuring the size of angels' feet.

All statement *abstracts*. For example, to say "This rose is red" abstracts a particular rose from the total environment, and its colour from the totality of its other properties. If a particular rose is red and I say that it is white, my statement is false in point of fact. The erroneousness or falsity of idealist statements, on the other hand, is not in the same way factual but consists in a *false abstraction*. Thus to say "Mr. Smith is at the office", when in fact he has cut work to watch a cricket match, is to make a statement in which the abstraction of an object (Mr. Smith) from its environment, and of its whereabouts from the totality of its properties and relations, has been quite properly done, and the object has merely been asserted to be located somewhere else than where it is actually to be found. On the other hand, to say (supposing Mr. Smith to have died) "Mr. Smith's soul is in Heaven" is to make an improper abstraction—for to abstract Mr. Smith's soul from Mr. Smith is to make an abstraction such that the resulting statements cannot possibily be checked; and similarly to speak of Heaven is to speak of a place abstracted from space and time is such a manner that there is no possible way of finding who is or is not present there.

The fundamental error of idealism, as a way of thinking, lies in its making false abstractions. This way of thinking is a habit, a method, a systematic use of false abstraction.

Thus for example, an idealist historian may faithfully report that William the Conquerer won the Battle of Hastings and that King John signed Magna Carta. He may make no misstatement of fact. He does not say that people did things which they did not do, or did not do things which they did do. Some historians do go wrong in that way too, but it is not in this that *idealism* consists. Idealism consists in *abstracting* "minds", "souls", "spirits", "ideas", "intentions", "tendencies", and the like, in such a way as to represent them as independent entities, independent 'forces, which are then the operative causes of historical events.

Now of course, people do have ideas and do act consciously; and if this characteristic of their activity is not taken into account, then their activity is misrepresented. But to represent "mind" or "consciousness" as though it were something which existed and operated independent of and prior to the total life activity of people who are conscious is to make a false abstraction. As Marx put it in the Preface to *Critique of Political Economy*, "it is not the consciousness of men that determines their being, but, on the contrary, their social being that determines their consciousness".

Similarly, Mr. Smith is conscious, and in that respect he differs from an automaton. To describe his mental processes and conscious motives is to abstract certain features of his life-process from the rest and to describe them, just as to describe, say, his eating habits and digestive processes is to make an abstraction. But it is not a false abstraction. What *is* a false abstraction is to say that his consciousness exists independently of his conscious activity in his material environment. To say he has a mind separate from his brain is rather like saying he has a digestion separate from his stomach.

These examples make it evident that idealism is not a way of thinking invented by idealist philosophers. What the philosophers have done is rather to generalise and systematise popular ways of thinking (embodied in superstitions, myths and religions) into elaborate theories about the universe and about man and human knowledge. But in so doing, they have not only theorised about minds and spirits, human and divine, but engaged in further flights of false abstraction which the unphilosophical would never attempt.

Thus, for example, Plato and all those philosophers who have been influenced by him right up to the present day abstracted the "forms" or "qualities" or "essences" of things, bestowed on them an idealised existence separate from and prior to things, and said that things are what they are because they partake of the form or essence. This doctrine is sometimes known as "realism" (though it is not very "realistic" in the common sense of that word), or better, "objective idealism". In modern philosophy there arose a quite different doctrine, often known as "subjective idealism" (its clearest exponent was the Anglo-Irish philosopher George Berkeley). While objective idealism supposed the supersensible and divine essences to be somehow apprehended and known by the intellect independent of the senses, subjective idealism arose from theorising about how we gain knowledge through our senses. It consists in abstracting the data of sense from the total situation in which a person is aware of his surroundings, bestowing on them an independent existence, and then saying that we have no reason to suppose that anything else exists and that what we call "material objects" are merely mental constructs out of sense-data.

The examples show how false abstraction differs from false statement of fact. At the same time, false abstraction does make a certain kind of misrepresentation of fact: it misrepresents the ways happenings are connected and determined. For in place of the real connection and determination of events it poses a fantastic connection and determination. For example, if you say that Mr. Smith cut work because of the sinful pleasure-seeking propensities of his soul, you have represented his action as being determined by what goes on in his soul, whereas in fact it is determined by what goes on in his brain. For this reason an idealist way of thinking may, and usually does, lead to overlooking happenings, and connections between them, which a materialist way of thinking leads one to search for and discover. Marx's materialist approach led him to study economic processes and relations of production which the idealists had ignored—because their idealist way of explaining what happened made them blind to the significance of these processes and relations. They excused themselves from having to make the kind of scientific investigation Marx made.

As Engels put it, materialism, or the materialist approach, consists in refusing to engage in "idealist fancy" or false abstraction, and resolving to comprehend the facts "in their own and not in a fantastic connection". This involves investigating the facts in such a way as to find out what their own real connections are. To engage in idealist fancies, on the other hand, is to excuse oneself from any such investigation.

3. THE CASE FOR MATERIALISM

The recommendation of the materialist approach is often opposed as a mere arbitrary dogma, and the materialist theoretical principles as incapable of proof. It is indeed logically impossible to prove from theoretical considerations alone that the materialist approach is requisite for the discovery of truth, and idealism productive only of fantasy. But that does not mean that materialism is to be dismissed as unproven. One great contribution made by Marx to the substantiation of the materialist approach was to have shown that its recommendation is a conclusion from the requirements of *practice*, and is grounded on *practical* considerations.

"The dispute over the reality or non-reality of thinking isolated from practice is a purely scholastic question", wrote Marx, in his *Theses on Feuerbach*. If you set out to reach conclusions about what exists or does not exist, about which is prior, thinking or being, and about how things are really connected, by a purely theoretical deduction from premises to conclusions, without any reference to practice and to what practice requires and what can be learned from it, then you can dispute for ever but can never prove any conclusion. Logic itself proves this. For it proves that no existential conclusion can follow from any but an existential premise, and that no existential premise can be certified by pure theory as self-evidently or necessarily true. There are and can be no theoretically certified premises from which one can conclude as to how the world must be and how true theory can be worked out and tested.

But theories are made by living people, who are not pure intelligences engaged in theorising, but practical agents whose practice leads them to theorise. "Social life is essentially practical", Marx continued. "All mysteries which mislead theory into mysticism find their rational solution in human practice and in the comprehension of this practice." The right approach to making theories, which will enable people in social practice to comprehend the facts in their own and not in a fantastic connection, has to be *learned* from trying to meet *the requirements of practice*, and is proved in terms of *practical* requirements and in no other way. It is a *practical* question, not an exclusively theoretical one—and has to be answered as such.

In theorising about practice Marxism brings into the practical argument in favour of materialism the conclusions of the empirical investigation of the actual conditions of human life. Marxism does not argue in terms of the bare abstract oppositions of "practice" against "theory", but in terms of a concrete analysis of human practice, which shows how theory and practice can be made one, in such a way that theories are consciously derived from practical experience and serve to inform practice.

What, then, is "practice"? What does this word mean in the context of the Marxist argument in favour of the materialist theoretical approach?

To talk of "practice", in this context, is to talk about certain activities (or certain aspects of the activity) of human beings. In other contexts one may well talk about the practice of chimpanzees in swinging through the trees, or of bees in building honeycombs, but in the present context "practice" means "human practice". The word is used to refer to certain unique kinds of activity performed by human beings.

Of course, if organic life has evolved on other planets in the galaxies, and has evolved forms similar in relevant respects to human beings on the earth, then what we say about human practice would apply equally to the practice of these similar organisms. They would be able to draw conclusions from their practice in the same way as we do. In general, *the laws of thought are the rules for drawing conclusions from practice*; and they would be the same for any thinking organism, just as the laws of nature would be. However, it will be convenient to ignore the possible existence of conscious intelligent life on other planets than the earth, and continue to talk only about ourselves—with the proviso that what we say about ourselves would presumably apply also to other organisms sufficiently like us.

Human practice is characterised by its being at once conscious, purposive and productive.

In *The German Ideology* Marx and Engels wrote that men "begin to distinguish themselves from animals as soon as they begin to produce their means of subsistence." It is from the labour process that the whole of human practice derives its distinctive human character—just as it is from the forces of production and the relations which people enter into in using them that human society derives its specific features. Writing of the labour process, Marx said in *Capital* (Vol. 1, Chapter 27) that it is "a process in which both man and nature participate, and in which man of his own accord starts, regulates and controls the material reactions between himself and nature . . . setting in motion arms and legs, head and hands, the natural forces of his body, in order to appropriate nature's productions in a form adapted to his own wants". Human labour, he continued, differs from the various constructive operations of other animals. "A bee puts to shame many an architect in the construction of her cells. But what distinguishes the worst of architects from the best of bees is that the architect raises his structure in imagination before he erects it in reality." From this is derived the distinctive character of human practice. The practical activities of the human body and its organs, in which individual men interact with objects environing them, are consciously directed to an end which already exists "in imagination". And by so acting people change external objects so as to adapt them to their wants.

In the *Theses on Feuerbach* Marx described human practice as "activity through objects"—it consists of men's conscious interactions with objects in the course of which they purposively turn objects to their own use. It is because of the way we turn objects to our use (i.e. act on them consciously, purposively and productively) that we form ideas of them—of their existence, their properties and relations, and of what we can do with them. Those ideas, Marx concluded, are first formed in human practice, and they can only be tested in practice, which he termed "human sensuous activity". It is in practice, and only in practice, that we can establish the truth about objects.

By calling practice "sensuous activity" Marx was calling attention to the circumstance that all our conscious action on objects depends on their acting on our sense-organs. The operations of the hands, to which he refers in describing the labour process, have to be initiated by and guided by sense-perceptions. It was with this in mind that Engels replied (in the Introduction to *Socialism, Utopian and Scientific*) to those philosophers who argued that there are no good grounds for supposing that any objects at all exist corresponding to our perceptions. "This line of reasoning", he said, "seems undoubtedly hard to beat by mere argument. But before there was argument there was action. . . . And human action had solved the difficulty long before human ingenuity invented it. . . . From the moment we turn objects to our own use we put to an infallible test the correctness or otherwise of our perceptions. If these perceptions have been wrong, then our estimate of the use to which an object can be turned must also be wrong, and our attempt must fail. But if we succeed in accomplishing our aim, if we find that the object does agree with our idea of it and does answer the purpose we intended it for, then that is positive proof that our perceptions of it and of its qualities, so far, agree with reality outside ourselves . . . the result of our action proves the conformity of our perceptions with the objective nature of the things perceived."

It is, of course, inherent in practice that it can be successful or unsuccessful—and that in varying degree. In so far as what people do fails to meet the end they set themselves, or fails to satisfy their wants, practice is unsuccessful. So there is always a kind of "trial and error" going on in practice. And in this we test and (if we have any sense) try to correct our ideas.

Human practice requires, and always must require, to be *informed*. By this I mean that in order to act on the objects surrounding us in a practical way, so as to contrive to turn them to our own use, we must first of all manage to obtain perceptions from which to conclude as to how things actually are, and then formulate (in language) concepts and theories about the properties and connections of objects in the light of which we can plan out what to do.

The information which we require for practice begins with sensations. But sensations, or sense-perceptions, are not themselves *information*, in the sense in which I am here using the word. On the other hand, all information is derived from and checked by perception.

Being conscious, purposive and productive, human practice has a social co-operative character. A man on his own can, of course, do all sorts of things; but that is only because he learns at least the rudiments of human practice in association with other men. To conceive purposes, to imagine something that can be made and to set about making it, people have to work together and learn from each other. They have to have evolved language, or the means of communication in articulate speech. The *information* which practice requires is *communicable*, and is *expressed in sentences and conveyed by language*. Sensations are not communicable; but aware through sensation of the objects of their practical activity, people formulate and communicate information about objects to inform and guide their practice.

A builder, for example, could not build anything unless he could see (or at least touch) his various building materials. But the mere sight of a lot of bricks does not by itself supply the information required for building. In this, as Marx observed, the human builder differs from, and shows his superiority to, various other animals which build things. For the nesting bird it suffices to see a bit of straw, and it picks it up and adds it to the nest: it acts instinctively, and does not require to be informed, as people do. Hence also it can get along with merely chirruping, and does not require to speak and be spoken to. The human builder, on the other hand, not only distinguishes the various materials of his trade by sight, but also requires such information about them as "This is a brick", "This is the hod for carrying bricks", "This is the mortar to stick them together", and so on. And as well as such *particular* information, he also requires information of a more *generalised* kind, such as "The bricks must be aligned like this or else the wall will fall down". True, a skilled man knows all this by heart, and does not keep repeating it to himself all the time, or asking his mates. He does not mutter to himself "This is a brick" every time he picks one up, or consult with his mates to decide what it is. Nevertheless it is on such communicable information that his skill is based.

Theory is required by men *to inform practice*. And while the word "theory" is commonly reserved for communications of a certain degree of generality, every item of information is, strictly speaking, an item of theory. The theory of an object generalises about it beyond whatever is immediately present to the senses at any time. Evidently therefore, such a statement as "This is a brick" is a theory—in just the same way as "This is a structure in which atoms are arranged in a certain pattern" is a theory: the second statement embodies more generalised theory than the first, that is the only difference. In fact, *all* statements are theories. And theoretical work or activity does not, rightly understood, consist exclusively in cooking up particular kinds of very generalised statements, but in arranging, co-ordinating, checking and criticising statements for the purpose of assembling information.

Theory to inform practice must fulfil, then, two very obvious conditions. First, it must deal with *sensible objects*, their properties and relations. For since our practice consists of interactions with objects that affect our senses, it is obvious that what informs practice is information about such objects. Second, what it says must be capable of being *tested* in the practical *experience* of our interactions with objects. This means that it must lead us to expect that certain observable happenings will result in other observable happenings: if they do not, then the theory is (so far at least) falsified.

Thus, for example, the theory that informs building operations deals with sensible objects, such as bricks. And what it says about them is capable of experiential test. The theory that "This is a brick" would be falsified if, on picking it up, it went off Bang! And the more general theory of building would be falsified if, in the absence of eathquakes or air raids, most of the buildings fell down. Obviously, a theory incapable of falsification would not impart any expectation regarding the objects we deal with in practice, and so would not inform practice. That is why the condition of falsification, which Dr. Popper so properly and vehemently stresses, is of such great practical importance in the making of theory.

The *practical* reason for keeping theory *materialist* is now evident. It is that only on that condition can theory inform and continue to inform practice.

But does not idealist theory also claim to inform practice, and to supplement in important ways statements about material things?

Let us suppose that someone asks the way to church, and is told: "Straight on and the second on the right—then you will get to the church." Having acted on this theory and found the church, he then asks the way to Heaven, and is told: "Pay two-and-sixpence and light a candle—then when you die your soul will go to Heaven." He acts on this theory too, and pays up and lights the candle. But it does not *inform* his practice in the way the other theory did, because in the first place it concerns his soul, which is not an object in any way accessible to the senses, and in the second place it cannot be tested in experience and is incapable of verification or falsification. He is not *informed*, but is simply handed out *instructions* which he has to take on trust. Information is capable of being tested in practice as you follow it up— but not the theory handed out in church. What is the faithful believer to do when he meets an atheist who tells him he has no soul and there is no such place as Heaven, or when he visits another place of worship where they tell him it is not of the slightest use lighting candles? He can only reaffirm his faith.

This example illustrates the difference between *informative* and *uninformative* theory. And it also shows how easy it is to suppose that uninformative theory is informative. It appears to be informative because it prescribes certain courses of action, just as informative theory does. "You want certain results? Then do something. You want to go to church? Then take the second on the right. You want to save your soul? Then light a candle." But it prescribes without informing. For the end which the prescription is prescribed to serve is defined as lying outside practical recognition, and whether it is achieved or not cannot be practically decided. It simply instructs you what to do, but offers no test of whether it leads to the results claimed for it.

All *idealism* bears this deceptive character. The idealist false abstraction is a pretence at information. It simulates information, and often stands as a substitute for it—but it does not inform. It is sham information. It is in this that its *falsity* consists. Information is true or false, and one can decide which by testing it in practice. But sham information cannot be tested. It does not present the same alternative of "true or false" because it is not susceptible to any decision procedure. It is "false", not in the sense in which a statement of fact is false when objects are related differently from how the statement says they are, but in the sense in which, say, a beggar on horseback is a false gentleman—it is not what it purports to be.

It is perhaps partly for these reasons that, in a scientific age, there is a growing tendency, at all events within the Christian religion, for religious believers to maintain that what is important, what really counts, in Christian teachings, are its precepts about the development of individual personality and human relations rather than its doctrines about another world. This is one of the reasons for the development of the contemporary "dialogue" between Christians and Communists, who on such questions find themselves in a good deal more agreement than either side previously supposed could be possible. What would be left of religion, and how long it could survive as an institution, supposing its precepts to be detached from the false abstractions with which they have always hitherto been associated, is a problem for the religious. So far as Marxists are concerned, we are not disposed to quarrel with people about what may happen to us after we are dead if we are able to reach a measure of agreement as to what to do so long as we remain alive. Marxists consider that to decide the latter questions we require only verified information about the conditions of our life in this world. Our grounds for always adopting a strictly materialistic approach in theory, and always rejecting the idealist approach, consist in the fact that only by adopting the materialist approach can we hope *to inform our practice*, whereas the idealist approach can never achieve anything but a pretence at information.

It may be said that we do not want merely to inform our practice but to discover "the truth", which serves higher ends than mundane practical ones. But what is this but to use the phrase "the truth" for the purpose of embellishing groundless fancies which serve to dictate modes of practice but not to inform them? We have no other way of seeking *truth*—that is, framing our ideas so as to correspond with the facts—than by seeking to inform our practice and testing our ideas accordingly.

Again, it is said that to adopt a view according to which man is a purely material being, with no "soul", is to adopt a very narrow view of human practice—for men are deeply concerned with "spiritual" things too, and impoverish themselves if they ignore them. Well, of course we are not concerned in practice only with material satisfactions, but with the satisfactions to be got from human relations, from love and companionship, and from cultivating all the higher human qualities of individuals. If by "soul" and "spiritual life" *these* things are meant, then of course it is no "fancy" to say that we possess souls and the capacity for spiritual life, and our practice includes our spiritual life too. But to recognise that does not require us to postulate immortal souls distinct from bodies. As a matter of fact, those who do so have so far signally failed to do much to raise the capacity for "spiritual life" of the majority of human beings. For if people's material life is impoverished, they do not get much chance to cultivate the things of the spirit—just as they do not do so either if they fail to appreciate the real character of human relations and concern themselves with nothing but their own individual material satisfactions. If only we can better inform our practice, in the materialist sense, by getting better to know ourselves, our needs, our dependencies on one another, we stand at least a chance of finding how in practice to cultivate all the higher human capacities, the things of the spirit.

3

THE MEANING OF DIALECTICS

I. DIALECTICS VERSUS METAPHYSICS

The materialist approach, as recommended by Marxism, has to be *dialectical.* While opposing "materialism" to "idealism", Marx and Engels opposed "dialectics" to what they called "metaphysics". This means that the necessary approach for working out informative theory is that of *materialist dialectics*—in opposition to the idealist error of false abstraction, and also to the sort of error denoted by the word "metaphysics".

In several passages of his writings Engels said what he meant by "metaphysics", or the metaphysical way of thinking, and by "dialectics" in contrast to "metaphysics". Although the account with which Dr. Popper has favoured us of what "dialectics" means in Marxist philosophy supposes that what Engels meant was something entirely different from what he said, I shall continue to assume that Engels nevertheless meant what he said—including what he said in those passages where he said what he meant.

"The metaphysical mode of thought," wrote Engels in *Anti-Duhring* (Chapter I), consists in "the habit of considering objects and processes in isolation, detached from the whole vast interconnection of things; and therefore not in their motion, but in their repose; not as essentially changing, but as fixed constants. . . ." Thus "in considering individual things it loses sight of their connections; in contemplating their existence it forgets their coming into being and passing away; in looking at them at rest it leaves their motion out of account. . . ."

In opposition to metaphysics, he continued, the dialectical way of thinking considers things "in their interconnection, in their sequence, their movement, their birth and their death".

As so defined, metaphysics consists in failure properly to connect. And dialectics, on the other hand, consists in properly *tracing out connections.*

Strictly speaking, Engels' addition of "sequence, movement, birth and death" to "interconnection" was redundant and unnecessary—a mere labouring of the point, done perhaps (though done in vain) for the benefit of those who study dialectics at mad tea parties where points are not always very clear. For quite evidently, if one fails to take account of "sequences, movements, births and deaths", one thereby "loses sight" of an essential element in "the whole vast interconnection".

To study "interconnections" is, therefore, a sufficient definition of the dialectical approach. So Engels, at the head of the chapter on "Dialectics" in *Dialectics of Nature* (Chapter 2), wrote that the study of the laws or principles governing the dialectical approach, and the dialectical understanding of the real world, should "be developed as the science of interconnections, in contrast to metaphysics".

Some may complain that in thus opposing "dialectics" to "metaphysics" Engels created confusions by using the latter word in a different sense from that in which it has often been used by other writers, both before and since. He used it in fact in a sense in which it was quite commonly used in Germany at his time, and which was employed by Hegel. And as he did explain quite clearly, and certainly more clearly than other German writers did, what this sense was, there is no good reason for finding his meaning obscure. By contrast, the other senses in which some philosophers have used the word "metaphysics" do leave a lot to be desired by way of clarification.

In the contemporary literature of would-be scientific philosophy, for example, the word seems often to stand for any doctrine that the particular philosopher disagrees with—and especially for any doctrine which says that the real world is other than it seems to be, and that the true nature of reality cannot be discovered by observation and experiment but only by pure reason. Of course, the dialectical materialist approach agrees with that of these other philosophers in finding such doctrines unacceptably "metaphysical"; but it finds many of their own doctrines equally so. What it objects to alike in their own "metaphysics" and in the "metaphysics" to which they are opposed is the failure to *connect* "appearance" and "reality", or the data of sense and the circumstances they reflect. Those whom many contemporary philosophers call "metaphysicians" consider "reality" as something quite separate from its "appearance"; but the "anti-metaphysical" philosophers consider the appearances in isolation and take them to be the complete reality.

At the same time, it should perhaps be admitted that, if we take into account how the term "metaphysics" originated long ago, the subsequent use made of this term to denote the antithesis of dialectics can be regarded as somewhat unfortunate. In its original use, the word "metaphysics", which is Greek in derivation and means "after physics", was the title given by the editors of the manuscripts of Aristotle to that philosopher's treatise on what he called "being as being". They gave this treatise that title for the simple reason that in their arrangement of his works it came next after his treatise on physics. It was largely as a result of the discredit into which Aristotle fell at the start of the modern age that the word subsequently acquired a perjorative significance, and was used to denote any sort of philosophical discourse which combines obscurity of expression with *a priori* reasoning. But the treatise of Aristotle to which the title was given was in fact a treatise about the universal interconnections of things, investigating in particular the connections between "substance" and "form", and "potentiality" and "actuality". To be fair to Aristotle, therefore, his "metaphysics" can properly be regarded as one of the first systematic essays in dialectics. So far from being guilty of the fallacy of metaphysics in the sense defined by Engels, that is to say, considering things apart from their connections, he sought to show how things must be understood in their connections. And so if by "metaphysics" we were to mean anything which follows up Aristotle's original treatise, then we would have to call any general statement of principles of dialectics "metaphysics".

In view of all this, and of the ambiguities attaching to the uses of the word "metaphysics", one might well wish to employ some other word to denote the mode of thought to which Engels opposed dialectics—and the simple expression "undialectical" at once presents itself. However, after its employment for more than a century in the sense defined by Engels, the word "metaphysics" has become so firmly entrenched in the discussion of dialectics that Humpty Dumpty himself could perhaps not now hope to press any other word into this employment. Its use need occasion no confusion, providing one bears always in mind the definition which has been given of it.

Having described the metaphysical or undialectical way of thinking (in Chapter 1 of *Anti-Duhring*), Engels said that what is wrong with it is that it "becomes one-sided, limited, abstract, and loses its way in insoluble contradictions". I have already quoted some of these contradictions when making the point that, far from welcoming them, the dialectician agrees with the formal logician in finding them highly objectionable. Metaphysics "loses its way" in contradictions, which become "insoluble" for it. Dialectics, on the other hand, finds the way to solve them by getting rid of them.

The undialectical way of thinking of things and their properties "in isolation, detached from the whole vast interconnection", leads to a formal counterposing of "is . . ." and "is not . . .".

Thus, for example, considering living creatures, as Engels put it, "each one separately", it would seem that they have the property of being "alive", which is the opposite of, and incompatible with, being "dead". However, if one considers what actually happens to them, in the real circumstances of their interactions with their environments, it is quite evident that death is a process. If that process continues long enough, the animal is quite definitely dead at the end of it; but during the process it survives in an intermediate condition. This fact is often illustrated nowadays at hospitals. Someone "dies", in the sense that his heart stops beating and he ceases to breathe, so that the processes of organic disintegration set in. But for a short time he remains sufficiently "alive" for the doctors to bring him back to life. Did he "die" or not? A less dramatic example of the same point is afforded by men who are losing all their hair. At a given moment, is such a man "bald" or "not bald"? The answer is that he is "growing bald", and that if he doesn't apply a hair restorer he will soon become completely bald.

Such examples are extremely simple and obvious, and as such not of great interest. As we shall see, the application of the same principle in other cases produces conclusions of greater interest. But meantime the simple examples make the basic point.

What is characteristic of the undialectical or metaphysical way of thinking, wrote Engels in the Preface to *Anti-Duhring*, is that it poses "rigid antitheses" and "sharp impassible dividing lines". It disconnects. But the continued investigation by the sciences of how things are *connected* in the real process of nature (and of society) means that these hard and fast antitheses and divisions "are more and more disappearing". Engels quoted a number of examples. "Since it has been proved that a body can be brought into a condition in which the liquid and gaseous forms cannot be distinguished from each other, the physical states have lost the last relics of their former absolute character. . . . And since biology has been pursued in the light of the theory of evolution, in the domain of organic nature one fixed boundary line of classification after another has been swept away."

Hence his conclusion: "The recognition that antagonisms and distinctions are in fact to be found in nature, but only with relative validity, and that on the other hand their imagined rigidity and absoluteness have been introduced into nature only by our minds—this recognition is the kernel of the dialectical conception of nature."

Hence he wrote in Chapter 1: "To the metaphysician, things and their mental images, ideas, are isolated, to be considered one after the other apart from each other, rigid fixed objects of investigation, given once for all. He thinks in absolutely irreconcilable antitheses. . . . For him a thing either exists or it does not exist: it is equally impossible for a thing to be itself and at the same time something else. Positive and negative absolutely exclude one another; cause and effect stand in an equally rigid antithesis one to the other."

But once one has grasped the point of dialectics, Engels wrote (*Ludwig Feuerbach*, Chapter 4), "one no longer permits oneself to be imposed upon by the antitheses insuperable for the old metaphysics. . . . One knows that these antitheses have only a relative validity. . . ."

In all these examples and explanations one looks in vain for the "thesis, antithesis and synthesis", and acceptance of logical contradiction, so beloved of Dr. Popper and other debunkers of dialectics (so beloved because so very easy to debunk). Engels' point in contrasting "dialectics" to "metaphysics" is quite simple, clear, and even painfully obvious. Metaphysics poses "absolutely irreconcilable antitheses", in the form of disjunctions: "Either it is . . . or it is not . . ., but not both." Such disjunctions do reflect distinctions and oppositions which are in fact to be found in the world. But they are nevertheless "only of relative validity". Dialectics consists in following up *the connections of opposites*, as discoverable in the real processes of nature and society. In these processes things come into being, change and pass away, not each separately, but in interaction and interrelation within "the whole vast interconnection of things".

When quotation from Engels removes the sort of objections to dialectics which, as we saw earlier, Dr. Popper lodged (for it is clear that Engels could not have meant what Dr. Popper says dialectical materialism means), a quite different kind of objection is sometimes lodged. This is the objection that what Engels said was obvious, and so obvious as to be trivial. The erroneous undialectical or "metaphysical mode of thought" to which he opposed dialectics, is a dead duck. No sensible person would ever think in such a way, so why make up a whole philosophy out of "dialectics" as opposed to "metaphysics"? "Dialectical materialism" turns out to be a mere truism.

The answer to this objection falls into two parts. The first part is that any philosophical principles which can be definitively established must always be, in a sense, mere truisms. Philosophies which appear as revelations of mysteries, revealed one knows not how, are, scientifically speaking, fraudulent. Valid philosophical points *must* be capable of being made "obvious", otherwise they cannot be valid. Hence Engels himself said (in *Dialectics of Nature*, Chapter 2) that, if only it is properly explained, dialectics must "become as simple and clear as noonday".

The second part of the answer is that the so-called "metaphysical mode of thought" is in fact anything but a dead duck, but is, on the contrary, widely engaged in with unfortunate consequences. To learn, formulate and inculcate the obvious principles of dialectical thinking is, therefore, far from unworthy of serious attention.

It is true that, as Engels said, all successful *scientific* thinking is, and must be, dialectical. All the same, to advise even scientists on the principles of dialectical as opposed to metaphysical thinking is not altogether the same as teaching one's grandmother to suck eggs. For what Engels also said is still worth quoting, even though not now so true as it was at the time he said it: "The scientists who have learnt to think dialectically are still few and far between, and hence the conflict between the discoveries made and the old traditional mode of thought is the explanation of the boundless confusion which now reigns in theoretical natural science and reduces both teachers and students, writers and readers, to despair" (*Anti-Duhring*, Chapter 1).

In more abstract and philosophical spheres the confusions that result from the metaphysical mode of thought, or lack of dialectics, are evident and notorious. One need not go back to the Middle Ages, or even to the eighteenth and nineteenth centuries, for examples. The most up-to-date kind of "logical-analytic" philosophy started off with the extremely "metaphysical" statements in which Russell and Wittgenstein enunciated the principles of so-called "logical atomism". "The existing world consists of many things with many qualities and relations", Russell announced in *Our Knowledge of the External World* (Chapter 2). "A complete description of the existing world would require not only a catalogue of the things, but also a mention of all their qualities and relations." And Wittgenstein elaborated this in certain famous propositions of his *Tractatus Logico-Philosophicus*: "The world is everything that is the case. . . . The world divides into facts. Any one can either be the case or not be the case, and everything else remain the same. What is the case, the fact, is the existence of atomic facts. An atomic fact is a combination of objects. . . . The object is the fixed, the existent. . . . The configuration of the objects forms the atomic fact. . . . Atomic facts are independent of one another." Russell and Wittgenstein saddled themselves, in their later activity, and their followers, with the unenviable task of trying to solve the numerous conundrums posed by these metaphysical statements.

In the philosophy of science, the "insoluble contradictions" posed by the metaphysical separation and counterposing of opposites supply further examples of the prevalence of metaphysics. Thus "particles" and "waves", "matter" and "energy", "determinism" and "indeterminism", continue to stand in "irreconcilable antithesis". In the discussion of ethics the metaphysical counterposing of "freedom of choice" and "determinism" still provides a subject for fruitless debate.

Finally, the metaphysical mode of thought is by no means without its influence in everyday and practical affairs. Take politics, for example. Engels said that metaphysicians adopt the precept from *The Gospel according to Saint Matthew* (5, 37): "Let your communication be Yea, Yea, Nay, Nay, for whatsoever is more than these cometh of evil." When people talk and act in terms of political formulas, and have a set of labels readymade to stick on to everything so as to judge it in accordance with its label, regardless of the actual changing circumstances in which both parties and individuals are acting and changing themselves by their actions, what is this but political metaphysics?

In the passages from which I quoted earlier, Engels mentioned some more difficult and interesting examples than the simple and easy ones with which we began.

"Closer investigation also shows us that the two poles of an antithesis, like positive and negative, are just as inseparable from each other as they are opposed, and that despite all their opposition they mutually penetrate each other. It is just the same with cause and effect: these are conceptions which only have validity in their application to a particular case as such, but when we consider the particular case in its general connection with the world as a whole they merge and dissolve in the conception of universal action and interaction, in which causes and effects are constantly changing places, and what is now or here an effect becomes there or then a cause, and vice versa" (*Anti-Duhring*, Chapter 1).

Again: "That which is recognised now as true has also its latent false side which will later manifest itself, just as that which is now regarded as false has also its true side by virtue of which it could previously have been regarded as true." And again: "One knows that what is maintained to be necessary is composed of sheer accidents, and that the so-called accidental is the form behind which necessity hides itself" (*Ludwig Feuerbach*, Chapter 4).

To get the point of dialectics one need only consider how many confused and confusing arguments have resulted from such abstract oppositions as "true" and "false", "cause" and "effect", or "necessity" and "accident". Fruitful discussion will always keep an eye open for the "latent false side" in propositions put forward as true, and for the element of truth in propositions condemned as false. Again, one may remember the confusion that results in discussion about social development when the idea that political actions are the effects of economic causes is divorced from the obvious fact that economic effects are caused by political actions. Or again, it is interesting to analyse the paradoxes and contradictions which accrue from saying that "everything happens by necessity", where "necessity" is supposed to exclude "accident". This last is a typical example of what many philosophers besides Marxists would recognise as a "metaphysical statement". The error in it results from counterposing the concepts of "necessity" and "accident" without analysing their interconnectedness; or, as some contemporary philosophers put it, not considering how such words as "necessity" and "accident" are properly used together in describing what actually happens.

2. MATERIALIST DIALECTICS

The account rendered of dialectics by Engels makes it quite clear that, for Marxism, the dialectical approach means considering things in their real interconnections, instead of separately—and therefore in their changes ("coming to be and passing away") instead of in abstraction from change.

There is the less excuse for Dr. Popper's making out that "dialectics" means nonsense about "thesis, antithesis and synthesis", because the actual use of the term by Engels and all competent Marxists in fact corresponds to its customary use over the years (not merely centuries, but millennia) by other philosophers.

Thus Plato, for example, stressed again and again the need for a "dialectical" approach, and for the understanding of "dialectic", precisely in order to avoid fallacies and contradictions resulting from thinking of things in a merely abstract way. Indeed, it was just this emphasis which accounts for the progressive quality of Plato's thought, despite his idealism and political reactionariness. His approach was the very reverse of metaphysical dogmatism; he was always inquiring, so that his Dialogues have remained living dialogues for over two thousand years, and will go on living so long as people go on thinking. In one place Plato illustrated "dialectic" by asking whether one of his fingers was short or long, and pointing out that it was short in relation to longer things and long in relation to shorter things. In other places he said that "dialectic" consisted in properly sorting out the relations of likeness and difference between things of a kind. Those who overlooked dialectic, he pointed out, got into absurdities and contradictions by posing what Engels afterwards called "irreconcilable antitheses". Thus a man who says his finger is not short but long gets involved in contradiction when he is made to admit that it is also short, and a man who says how different things are when he is made to admit how like they are.

Hegel's dialectic was derivative from Plato's; and similarly, his idealism was of the same "objective" type as Plato's—a resemblance duly observed by Dr. Popper in *The Open Society and its Enemies*, though he misrepresents Hegel on a scale that makes his misrepresentation of Marx seem almost like scholarly accuracy.

The purpose of dialectics, Hegel wrote (*Logic*, 81) "is to study things in their own being and movement". And to do this, he pointed out, we must study *the connections of opposites*—not simply hold them apart but connect them together. "We say, for instance, that man is mortal, and seem to think that the ground of his death is in external circumstances only; so that if this way of looking at it were correct, man would have two separate properties, vitality and—also—mortality. But the true view of the matter is that life, as life, involves the germ of death, and that the finite, being radically self-contradictory, involves its own self-suppression. . . . its own nature is the cause of its abrogation."

The difficulty in Hegel (as in Plato, but much more so) results from his *idealism*. He supposed that concepts or ideas are prior to things, and that the forms of relationship and development observable in the world are but realisations of concepts—so that the ways things are connected are deducible from the ways concepts are connected. A concept is correlated with and cannot be dissociated from its opposite (as "being" with "non-being", "quantity" with "quality", "continuity" with "discontinuity", "life" with "death", and so on). Hence (Hegel concluded) in the material world, where concepts are realised, opposites are indissociable. Quantitative changes consequently pass into qualitative changes, and the hard is soft, the short is long, the contin-uous is discontinuous, in the midst of life we are in death, and so forth. The artificiality and fallaciousness of Hegel's "dialectic" was due to the way he sought to deduce concrete connections of things from abstract connections of concepts. Thus in the notorious opening section of his *Logic* he claimed to deduce the temporality and change-fulness of things ("becoming") from the correlation of the abstract concepts of "being" and "nothing": because of this, he said, whatever has being must necessarily pass into nothing.

In a well-known passage (the Afterword to the second German edition of *Capital*) Marx said that with Hegel dialectics was "standing on its head. It must be turned right side up, if you would discover the rational kernel within the mystical shell." Instead of trying to deduce the interconnections in the real world from the development of con-cepts, we should try to develop our concepts in such a way as to reflect the interconnections in the real world. To do that is *materialist* dialectics.

Hegel (and, to a lesser degree, Plato) provides an object lesson in how a good dialectical, as opposed to an undialectical or metaphysical, approach can be turned into nonsense by being combined with ideal-ism. Materialist thinking, prior to Marx, likewise provides object lessons in how a good materialist, as opposed to idealist, approach can be turned into nonsense by being combined with metaphysics, or by being *un*dialectical.

Dialectical materialism is critical not only of idealism but also of metaphysical materialism. Marx and Engels included under the latter heading both ancient materialists, like Democritus and Epicurus, and modern ones like the French Encyclopaedists—the latter being also called "mechanical materialists" because of their idea that the laws of mechanics were fundamental for all material systems. All these mate-rialist thinkers persisted in thinking in terms of "rigid antitheses" and "sharp impassible dividing lines".

Thus ancient materialism posed the antithesis of space, as a sort of empty container, and matter, as what was to be found inside it. Democritus put forward the well-known metaphysical proposition, that what exists is "atoms in the void". This idea was simply taken for granted by the founders of modern physical science (Newton and others), and the subsequent scientific development of relativity theory and field theory (which *connect* space, time and matter) was necessary in order to try to get over the consequent theoretical difficulties.

Again, and especially in modern materialism, matter was separated from motion. Matter was thought of as either at rest or in motion, and some impulse had always to be given to it to get it moving. This led to the idea that God created matter and gave it its laws of motion, and then gave it a push so that thereafter material things kept moving.

Again, mechanical materialism took over from ancient materialism the metaphysical separation of mechanical motion, as spatial displacement of particles of matter, from all those forms of motion (such as chemical changes, or vital processes like sensations, perception and thought) which can be described only in qualitative terms. The former was then said to be the *real* motion, while the latter were only forms of appearance associated with it. The metaphysical separation of mechanical from other forms of motion was thus at the same time a metaphysical counterposing of appearance and reality. All that *really* happens in the world is that particles of matter move and interact according to the laws of mechanics. This led to the famous deterministic principle of Laplace, that from the position and momentum of every particle at a given instant could be calculated everything that would ever happen afterwards.

Such a metaphysical conception of matter and motion produced an equally metaphysical conception of the relation of matter and mind. Feeling, perceiving and thinking were regarded as nothing but subjective accompaniments of certain mechanical interactions. Thus, for example, the impingement of light on the retina causes a displacement of matter in the optic nerve, and this is "accompanied" by a "sensation".

Such metaphysical materialist conceptions were, of course, a gift to idealists. George Berkeley argued very convincingly, in his *Principles of Human Knowledge*, that the conception of matter put forward by "the most accurate philosophers" of his day (by which he meant metaphysical materialists) was "abstract and incomprehensible". It is not difficult to discredit metaphysical materialism, and then to claim that materialism is refuted.

In explaining what "materialist dialectics" means, Engels pointed out how metaphysical abstractions—counterposing one thing or aspect to another, and not connecting them—lead logically to absurd and unanswerable questions. Thus in Chapters 5 and 6 of *Anti-Duhring* he showed what absurdities arise from the metaphysical separation of space, time, matter and motion.

How could there be space and time without material events taking place in space and time? And what "matter" would be left if there were no such events? It is as absurd to talk of space and time separable from the relations of material things as it is to talk of anything existing outside of spatial-temporal relation, or (we may add) of space relations independent of time, or of temporal relations independent of space. "The basic forms of all being are space and time," Engels tersely summed up.

It is equally absurd to separate matter from motion. To do so is to talk as though "matter" were some sort of basic stuff or substance out of which things are made, and which is itself inert though things made of it will move if pushed. As against such absurdity Engels posed the principle: "Motion is the mode of existence of matter."

He then stressed the distinction and connection of different forms of motion of matter. There is not one single form of real motion (mechanical displacement), all other forms being mere appearances of it, but the investigation of the real motion of things involves connecting together the different forms of motion and studying transitions from one form into another. "Matter in motion" thus presents no simple picture of mechanical interactions. Simply to describe mechanical interactions, far from providing a complete picture of all that really takes place, is to abstract one single aspect—and then to present this abstraction as though it were the concrete reality.

"Motion in cosmic space, mechanical motion of smaller masses, the motion of molecules as heat or as electrical or magnetic currents, chemical combination or disintegration, organic life—at each given moment each individual atom of matter in the world is in one or other of these forms of motion, or in several forms of them at once", Engels wrote. Under definite conditions one form of motion produces another, and that other does not then replace the first but the totality of motion of the material structures concerned contains them both. Thus mechanical motions generate heat, physical motions pass into chemical, chemical combinations produce living organisms, and so on. But when heat is generated mechanical motion continues, chemical systems continue to obey the laws of physics, and living organisms exemplify the workings of the laws of mechanics. A person, for instance, who is acting voluntarily and purposively, is not thereby emancipated from the laws of mechanics, any more than his body ceases to be a physical structure and the processes in his tissues chemical processes. All the same, it is not true to say that a person's life is really nothing but a set of mechanical, or of physical or chemical, interactions.

Non-motion or "rest", Engels went on, "only has meaning relative to one or other definite form of motion". Absolute rest, or motionless-ness, is nonsense. So it is nonsense to suggest that matter may be either at rest or in motion, and only moves in response to an "initial impulse". One can no more separate matter from motion than from space and time. A body may be motionless in one or other respect, but it cannot possibly be motionless in all respects. Thus a body at rest relative to the earth is in motion relative to the sun; the internal motion of heat continues inside it; and so on.

In Chapter 1 of *Anti-Duhring* Engels explained in simple terms how the fallacy of metaphysical abstraction arises in the development of the natural sciences, and how the principles of materialist dialectics are necessary principles of the scientific way of thinking. And he repeated it all in Chapter 4 of *Ludwig Feuerbach*. It is indeed a pity that the rattle of the teacups prevented Dr. Popper from hearing these explanations.

In order to understand connections one has first to make distinctions. There is nothing wrong with "examining things separately": on the contrary, it is right to do so. Where metaphysics goes wrong is in sticking at the corresponding conceptions of distinctions and anti-theses, and failing to go on to study the connections.

For an adequate conception of things, Engels wrote in *Anti-Duhring*, we must study things in detail. And "in order to understand these details, we must detach them from their natural and historical connec-tions, and examine each one separately. . . ." So, he wrote in *Ludwig Feuerbach*, "it was necessary first to examine things before it was possible to examine processes. One had first to know what a particular thing was before one could observe the changes going on in connection with it." Science has to start with analysis, description and classifica-tion. But "when investigation had progressed so far, it became possible to take the decisive step forward of transition to the systematic in-vestigation of the changes which things undergo"; and so science in its later development has become "a science of processes, of the origin and development of things and of the interconnections which bind all processes into one great whole". Materialist dialectics is thus nothing but a generalisation of principles embodied in all scientific thinking, when it has advanced beyond the more primitive stage of analysis.

Once the point is made, it is very obvious indeed that no concrete or complete account of what is the case and what takes place can be content to consider each thing or aspect of things "in isolation" or metaphysical abstraction. It must take "the interconnections" into account. And when that is done, the kind of "antitheses" and mutual exclusion of "opposites" which come from undialectical thinking, together with the resulting puzzles and absurdities, vanish. Dialectical materialism makes this very obvious and very commonsensical point.

3. THE CONCRETE ANALYSIS OF CONCRETE CONDITIONS

"The world is not to be comprehended as a complex of ready-made things, but as a complex of processes," wrote Engels in Chapter 4 of *Ludwig Feuerbach*.

"This great fundamental thought," he continued, "is in its generality scarcely ever contradicted. But to acknowledge this fundamental thought in words and to apply it in detail to each domain of investigation are two different things." The general principles of dialectics—those "laws" which have been so often questioned, ridiculed and dismissed ever since Hegel first talked about them—are simply generalised guiding principles for this application.

And as Engels further said, "if investigation proceeds from this standpoint, the demand for final solutions and eternal truths ceases once for all; one is always conscious of the necessary limitation of all acquired knowledge, of the fact that it is conditioned by the circumstances in which it was acquired". The standpoint of materialist dialectics is thus one of continuous inquiry, opposed to all dogmatism —even though, according to Dr. Popper, the rules or dialectical laws of such inquiry constitute "a reinforced dogmatism".

To describe the world as "a complex of processes" is not, of course, to deny that there are "things". Engels made this perfectly clear when he wrote further that, in the processes of the world, "things apparently stable, no less than their mind-images in our heads, the concepts, go through an uninterrupted change of coming into being and passing away". The point is that "things" are not "ready-made", but are formed, transformed and dissolved in processes; and their properties, and their relations, are not fixed attachments of theirs, but come to be and cease to be exhibited by them in the course of the processes through which they go. If, for example, a stone has the property of being hard, and the relation of being harder than a heap of sand, that is because stones get formed out of certain processes—and if one takes this into account, it becomes evident that no stone is likely to remain hard for ever, but will grow crumbly and eventually crumble right away.

Stones are harder than heaps of sand, but sand may get formed out of crumbled stones, and can also itself get turned into sandstone.

To speak in terms of "complexes of things" is not always wrong. On the contrary, it is for many purposes the proper way of speaking. The point is that it is not the only proper way of speaking, but just one particular way. As I pointed out earlier, whatever we think, whatever we say, is always based on *abstraction*. To think and speak of "a complex of, things" exemplifies one particular *mode of abstraction*. This mode of abstraction is properly adopted for certain specific practical purposes. For other purposes it will not do. And it certainly will not do for the purpose of working out as complete and concrete an account as possible of what actually goes on in the world.

Let me take a very fragrant example, the scene of which is a commercial rose garden. Someone comes along to buy a dozen roses. In supplying this demand the rosegrower thinks only in terms of "ready-made things": he views his rosebeds simply as containing so many roses, some of this colour and some of that colour. In making up his accounts in the evening he continues to think in this same way: so many roses at so much per rose, so many labourers working so many hours at so much per hour, and so on. Nethertheless in seeing to everything that has to be seen to in his business he cannot always think in such an abstract way. He has to grow the roses, and in doing so does not think of them as "ready-made things" at all. His rose garden is no longer seen as "a complex of things", but as "a complex of processes in which things apparently stable go through an uninterrupted change of coming into being and passing away". So long as his only interest in roses was as commodities to be bought and sold, the "complex of things" mode of abstraction provided the proper way of thinking of them; it had to be supplemented by other kinds of concept as soon as his interest was widened to include also the concrete conditions under which roses are actually grown.

If from this humble rosegrower we turn to the philosopher, Lord Russell, we can see that his observation that "a catalogue of things" with "a mention of all their qualities and relations" would constitute "a complete description of the world", which I quoted as a typical example of a "metaphysical" statement, provides also an example of how deeply the commercial spirit has penetrated the thinking even of the British aristocracy. This whole type of metaphysics would, indeed, hardly have arisen had it not been for the development of commodity production and the separation of mental from manual labour.

When from viewing the world as "a complex of things" one proceeds to view it rather as "a complex of processes", in which things come into being and pass away in ever-changing interconnection, this procedure may be described as the passage from a more to a less abstract way of viewing things, or from a more *abstract* to a more *concrete* way of thinking. I cannot go here into the exact definition of "abstract" and "concrete", as technical terms of logic; it suffices to point out that a statement, B, is more concrete and less abstract than a statement, A, when everything A says is included in what is said by B, but not everything B says is included in what is said by A.

The "complex of processes" view is evidently more *concrete* compared with the more *abstract* "complex of things" view, for it includes whatever was included in the latter, and more besides. We do not think of processes as an alternative to thinking of things, but to think of processes is *to think of things in a much less abstract way*—in a way that more adequately reflects the actual concrete conditions of existence of things, the real interconnections. Thus whatever received reflection in the "complex of things" view is still reflected in the "complex of processes" view. When our rosegrower thinks of rosebeds in terms of the processes actually taking place there, he does not lose sight of the separate roses, or of their individual colours. Rather he sees them now (to quote Hegel) "in their own being and movement", instead of thinking of them in a more abstract way, in relative isolation from their actual conditions of existence.

Lenin, as I remarked earlier, wrote that dialectics was concerned with "the concrete analysis of concrete conditions". *Dialectics enters into thinking, and the principles of dialectics apply, whenever we require to make our thinking more concrete.* The dialectic of thinking does not consist in some artificially contrived performance of passing from "thesis and antithesis" to "synthesis" (wheoever but a charlatan or a pedant would undertake that?), but in passing from more abstract to more concrete concepts. Similarly, *the dialectic discovered in the objective world consists of those forms of interconnection within real processes which the concrete analysis of concrete conditions reveals, and which are ignored in more abstract metaphysical ways of thinking.*

The concrete analysis of concrete conditions demands the study of the forms of interconnection within the processes of the world, and it shows things as interdependent, changing, coming into being and passing away—and, moreover, as turning into their opposites, exhibiting contradictory aspects in different relationships and entering into contradictory relationships in which they suffer stresses and strains, conflicts and transformations.

Thus Marx wrote, in the Afterword to the second German edition of *Capital*, in connection with the analysis he had made of the concrete conditions of capitalist society, that dialectics "in its rational form is a scandal and abomination to bourgeoisdom and its doctrinaire professors, because it includes in its comprehension and affirmative recognition of the existing state of things at the same time also the recognition of the negation of that state, of its inevitable breaking up, because it regards every historically developed social form as in fluid movement, and therefore takes into account its transient nature no less than its momentary existence; because it lets nothing impose upon it, and is in its essence critical and revolutionary."

Of course, Dr. Popper does not like that. He represents dialectics, instead, as being doctrinaire nonsense. This he does by making out that dialectics is opposed to formal logic. But it is not opposed to *logic*, it is opposed to *metaphysics*.

The laws of logic are the laws of *consistency*. To advocate ignoring or breaking them is to advocate inconsistency. So of course, if that were what dialectics advocated, dialectics would be, as Dr. Popper says, nonsense. But, as we saw earlier, materialist dialectics advocates nothing of the kind. Its concern is with *a consistent account of how things are really connected*. It would be merely moronic to suggest that "the concrete analysis of concrete conditions" could be correct only if inconsistent. When Marx insisted on not only recognising "the existing state of things" but also "the negation of that state", he advocated no violation of the laws of logic. On the contrary, from the concrete analysis of the existing state of things the negation of that state follows logically. Marx was in fact very logical indeed. The scandal he caused "to bourgeoisdom" was due to his drawing the logical conclusions from a concrete analysis.

The laws of formal logic are of *absolute* validity, and *any* form of statement which sets them aside becomes thereby incoherent and inconsistent. The dialectical approach, therefore, certainly includes no suggestion that they may be broken with impunity for the purpose of a concrete analysis which treats of the real forms of interconnection of things—as though a statement of how things are connected could somehow break away from the norms of formal logic. Of course, if you ignore the ways things are connected—if you ignore, say, those connections of things which lead to an existing state of affairs generating

its own "negation"—you will reach wrong conclusions. That unfortunate result will not then be due to your respect for formal logic,
but to your disrespect for real connections. If you lack respect for
formal logic you can reach no conclusions at all.

What the dialectical approach does suggest and, indeed, insist on is
something quite different. Practical thinking (that is, thinking to inform
our practice) must always be logically consistent, but the laws of
logical consistency cannot by themselves provide sufficient principles
for its guidance. Formal consistency is not enough; though necessary
it is not sufficient. In other words, simply to say (as Dr. Popper says)
that the task of scientific thinking is to formulate generalisations consistent with observation, and then try to falsify them and, if they are
falsified, reformulate them so as to be consistent also with the new
observations, does not suffice. That must, of course, be done; but not
only that.

Generalisations about a given topic may be perfectly consistent—
consistent with observations, and falsifiable by observations—so that
by formal criteria there is nothing wrong with them; but even though
the thinking which employs only such criteria obeys the logical laws
of consistency with scrupulous care, and earns high rating from Dr.
Popper as science on account of its falsifiability, it is still hopelessly
inadequate for all but the most limited purposes of informing practice,
because it is still so "one-sided, limited and abstract". In order the
better to inform our practice we must formulate generalisations which
are not only consistent with observation, and falsifiable, but contribute
to the concrete analysis of the conditions observed.

Plenty of examples can be found of one-sided abstract generalisations, which illustrate also their obvious limitations. Such generalisations abound nowadays especially on social topics. Take, for example,
generalisations about the workings of the capitalist economy—which
are intended not only as descriptions of how things go, but also as
practical guidance for the direction of economic affairs, or for taking
advantage of economic circumstances for purposes of profit. What was
formerly called "the dismal science" of economics formulates such
generalisations, correlating all manner of observational variables in
the most scientifically complicated fashion, basing it all on statistical
inquiries, and correcting the generalisations whenever (as frequently
happens) they are falsified. These generalisations satisfy the formal
criteria of being based on systematic observations, being consistent
with the observations, and being falsifiable by other observations.

They tell us that when wages go up in excess of productivity such and such results tend to happen—and so on, and so on. Today in Britain such information is useful for persons trying to vet wage claims on behalf of the Prices and Incomes Board, or in the U.S.A. to establish Federal guide-lines on wages. But for the purposes of trying to find out how to organise human society to satisfy human needs, they are inadequate. For they just take the existing economic relations for granted, and describe how they work, without showing how they arose, develop and may be changed.

In the Afterword to the second German edition of *Capital* Marx quoted what he called a "striking and generous" account of his method of investigating economic processes written by a reviewer in the *European Messenger* of St. Petersburg. Marx investigated economic phenomena, said this reviewer, not only "in so far as they have a definite form and mutual connection within a given historical period. Of still greater moment to him is the law of their variation, of their development, i.e. of their transition from one form into another, from one series of connections into a different one. This law once discovered, he investigates in detail the effects in which it manifests itself in social life." "What else is he picturing", Marx commented, "but the dialectical method?" This method enjoins the concrete analysis of concrete conditions, and studies things in their real interconnections, in the processes in which they come into being and change, instead of being content with merely noting certain phenomena in abstraction from the processes in which they actually come into being.

The concrete analysis of concrete conditions has to be not only formally consistent, derived from observations and falsifiable by observations, but consonant with the principles of dialectics. It must comprehend the world "not as a complex of ready-made things but as a complex of processes"; it must not "in considering individual things lose sight of their connections", or "in contemplating their existence forget their coming into being and passing away"; it must not "be imposed upon by the antitheses insuperable for the old metaphysics", and must not simply note "the two poles of an antithesis" but also their inseparable connection; it must not in noting qualitative changes overlook their quantitative basis, nor in measuring quantitative changes ignore their qualitative consequences; it must not in dealing with one aspect of a relationship deny a contradictory aspect; it must, in short, always "study things in their own being and movement".

As I have pointed out, the one-sided abstract type of generalisation is perfectly adequate for certain limited purposes. For example, if you are a tradesman interested in things solely as commodities, it is adequate for your purposes to ignore the processes in which things come into being and cease to be. But for other purposes this will not do.

It is a striking characteristic of the modern development of the sciences, that the natural sciences, which are required to serve production, have had to give up the more limited kind of generalisation and investigate the dialectic of nature. For example, the biological sciences began by simply distinguishing the different characteristics of living species and noting how one characteristic is generally correlated with another—how horns and hoofs always go with a vegetarian diet, the frequencies with which the characteristics of parents are reproduced in their offspring, and so on. But they passed from this type of investigation to investigating how species evolve in interaction with environments, how living organisms are built of cells and their life consists of the disintegration and renewal of cells, and how the processes of heredity work. In this, said Engels, in the Preface to *Anti-Duhring*, "there could be no question of building the laws of dialectics into nature, but of discovering them in it and evolving them from it"; and in Chapter 1: "Nature is the test of dialectics, and it must be said for modern natural science that it has furnished extremely rich and daily increasing materials for this test, and has thus proved that in the last analysis nature's process is dialectical and not metaphysical."

The revolution which Marxism introduced into the social sciences was the same as that which took place in the natural sciences—the passage from abstract limited generalisation to dialectics, the concrete analysis of concrete conditions. But Marxism is not officially recognised by the capitalist scientific establishment. And so in the officially recognised social sciences the more limited type of generalisation has remained predominant. The practical reason for this contrast is not hard to guess. The Marxist analysis reveals the capitalist system in a light in which the successful bourgeoisie is not willing to see it, whereas more limited and abstract generalisations about costs, prices, wages, productivity, investment, and so on, provide them with sufficient information about its workings for their own profit-making purposes.

Thus *the same methodology which has paid off in the natural sciences is officially considered quite uncalled for in the social sciences.* Theories, like those of Dr. Popper, which formulate "criteria" for science simply and solely in terms of consistency and falsifiability, make out that limited and abstract generalisations are fully scientific. It then requires only a little ingenuity (or shall I say sophistry?) to talk about "reinforced dogmatism" and to make out that anything less limited and abstract is unscientific. Such limited criteria fulfil an extra-scientific function—they duly uphold the prejudices of the establishment.

In writing about Adam Smith, in *Theories of Surplus Value*, Marx remarked that Smith adopted two distinct lines of inquiry, which he never connected together. On the one hand, he "traces the inner connection between the economic categories—or the hidden structure of the bourgeois economic system". On the other hand, he was content with "only describing . . . the external phenomena". But this second line of inquiry was enough to satisfy "the man who is preoccupied and interested from a practical point of view in the process of bourgeois production".

The subsequent "vulgar" bourgeois economists developed only the second line of inquiry. Marx himself, following Ricardo, developed the first. And doing so, he also connected "the hidden structure" with "the external phenomena". Writing to Engels (April 30, 1868), he claimed that, at the conclusion of his analysis, "we have arrived at the forms of appearance which serve as the starting point in the vulgar conception. . . . But from our point of view the thing is now seen differently. The apparent movement is explained."

The same sort of development of two lines of inquiry can be seen in political theory. Political philosophers like Hobbes and, later, Hegel worked out "a theory of the state". Others (and one source of their inspiration will be found in the political essays of David Hume) considered such theories purely speculative and contented themselves with "only describing the external phenomena". This, to do them justice, they did with accuracy and care. They analysed, classified and minutely described different forms of state institution and different departments of state function. But the Marxist theory of the state again followed the first line of inquiry, theorising about "the inner connection". Briefly, it *connects* the development of states, and of state institutions and state functions, with the development of class divisions and class struggles.

According to Hegel, the state is "the realisation of the Moral Idea on earth". This is an idealist theory, employing false abstraction, incapable of empirical verification or falsification. So it has been very properly rejected by those who consider it better only to describe what states actually look like. The Marxist theory of the state, on the other hand, is a scientific and materialist theory, subject to the test of whether historical events confirm it or otherwise. For it investigates and verifies "the inner connection" in such a way that "the apparent movement is explained".

Many studies by non-Marxist political scientists in Britain and the U.S.A. are content today with no more than describing British and U.S. state institutions, for example, and how they work—adding eulogies in their praise together with some suggestions for their improvement. Marxist analysis takes all the facts into account, and duly displays them, but then explains how the state institutions are the means by which the social dominance of monopoly capital is maintained. That is a fact too. But when this "inner connection" is traced, as Marx said, "the thing is seen differently". The eulogies begin to sound a little hollow, the suggestions for improvement become rather more sweeping.

In general, if you accept existing economic relations and the existing political power structure as unchangeable, then abstract and limited generalisations about economic phenomena and state institutions are all that you practically require, and you will have no use for dialectics. If, on the other hand, you are practically interested in changing economic relations and the political power structure, you are compelled to replace such abstract generalisations by a more concrete analysis of the concrete conditions in which you live. You have resort to dialectics.

4. THE DIALECTICAL MATERIALIST THEORY OF KNOWLEDGE

The passage from more abstract to more concrete concepts, or concrete analysis of concrete conditions (in which materialist dialectics consists, and the principles governing which are the principles or laws of dialectics) is, viewed from the point of view of the development of human knowledge, a passage from knowing only "the forms of appearance" to the discovery of "inner connection" and "hidden structure". It is also a passage from knowledge useful only from the limited point of view of managing things as they are, to knowledge of how to change things.

And so Lenin, in his encyclopaedia article on *Karl Marx*, observed that "dialectics, as understood by Marx, includes the theory of knowledge, studying and generalising the origin and development of knowledge, the transition from non-knowledge to knowledge."

In considering questions about knowledge, and how to obtain and develop it, it is very important indeed to make clear that "to know" is not the same as to be "absolutely sure". This can be put, initially, as a rather obvious point about the normal use of words. If "knowing" were synonymous with "being absolutely sure", it would follow that we "know" hardly anything at all. I would then "know" that two plus two equals four, and that I myself exist, but not much else. This, however, is not what we generally mean by "know". For what we generally mean by "knowing" is something capable of *development*, whereas "being absolutely sure" is not capable of development. One is either possessed of absolute surety or else one is not. There is no development of it from being "less absolutely" sure to "more absolutely" sure. Hence what we generally mean by "knowing", and what it is interesting and important to study, is (as Lenin said) the *process* of knowing, "the transition from non-knowledge to knowledge"—from not knowing at all to knowing a bit, and then to knowing better. What counts as "knowing" in this process is certainly not identifiable with "being absolutely sure", and only very exceptionally ends in surety.

What we call "knowledge" must also be distinguished from "true belief". If, for example, there is life on Mars, the belief that there is life on Mars is true belief. But at the same time we certainly, as yet, *know* nothing of the matter. True belief only becomes knowledge when backed by some kind of investigation and evidence. Some of our beliefs may be true and others false, but we only start getting to *know* which are true and which are false when we undertake forms of systematic investigation.

In investigating and gathering evidence we are devising *tests* of the truth or falsity of beliefs or ideas, or of how far they are true. For nothing can count as "knowledge" except in so far as it has been properly *tested*. An essential part of the business of knowing is, therefore, the devising of appropriate methods of investigation and test.

What comes of the process of knowing would, then, be better described by such a phrase as "getting to know" than by unqualified "knowing"—for it seldom if ever reaches finality about anything, and contains few if any guarantees against error. The sort of tests we can devise are not *final* tests. To say we have got to know about something is not to say that our ideas about it have been finally certified as either true or complete, for the methods of investigation and test generally preclude such finality.

A great many philosophers, however, have supposed that we could not get to know about anything at all unless there were something we were sure about to start with. They have been unable to see how we can get to *know* without ever being *sure*. They have supposed, on the contrary, that whatever we know must be somehow or other based on, or deducible from, something we are sure about. We must *begin* by finding something we can be sure about—only so can knowledge develop.

As a result, there have been two sorts of theory of knowledge, both of which are wrong. On the one hand, philosophers have posited "first principles", or indubitable "data", which they claim to be sure about, and have then deduced all sorts of queer consequences from these and declared: "This is what we really know, the world must really be like this!" On the other hand, other philosophers have stressed human fallibility, and because they can find little they can be sure about have concluded that we "really know" hardly anything at all.

A grand source of error in the theory of knowledge has thus been the covert idea that knowledge must always begin from something we are sure about; and that to discover, therefore, whether we do or do not know something we think we know, it is necessary to find whether or not our belief in it is based on some form of certainty. But on the contrary, as Lenin said (setting forth the ideas of Marx about materialist dialectics), knowing, or getting to know, is a process in which there occurs "the transition from non-knowledge to knowledge". The process of knowing does not consist in the transition from being sure about one thing to drawing conclusions about another thing, but from not knowing about something, or being totally ignorant of it, to getting to know something about it.

Knowledge and ignorance are opposites. There are some things we do know something about, and other things we do not know anything about. And the process of getting to know is the transition from not knowing to knowing, and not simply from knowing something to knowing something else. It illustrates, therefore, the general dialectical principle of "the unity of opposites". But in the theory of knowledge nearly all philosophers have failed to appreciate this dialectic, and unwittingly adopted the metaphysical procedure of posing "rigid antitheses" and "sharp impassible dividing lines". They have opposed "not knowing" to "knowing", and supposed that knowing cannot come from not knowing, but that, on the contrary, whatever we get to know must be derived, somehow or other, from something we knew initially.

The route from not knowing to knowing *is found in human practice*. And if philosophers have not been able to discern .this route, that is because they have failed to notice the role of practice in the process of knowing. "In practice man must prove the truth, i.e. the reality and power, the 'this-sidedness' of his thinking' ", wrote Marx in the *Theses on Feuerbach*. Ideas that are formed for the information of practice, and then developed through investigation and tested in social practice, are the stuff of knowledge. Men pass from not knowing to knowing in their practical activity of developing their relations with one another and the external world, investigating the facts and the possibilities, and testing their conclusions. And in doing this they not only extend the scope of their knowledge, but also pass from one level of knowledge to another—from knowledge of particular properties of particular things, and relatively abstract generalisations about them, to the concrete analysis of concrete conditions.

Dr. Popper is, of course, quite right in stressing the necessity of applying *tests* in the development of scientific knowledge, and in stressing that none of these tests is ever final and that scientific theories are therefore always provisional. But in concluding from this that all scientific theories are alike "conjectures" awaiting "refutations" he is either concluding something which does not follow, or else using words in a very misleading way to mean something else than what those words would generally be taken to mean. To know is not to "conjecture", but neither is it to be "sure". Scientific knowledge is not conjecture, any more than it is final and complete certainty. The process of investigating the world and testing theories (which Dr. Popper lumps all together as alike "conjectures") is the process of getting to know—of passing from not knowing to knowing, and from not knowing well to knowing better.

In opposition to Dr. Popper's simplifications, and in opposition too to standard approaches to the theory of knowledge which Dr. Popper himself opposes, we may now try to sum up the dialectical materialist theory of knowledge in five cardinal points.

First, knowledge stems from experience, from the practical inter-actions of human individuals with their environments, in which people form judgements about objects and about themselves, and test and reformulate their judgements in the course of human practice. It is in thus connecting ourselves, in human practice, with things and with

examine the actual institutions—how they are constituted, and what the persons who administer them do. We must establish such facts as that there is a monarch, and discover what the Queen actually does. From this we may pass to a more concrete analysis and formulate (as was mentioned earlier) the theory that existing institutions of government are adapted to the function of preserving the dominance of monopoly capital. After that we shall have something more to say about the Queen than was comprised in the original observation of her behaviour—we shall have more to say than that she attends race meetings, confers honours, has a guaranteed income, and signs Bills.

Fourth, because knowing consists in the passage from not knowing to knowing, knowledge is always limited, partial, relative and subject to correction.

It is limited by the limits of the connections from which it springs. What is known is incomplete even in relation to its immediate object. Knowledge is limited by the conditions under which it was established, and is not only liable to be added to, but to be corrected when more is known.

Thus one should never say, without qualification, "This textbook summarises knowledge of the subject", but rather, "It summarises knowledge so far as it has been won by using certain techniques in certain circumstances". Consequently most scientific textbooks have to be periodically revised, and old ones replaced by new, not because their authors made mistakes but because knowledge has itself changed.

At the same time, knowledge is limitless in the sense that, whatever the limits resulting from the particular conditions in which we passed from not knowing to knowing, the discovery of new techniques and establishment of new connections may overcome them. Limits there always are, but no limit is finally known to be the final limit. The known is bounded by the unknown, but not by the unknowable.

Lastly, we can pass from knowing more and more about the processes which go on in the world, including our own individual and social life, to formulating the general principles or laws which have to be applied in and are exemplified by all knowledge, or genuine information.

This is the passage from *the discovery of matter of fact*, all statement of which is falsifiable, to *the demonstration of the necessary*, the correct statement of which, because it is necessary, cannot possibly be falsified. The principles of logic, which govern consistency of statement; the theories of mathematics, which are used for counting and measuring; and the principles of materialism and dialectics, which rule out fantasy and govern the concrete analysis of concrete conditions— are of this order.

All the processes we know are of the material world, they conform to logic, they exhibit number and measure, and they exemplify those forms of interconnection which we sum up as "dialectics". That this *is* so, we learn from getting to know about processes. That it *must* be so, is to be demonstrated by the tests applied in the development of logical, mathematical and dialectical materialist theory. In the development of such theory we are at one and the same time working out rules and criteria for the management of practical information, and testing the correctness and adequacy with which such rules and criteria are formulated.

5. REINFORCED DOGMATISM REINFORCED

Dr. Popper, as we have seen, regards dialectical materialism, or the materialist dialectic, as the fountain-head of the "reinforced dogmatism" of which he holds Marxism guilty.

"Hegelian dialectic, or its materialistic version, cannot be accepted as a sound basis for scientific forecasts", he writes (CR. 333). "Thus if forecasts based on dialectic are made, some will come true and some will not. In the latter case, obviously, a situation will arise which has not been foreseen. But dialectic is vague and elastic enough to interpret and to explain this unforeseen situation just as well as it interpreted and explained the situation which it predicted and which happened not to come true. Any development whatever will fit the dialectic scheme; the dialectician need never be afraid of any refutation by future experience."

There seems to be some little confusion in Dr. Popper's remarks as to whether they mean that the principles of materialist dialectics are valueless because they are *themselves* unfalsifiable, or that what is wrong with them is that their *application* leads to unfalsifiable pseudo-theories —theories so "vague and elastic" that "any development whatever will fit".

We have seen already that the second charge is certainly not true. Undoubtedly, as Dr. Popper says, some of the forecasts which Marx made when applying materialist dialectic in the study of social development have not come true, and yet Marx's social theory has proved "vague and elastic enough to interpret and explain" the failure of predictions in all those cases where such failure has occurred. But in that, Marx's theory is exactly like any other fundamental scientific theory. The sort of "dialectic scheme" (or rather, scientific analysis) which Marx worked out in *Capital* is testable, falsifiable and subject to correction and further working out in exactly the same way as any other scientific theory.

Does Dr. Popper mean simply that *general principles* of materialist dialectics, as the principles of an approach or method, have been so formulated as to be unfalsifiable? But if that is what he means, he is mistaken in suggesting that these general principles themselves imply "forecasts". If, as he says, "any development whatever" will fit them, then clearly no forecast is implied. In fact these general principles make no forecasts at all—and that is why no falsification of forecasts falsifies them.

Certainly, such a principle as the materialist one, that "the material world is to be explained from the material world itself", is unfalsifiable, and "any development whatever will fit". A particular materialist explanation of some phenomenon may be falsified, but that does not falsify the materialist contention that the correct explanation must be sought along materialist lines. Such a principle as this makes no "forecast" at all about particular events. It does not compete in the forecast stakes in the way the theories of the special sciences do, so naturally the sort of tests which are applicable to theories which do make forecasts are not applicable to such a purely methodological generalisation.

It is the same with principles of dialectics. They make no forecasts. For example, to say that things come to be and cease to be in processes makes no forecast about when or how any particular thing will come to be or cease to be. Someone who accepts this dialectical principle may make a whole series of totally false forecasts—that will not falsify the dialectical principle. Similarly with such a dialectical principle as that which says that qualitative changes are based on quantitative changes, and that at a certain point quantitative change results in qualitative change. This makes no forecast about any particular change. All such forecasts might prove false, but that would not falsify the general principle.

Materialism does indeed constitute "a sound basis for scientific forecasts", because theories not based on materialism operate with false abstractions. And materialist *dialectics* constitutes "a sound basis" because theories not employing it remain abstract and one-sided. But principles of materialism and materialist dialectics are obviously not "a basis" for forecasts *in the same sense* as scientific laws are a basis for forecasts. For example, the law of gravity is a basis for forecasts about what will happen to bodies in motion. At the same time, it is itself an exemplification of the materialist principle of explaining what happens in the material world from the material world itself, and in that sense its forecasts are "based on" applying the general principle of materialist explanation. But materialism itself, as a general principle, makes no forecast. The current formulation of the law of gravity might turn out to be mistaken, but that would not prove that materialism was mistaken. Similarly, laws of chemistry are a basis for forecasting chemical changes, and are themselves exemplifications of the dialectical principle of the connection of qualitative with quantitative change. They make forecasts "based on" applying that principle. But the dialectical principle itself makes no forecast. Particular chemical theories might turn out to be mistaken, but that would not prove that materialist dialectics was mistaken.

Dr. Popper has made great play with the words "basis" and "based on" for the confounding of materialist dialectics. But the basis for using such words should consist in being more careful in their use than Dr. Popper seems to be. The claim that general principles of materialism and dialectics must be "accepted as a sound basis for scientific forecasts" does not mean that those principles themselves make forecasts, so as to be tested, as scientific laws are, by whether or not the forecasts they make come true. What it means is that to make scientific forecasts we must study to comprehend the facts "in their own and not in a fantastic connection", and investigate the interconnections, the changes, the processes. If that is not done, forecasts may still be made, and some may come true and others not—as happens with the forecasts of prophets and astrologers; but they will lack what Dr. Popper justifiably calls "a sound basis".

The "sound basis" for forecasts lies in the materialist dialectical approach to investigating the facts. And that means that particular forecasts are based on scientific theories and scientific laws, which are arrived at by investigating facts and are tested in experience. Such forecasts are then based on the investigation, and on the investigation alone. This applies to all Marx's forecasts, both those which have turned out to be true and those which have turned out to be false.

But as Alice found at the mad tea party so we find with the critics of Marx, the type of exposition favoured by the March Hare and the

Mad Hatter only obscures plain meanings by playing on the more obvious sorts of ambiguities in words in common use. It is quite evident from what Marx and Marxists have said and done that dialectical materialism, as a methodology, is far from being either a reinforced dogmatism or a fountain-head of reinforced dogmatism. It is true that "any development whatever will fit the dialectical scheme", because "the dialectical scheme" is simply a scheme for investigating things in their connections and development. But it is not true that for that reason "the dialectician need never be afraid of any refutation by future experience". "The dialectician" is not a man sitting in an armchair who says "investigate the connections", but a man who investigates the connections. The outcome of his investigation stands or falls by how it will fit future experience, and if actual development does not fit his theories he must proceed to alter his theories so that they fit the development—in fact, he must carry on just like any other well-principled scientific inquirer.

Always ready to reinforce his refutations, Dr. Popper, immediately following the passage quoted above, proceeds to admit (as he does in other passages of his writings too) that Marx's teaching is *opposed* to "dogmatism" and in favour of genuine scientific inquiry. But what of it? Marxism is still a system of "reinforced dogmatism".

"Marx's anti-dogmatic attitude should be discussed", Dr. Popper writes (CR. 334). "Marx and Engels strongly insisted that science should not be interpreted as a body of final and well-established knowledge. . . . The scientist is not the man who knows a lot but rather the man who is determined not to give up the search for truth."

In this observation Dr. Popper transfers some of his own confusions into what "Marx and Engels strongly insisted"—for while insisting that no scientific knowledge could be "final" they certainly did not insist that it could not be "well-established", and while regarding science as a "search" they did not deny that those who search may occasionally find something. But let that pass. What is of interest here is the argument by which Dr. Popper makes out that "Marx's anti-dogmatic attitude" is transformed into "a reinforced dogmatism". Here it is.

"Marx's progressive and anti-dogmatic view of science has never been applied by orthodox Marxists within the field of their own activities. Progressive, anti-dogmatic science is critical—criticism is its very life. But criticism of Marxism, of dialectical materialism, has never been tolerated by Marxists. . . . Marx's anti-dogmatic attitude exists only in the theory and not in the practice of orthodox Marxism, and dialectic is used by Marxists, following the example of Engels' *Anti-Duhring*, mainly for the purposes of apologetics—to defend the Marxist system against criticism. . . . Thanks to dialectic the anti-dogmatic attitude has disappeared, and Marxism has established itself as a dogmatism which is elastic enough, by using its dialectical method, to evade any further attack. It has thus become what I have called a reinforced dogmatism" (CR. 334).

Here Dr. Popper develops his charge in a series of very sweeping statements, of which it can at least be said that none of them suffers from the fault of being unfalsifiable, since all of them are false.

He starts by telling us about the deplorable procedures of "orthodox Marxists". But if there are "orthodox Marxists" who "never apply Marx's progressive and anti-dogmatic view of science", that does not prove that the materialist dialectic which Marx regarded as the principle of scientific inquiry leads to dogmatism, but only that those who have become dogmatists have jettisoned the materialist dialectic of Marx.

There have indeed been and there still are such "Marxists". It was of some of them that Marx made his well known and often misquoted remark: "All I know is that I am not a Marxist." Dr. Popper can call such dogmatists "orthodox Marxists" if he likes—it is true that they sometimes call themselves so. That cannot alter the fact that a "progressive and anti-dogmatic view of science", such as Marxism advocates, precludes any rigid adherence to unalterable formulations of dogmas. And the fact is that in the development of the theory and practice of Marxism such "orthodoxies" have been regularly and relentlessly discredited.

"Marx's anti-dogmatic attitude" is acknowledged only in theory, never applied in practice, says Dr. Popper. Marxists have in practice so often experimented, rejected old schemes for new, and adopted theories about particular matters only to revise them, that a more common criticism is that their entire practice consists in a series of ideological and political somersaults. But Dr. Popper regards that as only another proof that Marxism is reinforced dogmatism. You can correct your previous analysis, alter your mind, change your policies— and still remain an "orthodox Marxist". "Thanks to dialectic", Marxism is "elastic enough" to evade refutation. Marxists refuse to apply the "anti-dogmatic attitude" to Marxism itself. Whatever betides, they insist on remaining Marxists.

What is the simple truth of all this?

Marxism has been well described as "not a dogma but a guide to action". When Dr. Popper talks about "Marxists" he is evidently referring, not simply to persons who accept in theory certain propositions enunciated by Marx, but to persons who contribute to and participate in the world-wide movement which accepts Marx as its first teacher. These are the persons who have allegedly refused to apply "Marx's progressive and anti-dogmatic view of science . . . within the field of their own activities".

What characterises and unifies Marxism as a movement (amidst all diversities and disagreements) is the aim of achieving a socialist society through the means of class struggle, and converting it into a communist society which will provide "to each according to his needs" by the employment of advanced technology. These ends and means of the movement are based on, worked out and justified in terms of Marx's original investigations of society and its laws of development. And these investigations in turn were guided by the dialectical materialist scientific principles of comprehending the facts in their own and not in a fantastic connection, in their movement and change, interconnection and development.

Obviously, anyone who decides that the principles employed and findings arrived at by Marx were fundamentally mistaken is not a Marxist but an anti-Marxist. And as obviously, if a sufficient number of those who are Marxists could be persuaded into "criticising" Marxism and becoming anti-Marxists, then Marxism would cease to exist as a force to be reckoned with, and the whole movement towards a communist society through the class struggle to establish socialism would fizzle out. Dr. Popper evidently regards this as a desirable outcome. So do many others—and they try to achieve it by a combination of criticisms of Marxism and punitive measures against Marxists. Marxists disagree, and so resist both the criticisms and the punitive measures.

Punitive measures have at some times and places been quite effective (though never for very long). But the same cannot be said of the criticisms. Marxists never tolerate criticisms of Marxism, Dr. Popper complains. True enough, they always answer them. I myself am answering some of them now. This dreadful intolerance of criticism, which Dr. Popper stigmatises as so contrary to the anti-dogmatic attitude of Marx himself, simply consists of listening to criticisms— and answering them. The critics, however, consider we should only listen—it is just too bad when we answer them back, and still worse when we make mincemeat out of them, as Engels did in *Anti-Duhring*. To reply to critics, and develop your own point of view at the same time—what a dogmatic thing to do!

Dr. Popper's objection to Marxism is that the Marxist movement has not yet found reason to revise its fundamental principles. What is so dogmatic in the Marxist movement is that it has continued to grow, and has not yet liquidated itself. It will not abandon its aims, and it will not renounce the idea that the means of class struggle are the means for attaining them.

There have been, of course, a number of people within the movement itself who have proposed to do so—but the movement has gone on without them. The so-called "revisionists" adopted Edward Bernstein's attitude that "the movement is everything and the aim nothing", regarding the communist aim as a utopian one based on dogmas, and the class struggle as a hindrance to the movement which could get to power more surely by class conciliation. This kind of "revisionism" has been justifiably described by Marxists as anti-Marxist. But the reasons for resisting "revisionism" are more cogent than simply that it is "revisionist". Why *not* "revise" Marxism in this way, or, in other words, liquidate the Marxist movement? Because revisionists have failed, as they claim, to show that Marxist theory is based on mistaken principles or that facts falsify it, and because, on the other hand, abundant experience shows that the proposals of the revisionists do not in fact lead to the practical results claimed for them.

The good reasons which Marxists have for defending the theory and practice of Marxism are not dissimilar. to those which, say, the directors of I.C.I. or Dupont would have for defending the theory and practice of the chemical industry, supposing some of the shareholders to object that a judicious employment of alchemy would be cheaper and easier. By diligent research and long practical experience I.C.I. and Dupont have found out something about what can be done with chemicals, and the necessary conditions for doing it. Similarly, Marxists have found out something about what can be done in society to satisfy human needs, and the necessary conditions for doing it— though the complexities and resistances met with in bringing about social changes are of another order than those involved in bringing about chemical changes.

The aim of the Marxist movement is socialism and communism, attainable through class struggle. Marxists have not yet found any reason to renounce this aim, either as a result of their own experience or of the objections urged by critics. If they did, or thought they did, the Marxist movement would stop, and communism would remain where the critics say it rightly belongs, in the realm of utopia.

At the same time, in order to move towards the aim, Marxists need to take at frequent intervals a long hard look at the conditions within which the movement is operating. They need to take into account, so far as they are able, all social changes and factors of change in all their complex interconnections. And on this analysis they have to base the policies pursued at different times and places, and the accounts rendered of particular situations. The Marxist dialectic is then exercised not "for the purpose of apologetics, to defend the Marxist system against criticism", but to effect that "concrete analysis of concrete conditions" without which the movement cannot find its way.

This analysis fails if it is not "critical". It fails if it is not checked and tested point by point, and if it is not thoroughly revised wherever and whenever circumstances change or experience reveals an error.

And of course it quite often does fail. It is but human to err, and Marxists often make mistakes—whether through inexperience, incompetence or dogmatism, or because they simply had not the time or means to conduct all the inquiries necessary. Their "reinforced dogmatism" then takes the form (luckily for the movement) of their not giving up the struggle or becoming anti-Marxists every time something goes wrong. Thanks to this reinforced dogmatism or, as it might better be phrased, clear-headedness and high morale, and thanks to the fact that the movement is so deeply rooted in social realities that whenever some go wrong others come forward to put them right, errors get corrected, and when circumstances change changed policies are adopted to meet changed circumstances.

It was for this reason that Lenin reinforced his dogmatism by .calling for continual "criticism and self-criticism". Lenin did, however, venture to remark, when annoyed by critics who jeered at the mistakes of Communists from the security of their padded cells in the capitalist madhouse, that the mistakes *we* make are like making "two plus two equal five", whereas the mistakes *they* make are like making "two plus two equal a tallow candle". When we make two plus two equal five we soon discover our error and find the right way of making them four.

In the international development of the Marxist movement, each generation is faced with conditions and tasks significantly different from those of the last. Circumstances change, and the very achievements, as well as the errors, of the previous generation present new tasks to the next. Similarly, these circumstances and tasks are different from one economic region to another, even from one country to another. In this way the "Marxism" of one time is not precisely the same as that of another time, and the "Marxism" of one place not precisely the same as that of another place. Besides errors which are peculiar to one time and place, the correct analysis, the correct definition of tasks, becomes different.

THE NECESSITY OF DIALECTICS

I. THE SCIENCE OF INTERCONNECTIONS

Dr. Popper's contention that dialectical materialism is a reinforced dogmatism comes from his failure to comprehend that the terms "dialectics" and "materialism", separately or together, do not stand for particular dogmatic theories but for the way of thinking or the approach necessary for working out non-dogmatic scientific theories. This applies equally whether the objects of investigation are processes of nature or of society—for there is no gulf between these. People are material organisms, and their individual and social activities are as much a part of the material world as are any other distinguishable types of material interactions. Dr. Popper is right, of course, in saying that Marx adopted an "anti-dogmatic attitude". He is entirely wrong in saying that to go on maintaining such an attitude demands "criticism of dialectical materialism". On the contrary, dialectical materialism is the principle of such an attitude, and consistently to maintain that attitude demands consistently maintaining dialectical materialism.

But, it will be objected, is not dialectical materialism itself a theory —the general philosophical theory of Marxism? And is not its intolerant assertion therefore dogmatic?

This objection depends only on equivocation. The word "theory" is ambiguous, and is here employed in two senses. There is theory in the sense of theory which informs or claims to inform practice; and theory in the sense of statement of the principles to be employed in informing practice. Scientific theories, religious theories, and also many traditional philosophical theories, are of the first sort. But the theory of dialectical materialism is of the second sort.

If the reader finds this confusing, I can only say that this ambiguity resides in the customary use of words, and that once it is pointed out the confusion vanishes. If one wanted, however, to use a technical term to point the distinction, the Greek prefix "meta-" could be adopted, and one could speak of "theory" and "meta-theory" (like those who now distinguish "mathematics" and "meta-mathematics"). Dialectical materialism would then be called the meta-theory of Marxism—the theoretical statement of the principles which Marxism advocates for the working out of all theory to inform human practice. But if one nevertheless prefers speaking English to speaking Greek, one will simply say (as is customary) that dialectical materialism is the general philosophical theory of Marxism.

As I have tried to explain, materialism is opposed to idealism, and dialectics to metaphysics. When theory is idealist it engages in false abstraction and its claim to inform us is a sham. When theory is metaphysical it is not necessarily an uninformative sham (though it may be that as well, if it is also idealist), but it is abstract and limited, in the sense that it considers objects and processes, and assigns properties and relations to things, only in abstraction from the concrete conditions in which they come to be and cease to be.

The principles of materialism, therefore, are the general ones to make theory informative, and the principles of materialist dialectics are the ones to carry forward informative theory into the concrete analysis of concrete conditions. And the general philosophical theory of dialectical materialism is the statement of the principles or rules of materialism and dialectics. This (like physics or mathematics) is not something that can be finally and completely formulated once for all. It has to be worked out and developed.

Materialism expresses what is necessary to keep theory on the ground and stop it flying away on the wings of false abstraction. We must also make sure that all sides, all aspects of the concrete conditions to be investigated are properly related to and connected with each other. This is the business of dialectics. Dialectics expresses what is required in theory to connect the data properly, to assemble properly the various items of information, or to process the information, so as to make analysis concrete and avoid one-sidedness. To state the general principles or laws of dialectics is, then, to state those most general *laws of interconnection* which are *and must be* exemplified in processes. These laws do not state what is going to happen or not happen in particular cases, but they state the *forms* of interconnection in the real world, which are exemplified *whatever* happens, and which it is the job of every concrete analysis to trace out.

Can we discover such laws? Marx and Engels were of opinion, and said so clearly, that examination of the findings of science does lead to the conclusion that there are such laws which are universally exemplified. They were of opinion that such general concepts as those of "the unity of opposites" and "the transformation of quantitative into qualitative changes" express, however imprecisely in their initial formulation, universal laws which are always found exemplified in all the processes of both nature and society. That is to say, whatever process we may consider, the concrete analysis of what is going on always reveals the inseparable connection of opposite sides or aspects, the conflict or struggle of contradictory elements, the occurrence of qualitative changes as a result of quantitative changes, and so on. Of course, if the concepts are imprecise, and the terminology employed loose or ambiguous, these are defects of exposition which future work ought to be able to remedy.

In their works Marx and Engels provided numerous illustrations of what they conceived to be the correct application of such general concepts of dialectics, as well as providing explanations (which I have quoted) of what they meant in general by "materialism" and "dialectics". But they nowhere undertook any systematic working out of the "laws of dialectics" in their generality. What they did— and Engels especially in the chapters on the laws of dialectics in *Anti-Duhring* and *Dialectics of Nature*—was to cite *examples* of phenomena corresponding to these laws.

Engels made the purpose of these examples perfectly clear. He was arguing against Duhring and others who had said that "dialectics" was nothing but a farrago of empty phrases. He cited examples to demonstrate that this was not so, but that the sorts of movements and interconnections described as "dialectical" do occur. He demonstrated that such concepts as "the transformation of quantity into quality" and "the negation of the negation" really are, as he said they were, "abstracted from the history of nature and society", because many concrete examples of such modes of interconnection are in fact to be found in "the history of nature and society".

Such examples did demonstrate what Engels set out to demonstrate. But of course, the mere citing of examples did not and could not demonstrate the universality and *necessity* of the laws of dialectics. Examples can serve to make clear the meaning of concepts, and to refute criticisms based on misunderstanding their meaning or on saying that they are meaningless. But no list of examples, however long, could suffice to establish the universal validity of concepts. Nor could examples demonstrate that the "laws" exemplified were the complete laws, that there were no others.

These are elementary points of logic which anyone who discusses dialectics ought to understand, though some apparently do not. There is no reason to include Engels among the latter. On the contrary, what he wrote makes it clear that he understood such points of logic very well. And he accordingly stated (I have already quoted this statement, but now I add my own italics): "Dialectics is to be *developed* as the *science* of interconnections."

A *science* is meant to comprise, one would suppose, a good deal more than a list of examples. Engels also said that he was "not concerned with writing a textbook of dialectics", and that in citing examples of dialectical laws he did not "go into the inner connection of these laws with one another". The "science of interconnections" would have, however, not only to state a set of laws but show how they were connected, and it would all have to be worked out and demonstrated by appropriate methods of formulation and test.

That there is work to be done here was likewise emphasised by Lenin. In his notes *On the Question of Dialectics* Lenin criticised G. V. Plekhanov on the grounds that, in his exposition, laws of dialectics were only "taken as the sum-total of examples". "The same is true of Engels," Lenin added, "but it is in the interests of popularisation." He then stated that the "principal" law of dialectics, "the unity of opposites", ought to be expounded and demonstrated "as a law of cognition *and* as a law of the objective world".

At all events, unless it can be so expounded, and ways found of testing the exposition at every link and every step, dialectics can hardly claim the status of "the *science* of interconnections".

Materialist dialectics asserts "the unity of opposites", and that there are "contradictions" in all the phenomena of nature and society, as universal truth. Examples, as I have just said, may help to illustrate what is meant, and to show that the concepts are not empty ones. But they cannot by themselves suffice to demonstrate the universality of the concepts, or to explain why it *must* be so. What is required, as both Engels and Lenin after him stated very clearly, is for more work to be done on the actual derivation and basis of these concepts, so as to show *why* "concrete analysis" should *always* exemplify, say, the unity of opposites and the discovery of dialectical contradiction.

If Dr. Popper wants to criticise Marxists, he could well point out that we have been slow to follow up the very clear theoretical directives of both Engels and Lenin for the systematic study of materialist dialectics, which would make it more than "the sum-total of examples" and develop it as the real "science of interconnections". But wanting to make out that Engels was only interested in "apologetics" and that dialectics is all nonsense anyway, he has not thought fit to assist us with any such constructive criticism.

2. THE UNITY OF OPPOSITES

The fundamental concept of dialectics is that of the unity or inseparable connection of opposites. This has been stated by nearly all who throughout the history of philosophy have variously discussed "dialectics". At the start of the present discussion, when examining the distinction of "dialectics" from "metaphysics" as a method of thinking, the point emerged that "dialectics consists in following up *the connections of opposites*".

The idea that everything that comes to be is the product of the mutual interaction and interpenetration of opposites, and holds them within itself, is a very ancient one, being founded on universal experience. Thus, for example, in very ancient Chinese philosophy the world and everything in it was said to be the product of the action and conflict of eternally opposite forces or principles, manifesting themselves in all the particular oppositions to be found in the universe. Every unity necessarily divides into two opposite components contained within it, and development results from the interaction of these inseparable opposites into which it divides. Undifferentiated unity would be motionless: motion arises and continues as a result of "the division of the One" into conflicting opposites. Something of the sort has, indeed, recently been repeated by Mao Tse-tung and his followers in China. For this way of thinking, the existence of opposites and their inseparable connection is the fundamental fact of the universe. It is an ultimate mystery for which there is no accounting. It just *is* so.

It is certainly true that a fundamental opposition is always to be found in every process or aspect of processes we may consider. For example, in vision the light and the dark, black and white; in touch the hot and cold, rough and smooth, hard and soft; in magnetism, opposite poles; in all motion, forwards and backwards, up and down, right and left; and so on. However, in considering such examples of opposition we would be well advised to avoid the fallacy of *false abstraction* into which both the earliest philosophers and some of their later followers seem to have fallen. Thus, for example, the opposite terms "light" and "dark" do not stand for eternal and primeval forces of Light and Darkness the war between which produces the phenomena of variations in light and shade. On the contrary, the opposition between "light" and "dark" is simply the logical opposition of abstract terms employed in the description of the phenomena of vision familiar to us in changes of light and shade, and from light to dark.

In general, any terminology adapted to the statement and description of *changes* (or in other words, any language, or any apparatus of workable concepts) is sure to reveal in logical analysis a structure of opposite terms. It is a logical necessity. Why is this? It is because to specify a change one must specify a direction of change—from this to that. The total complex of observable changes includes many different aspects of change, each of which can be considered in abstraction. For instance, there are changes in colour, in shape, in relative motion, and so on. To specify *what* change is taking place in any particular case under a given aspect of change, one must be able to specify a *direction* of change, and then that the change is taking place *either* in that direction *or* in the *opposite* direction. Every possible direction of change *necessarily has its opposite*. It follows that in specifying the changes taking place under any aspect of possible change, we always find ourselves confronted with opposites, two *opposite directions of change*, under which the totality of possible changes can take place.

Suppose, then, that instead of specifying changes we are concerned with comparisons. The respects under which things may be compared are the same as the respects under which they can change. And comparisons are the same thing as estimates of what change would be involved in changing the state of the one thing compared into that of the other. So of course the opposites of directions of change also appear as the opposites of comparison. Hence in comparing shades, for example, we have the "opposites"—dark and light, black and white. They appear not as opposite directions of change but as opposite qualities.

The most elementary instances of the principle of "the unity of opposites" are those afforded by the logical principle that to specify changes we have to specify them under opposite directions of change peculiar to each aspect of change. All those elementary examples of inseparable opposites like black and white, hot and cold, wet and dry, up and down, north and south, and so on, quoted to illustrate the principle of the unity of opposites, are examples of the principle that possible changes go in opposite directions. If, then, dialectics is (as Lenin said) "the concrete analysis of concrete conditions", and the principles or laws of dialectics are the principles or laws which have to be applied in passing from a more abstract to a more concrete account of things, the most elementary principles of dialectics are those concerned with the use of concepts of opposite directions of change when specifying changes and engaging in comparisons.

These principles are very elementary and seemingly trivial. And so it cannot but seem something of an anti-climax when one arrives at them as a result of eliminating false abstractions from the impressive but obscure and mystical conception of the eternal law of the division of unity into inseparable and contradictory opposites, whose omni-present conflict produces all the phenomena of the world.

However, lest it be said that we are reducing dialectics to the commonplace, we should go on to observe that a good deal more is involved in the thorough working out of the principle of the unity of opposites. In this, a great deal of muddle can be created, not only by false abstraction (such as that engaged in by most ancient and some modern exponents), but also by muddling up together different types of example. For instance, if to the examples of "opposites" expressive of opposite directions of change (which I cited above) are added further examples of "opposites" such as "male and female" or "capitalists and workers" or "socialised production and private appropriation", then the whole conception of opposites and of their connection is confounded by the confusion and indiscriminate lumping together of *different types* of opposition and of the unity of opposites. This shows that the principle of "the unity of opposites" is not one single universal law which can be expressed in a single formula, but *a whole branch of philosophical inquiry* which needs careful working out.

So far as it relates to opposite directions of change, the principle of the unity of opposites expresses only what is logically necessary in the conceptual representation of changes. Further working out of the same principle can proceed on the same basis.

I have already remarked several times upon the procedures of *abstraction* characteristic of all thinking. All thinking proceeds by *abstractions* out of the concrete processes amid which we live, and then represents them in terms of these abstractions and of com-binations of abstractions. I pointed out that "all statement abstracts", and cited as an example the statement "This rose is red", which "abstracts a particular rose from the total environment, and its colour from the totality of its other properties". I then pointed out that there are different "modes of abstraction", which are "properly adopted for different practical purposes". For example, to talk about, say, colour is evidently one mode of abstraction, to talk about shape or size another, to talk about relative motion yet another.

Principles of dialectics come in when we pass from more abstract to more concrete statement. They come in as *the principles of properly combining or assembling different modes of abstraction* in the concrete analysis of concrete conditions. The most elementary exercise in abstraction characteristic of our thinking is that of abstracting the different aspects of observable change and the opposite directions of change under these different aspects. In terms of these abstractions we state the changes and possible changes things undergo, and make comparisons by means of which we state the properties of things and relate them to each other by comparison of their properties. The most elementary exercise of dialectics is, therefore, the exercise of properly combining in the concrete analysis of concrete conditions the abstract conceptions of aspects of change and of opposite directions of change.

But this is only the beginning of the story of the adventures of dialectical thinking, not the end.

"The world is not to be comprehended as a complex of ready-made things, but as a complex of processes." It will be remembered that Engels called this statement (which, as he said, is so obvious that it is seldom contradicted) a "great fundamental thought". It follows from it (as I pointed out in an earlier chapter) that to talk about "things" and "complexes of things" is merely one mode of abstraction, adequate for some practical purposes but far from adequate for others. Quite evidently, to talk about the complex of processes going on, and to say how out of it there emerge the various complexes of things which we observe and which come and go and change in processes, is to talk more concretely than simply to say "There are such and such things"—which is true enough, but a much more abstract statement. Therefore the concrete analysis of concrete conditions always demands that we should *combine* modes of abstraction which deal with "things" and modes of abstraction which deal with "processes". This involves rather more profound questions than those hitherto considered.

As the ancient philosopher Heraclitus put it, "everything flows". Or as Hegel put it, nothing just "is": all "being" is "becoming", a ceaseless coming to be and ceasing to be. A feature of conceptual consciousness, derived from the use of language, is, however, that as reflected in statements the passage of time is apparently arrested. If you make a remark like, for instance, "He came in at the door", a particular event, a particular state of affairs, is, so to speak, taken up out of time and fixed in the combination of symbols. However, to reflect (however inadequately) the actual passage of time amd the actual spatial-temporal interconnection in that passage, from which momentary states of affairs, relations of things, and so on, are abstracted and fixed in repeatable images, it is necessary to say how particular things, complexes of things, facts and events come to be and cease to be *in processes.*

For this reason there are always *two* fundamental and inseparable *modes of abstraction* employed in the reflection of concrete reality in thought—that mode which, in Engels' words, produces only an abstract picture of "a complex of ready-made things", and that which then contributes to a more concrete picture of "a complex of processes".

As we saw earlier, the more concrete picture of "a complex of processes" *includes* what was presented in the abstract picture of "a complex of things". Evidently, therefore, the picture of "a complex of processes" is composed by *combining* with the products of the mode of abstraction which gives only "a complex of things" the products of that other and complementary mode of abstraction which gives "processes". To reflect concrete reality, flowing in time, we have therefore to *combine* these abstractions in the picture of things coming to be and ceasing to be in ever-moving interrelationship in processes.

It follows that for the adequate representation of concrete reality there is always required, as a strictly logical or logically necessary requirement, the combination of what may loosely be called "complex of things" concepts with "complex of processes" concepts—which are thus logically paired together. This, I believe, is the rational explanation of a remark by Hegel with which he introduced what he called "The Doctrine of Essence" in the Logic section of his *Encyclopaedia of the Philosophical Sciences*, a remark so obscure it may well have made Dr Popper groan (and not only him): "The terms in Essence are always mere pairs of correlatives." The truth is, and this is a profound principle of dialectical thinking, that we must always *connect* the "opposite" but complementary and inseparable aspects or features which concrete reality presents to us—of flow and arrested flow, fluid process and fixed momentary state, unrepeatable passage and repeatable pattern— in the concrete analysis of concrete conditions. Hence we get the logically necessary correlation in pairs of such categories as those of "property and relation", "form and substance", or "quality and quantity". The first term in each pair is the "complex of things" category, the second, its correlative or opposite "process" category; the second the category of flow, the first of arrested flow.

Thus, for example, things are conceived of as having *properties* which "belong" to them: and at the same time, when considered in their movement, they enter into all manner of complex *relations* with other things. The "metaphysical" way of abstract thinking just sets down properties and relations side by side, as it were. There are properties and (also) relations. On the other hand, the concrete analysis of concrete conditions (in which principles of dialectics emerge) is concerned with tracing out how things come to manifest various properties as a result of the ever-changing relationships which occur in processes. Thus the properties of things change with changing relations: what is true of a thing in one relationship is not true in another, what is true in one set of circumstances is not true in another.

Again, consider the pair of "opposites": "form and substance", or "form and content". This involves consideration of the way in which the occurrence of processes, which may loosely be said to constitute the "substance" or "content" of things, always produces, and is circumscribed within, certain patterns or "forms". (Unfortunately, the terms provided by ordinary language are far from precise and invariably ambiguous, so that unless we are to embark on a long discussion in which a whole series of technical distinctions and definitions are included these points about dialectics can only be hinted at in a rough and ready way; this is the best that limitations of time and space allow us here.) We find that substance determines form, and form limits the development of substance. For undialectical thinking, however, forms are considered abstractly, apart from the processes which take on such forms—as when, for example, political theorists analyse forms of state (such as constitutional monarchies, republics, democracies, despotisms) in abstraction from the processes of class-domination which are carried on under such forms. On the other hand, it is equally metaphysical to consider processes in abstraction from the forms they take on—as though one should generalise about, say, the course of the class struggle without realising that its character and outcome is vitally affected by whether it is waged under the form of a democratic process or of a struggle against a fascist dictatorship.

Again, the famous dialectical principle about "quality" and "quantity" comes in here. Things and complexes of things present to us distinctive *qualities*—they are of distinct "kinds", they exemplify distinct "laws" in the manner in which they affect us and affect other things. At the same time, in the processes out of which qualitative differences emerge there are *quantitative* measurable changes of increase and decrease, in the course of which the proportion or balance between various factors is altered. For example, if pressure piles up inside a boiler while its ability to contain the pressure remains constant, the balance of forces is altered and an explosion occurs. Or if extra atoms are added to a molecule there is a chemical change, because the balance of the molecule is altered and it reacts differently in its relationships with others. Thus qualitative characteristics depend on quantitative relations, and quantitative changes invariably lead up to qualitative changes. To consider quality and quantity, on the other hand, as distinct and unconnected—to consider qualities apart from quantitative relations, or to consider quantitative relations apart from the qualities which accrue from them—is mere metaphysical abstraction.

These sorts of consideration lead to a result of very great interest. For when in the analysis of specific cases we seek to *connect* the *opposite* aspects under which processes of change and development are to be considered, we come upon the so-called "dialectical *contradiction*", or "the *struggle* of opposites". As Lenin remarked in his *Philosophical Notebooks* (true, the language is rather obscure and it should be remembered these were only notes which he made for further work which he never did): "The condition of the knowledge of all processes in the world . . . is the knowledge of them as a unity of opposites. Development is the 'struggle' of opposites."

When we consider, for example, how the properties manifested by things are conditioned by the circumstances of their existence, or the relationships occurring within processes; how form is conditioned by substance, and substance by form; how qualities depend on quantities, and so on—then we find necessarily and always in processes of change and development the incidence of "struggle" or "contradiction". For changing relations destroy existing properties which nevertheless persistently manifest themselves for as long as possible, quantitative changes break up old qualities and bring new ones to birth, and processes break out of old forms which nevertheless, so long as they persist, limit the development of those very processes.

It is, I believe, along these lines that we can expect to show *why* "concrete analysis" must (as Marxism says) always and necessarily exemplify the discovery of "contradictions". But before proceeding further we should perhaps at this point listen again to Dr. Popper, who has, as usual, a "devastating criticism" to offer.

Generously endeavouring to explain, if not excuse, the mental aberrations of Marxists, Dr. Popper has accounted for the dialectical conception of the unity of opposites and of contradiction as follows: ". . . if we look a little closer into these so-called contradictory facts, then we find that all examples proffered by dialecticians just state that the world in which we live shows, sometimes, a certain structure which could perhaps be described with the help of the word 'polarity'. An instance of that structure would be the existence of positive and negative electricity" (CR. 329).

So, according to Dr. Popper. what dialecticians have done is to notice that polarity "sometimes" occurs, cite examples of it, and then turn this into a universal necessary "law" of dialectical "contradiction" or "unity of opposites". First, as we saw earlier, he made "dialectical contradiction" mean "logical contradiction". Now, regardless of the inconsistency (for inconsistencies seem to trouble Dr. Popper as little as he says they trouble Marxists), he makes it mean "polarity".

But in the first place, many examples of "contradictions" have been "proffered" which have little in common with the polar opposition of positive and negative electricity—such as the contradiction between socialised production and private appropriation which is proffered as the basic contradiction of capitalism. In the second place, such polar oppositions as that between positive and negative electricity do not merely exemplify types of "structures" which "sometimes" occur in "the world in which we live", and might perhaps not occur at all in some other world, but types of "structures" which must *necessarily* occur if bodies move in space.

Let us look for a moment at some phenomena which "could perhaps be described with the help of the word 'polarity'". A rotating sphere must have a north and south pole, for there cannot possibly be the one pole without the other and there must be both, opposite poles one at each end of the axis about which the sphere rotates. Similarly, if there is a flow of electricity there must be positive and negative charges. Where there is motion the description of it, whatever it is, is bound to involve polarity—if only because the concept of motion in one direction is tied with that of motion in the opposite direction. In this criticism of dialectics Dr. Popper has made a double error. In the first place, he has failed to notice that quite different types of relation fall under the heading of "unity of opposites", and has tried to convict Marxists of basing their ideas on a confusion of types of which it is he himself who is guilty. In the second place, he has confused *logical necessities* with mere "matters of fact", when he supposes that such "structures" as those described "by the help of the word 'polarity'" are simply "structures" which "sometimes" as a matter of fact occur, and not structures which must *necessarily* occur.

It is of importance to make clear that there are *necessities* exemplified in the types of connection we discover in "the concrete analysis of concrete conditions"; and the working out of the general principles of dialectics means the working out of these *necessities*. Considerations about the type of "polarity" exemplified by "positive and negative electricity" belong to the more elementary part of this, being concerned with what is necessarily involved in the description and analysis of physical motions. The necessities considered under the heading of "dialectical contradiction" involve further considerations about the structure of *all* processes, going beyond the consideration of "physical" aspects alone. Then it is found that it makes not the slightest difference what sorts of process one is considering, whether they be processes of nature or of society—the concrete analysis, the scientific analysis and explanation, of processes always takes the form of the exhibition of specific contradictions, of "the struggle of opposites". In general, the complete account or concrete analysis of processes must always be stated in terms of "the unity and struggle of opposites". This is, indeed, the logical structure of explanation or concrete analysis.

In the case of social development, for example, characterised by the conscious strivings and clashes of people, the basic contradiction which has to be taken into account in describing and explaining this development is that between the way in which men combine together to satisfy their needs by their intercourse with nature, and the forms of their own social organisation. It is on the basis of this contradiction that there develop the various conflicts and struggles of men with men—which are conscious struggles, unlike anything that takes place in nature as distinguished from human society.

It is the universality of contradiction, the universal truth that in the connection of its different sides or aspects all process exhibits the unity of opposites, and that all development is the development of the consequent contradictions inherent in things and processes, that accounts for the incidence of those sudden changes, radical transformations and breaks in continuity which are such a marked feature of the world as we know it. As Hegel used to say, the contradictions within a given state of affairs result in its eventually giving rise to "its own negation".

Needless to say, the word "negation" is here used, as was customary with Hegel, in a peculiar sense, not to be confounded with that defined in formal logic, but not for that reason particularly recondite or obscure. In formal logic, the negation of an expression is obtained by a formal logical operation—so that one can write down the negation, according to the rules of formal logic, without any investigation of what actually occurs. The sense of the word "negation" in which Hegel spoke of a given state of affairs having "its own negation" is quite different—for here the negation is not deduced by logic but is discovered as a result of investigating actual processes and finding out where they lead. In this sense, a given structure or a given state of things has "its own negation", which is on the one hand opposed to and incompatible with it, and on the other hand is linked with it in as much as neither occurs without the other—the one issues in the other, as "its negation", and the other comes into being only as such a negation. As Hegel observed, the connection of life and death, for example, is of this type. The processes of life give rise to death, and death only happens as the termination and negation of life. To understand life, as to understand death, we must, in our concrete analysis of real processes, have reached an understanding of this connection. In general, where B is thus "the negation" of A, we misunderstand and misinterpret what actually happens in the processes where A or B occur if we merely consider A and B as opposed and incompatible without grasping their "dialectical connection". It was in this sense that Marx regarded socialism as "the negation" of capitalism.

As Hegel further said, in definite conditions the "negation" is in turn "negated", so as to produce a new version of the original structure or state of affairs. The Hegelian terminology is, as usual, puzzling, because of the ambiguity of the word "negation" which is used differently in the context of dialectics and in the more familiar context of formal logic. But the fact is undoubted. Of many irreversible but at the same time cyclical processes we can say (as Marx said when he showed how the working owner of means of production, expropriated by capitalists, would have the means of production restored to him when capitalists were expropriated), "it is the negation of the negation". In such cases the original condition is not simply restored, it is recreated in a new enriched form, "on a higher level"—as when the individual owners of a few simple tools are eventually replaced by the joint owners of gigantic productive powers. In such cases, we will not fully understand the character of new structures unless we understand them as the products of such processes, *in their connections with their conditions of coming into being*, as "the negation of the negation".

3. THE TEST OF DIALECTICAL MATERIALISM

I shall now try to sum up those very good reasons which Marxists can find for maintaining the truth, and the necessary truth, of dialectical materialism, and for confidently seeking to develop it.

As I have tried to show, the principles of materialism and of materialist dialectics are intended to serve us as the most general guiding principles for understanding the problems of life—for comprehending the facts in their own and not in a fantastic connection, and effecting the concrete analysis of concrete conditions, in the way that is necessary for seeking to answer the problems of life.

For drawing inferences we rely on the principles of logic, for measurement and calculation we rely on the principles of mathematics, for investigating phenomena we rely on the principles of scientific method. Our reliance on these principles does not make us "reinforced dogmatists". Nor does general reliance on the principles of materialism and materialist dialectics make us reinforced dogmatists. No, for we have very good reasons for all such reliances, and the principles relied on are all great human discoveries which have been and continue to be tested by the most rigorous tests.

Of course, mistakes can always be made, and sometimes have been made, in the formulation of principles. That the principles of logic, for example, are necessary inviolable truths does not mean that logicians, who try to work out these principles, cannot get them wrong. On the contrary, the fact is on record that Aristotle—the first man who tried systematically to work out the principles of logic—not only did not establish them all, but some of those he thought he had established were wrongly formulated and were not, exactly as formulated, valid logical principles at all. The point is that where mistakes are made, they can be detected and corrected. Methods of *test* are applicable in the formulation and working out of principles. This goes for principles of materialism and dialectics equally with any others.

Dr. Popper is, then, undoubtedly in the right about the necessity for finding *tests* for everything we propose to maintain. There must always be tests. And if we maintain propositions without being able to say how to test them, and without submitting them to test, then at the best we are mere dogmatists or people of extreme gullibility, and at the worst victims of superstitions, employing meaningless formulas as incantations. Rationality, with its implications of over-coming dogmas, ignorance and superstitions, demands discussion and investigation, and the decision of questions on the basis of testing the proposed answers.

It is quite true (as I have said already) that the Marxist movement has suffered from dogmatists—with a division of labour between some who loudly proclaim dogmas and others who obediently repeat what they are told. However, dogmas get discredited, and Marxism is opposed to dogmatism. To be a Marxist you are not required to subscribe to anything without reason, not to accept any formulation as so authoritative that it cannot be modified, or indeed rejected altogether, as a result of discussion. And considering the amount of discussion that has gone on, and continues to go on, about the formula-tion of even the most fundamental principles of Marxism (to which this present work is intended as a modest contribution), there are certainly no grounds for asserting that Marxism imposes a dogmatic uncritical attitude towards even the basic principles of Marxism itself.

So now we must ask: What are the tests, what are the reasons for the principles of materialism and materialist dialectics? Dr. Popper asserts that there aren't any. I propose to show that there are.

To know how to test the concepts and principles of dialectical materialism it is first of all necessary to be clear about what *types* of concepts and principles these are. For different types of statements require different types of test. As many contemporary philosophers have astutely observed, confusions result from taking statements of one type to be statements of another type; and if tests appropriate only for one type of statement are applied to another type of statement, then, as the saying goes, confusion becomes worse confounded.

Not all statements are testable "by experience" in the same way as are statements of the empirical sciences and, in general, factual or what I have called "informative" statements. Dr. Popper himself stresses it. He insists (very properly) that statements which cannot be tested by experience and which, in that sense, are "unfalsifiable", must be excluded from the body of empirical sciences. But he does not therefore conclude that no empirically unfalsifiable statements are ever to be accepted. On the contrary, theorems of formal logic and of mathematics, for example, are empirically unfalsifiable. But that does not mean we should have no use for them. It simply means that formal logic and mathematics are not *empirical* sciences.

For example, a physicist having expressed a certain connection between observational variables in an equation proceeds to perform calculations from which he arrives at a conclusion which he submits to experimental tests. There is clearly a distinction between the experimental procedure he adopts to test his hypothesis about the connections of physical quantities and the mathematical procedure he adopts to deduce one formula from another. He checks his hypothesis empirically, whereas he checks the correctness of his mathematics by making sure that each step in the calculation is vouched for by valid rules of calculation. And the correctness of the laws of calculation is not established empirically like the correctness of physical laws.

Suppose that what he calculated should happen does not happen: this would falsify his physical hypothesis, but not the laws of mathematics which he used in working out his hypothesis. For the latter are not empirically falsifiable. Here is a very simplified instance to illustrate this point. Suppose that having put two apples in a box and then two more I use the mathematical rule "$2 + 2 = 4$" to calculate that later on I shall find four apples in the box. Suppose that in fact I find only three: this does not falsify the arithmetical theorem that $2 + 2 = 4$, but only falsifies my hypothesis that four apples put into the box would stay there. I should conclude that someone must have taken one out when I wasn't looking.

It may be added that the empirical unfalsifiability of mathematical theorems does not imply (as some philosophers have assumed) that mathematical ideas are or could be arrived at and defined independently of experience. On the contrary, our ideas of numbers are derived from the practical experience of counting, and unless we observed numbers of things and counted them we would never be able to arrive at the definition of the series of numbers and formulate and prove theorems of mathematics. But that mathematics is thus a product of experience and practice, and is used for practical purposes, does not imply that theorems of mathematics are established experimentally or are falsifiable in experience.

The point is that certain empirically unfalsifiable statements may yet admit of very rigorous tests. Wrong theorems of logic or mathematics can be corrected, and correct ones *proved*. There are highly developed techniques for correcting and proving empirically un-falsifiable statements, just as there are highly developed techniques for empirically testing empirically falsifiable statements. The theorems of logic and mathematics are types of statement which admit of proof but not of empirical test, just as the statements of the empirical sciences are a type of statement which admit of empirical test but not of proof.

What Dr. Popper objects to, and what Marxists object to as well, are statements which do not admit of any genuine test at all. These include statements which involve what I have called "false abstraction". These statements are neither empirically falsifiable nor are there non-empirical ways of establishing or refuting them. It is true that a great deal of argument and discussion goes on about such statements—for instance, the debates of theologians. But the trouble with this sort of argument is that it always, in the last resort, relies on dogmatically imposed authority. The argument applies tests of a sort, in which statements are tested by reference to some set of master statements. But how are the master statements tested? Only by finding out which master statements are supported by the loudest voices or most alarming excommunications, or, in more liberal circles, which are deemed most morally uplifting or most comforting. Dr. Popper seems to be of opinion, and Marxists who follow Marx most certainly are of opinion, that the test for whether statements are to be accepted for our practical guidance lies in whether there are ways of genuinely testing them.

According to Dr. Popper, *philosophical* theories are empirically unfalsifiable. One cannot but agree with him on this point, for empirically falsifiable theories would be subject to the tests employed by empirical sciences and so would come under the heading of "empirical science" rather than "philosophy". Historically there was, to begin with, no clear division between philosophy and the empirical sciences, but only a general speculation about "the nature of things". As the empirical sciences developed, however, they separated off from philosophy; and so the division has been introduced between empirical sciences, the statements of which are empirically tested, and philosophy, the statements of which are tested, if genuinely tested at all, by different means. Indeed, the division of philosophy from the empirical sciences was largely the result of the systematic development of scientific method, systematically using techniques of empirical test; certain discussions not subject to such tests were channelled off from the sciences into the separate province of philosophy.

Recognising this division, Dr. Popper says it is nevertheless possible "to examine critically" empirically unfalsifiable philosophical theories (CR 198). Of course, "critical examination" entails criteria for rejection. So Dr. Popper proceeds to suggest criteria for deciding to reject certain philosophical theories. These lead to the rejection of all (in Marxist terminology) idealist and metaphysical theories. We agree: I have already tried to indicate the grounds for rejecting these theories.

The question has to be raised, however, whether there are valid grounds for *accepting* any philosophical theory. Dr. Popper's whole stress is on finding good reasons to *reject* philosophical theories. However, if the criteria employed in "critical examination" are so devised that *any* theory is eventually *rejected*, such criteria are evidently as worthless as they would be if there were no criteria for rejection at all. We require to know not only what makes a philosophical theory unacceptable, but also what makes it acceptable.

Dialectical materialism (so Marxists contend) is a philosophical theory of such a kind that good reasons can be found for accepting it. That does not mean we are against "examining it critically". It does mean that we are against the assumption that "critical examination" is always tantamount to rejection.

General principles of materialism are empirically unfalsifiable. So are general principles of materialist dialectics. How could one set about falsifying them? They do not entail any predictions of what will happen in particular circumstances, and so nothing that happens will ever falsify them. But these statements are not empty ones (owing their appeal merely to an impressive combination of words with emotional resonance, like "The All is One" or "God is Love", which will likewise never be empirically falsified). What gives them practical content is their function of stating guiding principles for formulating, assembling and concretising information. And it is in relation to that function that they are tested.

The logical type of a statement is given by the function it performs in human practice. And principles of materialism and dialectics are distinguished from statements of empirical sciences, and from theorems of logic and mathematics, precisely by their logical type and practical function. In them is discovered the correct form for philosophical, as distinct from empirical, formal-logical or mathematical statements. And in that form, philosophy, the general principles of materialism and of materialist dialectics, can be and should be developed as a science, so worked out as to be tested at every step and the findings confirmed.

I shall now try to define the logical type of the philosophical statements of dialectical materialism, so as to characterise them as a distinct type of statement, and in doing so to indicate how they may be tested. The object of the exercise is to distinguish them, on the one hand, from statements of the empirical sciences, and of logic and mathematics—all of which have their own specific types of test; and on the other hand from those statements, made in other philosophies, which are to be rejected because so formulated as to evade any positive test. I must premise, however, that I shall attempt this here in only a very rough and ready way. To go into these questions with all the exactitude and attention to detail proper in a logical treatise would require much more space and time than is available here at present.

To distinguish the type of philosophical statements made by dialectical materialism and how they are to be tested, it will be convenient to introduce one new technical term—*category*. This is defined in terms of "mode of abstraction".

The statements which result from different modes of abstraction employ different categories; conversely, the different categories we employ in making statements, or in terms of which we formulate our information are the products of different modes of abstraction. To distinguish modes of abstraction is to distinguish the categories wherein the products of such modes of abstraction are expressed, and to distinguish categories is to distinguish them as products of different modes of abstraction.

Thus, for example, to talk of "things" is, as I have said, one particular mode of abstraction; and this mode of abstraction gives us the category of "thing". To talk of "processes" is another mode of abstraction giving us the category of "process". Similarly, "causality" is a category in as much as when we distinguish and relate causes and effects we are dealing in a special mode of abstraction. Thus to discuss causality in a philosophical way is to discuss how the category of causality is properly applied, and is quite distinct from the empirical investigation of causes and effects. Again, the modes of abstraction which result in our distinguishing "properties" and "qualities" give us the categories of "property" and "quality"; and the modes of abstraction which result in our distinguishing "relations" and "quantities" give us the categories of "relation" and "quantity".

It is evident that there is and must be a connection between all legitimate modes of abstraction, inasmuch as they all abstract (to express it loosely) different interconnected aspects of one and the same concrete reality. These connections, in their generality, may be expressed as category-connections. Thus categories are connected by the way they complement and supplement one another in the reflection of concrete reality; and (as noted in an earlier chapter) one result of this is the dialectical pairing of categories in the formation of pairs of "opposites".

In writing thus of categories, I am using the word "category" in a *specialised* sense. I am using the word as a specialised technical term for the purpose of discussing certain questions of philosophy. In everyday language, on the other hand, the word "category" is often used in much wider and looser senses, with which I am not here concerned. For example, we often speak of, say, engineers, miners and steel-workers as distinct "categories" of worker—that is to use the word "category" to apply to different trades associated with the division of labour in modern industry. Thus (like Humpty Dumpty) I am defining only how I propose to use the word "category" in this present dis-cussion, whereas both I and other people often legitimately use the same word in quite different ways in other contexts. However, my use here of the word "category" is not, I am sure, a mere personal idiosyncrasy: it corresponds pretty closely to the way this word has been traditionally used by many philosophers.

What I am talking about now when I use the word "category" is much the same as what Aristotle was talking about at the beginning of scientific philosophy when he wrote a treatise called *The Categories*, and as Kant was talking about when he spoke of "substance" and "causality" as "categories". But while I am talking about what Kant talked about, what I am saying about the subject is quite different from what *he* said. For I am trying to express the standpoint of dia-lectical materialism, which is opposed to that of Kantian or any other brand of idealism.

Kant said that the categories could be "deduced *a priori*". He said that they were somehow inherent in the mind, and that far from deriving them from the objective material world we project them from our own minds into the world—thus making the world appear to us, as a "phenomenon", very different from what it is "in itself". Hegel "corrected" Kant only by denying that the mind of "the finite individual" produces its own categories for itself; he said that the categories are eternally present in the thinking of the Absolute Spirit, from whence they are all derived—a correction which, one may well protest, only makes what was mystifying already a great deal more mysterious.

In saying that categories are products of different modes of abstraction I am saying the exact opposite of what Kant and Hegel said. I am adopting a materialist as opposed to an idealist approach to the question of categories. The categories we employ in stating information about the world reflect the world we are informing ourselves about. The interconnections of categories in informative statement, as we proceed to fit together relatively abstract items of information into the concrete analysis of concrete conditions, reflect the forms of interconnection of the different features and aspects of the material world. As Marx put it in the Afterword to the second German edition of *Capital:* "The ideal is nothing else than the material world reflected by the human mind and translated into forms of thought."

Statements formulated with such a high degree of generality as to deal purely with connections of categories, rather than state facts which come under those categories, may be called *category-statements*. For example, "Qualities depend on quantitative relations" is a category-statement—as distinguished from, say, "The chemical properties of molecules depend on how many atoms are combined in them", which is a statement of fact exemplifying the connection of categories stated in the category-statement. The category-statement is empirically unfalsifiable, whereas the factual statement exemplifying it is of the empirically falsifiable type. It will be seen, too, that category statements are arrived at by a procedure of abstraction from statements of facts: the categories are abstracted from the facts. Categories are therefore in no sense "derived or known *a priori*". They are not present in the mind or known independent of experience or prior to experience, but derived from or abstracted from experience. They are not imposed by the mind upon the known world, but abstracted by the mind from the material world as it is known to us in experience.

The general philosophical principles of materialism and materialist dialectics may now be typified as category-statements. That is their logical type, as distinguished from other types of statements. It is as category-statements that they are of use to us, and it is as category-statements that they may be scientifically derived, formulated and tested.

In formulating these principles it has been customary to distinguish "materialism" from "dialectics". This distinction has its basis in the conditions of our conscious activity, which create (as I tried to indicate when discussing "materialism versus idealism") the distinction and opposition of "material" and "ideal". Principles of materialism are those of the real connection of the material and the ideal. The principles of materialist dialectics comprise all those further principles of inter-connection which come to light in the concrete analysis of concrete conditions. But so far as the logical type of the principles is concerned, there is no distinction: materialism and materialist dialectics are all of one piece. To suppose dialectical materialism to be some kind of artificial conjunction of two logically separable elements is, therefore, a crude error (an error which has, nevertheless, sometimes been made in expounding it as a philosophy). Historically, philosophical materialism and dialectics were separately developed—materialism in a metaphysical way, and dialectics mystified by idealism. By bringing them together Marx eradicated the twin fallacies of metaphysics and idealism, and laid the basis for a single unified development of philo-sophical principles.

How, then, are these principles established and tested?

First I shall repeat that, as Lenin stressed, they are *not* to be established simply by "examples". Some Marxists do seem to have supposed that materialism and materialist dialectics are sufficiently established by citing a lot of examples to bear them out and none to contradict them. But this is to make the logically untenable supposition that very general statements embracing category-connections rest on the same sort of evidence as do the statements of empirical sciences. And then it is easy for logically trained critics to put Marxists on the spot. First it can be asked: Have we in fact examined all relevant cases? We certainly have not. But second, our claim to establish our points by citing positive instances is bogus. For what would happen if we *did* meet an apparently negative instance? If there arises a case where materialist explanation is lacking (for instance, some of the cases produced by so-called psychical research) it can be pleaded that the lack of it is only due to our not yet knowing enough; and if there arises a case where, say, a quantitative change does not lead to a qualitative one it can be pleaded that that is only because the quantitative change did not go far enough. Thus generalisations which claim the support of universal experience turn out to be so devised (just as Dr. Popper has said) that any experience which fails to support them may be dismissed as irrelevant. Principles of materialism and of materialist dialectics are empirically unfalsifiable. So it is absurd to claim to establish them as though they were ordinary empirical generalisations.

To formulate and establish valid philosophical principles we must engage in that type of abstraction and generalisation which results in category-statements. And to establish that these statements are genuine it must be shown that they are *necessary* in the formulation and assembly of genuine information. Of course, it is just because they are necessary that genuine category-statements are unfalsifiable by experience. On the other hand, many statements unfalsifiable by experience are far from expressing genuine necessary principles—there are empty statements, statements of false idealist abstraction, and so on.

In scientific philosophy we must, first, abstract the categories employed in informing ourselves about the world. That is how we arrive at the content of our philosophical statements.

Second, we must work out how, in seeking a concrete analysis, we pass from one set of categories to another, and how we connect them. That is how we make our exposition scientifically systematic and coherent, and not a mere jumble of separate "principles".

Third, we must check up that every conclusion is in fact abstracted from the actual procedures and findings of scientific knowledge, and is a necessary principle in these procedures, in the sense that they could not get on without at least implicitly accepting it. That is how we test our conclusions.

Let us briefly consider in this connection the test of the materialist dialectical principle about quality and quantity. Scientific procedures do in fact investigate the basis of observed qualities in quantitative relations—the principle really is adopted in scientific work. But it is not a principle which just so happens to be sometimes adopted, it is a necessary principle. For to investigate the quantitative basis of qualities, whether successful or not, is the only and necessary way of discovering how qualitative changes are determined and controlled. To suppose otherwise would be to suppose that the material processes of the structures exhibiting qualities do not affect those qualities. And if that were so, we could not inform ourselves of how qualities are determined. If, therefore, we are to try to so inform ourselves, it can only be by investigating quantitative relations.

Philosophical principles are principles of "interconnection". The right way of working them out and testing them must, in short, be such as to ensure: first, that they do relate to the actual information we possess and use, and are not merely cooked up out of metaphysical

THE NECESSITY OF DIALECTICS

or idealist abstractions; and second, that they do state *neccesary principles* governing the formulation and assembly of that information.

Is it, then, possible to finalise, once for all, a complete system of the principles of materialist dialectics? I do not think so.

Aristotle, Kant and Hegel all supposed it possible to write down a complete list of categories. Professor Gilbert Ryle, the editor of the philosophical journal *Mind*, has described this idea as "scholastic": to compile "a decalogue of categories" is, according to him, to try in a dogmatic scholastic way to circumscribe the range of our concepts. I think Professor Ryle is right. It does not seem to me that one can say: There are just so many possible modes of abstraction, and these are the ones. Nor can one say: The totality of forms of interconnection in the material world comprises exactly these, and no others. Lenin was apparently of the same opinion when he wrote (in his article on *Karl Marx* contributed to a Russian encyclopaedia) that "the indissoluble connection of all sides of every phenomenon . . . constantly discloses new sides".

Hence to assert that there are exactly three, four, or any other number, of "laws" to which the principles of materialist dialectics may be reduced, is a mistake. Of course, "in the interests of popularisation" and illustration it is both useful and legitimate to cite certain "laws" (as Engels did). But that does not mean that those particular "laws" provide formulas under which everything that ever happens or ever comes to interest us is to be subsumed. As for "the unity of opposites", this is less one law amongst several than a general prescription for the form that all interconnection takes. But if one proceeds to consider, in a general way, the cases of "the unity of opposites", there is no end to them; and each case has "its own dialectic", requiring its own special study.

Hence materialist dialectics is not a subject which can be completed by writing down and learning a few (or even a large number) of formulas in a textbook. And in that respect it is exactly like any other scientific discipline, whether the empirical sciences or the "exact" sciences of logic and mathematics. We should not expect ever to work out a final system of category-statements, sufficient for all purposes.

4. THE PHILOSOPHY OF IDENTITY

The value of philosophy is not that it tells us all about "the nature of reality" and sums it all up in a few formulas, but that it embodies a

continued scientific activity of working out principles of how to
think so as to inform ourselves and, informing ourselves, arrive at
rational judgements about our human ends and the means to attain
them. It does that, and in doing so arms us against idealist illusion
and metaphysical abstraction. Such, at all events, is the value of
dialectical materialist philosophy.

It may be thought, however, that there are inconsistencies to be
found in the way in which Engels, in particular, described the ideas
and aims of dialectical materialism.

Distinguishing philosophy from the empirical sciences, Engels wrote
in the first chapter of *Anti-Duhring* that "what independently survives
of all former philosophy is the science of thought and its laws—formal
logic and dialectics". So he very clearly coupled dialectics with formal
logic in "the science of thought and its laws", implying that laws of
dialectics are laws of thought. But in the preface to the same work he
wrote that "there could be no question of building the laws of dialectics
into nature, but of discovering them in it and evolving them from
it . . . Nature is the test of dialectics." This implies that laws of dialectics
are laws of the objective world. But can the same laws be laws of
both?

Engels evidently thought they could, for in *Ludwig Feuerbach*
(Chapter 4) he wrote that dialectics comprises "the science of the
general laws of motion both of the external world and of human
thought". And in *Dialectics of Nature* (Chapter 2): "It is from the
history of nature and human society that the laws of dialectics are
abstracted. For they are nothing but the most general laws of these
two aspects of historical development, as well as of thought itself."

In similar vein Lenin asserted that dialectics must be demonstrated
"as a law of cognition *and* as a law of the objective world".

To all this it may be objected, first, that there seems to be an initial
uncertainty as to whether materialist dialectics formulates "laws of
thought" or "laws of the objective world"; and second, that to say it
does both makes the dogmatic assumption that these "laws" are
identical.

Such objections are (as we might have expected) rather vehemently
lodged by Dr. Popper.

The equation of laws of thought with laws of the objective world
is called by Dr. Popper "the philosophy of identity", with its pernicious
source in Hegel. "Hegelian dialectic is based on his philosophy of
identity. If reason and reality are identical and reason develops

dialectically . . . then reality must develop dialectically too. The world must be ruled by the laws of dialectical logic" (CR. 329). With Hegel, Dr. Popper concedes, this notion might appear "plausible and understandable"—for if, as Hegel asserted, "reality" is the creation of "reason", then one would expect the laws of the objective world to be identical with the laws of thought. But all the same, the whole "philosophy of identity" is, so Dr. Popper assures us, an "utter absurdity". And it becomes "even worse" when "dialectic idealism" is replaced by dialectical materialism. "Its holders then argue that reality is in fact of a material or physical character . . . and by saying that it is identical with reason or mind . . . imply that the mind is also a material or physical phenomenon—or, to be less radical, that if the mind should be somewhat different from it then the difference cannot be of great importance" (CR. 331).

Just as King Midas reduced what he touched to gold, so Dr. Popper reduces what he discusses to nonsense. Dialectical materialism appears to him so absurd only because of the utter absurdity of his exposition of "the philosophy of identity".

An impartial consideration of the logical character of category-statements (of which the philosophy of dialectical materialism consists) will show how and why they are at one and the same time "laws of thought" (not, of course, in the sense of psychological laws but of "normative" laws) and true of the objective world. This has nothing whatever to do either with any Hegelian notion of the identity of "the rational and the real", not with any Dr. Popperite notion (for it certainly is not a Marxist or materialist one) that "the mind is also a physical phenomenon", or that the distinction between mental and physical phenomena "cannot be of great importance".

Let us consider once more the stock example of the dialectical law or category-statement about quality and quantity. This is "a law of thought"—not, of course, in the sense that it states a psychological law to the effect that whenever one thinks of a qualitative change one must think of a quantitative one, as whenever Mrs. Shandy thought of the clock being wound up "the thoughts of some other things unavoidably popped into her head"—but in the sense that it states a general principle of how to connect the qualitative and quantitative aspects of reality. It is also "a law of the objective world", inasmuch as quantitative and qualitative changes take place whether we are thinking of them or not, and are connected in the way stated in the law. This law can in fact be expressed equally well either way round:

one can say that qualitative and quantitative changes are connected, and therefore we should always think of them as connected; or that we find a necessary connection between the categories of quality and quantity, and therefore qualitative and quantitative changes are connected. And the same goes for category-statements in general.

These sorts of stated connections are discovered in the objective world—and they certainly would be fancy ones and not real unless they were there discovered. They are "abstracted", just as Engels said. And having been so abstracted they are formulated as "laws of thought" and tested, not as empirical laws are tested but as category-statements are tested—as Engels also implied when he wrote about "the science of thought and its laws". Exactly as Engels said, materialist dialectics is "the science of interconnections" or (in his slightly Pickwickian use of the word "motion") "the science of the laws of motion both of the external world and of human thought". Exactly as Lenin said, dialectics is "a law of cognition *and* a law of the objective world".

It has often been considered puzzling that by a process of thinking, of combining and recombining concepts, we should be able to arrive at conclusions which are practically reliable—that by working out in our heads what is going to happen we should arrive at a conclusion duly verified by what does happen. For example, if an artificial satellite is put into orbit we can, simply by calculations, know where it is to be found at any moment of time. Is it not strange that things should actually and regularly behave according to our ideas of them?

According to Hegel's "philosophy of identity" the only possible explanation for such a state of affairs is that the material world was created by a divine intelligence. Material things correspond to ideas of them because they were created in accordance with ideas. And this is, indeed, the fundamental standpoint of "objective idealism". It is a sophisticated version of the old "argument from design" by which theologians sought to prove the existence of God. How extraordinary that the grass feeds the cow and the cow's digestive processes turn it into milk to feed us! This could only happen because God designed it that way! But there is another explanation. The cow evolved by a process of natural selection in an environment where grass was growing and when people came to live in such places they found in the cow an animal which they could learn to domesticate as a source of food. Similarly, if our ideas correspond to things outside us, there is another explanation than that things were specially created to correspond to ideas. It is that we learned by trial and error to make our ideas correspond to things, because unless they did so our ideas would be useless to us, and worse than useless.

The point of the materialist "philosophy of identity" was put in a very clear and simple way by Engels, in Chapter 3 of *Anti-Duhring*. Puzzles arise, he said, from "accepting 'consciousness', 'reasoning', as something given . . . in contrast to being, to nature. If this were so, it must seem extremely remarkable that consciousness and nature, thinking and being, the laws of thought and the laws of nature, should be so closely in correspondence. But if the further question is raised: what then are thought and consciousness, and whence they come, it becomes apparent that they are products of the human brain and that man himself is a product of nature, which has been developed in and along with its environment; whence it is self-evident that the products of the human brain, being in the last analysis also products of nature, do not contradict the rest of nature but are in correspondence with it."

There is neither inconsistency nor any other sort of "absurdity" in the dialectical materialist "philosophy of identity". The so-called "philosophy of identity" certainly appeared a rather odd one in the writings of Hegel, when he asserted that categories existed eternally in the realm of the Absolute Idea and were materialised in processes in space and time. There is nothing at all odd in it, as propounded by Marx. As he explained, "the ideal is nothing else than the material world reflected by the human mind and translated into forms of thought". So since the categories of thought are abstracted from the material world, and reflect it, there is nothing surprising in universal truth about the material world being correctly stated in the form of category-statements. By rationally demonstrating "the laws of thought" we demonstrate the laws of the objective process reflected in thought.

Dr. Popper represents "the philosophy of identity" and dialectical materialism as an absurd ideology, trapped out as a "reinforced dogmatism" so as to defend itself from every rational criticism. Closer examination shows, however, that it is a rational exercise in the principles of practical thinking, reinforced only by its demand for continual critical test.

It was no accident at all that it was Marxism, the ideology of the modern working-class movement and of communism, which first developed the consistent criticism of all idealism and metaphysics, found the basis for "the science of thought and its laws", and demanded that every statement and every principle used to guide human practice should be critically tested and never accepted on authority. It is true that there have been, and still emerge from the woodwork, exceptionally "orthodox" Marxists who like to set up texts as authorities, and consider it detrimental to Marxism that these texts should ever be tested (since to test is to question), and still more so that any development of Marxist ideas should take place. But the aim of the emancipation of humanity from exploitation, and the advance towards communism, demands that everything should be tested, and that ideas should be continually developed—for its success demands a grasp of things as they are, and not as someone may have said they are. The true militant is always questioning. He will allow himself to be imposed on by no dogmas, whether of the "right" or of the "left": for they are all blinkers preventing him from taking stock of the world around.

And now we may pass on to see how the principles of dialectical materialism apply to the understanding of society, of human life and human needs, and of the means to satisfy human needs. What sort of dogmatism and accompanying misdirection of human affairs does it produce?

PART TWO

PREMISES FOR POLITICS

HISTORICISM AND HISTORICAL PREDICTION

I. THE DOGMATISM OF HISTORICISM

Historical materialism, the Marxist theory of man and society, is the application to social problems of the general theory of dialectical materialism. And since dialectical materialism enjoins us to study things in their real changes and interconnections, the conclusions of historical materialism about social affairs, about the laws of social development, and about what we can do now to solve the pressing problems of contemporary society, are reached as a result of doing precisely that.

Having stigmatised the general philosophy of Marxism as "reinforced dogmatism", Dr. Popper proceeds to explain how this general dogmatic approach produces the particular form of dogmatism which he finds characteristic of Marx's social theories—the dogmatism of "historicism". He presumes, reasonably enough, that dogma produces dogma—so that with an absurdly dogmatic philosophy there goes an absurdly dogmatic theory of man and society. Just as dialectical materialism allegedly replaces the scientific study of the different aspects of real processes by a dogma that the process as a whole must go through the dialectical sequence of "thesis-antithesis-synthesis", so does Marx's historicism replace the scientific study of social affairs by the dogma that society must necessarily pass through a pre-ordained dialectical progress from primitive communism through class-society to the final communist millennium. But just as Dr. Popper's interpretation of dialectical materialism as "reinforced dogmatism" and of "the dialectic" as a scheme of "thesis-antithesis-synthesis" is an absurd travesty, so is his interpretation of historical materialism as embodying what he calls "historicist" dogma.

Dr. Popper defines historicism as "an approach to the social sciences which assumes that historical prediction is their principal aim, and . . . that this aim is attainable by discovering the 'rhythms' or the 'patterns', the 'laws' or the 'trends' that underlie the evolution of history" (PH. 3). Marx, he assures us, was "a famous historicist" (PH. 8).

Why should one not aim at "historical prediction"? The point is that the historical predictions engaged in by historicists are entirely unlike the more modest predictions normally made by the sciences. For "ordinary predictions in science are conditional. They assert that certain changes (say, of the temperature of water in a kettle) will be accompanied by other changes (say, the boiling of the water)." Historicist predictions, on the other hand, are "unconditional historical prophecies" (CR. 339).

Thus historicism considers it "the task of the social sciences to furnish us with long-term historical prophecies" (1–OS. 3). It ceases to be a science and becomes "a wider philosophical scheme . . . the view that the story of mankind has a plot, and that if we can succeed in unravelling this plot, we shall hold the key to the future" (CR. 338). "Historicism is out to find the Path in which mankind is destined to walk" (2–OS. 269).

Historicism has its own method for "unravelling the plot" and discovering the destined "Path". This is the historical method. "The way of obtaining knowledge of social institutions . . . is to study its [sic] history" (2–OS. 37). "We can obtain knowledge of social entities . . . only . . . by studying social changes" (2–OS. 7). To know what is destined to happen in society one must study the origins and development of society, and so discover the "rhythms, patterns, laws and trends" which are at work and which will infallibly determine the future.

And historicism has also its practical political application. The historicist tries "to understand the laws of historical development. If he succeeds in this, he will, of course, be able to predict future developments. He might then put politics on a solid basis, and give us practical advice by telling us which political actions are likely to succeed or likely to fail" (1–OS. 8). "Sociological study should help reveal the political future, and . . . could thereby become the foremost instrument of far-sighted practical politics" (PH. 42).

Marx, then, as "a famous historicist", studied social changes with a view to making "unconditional prophecies". Regardless of the fact that genuine science can make only "conditional predictions", Marx thought that his "philosophical scheme" could "put politics on a solid basis". He thought he knew what was fated to happen, and could base politics on preparing for it.

Having thus charged Marx and Marxists with the fallacies of historicism, Dr. Popper proceeds to bring three more charges of theoretical misdemeanour, which he expounds as companion errors which go with historicist dogma. These are "essentialism", "holism" and "utopianism".

"Historicism" is tied up with "essentialism". For the belief in "unconditional historical prophecies", incompatible with genuine science, is dependent on the belief that the "essences" of things unfold themselves in an inevitable historical development, so that if one can but discover "the essence" one infallibly knows what is going to happen. "It is argued that the task of social science is to understand and explain such sociological entities as the state, economic action, the social group, etc., and that this can be done only by penetrating into their essences" (PH.30).

"I use the name methodological essentialism," writes Dr. Popper, with polysyllabic orotundity, "to characterise the view . . . that it is the task of pure knowledge or 'science' to discover and to describe the true nature of things, i.e. their hidden reality or essence" (1-OS. 31). According to essentialism, "the best, the truly scientific theories, describe the 'essences' or the 'essential natures' of things—the realities which lie behind the appearances" (CR. 104).

The essence (so Dr. Popper explains the doctrine of "essentialism" and its connection with "historicism") reveals itself in a certain pattern of development. For "in order to become real or actual, the essence must unfold itself in change" (2-OS. 8). Thus "applying this principle to sociology we are led to the conclusion that the essence or the real character of a social group can reveal itself, and be known, only through its history" (PH. 33). By studying the historical pattern of development of society, therefore, one penetrates to the essence of society—and having grasped the essence one can then understand the necessity of that particular pattern of development, and can infallibly predict its continuation. "Change, by revealing what is hidden in the undeveloped essence, can only make apparent the essence, the potentialities, the seeds, which from the beginning have inhered in the changing object. This doctrine leads to the historicist idea of an historical fate or an inescapable essential destiny" (2-OS. 7).

Being guilty of historicism, then, Marx and Marxists could not but be also guilty of essentialism. Marxism means that the inescapable destiny of man in society is predetermined by the social essence of man. By studying human history one can discover what this essence is, and so acquire the power of making unconditional prophecies.

Error, like crime, has its own crazy logic; and Dr. Popper goes on to explain that, once guilty of historicism and essentialism, Marxism could not but degenerate further into "holism" and "utopianism". One would almost suppose that Dr. Popper imagines himself digging into the very depths of the essence of Marxism. A fine lot of nonsense he digs up, and no wonder, for he buried it all there himself.

"The strongest element in the alliance between historicism and utopianism is, undoubtedly, the holistic approach which is common to both," writes Dr. Popper (PH. 74). "Historicism is interested in the development, not of aspects of social life, but of 'society as a whole'."

We must study "society as a whole", says the essentialist-historicist, and study particular "aspects of social life" only as their development is determined by that of the whole. The trouble with this injunction, says Dr. Popper, is that "if we wish to study a thing, we are bound to select certain aspects of it. It is not possible for us to observe or to describe a whole piece of the world, or a whole piece of nature; in fact, not even the smallest whole piece may be so described, since all description is necessarily selective" (PH. 77). It is not the development of the whole which determines that of particular aspects, but the development of particular aspects, and their complex interaction, which determines the development of the whole.

Historicism and essentialism, demanding a "holistic approach", become thereby involved in "utopianism". For "holists not only plan to study the whole society by an impossible method, they also plan to control and reconstruct our society 'as a whole'" (PH. 79). And that is utopianism. Thus Marx's "unconditional historical prophecies" about the development of "society as a whole" became a "utopian blueprint". "He predicted, and tried actively to further, a development culminating in an ideal utopia" (PH. 74). "Marx saw the real task of scientific socialism in the annunciation of the impending socialist millennium" (2–OS. 86).

But unfortunately, utopianism, based on "an impossible method", can never lead to the realisation of utopia. "Even with the best intentions of making heaven on earth it only succeeds in making it a hell— that hell which man alone prepares for his fellow-men" (1–OS. 168). Marx's theoretical misdemeanours have encouraged Communists, Dr. Popper subsequently explains, in their nefarious work of suppressing individuality, instigating violence and tyranny, and perpetuating a "closed society".

We had best remember now that, with Dr. Popper, we are still in Wonderland, where everything is queer and the meanings of words get twisted. As soon as the charge was read the King of Hearts told the jury "Consider your verdict". But that was too much, even for the White Rabbit. "Not yet! Not yet!" the Rabbit hastily interrupted. "There's a great deal to come before that!" There is indeed a great deal to be said on the topics expounded in Dr. Popper's charge. But to say it we must leave Wonderland and take a look at how things are in the real world, and cease to discuss general philosophical principles but rather apply them in the concrete analysis of concrete conditions.

2. MEN MAKE THEIR OWN HISTORY

According to Marx: "Men make their own history, but they do not make it just as they please; they do not make it under circumstances chosen by themselves, but under circumstances directly encountered, given and transmitted from the past" (*The Eighteenth Brumaire of Louis Bonaparte*, Ch. 1).

In other words, men make their own history by their own actions—no "fate" makes it for them. But men in their actions respond to whatever circumstances they find themselves in. They directly encounter circumstances given and transmitted from the past—that is to say, created for them by past generations; change these by their actions; then again respond to the changed circumstances; and so on, for as long as mankind endures.

This may be called "reinforced dogmatism", but it sounds more like reinforced common sense. What are some of the implications, as regards human action and its possibilities?

It means, in the first place, that while men make their own history, what they can and cannot do at any place and time depends not simply on their own desires and decisions but on the circumstances in which they are placed. It is in this sense that they do not make their history "just as they please". Obviously, as Marx said, people cannot choose their own circumstances—one does not choose to be born, nor to be born into one set of circumstances rather than another. Choice applies to what to do in whatever circumstances one finds oneself; and the circumstances limit the choice of action. But because of this, circumstances not only limit what men *can* do, but condition what in practice they *want* to do; people's desires, aims and ideals are conditioned by their circumstances; what one effectively wants to do, or would like to see done, takes its start from the circumstances in which the wish is born. It means, too, that men's ways of thinking—the scope of their ideas, the ways they conceive of themselves and of the world about them—are conditioned by circumstances. And lastly, it is obvious enough that, while men may choose and decide what to do in given circumstances, they cannot choose or decide what *effects* their actions, once embarked upon, are going to have. Men can act with the intention of bringing about certain effects; whether these effects actually take place, or whether something quite different happens, does not depend on the intention of the action but on the action itself, and the circumstances in which it was performed.

It was on no deeper or darker philosophical presuppositions than these that Marx and Engels proceeded to consider how, in actual fact, "men make their own history".

At the start of their first mature work on this subject, *The German Ideology*, they remarked that "the first premise of all human history is the existence of living human individuals. Thus the first fact to be established is the physical organisation of these individuals and their consequent relation to the rest of nature". Having established that fact, they went on to inquire how the innumerable actions of innumerable human individuals could come to make human history.

The "physical organisation" of human individuals is, of course, a consequence of the natural evolution of species; and "their relation to the rest of nature" is a further consequence. The unique physical characteristics of the human species, namely, the upright stance, hands and brain, lead to their unique relation to the rest of nature, namely, obtaining their requirements from nature by means of social production. Human psychology is, then, a further consequence—the product of individuals with this physical organisation living in society.

In order, then, to carry on their relation with the rest of nature—in other words, in order to live, since organisms live only by obtaining their requirements from nature—people devise instruments of production, learn the skills to use them, and enter into social relations of production. They evolve their social mode of production, which consists of employing certain forces of production and instituting definite relations of production in order to deploy the social productive forces and distribute the product.

This is how the past generations create the circumstances with which the next generations have to cope. What they do, by their social activity in the physical environment, is in the first place to equip their successors with certain forces of production and provide them with a physical environment changed and refashioned in various ways by the past application of those forces of production. In the second place, they settle them in definite relations of production within which the forces of production are deployed. Finally, they hand on to them a whole heritage of institutions, customs and ways of life, knowledge, ideas and culture, and leave them to continue a whole set of undecided conflicts and arguments and uncompleted activities.

In the study of history the successors look back on how the predecessors managed to make things turn out the way they did—at least, that is how history must be regarded if its study is to prove of any practical advantage, and that is how Marx and Engels evidently regarded it. "All history must be studied afresh, the conditions of existence of the different formations of society must be examined in detail," wrote Engels to C. Schmidt (August 5, 1890). And he told his correspondent that "our conception of history is above all a guide to study". The materialist conception of history is a guide to study in the same way that any other scientific conception is a guide to study. Our conception of human physiology, for example, is a guide to study, because it tells us what to look for in order to be able to explain how the phenomena are brought about—in a case of epilepsy, say, to look for the brain lesion responsible for the condition, rather than for the evil spirit. And so with the materialist conception of history. Marx and Engels pointed out that, whatever people do in society, they can only do it on the basis of being mutually involved in a mode of production—for without that, they could not live or do anything at all. As they change their forces of production, and consequently create problems for themselves the solution of which requires changed relations of production, so do people modify in various ways the character of all the rest of their activity.

It is because people live by social production that human societies have a history different in kind from, say, the history of a community of ants. Ants could not, of course, study their own history in any case, since they are not physically equipped for studying. However, outside observers could quite well study the history of a given community of ants, and in it would be recorded not only the common round of hatching out the eggs, and so on, but also such "historical" events as floods and other catastrophes, wars with neighbouring anthills, and great migrations of ants. It is a shortcoming of some human historians that they study the history of men just as though men were nothing but a talkative kind of ants. But it is not only speech and the element of individual consciousness or purposive activity that distinguish men. Human history differs from the history of ants by exhibiting a type of historical development which is peculiarly human; and this is due to the social production by which men live. The mode of production changes. Ants always get their living in the same way; but not so human beings. People acquire new productive forces, and change their relations of production. And this introduces a quite new factor into human history. Human history is the history of how men acquired and used forces of production, and adapted their relations of production to the requirements of developing their forces of production; it is the history of how men did this, and what activities, difficulties, defeats and victories, constructive enterprises and wars, they involved themselves in doing it.

Dr. Popper explains that the historicist "sees the individual as a pawn, as a somewhat insignificant instrument in the general development of mankind" (1–OS. 7–8). But the materialist conception of history, as a way of studying and understanding human history, does not mean, as Marx and Engels themselves made abundantly clear, that history is made in any other way than by the activities of human individuals. It does not mean that what individuals may think and do counts for nothing, that they are all mere "pawns", and that what alone counts is the inexorable development of "the different formations of society". For to talk about the "social formation" is simply to talk about how individuals, having socially acquired certain productive forces, involved themselves in certain production relations. What it does mean is that, to see how the circumstances of the new generation were transmitted to them by the old, we have to see how the forces of production were developed and how the relations of production were managed; and that to see what the generation can or cannot do in such circumstances, and how their practical outlook is consequently generated, we have to see what can or cannot be done by way of preserving or changing both the relations of production and the forces of production deployed within them.

The Marxist materialist conception of history is, then, the scientific conception of how the old people bring into being the circumstances which the young people are born into and have to cope with. Like other scientific conceptions in other spheres, it is of great practical value. In the first place, it assists us in making an accurate assessment of just what our circumstances are, and dispelling illusions about them. In the second place, by the historical study of how social circumstances are brought about we can reach conclusions as to what sort of things can and cannot be done to cope with them.

3. HISTORICAL PREDICTION

How far, we may now ask, does the study of history enable us to predict the future? And what sort of predictions does it enable us to make?

Marxism means making "unconditional long-term historical prophecies", Dr. Popper tells us; and the "principal aim" of Marxists in studying history is to deduce such prophecies from it.

The principal aim of Marxists in studying history is not to prophesy but to understand, and to direct practical action in the light of understanding. "Men make their own history", said Marx. We study history to try to understand how we make it, and consequently how to go on making it without illusions that it can be made in some other way than that in which it is in fact made.

Obviously, so far as the past is concerned, history is not predictive but descriptive and explanatory. We do not study the events of, say, a thousand years ago in order to predict the events of, say, nine hundred years ago—for when we study the earlier events we already know what the subsequent events were. We study the past sequence of events in order to try to discover explanatory generalisations about how later events issue from earlier ones. Marx's discovery was that to explain the historical sequence we must always, first, examine the mode of production and how it develops, and second examine how people acted socially in order to adapt their production relations, and their institutions and ideas, to their forces of production.

This descriptive-explanatory approach to the study of history does not represent history as the automatic consequence of the operation of inexorable "laws"—like, for example, a closed mechanical system in which a later state inexorably ensues from the earlier by the operation of the laws of mechanics. It is often said that, for the materialist conception of history, everything happens "according to laws". If that means that the materialist conception of history formulates explanatory generalisations about how human society always develops, well and good; that is just what the materialist conception of history does do. But to suggest that there are "laws" governing human actions such that, given certain circumstances, all the ensuing events are uniquely determined by those laws, is obviously mere empty talk. What are these laws? Where are they stated? Where is their verification to be found? You can read right through the historical works of Marx, and of all other competent Marxist historians (and, indeed, of all reputable historians, whether Marxists or not), and not meet with any formulations of any such laws. Such a theory of "laws" is in fact a hangover from the days when it was thought that the entire material world was a closed mechanical system—and it has, needless to say, very little in common with the scientific ideas of dialectical and historical materialism. It has to be given up because no one can discover such laws, and the idea that there must be such laws is a groundless dogma.

The historical works of Marx himself, and of Marxist historians (as can easily be verified by reading them), do not proceed by trying to show how the later events necessarily followed from the earlier ones in accordance with inexorable laws, but by showing how people, in the development of social production, became involved in certain contradictions and problems, and how they acted to resolve those contradictions and problems. And the basis is always the adaptation of relations of production to forces of production.

It is to this guiding idea that the materialist conception of history owes not only its descriptive-explanatory power as regards the past, but its prescriptive power as regards the present. It is a guide to study of the present in its emergence from the past, so as to conclude what are the historical issues of today and what best to do to develop social relations in order to plan social production to satisfy human needs. Just that is the object of Communist theory and practice.

Any social situation contains certain historical issues, or historical tasks. And these may be defined by the historian objectively, irrespective of the particular terms in which the individuals of the time, through their ideological agencies, may present them to themselves. "Just as our opinion of an individual is not based on what he thinks of himself, so can we not judge of . . . a period . . . by its own consciousness; on the contrary, this consciousness must be explained rather from the contradictions of material life, from the existing conflict between the social forces of production and the relations of production", wrote Marx, in the Preface to *Critique of Political Economy*.

It is not, as everyone knows, the historian's object to search out and record every single event of the past. He is primarily concerned with the "historical" events—though just what makes an event historical is a point not clarified by all historians. For Marxist historians, the key to understanding any period is to discover the main historical issues of that period—and these proceed from and relate to the development of forces of production and the adaptation to it of production relations and social institutions and ideas. Thus, for a Marxist, the question of whether King Valoroso should award the Order of the Cucumber to his son-in-law, Prince Bulbo, was hardly an historical issue—even though the Court Journal, and historians who base their histories on court journals, might regard it as an issue of great importance. The historical events—the ones that constitute, so to speak, the fabric of history—are those public events which mark a response to historical issues and affect the issue. But of course, in a certain sense, *any* event is of interest to historians, because even the most trivial ones illustrate the sort of people there were, and their habits, and so are relevant to understanding historical events; and often an accidental concatenation of small events can build up an effect which decisively alters the way issues are tackled.

Looking at the overall development of human society from the earliest times, Marxism sees it as the progressive posing and tackling of a series of issues stemming from the development of productive forces, and the adaptation to that development of the relations of production. In many cases, as Marx made clear in his *Pre-capitalist Economic Formations*, this adaptation has been unsuccessful, and has led to a dead end rather than to further progressive development. The thread of human progress can be traced through those communities which successfully adapted their relations of production to the requirements of developing their productive forces. The overall history of human society is, then, "a law-governed process" in the sense that it exemplifies this general law of development. It is not, and could not be, a "law-governed process" in the strict-determinist sense that there are pre-ordained laws which allow nothing to happen except what does happen.

With human affairs, as with other things, a conception of how they go enables us to make predictions about future events. But the *test* of the adequacy or otherwise of a conception of how things go does not lie (as Dr. Popper seems sometimes to suggest) only in waiting to find out whether or not predictions are verified. We also test the conception of how things go by examining the record of how they have gone—and "refutations" may be as readily sought in the past as awaited in the future. For this reason we can always claim that scientific conceptions are pretty well established by what has happened already, without having to join Dr. Popper in regarding them all as mere "conjectures" about the future which may well be falsified at any moment. This applies to our conceptions of how, say, physical and chemical processes go—and also to our conceptions of how social processes go. The warranted assertibility (to adopt a useful phrase invented and misused by the pragmatists) of our conceptions of how things go depends on the thoroughness with which we have investigated how they have gone.

Our conceptions are further tested and, if need be, modified, by the verification or falsification of the predictions they enable us to make. The purpose of predictions is not, however, simply to test our conceptions. It is to direct our actions. For unless we made predictions we could never direct our actions at all. For example, we could not direct the making of tea unless we could predict that water boils when heated, and that boiling water poured onto dried tea-leaves produces tea. In directing our actions, therefore, it is important to possess conceptions the assertibility of which is pretty well warranted already, so that the predictions derived from them may be acted on with a reasonable degree of confidence and not be regarded as only "conjectures". To furnish such a conception of human affairs is the aim and claim of the materialist conception of history.

We can and always do rely on being able to make a whole number of predictions to direct human activities. We rely on being able to say: "If A happens, B will happen", or "Since A has happened, B will happen unless C intervenes", and so on. We rely, in other words, on what Dr. Popper calls "conditional predictions". These may often be usefully expressed, as he has said, in the form of prohibitions: "A B cannot happen; hence since A has happened, B will not happen". Experience and study warrant us in making many such predictions about physical, chemical and biological processes; and (as practically everyone, including Dr. Popper, agrees) experience and study warrant us in making many such predictions about human activities too.

Does the materialist conception of history claim a warrant, however, for any other kinds of predictions—long-term "unconditional" ones, as Dr. Popper expresses it? Does Marxism propose to justify statements of the form: "So and so will happen, regardless"? Such statements are, as Dr. Popper rightly says, foreign to the natural sciences. Does Marxism unscientifically propose to introduce them into the social sciences?

Marx's discovery of the general "law of historical development" does lead to a "long-term" prediction. And Dr. Popper rightly says that this long-term prediction is regarded by Marxists as of very great theoretical and practical importance. The logic of this long-term prediction is quite simple. In order to go on developing their forces of production people have always to adapt their production relations to their productive forces. Hence if the present-day forces of production go on being developed, the relations of production will be adapted to them. The existing capitalist relations fetter production. If production is to go on developing these fetters will be removed and socialist and, later, communist relations of production established.

Obviously, this long-term prediction depends not only on "the general law" but also on the hypothesis that capitalist relations fetter production and that the removal of the fetters of private appropriation equals social appropriation. The latter, less general, hypothesis, is verified in terms of contemporary history, just as the more general hypothesis is verified in terms of universal history. So what is there "unscientific" in the consequent long-term prediction? It would be absurd to say that only "short-term" predictions are scientific. Scientific thought ventures on long-term predictions in other spheres covered by scientific hypothesis, so why not in the sphere of human activity? Of course, if hypotheses are found to be wrong, then the consequential predictions, whether short-term or long-term, have to be modified. But in so far as confidence in the hypotheses is warranted, so is confidence in predictions, long-term and short-term. This goes for Marx's hypotheses like anyone else's. Of course, those who have a stake in maintaining the capitalist system do not like Marx's long-term prediction of its displacement. But that is a complication which merely introduces extra-scientific disputes into a scientific question. Scientifically speaking, the logic of Marx's long-term prediction is impeccable.

Dr. Popper does not, of course, deny that long-term prediction is sometimes permissible in the sciences. But he maintains that the conditions for it are not present in the social sciences. "Long-term prophecies", he writes (CR. 339–40), "can be derived from scientific conditional predictions only if they apply to systems which can be described as well-isolated, stationary, and recurrent. These systems are very rare in nature; and modern society is surely not one of them. . . . Society is changing, developing. This development is not, in the main, repetitive."

Of course society develops, and the development is not repetitive. That does not mean that there cannot possibly be a discoverable law of development. On the contrary, Marx discovered the law—the law of the adaptation of production relations to productive forces. And clearly, if this law describes the way society develops, then the development is non-repetitive. Non-repetitive development does not mean that there is no law, nor that the law cannot be formulated in such a way that from the analysis of the present stage of development a prediction of the next stage can be made. Evidently, therefore, Dr. Popper is mistaken in his dogmatic and unsupported statement that long-term prediction can apply only to "well-isolated, stationary and recurrent systems".

His argument depends on a simple confusion between long-term prediction and what he calls "unconditional" prophecy. It is quite true that only in the case of a "well-isolated, stationary and recurrent system" ("very rare in nature", as Dr. Popper rightly says) could it be guaranteed that no outside or non-recurrent factor was ever going to interfere in the working of the laws normally governing the system. Society is not a system of that kind, and Marx's long-term predictions about society only predict that the continued development of production will bring socialism—because, in the long term, the condition for it is the removal of the fetters of private appropriation. People have always so far managed to overcome, eventually, obstacles to the continued development of their productive forces; and if they go on doing so, then socialism will come, and only if socialism comes will they be able to go on doing so. That is the prediction. It is conditional, not unconditional. It does not say that nothing can ever possibly prevent the advent of socialism. On the contrary, if people should destroy their productive forces, along with most of the human race, in a nuclear war,—then many nations may never achieve socialism. Again, an invasion of hostile forces from outer space might prevent our achieving socialism. We may think the latter catastrophe unlikely, and have confidence in our ability to prevent the former, or even to cope with its consequences if it happens—and so live in confident expectation that the long-term prediction of socialism will come about, because examination of the existing state of affairs shows that the conditions for its being brought about are present. That is the practical attitude of Communists. But it does not turn long-term scientifically-based prediction into unconditional prophecy.

4. PREDICTION, PROBABILITY AND INTENT

The long-term prediction of socialism is a prediction about human actions and the results of human actions. In this it differs, obviously, from predictions about the operations of natural forces. As Engels, perhaps rather tritely, remarked (*Ludwig Feuerbach*, Ch. 4): "In nature there are only blind, unconscious agencies acting upon one another. In the history of society, on the other hand, the actors are all endowed with consciousness, are men acting with deliberation or passion, working towards definite goals; nothing happens without a conscious purpose, without an intended aim." The long-term historical prediction is, then, a prediction about what "men acting with deliberation or passion, working towards definite goals" will do, and what results will accrue from their doing it.

It is sometimes suggested that just because men act "with deliberation or passion" it is impossible to make any predictions about them. Each man decides what to do for himself, or acts from his own private passions, so no over-all predictions can be made. That is absurd. We all constantly make predictions of the form: "In such and such circumstances, such and such people will act in such and such a way, and such and such results will follow", and if we could not rely on any such predictions we could not manage our social lives.

Predictions about human actions do not imply that human beings act, and act on one another, in the same way as non-human or "natural" agencies do. They act deliberately, they are moved by passions, they form intentions and set themselves goals—and it is these sorts of actions, and the results of these sorts of actions, that we predict.

For example, when a sufficient number of people are brought together as wage-workers they start talking together about how to improve their conditions, form organisations and formulate common demands. They always do this, and we can predict that they will. Such a prediction does not imply that the individual workmen are "pawns", whose deliberations and passions count for nothing. On the contrary, the prediction is a prediction of their deliberations and passions. In such circumstances enough workmen will feel passionately fed up and voluntarily organise as to constitute an effective organisation which can coerce or at least discount the opposition of those who feel contented and do not voluntarily organise.

Such predictions are (as the above example makes evident) based on estimates of probabilities of what will happen as a result of the inter-

action of a large number of interdependent variables. The same is true
of predictions about the behaviour of single individuals. When we
predict what a certain person will do, we are estimating the probable
outcome of all the various motivations and counter-motivations he
experiences.

Nearly all predictions, whether they concern human beings or not,
are similarly based on estimates of probability. Thus, for example, the
prediction that a kettle of water placed on a fire will boil is (as modern
science has shown) based on the estimate that more heat will pass from
the fire into the kettle than from the kettle into the fire, and that when
enough has passed the agitation of the molecules of water in the kettle
will produce the phenomenon of boiling. Predictions about working-
class organisation and other human activities depend on the same kind
of estimates of probability.

There is nothing especially uncertain or "conjectural" about such
estimates. On the contrary, it is by such estimates that we guide our
lives, and, if due care is exercised in arriving at them, they are extremely
reliable. Such reliable estimates can be arrived at about our own
actions, as well as about what goes on in the physical environment.

In the interpretation of the past, it is precisely such estimates of
probability that explain the overall progressive course of human
history. Not all communities have developed their forces of production, but some have—and so a progressive overall development has
taken place, with new relations of production adapted to new forces of
production, up to humanity's arrival at its present predicament. With
so many people carrying on social production for such a long time, it
was so probable as to be, practically speaking, inevitable that at least
some would on occasion enter into favourable circumstances when
they could improve on existing forces of production—and so the
progressive development took place, and is likely to continue. This is
the scientific explanation of human progress—what would probably
happen happened.

To explain why some particular development—the "classical"
slave empire, say, or modern capitalism—took place exactly where,
when and how it did, one has, of course, to ascertain a lot of relatively
coincidental facts: if something else had happened earlier (as it well
might), this development could have taken place somewhere else and
in a different way. But overall it was so probable as to be practically
inevitable that a great slave empire would develop somewhere, and
that, later on, capitalism would develop.

Moreover, when such developments take place they tend to be unique. This is because whoever achieves the development either prevents anyone else repeating it, or if others do follow suit the fact that it has been done already alters their circumstances and makes them do it differently. Thus, for example, the achievement of capitalism in one set of countries prevented a similar development in regions which they colonised. Again, the head start which Britain gained in capitalist development affected the conditions in which Britain's competitors had to operate. Again, the achievement of socialism in the U.S.S.R. affects the whole character of the road to socialism in the rest of the world.

The same sort of considerations explain, incidentally, the role and the uniqueness of "great men". When once one individual has come to perform a "great man" function, he deprives others of the chance of doing the same thing. Napoleon, for example, was unique, not only because of his individual personality, which impelled him to the top after the French Revolution, but because there could in any case be only one emperor of the French.

In explaining social development and predicting its continuation, therefore, the materialist conception of history does not, as a scientific conception, need to invoke any inexorable "fate" or "destiny" brooding over human affairs and directing them. We conduct our affairs without that. And still the conduct of our affairs is, like other things, explicable and predictable.

The same principles which explain how people acted in the past explain how they are acting now, and serve to predict how they will act in the future. Predictions about human affairs, however, very clearly differ from predictions about natural processes, as well as from explanations of past affairs, in that the people making the predictions are themselves agencies in the processes through which the predictions will be realised. To predict something which you yourself are going to do—or at least, if not you yourself individually, the people with whom you associate and with whose interests you identify your own—is equivalent to *a statement of intent*. For instance, to predict "It is going to rain" is simply to state what you expect to happen; but to predict, "I am going to put on my raincoat" is a statement of intent. You would not predict you would put on your raincoat if you did not intend to do so.

In making such predictions, whether ones like "I shall put on my raincoat" or "We shall achieve socialism", we rely on an analysis of the objective circumstances to which the predicted action is to be the response. If that analysis proved mistaken, the predicted action would either not take place, or, if it did, would not have the expected results. If, for example, my analysis of the weather proves mistaken, I shall either not put on my raincoat or, if I do, it will only weigh me down and not keep me dry. Again, the analysis of circumstances may be mistaken in such a way that the intention expressed is not in the circumstances a practicable one. For instance, if I had lost my raincoat, the prediction that I would put it on would not be fulfilled; in making the prediction I would have simply forgotten that I had lost the raincoat.

In stating intentions, then, one generally reckons to have reasons (based on an analysis of circumstances) for considering the intention practical, and for considering that its fulfilment will bring certain advantages or avoid certain misfortunes. If one learned that the intention was not practical, or that it would not bring the expected advantage or avoid the feared misfortune, then one would abandon the intention and the prediction would not be fulfilled.

Evidently, therefore, the fact that predictions about future human actions may also be statements of intent does not mean that such predictions are not founded on an objective analysis of circumstances; nor does the fact that such a prediction is founded on an analysis of circumstances mean that the carrying out of the predicted action is done under the impulsion of fate, and not voluntarily to fulfil a stated intention. It is obvious that such predictions can be well founded; and also that, however well founded they are, they can only be fulfilled on condition that the people whose intentions are expressed in the prediction continue to try hard to carry out their intentions.

The Marxist prediction about socialism exhibits all the above characteristics of a prediction which is also a statement of intent. In this it certainly differs from, say, an astronomer's prediction of an eclipse. It likewise differs from certain other predictions about human affairs—for of course, not all such predictions contain this element of being a statement of intent. For example, when Louis XV of France made his famous prediction, "Après moi la deluge" (a well-founded prediction which came true), he was simply stating what he expected other people to do; and the "fatalistic" character of his prediction was due to his (correct) opinion that he and his friends could not stop them doing it. Marx's prediction about socialism, on the other hand, was also a statement of intent, and intended for adoption as a statement of intent; and the conditions for its realisation included the condition that it should be widely adopted as an intent, and stuck to—for otherwise, socialism would certainly not come about. It could only come about by people purposively struggling for it. On the basis of the same analysis of circumstances which made Marx voice the intention of socialism, he concluded that a sufficient number of people would adopt it.

Obviously, this prediction by Marx includes features not to be found in such a simple prediction as "I shall put on my raincoat", though it does have in common with the latter the feature of expressing an intention based on an objective analysis of circumstances. For Marx's prediction predicted what other people were going to do. It is a "we" prediction, not an "I" prediction; and of course, every "we" prediction is also a "they" prediction.

In this respect it may be compared with, say, a prediction made by the first Everest expedition that "Everest will eventually be climbed". Such a prediction expresses an intention of climbing Everest, coupled with a conclusion of the practicability of eventually getting to the top and of the desirability of doing so. It relies also on the prediction, based on estimates of the probabilities of human actions, that a sufficient number of people will always want to get to the top of Everest, and will devote enough care to the preparation of adequate techniques as to ensure the eventual achievement.

It may also be noted that the same prediction could be made by observers who had themselves no intention of climbing Everest. Those observers would note that the intention had been formed, that it was practicable, and that a sufficient number of people supported it as to ensure its eventual success. But that the prediction can be made on good grounds by mere observers does not make it fatalistic. For the prediction would never be realised unless there were people who intended to climb Everest and who adopted it as a statement of intent. Observers could have no conclusive grounds for predicting the climbing of Everest unless climbers intended to climb it and themselves predicted, as a statement of their intention, that the climb would take place and go on taking place until they reached the top. True, in this example observers of the habits of climbers might venture to predict that Everest would eventually be climbed, even before any climbers had themselves formed the intention of climbing Everest and organised an expedition. All the same, the realisation of the prediction would depend on the climbers forming the intention of attempting that particular climb, and organising to achieve it.

It may also be noted, in all these examples, that the objective analysis of circumstances on which such predictions are based includes, if the predictions are well-founded, a causal explanation of why the intention the fulfilment of which is predicted came to be formed and will go on being held. Thus in the case of putting on a raincoat, for example, the explanation of the intention is that to go out in the prevailing rainy conditions tends to give one a cold. In the case of climbing Everest, the explanation of the intention is that climbers find it intolerable to be confronted with mountains they have not climbed. And in the case of socialism, the explanation of the intention is that under capitalist conditions a great many people find intolerable the fetters capitalist relations place on the satisfaction of human needs.

These considerations show that Marx's "long-term" prediction of socialism can claim, just like many simpler and shorter-term predictions, to be well founded on an objective analysis of circumstances. This analysis, is, by the nature of the case, complicated and difficult. It requires in practice to be continually developed and checked. And of course, if any part of it were shown to be quite wrong, then the foundation for the prediction would be weakened, if not destroyed. But as originally worked out by Marx, and continued by his successors, it does provide a very firm and sound foundation for the prediction of socialism.

In the first place, the prediction is founded on recognition of the general law of social development—that production relations are adapted to productive forces. Secondly, it is founded on an investigation of capitalist production relations and how they fetter productive forces. Thirdly, it is founded on the demonstration that socialised production, of the sort developed in modern industry, requires social appropriation—so that the only way to develop modern socialised production to meet social needs is to establish socialist relations of production. Fourthly, it is founded on an analysis of the class struggle which ensues from capitalist production relations, in which the intention of achieving socialism corresponds to the class interests of the majority of working people—so that there are good grounds to expect that in the long run the forces activated by that intention will grow stronger in comparison with those opposed to it. Fifthly, it is founded on a very practical working out of the principles of the strategy and tactics of the class struggle for socialism.

So as Marx claimed all along, the scientific study of society, its history and how men make their own history, provides the foundation for a long-term prediction of socialism. This is not, however, like the predictions of astronomers who predict events which are going to happen irrespective of human intentions and strivings. From the nature of the case, being a prediction of the eventual outcome of a struggle in which the makers of the prediction take part, it has the characteristics of a political policy and a political propaganda. Marx himself cited very good reasons to consider the policy sound, and to persevere in it. And these very good reasons (provided they are stated properly) serve as very good propaganda for the policy.

It is further evident from all this that the realisation of the prediction of socialism depends on the building of an organisation, activated by scientific socialist policy and with sufficient centralisation, unity and discipline as to function in a consciously controlled way—in short, on a political party of the working class. Marx himself made this very clear. And it was underlined by Lenin, especially in his pamphlet, *What is to be done*, where he pointed out that the merely "spontaneous" behaviour of people demanding some improvement in their conditions could never result in socialism; for that, political organisation was required, activated by scientific socialist theory.

Indeed, we cannot make *well-founded* long-term predictions about social events *unless* we can at the same time build effective organisation intended to carry them out. For without this, the people making the predictions would be like architects predicting the erection of some building without taking any steps to mobilise a labour force and provide it with building machinery. It is, indeed, for this very reason that, in the past (and also, for many of our fellow citizens, in the present), people have not been able to make well-founded long-term social predictions. For the sort of organisation necessary for carrying them out could not be projected. They have occasionally hazarded long-term predictions, but these were not well founded. Thus, for instance, no great confidence can be reposed in the sort of long-term predictions at present engaged in by various capitalist economic planning agencies if only because in the prevailing capitalist conditions the machinery does not exist and cannot be created for effectively controlling their realisation.

The well-founded scientific long-term prediction of socialism propounded by Marx was thus a novelty in human affairs. This novelty was introduced by him (as one would expect such a novelty to have been introduced) when and only when the social conditions for its introduction were realised. The formation of the modern working class brought into being for the first time in history the basis for mass organisation which could effectively pursue a policy of bringing relations of production into accordance with the social forces of production in a controlled way, guided by the scientific study of the structure and mode of development of human society. Naturally, therefore, the scientific theory of society, on which the modern revolutionary socialist movement relies, was worked out when and only when that organisation began to be created; and not independently of the work of creating and directing the organisation, but as an integral part of it. This means that for the first time in history men have begun to take the future into their own hands, in the sense of being able to build an organisation which could so understand the issues as to predict where it was going, and go there.

Such, then, being the logical character of the long-term predictions scientifically worked out by Marxist social theory, we can also reach some conclusions as to the necessary *limits* of predictability.

I have already pointed out that well-founded social predictions are not "unconditional" but conditional, that they are based on estimates of probabilities, and that their realisation depends on the existence of effective organisation to create the conditions for carrying them out and to carry them out.

In the first place, therefore, we cannot predict anything beyond what the organisation can carry out. Marx's predictions concerned the work of Communist organisations in bringing about first socialism, and then the transition from socialism to communism. It is clear enough that, when the latter goal is realised, the communist organisation will have completed its function. So what people do after that will be up to them. We can certainly predict that the principal causes of present social ill. will by then have been finally removed and that, having established social appropriation to match social production, people will not go back again to private appropriation. But while on these grounds we can express the confident hope that, when communism is established, people will manage much better than they did in the past, or do now, we cannot possibly predict just how they will manage, or what exactly they will decide to do, or what new difficulties they will meet and how they will cope with them.

In the second place, because of the way social life depends on developing and deploying forces of production, prediction is limited to what can be done with the forces of production at present under development. It is true, of course, that on the basis of existing technology certain predictions can be made about probable technological advance in the future. In other words, certain discoveries can be seen coming; and this, of course, is the basis for planned research. For example, once certain fundamental discoveries of nuclear physics had been made the technology of nuclear energy could be seen coming, and so research was devoted to its development. So, at the present day, we can see coming a very big development of the technology of nuclear energy, automation and electronic computers, and space travel, and can forecast various ways in which these technologies will be used. However, this kind of technological forecasting is limited. We cannot possibly predict the content of entirely new discoveries— for obviously, if we could predict them we would have discovered them already. Hence we cannot predict what new technologies will be invented, after the present ones have been more fully developed. And so we cannot predict what human life will be like in the event (and it is in the long-term the very probable event) of new fundamental discoveries. People in the Stone Age could not have predicted the discovery of iron. And we remain in a similar position.

5. NECESSITY AND INEVITABILITY

Marx "was the first to put sociology on a scientific basis", wrote Lenin in *What the Friends of the People Are*, "by establishing the concept of the economic formation of society as the sum-total of relations of production, and by establishing the fact that the development of such formations is a process of natural history."

That the evolution of social-economic formations is like natural history means that the past course of social evolution is explained like natural history. Just as the evolution of species is explained by the necessity of organisms being adapted to their environments, so is the evolution of social formations explained by the necessity of production relations being adapted to productive forces. In social evolution, presumably, this adaptation will continue, just as species will continue to be adapted to their environments.

In predicting the future we presume that it will be explicable on the same lines as the past. Nevertheless, this does not mean that prediction of future social events is like prediction of natural events. For our own role in the process of bringing about those events is different. A similar distinction must be made, of course, regarding predictions of natural events subjected to human interference.

Science, which is something which people do, must always take into account the relation of the people doing the science to the processes which the science is about. Men make their own history. Therefore the relation of people trying scientifically to understand social processes to the processes they are trying to understand is different from that of the same people to natural processes. And therefore, this difference must be taken into account in thinking scientifically about social prospects.

It is true that some people (those whom Dr. Popper calls "historicists") try to take what may be called a "god's eye" view of human affairs, and to predict the future of these little creatures crawling over the face of the earth as though they themselves and their contemporaries were not engaged in making that future. However, the god's eye view is not the scientific view. Some see in the crystal ball visions of utopia, others catastrophe, or unending cycles of decay and regeneration. But none of their prophecies are, or can be, well founded—because they do not take into account how people actually make history, and do not back their predictions with practical proposals for an organisation to carry them out. Instead, they imagine themselves as looking down on society from a stance outside society—which is as absurd as a physicist imagining himself as looking at the physical world through an instrument which is not itself physical.

In his criticisms of "historicism" Dr. Popper justifiably questions the assumptions of crystal-gazers. Evidently, his criticisms have no bearing on the scientific study of society, and the proposals for and predictions of future social activity, made by Marx. Marx did not gaze into any crystal. Nor did he imagine himself as looking down on society, like a man who watches a carpet being unrolled, and who predicts the pattern on the next bits to appear from what he has seen of the pattern so far. From studying history Marx concluded that men make their history by adapting their production relations to their productive forces. He worked out how we can do this today, made practical proposals for organisation for doing it—and predicted that it would be done. As Lenin said, he "put sociology on a scientific basis", and so put political policy-making on a scientific basis too.

It is, of course, always possible to make fairly reliable short-term predictions of social events from the standpoint of a mere observer, by estimating what some people are doing or going to do, and what others may do to stop them. If, for example, it looks either as if no one can stop them, or as if no one wants to stop them, then a fairly confident prediction can be made that what they are doing will be done. Marx's prediction went far beyond this, because it concerned the future social-economic formation. Such a prediction can only be scientifically grounded when it is grounded, first, on an accurate idea of the general conditions governing the evolution of economic formations, and second, on proposals for what sort of organisation is required to bring the new formation into being and how the organisation should be conducted. And that is how Marx's prediction was grounded.

Marx did not speak as a prophet or fortune-teller, who tells people: This is fated to happen, so prepare yourselves! He spoke as a practical organiser, who says, with good grounds for saying it: Do this—and you will win.

Where, then, is the "historicism" in Marx, which Dr. Popper so vehemently censures? Where is the vaunted discovery of "the plot" which the moving finger writes, of "the path" which people willy-nilly tread, of "the destiny" which pursues us? And where is the "unconditional prophecy"? Only in Dr. Popper's fertile imagination. Marx, the "famous historicist", was not "an historicist" at all. He was only, as Lenin said, "the first to put sociology on a scientific basis".

Historicism, as defined by Dr. Popper, is an idealist concept. The concept of "the plot" which is unfolded in history and "the path" laid down for us, is the concept of a pre-existing idea which is realised in time in the material world. It is, indeed, at bottom, a theological concept of creation: "in the beginning was the Word". Those who think they can say what the future will be because they think they know "the plot" and "the path" are frauds who pretend to powers of prophecy not given to other men because they imagine themselves to be *en rapport* with the eternal. Despite his rationalism and empirical method, Hegel, the idealist, was certainly "an historicist" in Dr. Popper's sense. In opposing Hegel's idealism, Marx opposed to Hegelian "historicism" the scientific materialist theory of how men make and will make history.

That Marx made use of "the historical method" is undoubted. As Dr. Popper quite rightly says, Marx considered that "we can obtain knowledge of social entities only by studying social changes". And it is a puzzle to know how else we could "obtain knowledge of social entities". Dr. Popper, however, proceeds to call Marx's historical method "historicist", and says Marx studied social changes so as to discover therein "rhythms, patterns, laws and trends" and so predict the future. He makes out that Marx was the man who traces the pattern in the unrolling carpet so as to predict what the next piece of the pattern will be like. The prediction, of course, must be quite groundless unless one has grounds to believe that the carpet was made by a manufacturer who imposed a pattern on it. Human history is not at all like an unrolling carpet.

Marx did not look at history to find the superimposed pattern. He studied social changes to obtain knowledge of how men make such changes, so as to work out how we can make changes now, and what conditions they must fulfil to satisfy our needs. Like any scientist, he wanted to find out what are the conditions of our lives and what we can do about it. That was Marx's historical method, and the object of his applying it.

The crunch of this whole argument concerns Marx's conception of "the class struggle" and of the "necessity" and "inevitability" which, he maintained, attaches to it and its outcome. Explaining to a corrrespondent (J. Weydemeyer, March 5, 1852) what he claimed to have scientifically established by his historical method, Marx wrote:

"No credit is due to me for discovering the existence of classes in modern society, nor yet the struggle between them. Long before me bourgeois historians had described the historical development of the struggle of the classes, and bourgeois economists the economic anatomy of the classes. What I did new was to prove:

(1) that the existence of classes is only bound up with particular historical phases of the development of production;

(2) that the class struggle necessarily leads to the dictatorship of the proletariat;

(3) that this dictatorship itself only constitutes the transition to the abolition of all classes and to a classless society."

There you have it, Dr. Popper may say. What did I tell you? Marx *was* an historicist. It may be in fact true that history is "the history of class struggles". And "bourgeois historians" who modestly attempted to do no more than describe what happened, and did not aspire, like historicists, to be prophets, may have done well to describe those class struggles. But Marx goes farther. He asserts that class struggles are "bound up with the development of production" and so constitute the necessary pattern of history, and that the continuation of this pattern will "necessarily" or "inevitably" lead to "the dictatorship of the proletariat" and then to "a classless society". What is this but unconditional historical prophecy, derived from a claim to have discovered the pattern, the rhythm, the plot and the plan of history?

Let us examine the plain meaning and implications of Marx's statement of his position.

First of all, Marx in his theory of class struggle drew attention to inescapable circumstances in which people have had, and still have, to act; and to inescapable issues which they have had, and still have, to settle. There is no help for it—there are the circumstances, there are the issues, as objective facts of human life which cannot be evaded. Because class divisions bring class antagonisms into the way people have to get their livelihood, the class struggle has become necessary or inevitable, in the sense of unavoidable. And Marx was able to explain why this has happened. It is because the production relations into which people entered once they began to raise their productive forces above the level of the Stone Age have included class contradictions.

Exactly as Marx said, "men do not make their history just as they please, they do not make it under circumstances chosen by themselves". They have to enter into relations of production in order to use their productive forces with the same necessity as they have to use their hands to fashion their implements of production. Such things are, for us, necessary, inevitable, unavoidable. To know what are our actual circumstances, what are the issues, and what we can and cannot do about them, science must distinguish the accidental in our circumstances from the necessary, the avoidable from the unavoidable. Not to do so is to draw back from scientific analysis and decline to face facts.

Secondly, having demonstrated the necessity or unavoidability of the class struggle, Marx concluded that the class struggle provides the dynamic whereby historical issues are decided. The given relations of production contain the class divisions, and action to change the relations of production is action to change the class relations, that is, class struggle.

And finally, his analysis of the capitalist production relations and the class struggle under capitalism led to the conclusion that these relations and the corresponding class struggle will persist until such time as the working classes succeed in winning the political power to institute social ownership and social appropriation, which means expropriating the capitalist class. That is what he called "the dictatorship of the proletariat". This is the only way to settle the issue of adapting production relations to modern forces of production, and when it is accomplished there will be "a classless society".

That "the class struggle *necessarily* leads to the dictatorship of the proletariat" has the plain meaning that this is the only way in which it can be finished. It cannot but go on until that outcome takes place. From the very circumstances of its existence the working class cannot but continue to oppose exploitation, and the only way it can get rid of what it opposes is by winning political power and using that power to reorganise social relations. And so, apart from what *The Communist Manifesto* described as "the mutual destruction of the contending classes" (which could take place nowadays in a nuclear war), or outside intervention (such as an invasion from outer space, or a cosmic catastrophe), the dictatorship of the proletariat and the transition to a classless society is the unavoidable, that is, necessary or inevitable, outcome.

It is clear that this theory of the necessity of the class struggle and of the dictatorship of the proletariat is no "unconditional prophecy" but a straightforward scientific analysis. It is a scientific analysis which supplies a programme and a guide to action for the working-class struggle, based on sober scientific recognition of the whole social situation. To argue that the theory is wrong it would have to be argued that the general idea of adaptation of relations of production to forces of production is wrong, and that the analysis of capitalist relations of production is wrong. But Dr. Popper, with his critique of "historicism", dodges the issue by arguing that the very concepts employed by the theory are "historicist" rather than scientific. He can do this only by making out that the theory means something different from what it says.

To know the meanings of words as they are used in statements one must always take those words and statements in their context, with their implications. The secret of the mad tea party type of discussion lies in refusing to do this. Certain philosophers have tried to define senses of the words "necessity" and "inevitability" which give us *absolute* or "inexorable" necessity in nature and human affairs, and *absolute* inevitability. A model for this was the well-known theorem of Spinoza, that "the effect follows from the cause with the same necessity as the three angles of a triangle make two right-angles". It is evident, however, that the word "necessity" has a different sense when we talk about some event "necessarily happening" from what it has when we talk about "the three angles of a triangle necessarily making two right-angles". This is evident, for one thing, because for angles to add up to two right-angles is not an event; and for another, because to say "so and so necessarily happens" is not incompatible with saying "under other imaginable circumstances something else could have happened".

For discussing what happens, the relevant categories are those of *possibility* and *impossibility*—and these are the categories employed by the sciences, including the science of society. Scientific thinking reaches conclusions about what is possible and what is impossible *relative to a given set of circumstances*. On the other hand, "inexorable necessity", "absolute inevitability", "fate", "destiny", and so forth, are absolutes; the inexorably necessary is supposed to happen, and "the destined path" is inexorably taken, regardless of circumstances. Such absolutes are alien to science, and apply only in the fantastic world of false abstraction.

Of "necessity" it may be remarked that the opposite of "impossibility" is "possibility" and not "necessity". In the context of possibility, as defined by science, the word "necessary" has the sense of "impossible without" or "impossible unless". Thus the class struggle necessarily leads to the dictatorship of the proletariat because that is the only way it can finish, and because the class aim of emancipation from exploitation is impossible to realise without establishing first a system of political power to abolish exploitation.

Successful politics, then, demands *the appreciation of necessity*, that is to say, of *the necessary conditions* without which the possible cannot be achieved, but with the satisfaction of which it will be achieved. And this appreciation is afforded by social and political science. The essential teaching of Marxism for working-class politics is that emancipation from exploitation and class struggle can only be achieved through the dictatorship of the proletariat. Marx was talking about unavoidable conditions of human action, about the only ways in which unavoidable issues can be finally settled.

In the light of these considerations about necessity and inevitability, and the preceding analysis of the logical character of scientific social prediction, we can now, I think, detect the further misunderstanding which Dr. Popper perpetrates when he concludes that Marx's "historicism" was in contradiction to what he calls Marx's "activism". Dr. Popper says that to speak of what the class struggle "necessarily" leads to, and to make a long-term prediction, is incompatible with the "activist" point of view which promotes organisation for realising the prediction and admits that without the organisation the prediction will not come true. For if something is fated to happen, or will happen with inexorable necessity, why advocate going to any trouble to make sure it does happen?

"The historicist method", writes Dr. Popper, "implies . . . that society will necessarily change . . . through stages predetermined by inexorable necessity." Hence "it teaches the futility of any attempt to alter impending changes; a peculiar variety of fatalism. . . . Admittedly, the 'activist' exhortation 'The philosophers have only interpreted the world in various ways: the point, however, is to change it', may find much sympathy with historicists. . . . But it is in conflict with the most significant doctrines of historicism. For as we now see, we may say: 'The historicist can only interpret social development and aid it in various ways; his point, however, is that nobody can change it.' " (PH. 51-2).

Dr. Popper begins by merely begging the question, since, as we have already seen, Marx's method was not "historicist", nor did his conclusions imply that historical necessity is "inexorable". But he ends with sheer nonsense. When Marx said "the point is to change it" he clearly meant that the point is, by understanding the way changes operate, to bring about controlled changes. He did not mean to change the ways things change. It is quite true that nobody can change the basic ways human beings have to set about their affairs—we cannot "change social development" in such a way as to do by will-power or magic things which hitherto we have done with our hands; nor can we change it in such a way that we do not have to adapt relations of production to forces of production; nor, when modern forces of production are fettered by capitalism, can we change this situation into one in which capitalist relations cease to act as fetters. But this does not imply that we cannot "change the world" in a controlled way, if once we arrive at an objective analysis of circumstances and of the means and limitations of our actions. It does not mean that we cannot with the aid of scientific analysis effectively organise to "make history"; though it does mean, of course, that we still cannot "make it just as we please". But no one but a fool would think that either individually or collectively people have power to do "just as they please".

As regards the "peculiar variety of fatalism", the judgment about whether a scientific analysis of social circumstances implies "fatalism" and "the futility of any attempt to alter impending changes" depends entirely on one's point of view and what changes one wants to make or prevent. From the point of view of someone who proposes to rise on the wings of a dove, the Newtonian theory of gravitation no doubt propounds "a peculiar variety of fatalism". It says you just can't do it.

From the point of view of the capitalist class, Marx's theory is certainly "fatalistic". It says: You cannot contrive a managed capitalism, you cannot do away with the class struggle, you cannot keep the system going indefinitely. It does not go so far as to say, You can do nothing to block socialist advance; but it does say, You can never block it once for all, but will have to keep on blocking it until finally it blocks you. As a further offence against capitalism, it offers practical advice to socialists as to how to demolish capitalist blocks. From the point of view of the working class, on the other hand, it is not "fatalist" at all. It explains the situation, says what to do, and predicts that it will be done.

Dr. Popper's critique does no more than voice the natural dissatisfaction of capitalist apologists with an objective analysis of capitalism and its possibilities of development. *Any* scientific analysis is bound to be "fatalistic" from the point of view of those interested in doing what cannot be done.

6. SCIENCE AND UTOPIA

After what has been said about "historicism", it is perhaps unnecessary to add much more in relation to Dr. Popper's further allegations about "essentialism", "holism" and "utopianism".

According to Dr. Popper, Marxist science claims to discover and describe the "hidden reality or essence" which "must unfold itself in change". Well, Marxist science certainly does claim to discover and describe processes going on amongst men in society, relations into which men enter with nature and with one another, which men cannot avoid entering into and conducting, and which do, inevitably, whether men are aware of it or not, determine the character of the social changes they make and condition their conscious activities. In this respect, however, the discoveries of Marxist science about men are no different in kind from the discoveries of any other empirical science about anything else.

Chemists, for instance, observing chemical phenomena, and wishing to explain them, try to discover processes and relations which determine and condition the phenomena. They try to discover "what is really happening" when those phenomena happen. In this sense chemistry (like all other branches of natural science) certainly claims to discover "the hidden reality" or, as Dr. Popper has also expressed it, "the realities which lie behind the appearances". But no one accuses chemists of "essentialism".

Marx said that men always enter into relations of production in order to deploy their forces of production, that this has involved them in class struggles, and that "history is the history of class struggles". This is how men carry on. Indeed, it is how men inevitably or necessarily or "essentially" carry on, in view (as Marx and Engels said) of "the physical organisation of the individuals and their consequent relation to the rest of nature". This fact was "hidden", and it required some research to uncover it. It was a scientific discovery, like other scientific discoveries. It was no more a product of "methodological essentialism" than any other scientific discovery. It was no more a discovery of "the hidden essence" than any physical, chemical or biological discovery discovers "essences". Marx was not concerned with "essences" but with real relations of human individuals, which, as he and Engels said in *The German Ideology*, "can be verified in a purely empirical way".

Finally, we come to "holism" and "utopianism". According to Dr. Popper, "holism is interested in the development, not of aspects of social life, but of 'society as a whole' ", and considers that one can only properly understand particular "aspects" by seeing how they are determined by "the whole". And "utopianism" is bound up with "holism", because "the utopian" does not aim at changing particular "aspects" but "the whole".

Marx was certainly "interested in the development of society as a whole". He was interested "in the development of society as a whole" in the same way as a biologist, for instance, is interested in the development of the organism as a whole. That does not make either the Marxist or the biologist into a "holist". Neither is interested in the "the whole" to the exclusion of "the aspects", for each knows perfectly well that "the whole" is the product of the complex interactions of the parts.

The biologist understands the organism as a complex of interrelated living cells, and similarly the Marxist understands society as a complex of interrelated living individuals. The living parts live in interrelation. Of course, it is their mode of interrelation which determines the overall character and behaviour of the whole, of the organism or of the society. And at the same time, the ways in which the parts are interrelated, and interact and function, as parts of the whole, determines the specific character and properties of each part. A cell which is a cell of some organism is a bone cell or a nerve cell or a muscle cell, and so not the same as a cell that lives all on its own; just as an individual person gets his individuality from his being born into, educated in and functioning in a society, and would not have this individuality outside society. An organism is not formed by fully-fashioned individual cells, each complete independently of the organism, coming together to form an organism; nor is a society formed by fully-fashioned individuals, each a complete human person independently of social life, coming together to form a society. Further, just as the organism grows and changes by a process of all the cells functioning and relating themselves to one another to obtain the means of life from the environment, so does society grown and change by a process of all the individuals functioning and relating themselves to one another to obtain the means of life.

Marx's investigation of society led him, however, to conclude that a society is nevertheless in important respects not much like a biological organism. The individuals who make up society are human organisms, so naturally the relations they enter into as human organisms obtaining their means of life by social production are of an entirely different kind from those the cells of a living organism enter into as cells of that organism. His views about society were arrived at by investigating the relations individuals enter into in forming a society, and not deduced from some abstract comparison of societies with organisms.

His analysis of the social process, that is, of the relations individuals enter into in order to obtain the means of life, and of the consequences of their entering into those relations, led him to the conclusion that, to "change society", the key thing to do is to change the relations of production in adaptation to productive forces. He concluded that then, when that is done, "with the change of the economic foundation the whole immense superstructure is more or less rapidly transformed". And this conclusion, a consequence of the analysis, is verified by the facts of history—a verification which thus verifies the analysis of which it is the consequence.

In what way is this conclusion from a normal type of scientific analysis either "holist" or "utopian"? Marx did not say that one must first change "the whole", and that only by that means could one change "the aspects". Of course, it is as absurd or utopian to seek to change "the whole" without studying and doing something about "the aspects" as it is to seek to "understand the development of the whole" without studying the aspects in their complex interrelationship. What Marx did do, and what Marx did say, was precisely what normal scientific method requires us to do and say. He studied the various aspects of society to find out how the whole is constituted and develops; and out of this study he discovered what are the key relations determining overall development, and said that, to change society, one must concentrate on finding how to change those key relations.

On the other hand, it is not very difficult to see that the opposition which Dr. Popper has inferred, between Marx's alleged "holism" on the one hand, and the alleged "anti-holism" of science, is an absurdity. Societies have in fact in common with living organisms the feature that in each there occur certain kinds of "life process" (for example, the circulation of the blood in animals, and the processes of economic exchange in commodity-producing societies), the disruption of which is followed by the death or distintegration of the whole. It is essential in any sort of scientific account of processes of this description that the given process should be studied "as a whole"—to find out, that is to say, how the parts interact in order to produce the whole process, and why, if the whole disintegrates, the parts can no longer exist as before, being no longer parts of the whole. This entails, in particular, investigating the mechanisms of "feed-back" by which what happens in one part produces effects which react back on other parts, so as to keep the whole intact. Clearly, such feed-back processes are characteristic of the organism or of the society "as a whole", and cannot be studied except in the context of studying how "the whole" is maintained and develops. When Marx studied capitalist society, examining at one level the processes of the circulation of capital, and at another level those of the class struggle, he was studying how the "life process" of society goes on under capitalism, was discovering the disruptions it undergoes, and accordingly working out proposals as to what should be done and what changes should be made in order to enable social production and consumption to continue without these sorts of disruptions.

So when we examine Marx's methods, ideas and conclusions, we find that all Dr. Popper's clamorous allegations about "historicism", "essentialism", "holism" and "utopianism", which have so greatly impressed so many people whose prejudices made them want to be impressed, are sheer misrepresentation and mythology. In telling us what Marxism means, Dr. Popper produces only a very stupid travesty of Marxism. This, he asserts, amounts to a "devastating criticism" and destroys all the scientific pretentions of Marxism once for all.

Certainly, the Marx whom Dr. Popper puts up to prosecute for ideological errors in Wonderland shows very little understanding of the concepts or methods of the sciences. But as we have seen, and as we shall see again and again in what follows, the real Marx is perfectly conversant with the methods of science and with various scientific truths which Dr. Popper proclaims with the intention of confounding him; and the real Marx drew scientific conclusions which Dr. Popper, for all his parade of a truly scientific outlook, only misrepresents and evades. It is in these misrepresentations and evasions contained in Dr. Popper's refutations of Marxism that misunderstandings about the character of scientific method and of scientific conclusions are to be found. As for Marx, he approached the investigation of social phenomena, and the proposal of social remedies, in a thoroughly scientific manner.

2

SCIENCE APPLIED TO POLITICS

I. PROBLEMS OF SOCIAL SCIENCE

Marx applied the normal methods of scientific inquiry to the study of human society, and formulated the fundamental hypotheses underlying all social sciences..His credentials are similar to those of any other foundation-layer in other sciences. His propositions can all be tested and, far from propounding a theoretical system to answer all questions and account for everything finally and completely, he began an investigation for others to carry further.

But that Marx applied scientific method, already well established for the study of nature, to the study of society, does not mean that he set about the job as though there were no difference between studying natural and social processes. For different kinds of processes different techniques of inquiry have to be devised, with different kinds of hypotheses and appropriate methods for testing them. Social processes, unlike mechanical, physical, chemical or biological processes, are the results of self-conscious agents "acting with deliberation or passion". Possibly one may study how deliberations and passions are engendered in individuals as one may study how, say, chemical reactions are engendered. But the way in which the actions of human beings make up the processes of society precludes the systematic investigation of the latter by artificially setting up experiments, as is done in, say, chemistry. As Marx said in the Preface to *Capital*, here "neither microscopes nor chemical reagents are of use. The force of abstraction must replace both".

Moreover, not only do the phenomena investigated thus differ in the way they are brought about, but there is the further difference that to investigate social activities is itself a social activity and introduces a new factor into the phenomena investigated. Physicists have had to reckon with the fact that to investigate electrons a beam of electrons is employed, so that the investigation interferes with what is investigated. Nevertheless, to use electrons to investigate electrons does not alter the ways electrons behave by creating for them the power to do what they otherwise could not do. When people, on the other hand, gain knowledge of their own social relations and their mode of development, that gain of knowledge is the gain of a new power for changing and developing their social relations.

That Marx succeeded where others had failed in finding how to study society scientifically was due, amongst other things, to his recognition that studying social processes is not at all the same thing as studying natural processes.

In his observations about scientific method Dr. Popper has very rightly and properly pointed out that the old idea of empiricist philosophers, that science proceeds simply by accumulating "observations" and then making "inductions" from observations, does not correspond to the logic of scientific inquiry. That is not how science proceeds, or could proceed. "Science starts from problems, and not from observations," he writes. "The conscious task before the scientist is always the solution of a problem through the construction of a theory which solves the problem . . . every worth while new theory raises new problems . . . the most lasting contribution to the growth of scientific knowledge that a theory can make are the new problems which it raises, so that we are led back to the view of science and of the growth of knowledge as always starting from, and always ending with problems—problems of an ever-increasing depth, and an ever-increasing fertility in suggesting new problems" (CR. 222).

As I said at the beginning of this book, Marx laid the foundations of social science by finding the right problems to tackle. To find the problems of science is also to define the subject-matter of science. Formulating the problems, Marxism at the same time enables us to define the subject-matter of the inquiry. It thus becomes a true scientific discipline.

Human society consists of nothing but interrelated human individuals. So naturally, social science is an inquiry into what human individuals do, and how they are able to satisfy their needs in their social intercourse. But the problems and subject-matter of social science are not those of the physiology and psychology of human individuals, their individual activities and reactions. Individuals create and sustain society by entering into social relations with one another, and it is the *social relations* which are the subject-matter of social science and set its problems.

Dr. Popper has criticised under the name of "psychologism" the view that the fundamental question for social science is to understand the psychology of human individuals, and that all social phenomena are direct effects of psychological causes. Crude examples of psychologism are the theory that individuals need a father-figure, and so we get monarchies; and are aggressive, and so we get wars. The fact is that social phenomena, such as monarchies and wars, are consequent upon the social relations into which individuals have entered. Indeed, individuals acquire their human individuality only in social relations, and behave differently in different social relations; though naturally, as Marx and Engels also pointed out, to explain the social relations and what people do in them we must always take into account "the physical organisation of the individuals and their consequent relation to the rest of nature".

"Perhaps the most important criticism of psychologism is that it fails to understand the main task of the explanatory social sciences", writes Dr. Popper (2–OS. 94). "This task is . . . the discovery and explanation of the less obvious dependencies within the social sphere." He justly praises Marx for opposing psychologism. But what he fails to note is that, opposing psychologism, Marxism has well defined "the main task of the explanatory social sciences", leading to "the discovery and explanation of the less obvious dependencies".

The main task of the explanatory social sciences is to describe and explain social relations, in abstraction from individuals who enter into them. The dependencies discovered and explained are *the dependencies of social relations*. Clearly, to speak of social relations is to speak of what numbers of unspecified individuals do in association. A social relation is a relation of individuals. But to describe social relations does not require specification of the individuals who enter into them, and social relations persist while individuals come and go.

This shows, incidentally, why Marx spoke of "the force of abstraction" as replacing, in social science, microscopes and chemical reagents. A relation cannot be laid out under a microscope, nor can it be separated out and put to work like a chemical reagent. To study social relations independent of the individuals who enter into them requires "the force of abstraction". Dr. Popper himself recognises this. "In the social sciences . . . we cannot see and observe our objects before we have thought about them", he says. "For most of the objects of social science, if not all of them, are abstract objects . . ." (PH. 135). Marx put it rather more clearly—but the point is the same.

As we have seen, Marx's fundamental propositions for the social sciences were arrived at by asking what is the necessary condition for people to enter into social relations at all. People must socially produce their material means of life, and enter into relations of production corresponding to their social forces of production. Having reached that conclusion, he went on to study how people change their relations of production, and this entails the study of the interdependencies of social relations in processes of social change. The key problems for social science, he showed, are not problems of the actions and motivations of individuals but of the formation and interdependence of social relations. Social relations change and develop. The problem of how the change and development is brought about and of the laws which govern it, the main problem of the scientific understanding of society and its history, is the problem of analysing and sorting out the interdependence of social relations. The laws regulating society and its development are expressed as generalised statements of such interdependence.

Social science thus abstracts from individuals and deals with social relations. It is not concerned with individual but with aggregate humanity—with the consequences of the interactions of large numbers, and not with the individual peculiarities of this and that person. The laws which it formulates, therefore, to the effect that some social relations depend on others, which are laws governing all change in social relations, are laws applying to aggregates of individuals, not to the individuals who make up the aggregates. And (as I have already said) the predictions which it enables us to make are predictions about the overall consequences of large numbers of individual interactions.

All this seems, in principle, not only fairly clear but also in fair accord with Dr. Popper's own justified remarks about scientific method. Dr. Popper, however, now proceeds to some further criticism of Marx's allegedly "historicist" views about the laws governing social processes.

According to historicism, he says, "sociological laws, or the laws of social life, differ in different places and periods" (PH. 5). Consequently "the only universally valid laws of society must be the laws which link up successive periods. They must be laws of historical development which determine the transition from one period to another" (PH. 41). Historicists, of whom Marx was a famous one, think they have found the one great law which determines social development—and this law is an "evolutionary" law, which says that social development follows a certain course in the sequence of periods and the transition from one period to another.

Such a claim, says Dr. Popper, is very easy to refute. "Can there be a *law* of evolution?" he asks. "I believe that the answer to this question must be 'No', and that the search for the law of the 'unvarying order' of evolution cannot possibly fall within the scope of scientific method, whether in biology or in sociology. My reasons are very simple. The evolution of life on earth, or of human society, is a unique historical process. Such a process, we may assume, proceeds in accordance with all kinds of causal laws, for example, the laws of mechanics, of chemistry, of heredity and segregation, of natural selection, etc. Its description, however, is not a law, but only a singular historical statement. Universal laws make assertions concerning some unvarying order . . . i.e., concerning all processes of a certain kind . . . But we cannot hope to test a universal hypothesis nor to find a natural law acceptable to science if we are for ever confined to the observation of one unique process. Nor can the observation of one unique process help us to foresee its future development" (PH. 107–8).

But these remarks have no more relevance to the "sociological laws" or laws of "social evolution" discovered by Marx than they have to the laws of organic evolution discovered by Darwin.

Darwin's explanatory theory about organic evolution did not consist in propounding "the law" that organic evolution "invariably" or "universally" proceeds from marine invertebrates, through fishes, reptiles and mammals, to man. Of course, organic evolution on the earth is a unique process, so there cannot be a "universal law" that it "always" proceeds in one "unvarying order". Darwin's explanatory theory was the theory of natural selection, which explains how the unique evolution has taken place. Similarly, Marx's explanatory theory about social evolution did not consist in propounding the "law" that society *always* develops from primitive communism, through slavery (not to mention the Asiatic, Slavonic, Germanic and other odd modes of production) to feudalism and capitalism. Society has not *always* developed like that, it has only happened once. His explanatory theory was a theory about the interdependence of social relations, with the basic dependence of production relations on the forces of production and of other relations on production relations, which not only explains how the unique evolution has taken place but how to continue it in the direction of satisfying human needs. Marx's theory showed cogently enough why social organisation had to start at the level of primitive communism, how private property developed and what effects it had, why certain conditions had to be achieved before others could be entered into (for instance, why feudalism had to precede capitalism), and, finally, that we can only solve the contradictions of capitalism by advancing to socialism. But as usual, Dr. Popper refutes Marx by making out that Marx talked "historicist" nonsense.

Having done so, however, Dr. Popper proceeds to talk nonsense himself. Because social evolution is a unique process, he concludes that "history is characterised by its interest in actual, singular, or specific events, rather than in laws or generalisations", and that this distinguishes "historical" from "theoretical" or "explanatory" sciences (PH. 143). The historian, interested in one unique sequence, cannot hope to find any "universal law" governing the sequence. But why ever not? The historical sequence is in fact governed by the law that people always adapt their relations of production to their forces of production. Why should not historians be interested in such a law? It is universally true, and without it they cannot explain the sequence but only describe it.

Finally, if one takes into account the laws which Marx actually discovered (as distinct from those which Dr. Popper invents in order to refute), it is evident that the idea that "sociological laws differ in different places and periods" and that "the only universally valid laws of society must be the laws which link up successive periods" is as nonsensical as all the rest of Dr. Popper's infelicitous lucubrations. The basic law which Marx formulated is always valid, whether in the development of a single "period" or in the transition from one to another. Of course, when a specific set of social relations come into being there are interdependencies between them which do not operate in other circumstances, when those relations are not present (for instance, under capitalism there are laws about, say, costs and profits which came into operation only when capitalist relations began to be formed). However, that means that "the laws which link up successive periods", far from being "the only universally valid laws", operate only in the specific link-up (for instance, the specific laws in operation in the transition from feudalism to capitalism are peculiar to that specific transition).

The way in which a unique unrepeatable irreversible process of development can happen in accordance with universal laws is really quite simple. It does not mean, as Dr. Popper makes out Marx "the famous historicist" meant, that the process "always" follows a certain order. That is obviously nonsense, for if it only happens once then it does not "always" happen. The *order* of the process, the order in which stage follows stage, the necessity of one stage preceding or being followed by another, is the consequence of the working out of the laws—it is what the laws explain and so is not itself "the law". The laws are of the form that certain relations always depend on certain other relations. Whatever relations are formed, their laws always operate. According to Marx's theory of "sociological laws" relations of production depend on forces of production; people change their forces of production in the development of their productive intercourse with nature, and so change their relations of production; and so the unique irreversible stage-by-stage development of social-economic formations of human society takes place. This makes good scientific sense and is empirically verifiable in terms of what people do.

No more than the operation of sociological laws means that every social event and social change is predetermined or "fated", does it mean that people are moved about like "pawns" in the grip of historical necessity. On the contrary, as Engels said, and as we know from experience anyway, "nothing happens without a conscious purpose, without an intended aim", and people face choices and act of their own volition. But relying on certain productive forces, to live by which they have entered into certain production relations, what people do and can do—what they intend to do and what actually comes of their doing it—is conditioned by the relations into which they have entered with nature and with one another for obtaining their means of life, and the interdependencies of these relations. That is an objective condition of life from the limitations of which we can no more escape than we can from the limitations of our mortal bodies. But the better we understand such objective conditions, the less do they appear as limitations. The better we understand what cannot be done the better do we understand what can be done, and how to do it.

Speaking of the conscious volitional character of human actions, Engels went on to say (Ludwig Feuerbach, Chapter 4), that nevertheless "that which is willed happens but rarely; in the majority of instances the numerous desired ends cross and conflict with one another, or these ends themselves are from the outset incapable of realisation or the means for attaining them are insufficient". Consequently "the many individual wills active in history for the most part produce results quite other than those they intended—often quite the opposite; their motives therefore in relation to the total result are likewise only of secondary significance".

To explain what happens in history it is not enough to say that people act from certain motives. Their actions are, of course, motivated; and the explanation of what happens includes the description of the motivations. But motives "cross and conflict" and, as it works out, what happens is, more often than not, what no one intended. To explain both human motivations, and the results, both intended and unintended, of their motivated actions, it is also necessary to take into account the interdependence of social relations, which exhibit laws quite independent of anything people may intend or think.

In remarking that the task of the social sciences is "the discovery and explanation of the less obvious dependencies within the social sphere", Dr. Popper proceeds to conclude that "the main task of the social sciences . . . is the task of analysing the unintended social repercussions of intentional human actions" (2–OS. 95; he must think this definition definitive, for it is repeated in italics in CR. 342).

This conclusion only illustrates once again Dr. Popper's unfortunate tendency to talk nonsense. Why ever should the task of the social sciences be restricted to tracing the *unintended* social repercussions of intentional actions? For the better we can discover and explain "the less obvious dependencies within the social sphere" (dependencies of social relations), the better can we judge what can and cannot be done, and so the less will the social repercussions of our intentional actions be unintended. Put together, Dr. Popper's two definitions of the task of the social sciences make nonsense. For success in carrying out the first task eliminates the second.

In studying the laws of development of society (or "dependencies within the social sphere"), and pointing out that their operation explains the results of human actions irrespective of intentions, Marx and Engels made it quite clear that, once these laws are understood, it becomes possible to project plans of action, based on an objective analysis of circumstances, in which the results will be brought more and more, in a controlled way, within the scope of the intentions. As with other sciences, success in social sciences increases our power to fit our intentions to our capabilities and to bring about what we intend. All knowledge is power. It follows that knowledge about our own social activities makes possible a change in the character of our social activities. When we have enough of it, and have built an organisation for using it, we can base our intentions on knowledge of our circumstances and needs, and carry them out.

2.   SOCIAL SCIENCE AND POLITICS

Politics, it has been well said, is the art of the possible. This description of politics makes it clear how social science applies in politics. For in science we discover what is possible and what is not, and how what is possible gets brought about. In social science, the study of social relations, we discover the conditions and possibilities of human action in the management of social life. We discover how given social relations limit possibilities. We discover the conditions for changing social relations and what possibilities such changes open up. We discover how social relations establish class distinctions and divergent or antagonistic class interests, and what possibilities there are for the pursuit of those interests.

Politics is a social activity—an art or a science or however one likes to describe it—which certain people undertake in definite social circumstances on behalf of definite interests. It is concerned with government, with the management of people by means of the control and direction of institutions.

In politics divergent interests are pursued. It is a struggle between political rivals, each with his own policy or his own politics. And, underlying all other political divisions, there are always the divisions of class interests. For the most part politics consists of a complicated game of move and counter-move, in which each party seeks some immediate advantage or to avoid some immediate danger; and while all parties may claim a far-sighted vision of what they will achieve in the future, in practice they simply follow their noses as they smell out where their interest lies. The political struggle is waged in the name of all kinds of principles, ideals and universal ends. But in effect each party pursues its particular sectional interest. As Marx caustically observed in *The Eighteenth Brumaire of Louis Bonaparte* (Chapter 3): "As in private life one differentiates between what a man thinks and says of himself and what he really is and does, so one must distinguish still more the phrases and fancies of parties from their real interests, their conception of themselves from their reality . . . Thus the Tories of England long imagined they were enthusiastic about Monarchy, Church and the beauties of the old English Constitution, until the day of danger wrung from them the confession that they are only enthusiastic about ground rent."

Political parties, in the form of more or less permanent organisations with membership, officials, programme and rules, are products of modern democracy. Combinations of place-seekers are as old as government itself. But with democratic institutions, rulers and would-be rulers had to do more than gang up together in order to rule. In many cases they have felt and (judging from television performances) some continue to feel the same disdain for the electorate as Shakespeare depicted Coriolanus as feeling when he had to "stand here and beg of Hob and Dick" and wished the plebs would "wash their faces and keep their teeth clean". But more astute than Coriolanus, they have managed to build party organisations to nominate rulers, campaign for support of them, and make Hob, Dick and their wives think their views are being consulted.

Parties are not necessarily formed with the open intention of promoting the interests of any one class. But they can be neither stable nor long-lasting except as political organisations of a class. A party which no interest could regard as its own would stand little chance in politics compared with the parties of each interest. For only when the ideas of a party and the policies it carries out correspond near enough to a class interest is the support forthcoming to maintain the party organisation. A party is kept up by a class interest, and bases its practical calculations of policy on the promotion of that interest in interaction with others. Hence the complicated interplay between politicians concerned with office and citizens concerned with the uses to which the power of office is put, leads to the result that a class sets up its own political parties, and political parties act as the political representatives of classes. By means of politics a class promotes its economic interest, and by the control of political power establishes and augments its economic power.

In these conditions Marx and Engels stated, as long ago as 1850 in the *Address of the Central Committee to the Communist League*, the need "to establish an independent . . . workers' party and make each section the central point and nucleus of workers' societies in which the attitude and interests of the proletariat will be discussed independently of bourgeois influences".

The object of political parties is power—to hold office in the power-institutions so as to carry out a policy. Without a political party a class cannot win power. Various organisations which work for the economic interest of a class, or which in connection with this or that item of public policy aim at bringing pressure to bear on those who hold power, or which undertake ideological and cultural work, are of vital importance in the life of a class. But their action is dispersed and, without a political party, does not add up to a struggle for power. So a class which is to come to power, and so be able to transform society in its own image and in its own interests, must organise politically. Accordingly in Rule 7a of the First International, drafted by Marx and adopted at The Hague Congress in 1872, it was laid down that "in its struggle against the collective power of the possessing classes the proletariat can act as a class only by constituting itself a distinct political party, opposed to all the old parties formed by the possessing classes".

Politics is often described as a dogfight: the introduction of *science* into this dogfight was a consequence of the birth of the working-class movement and of socialist politics. The working-class movement brought something new into politics, because it meant that for the first time the masses of working people could constitute a permanently organised political force in opposition to their rulers, and this in turn meant new forms of democratic organisation and new ideas of democratic government. To begin with, the working-class organisations tended to seek no more than immediate demands for improved working and living conditions, and to support one or other of the traditional ruling parties in pursuit of these. But with working-class organisation, itself the natural product of the development of modern forces of production, the aim became practical of finally doing away with all exploitation of man by man, and planning social production for the satisfaction of the needs of all.

So the science of socialism was evolved, to demonstrate the practicality of this aim and the means to achieve it. The working-class movement could not successfully pursue its long-term interest unless it based its politics on science.

The theory of scientific socialism had to be worked out and its fundamental principles stated; then to be learned, studied, applied, tested in practice and developed. The working out of the theory can be said to have been commissioned by the newborn working-class movement, in as much as it was that movement that needed the theory and groups of workers began to discuss the problems of revolutionary policy and organisation. But the synthesis of vast data drawn from experience into a scientific theory could not emerge as it were spontaneously out of the mass movement itself, since it required long and exacting work of scientific research. This work could only be done by scholars, by intellectuals. The men who originally worked on the theory did not themselves work in factories or mines. But they could do the job only because they were aware of what went on in factories and mines, and devoted their activity entirely to the cause of the workers' movement with which they identified themselves. They were able to create the theory of scientific socialism because, first, they were from the outset concerned with the injustices and contradictions of society as they found it and were resolved to find a solution; second, they could draw on the past heritage of progressive science and philosophy and could see at the same time the insufficiency of past ideas to the present problems; and third, they recognised in the working-class movement the movement of the future. The founders of scientific socialism were not separate from the working-class movement, teachers who stepped in to give instruction, but workers in it and leaders of it. They worked out the theory for the movement, introduced it into the movement, and then fought for its acceptance and understanding.

Scientific socialism, like other scientific theory, can only be developed in its use. Its development could take place only in the working-class movement, and the movement could only become united and capable of achieving political power when it had made the theory of scientific socialism its own. A political party is the only organisation which can thus carry science into the movement. And only by doing so can a political party provide the political leadership for the mass movement to win power and build socialism.

A working-class party should consciously set out to serve the interests of the class. As Marx and Engels made clear in *The Communist Manifesto*, this does not mean, in the case of a party capable of leading the class to win power, that it bases its policy on nothing but the clamour of immediate and sectional demands, but that it "brings to the front the common interest" and "in the movement of the present takes care of the future of the movement".

The party's standpoint is a class standpoint. It does not claim to adopt a god's-eye point of view in forming its judgments, but the point of view of the working class. This does not mean, however, that the party accepts the ideas of workers, whatever they may be. On the contrary, many ideas in workers' heads are implanted there by their rulers, or are merely the crude reflections of degrading conditions of life and help to perpetuate them. So the workers' party must try to lead workers to change their ideas. For Marxism, a class standpoint in ideas is not the mere echo of the ideas which most members of a class happen to entertain at a particular time and place. A class standpoint in ideas means developing ideas in conformity with the objective requirements of the class for developing its way of life, its means of liveli-hood.

In *The Eighteenth Brumaire of Louis Bonaparte* (Chapter 3) Marx explained that "the relation between the political representatives of a class and the class they represent" consists in the fact that the former work out in their ideas "the same problems and solutions to which material interests and social position drive the latter practically". In the case of the political representatives of the small-trading class, about whom Marx was writing, he concluded that this meant that "in their minds they do not get beyond the limits which the class does not get beyond in life". In the case of working-class ideas it is not so much a matter of not getting beyond limits as of getting beyond them. Whether most workers know it or not, the "problems and solutions to which material interests and social position" drive the working class are problems of escaping from exploitation and solutions by making social production serve social welfare. And these are the problems and solutions which the political representatives of the class have to work out in ideas. Whereas the other classes are driven to try to keep *inside* the limits within which they live, and their political representatives wear blinkers so as not to see beyond them, the work-ing class is driven to try to *get out of* the limits within which it lives, and the job of its political representatives is to think out the corres-ponding problems, the solution of which demands the strict metho-dology of science.

Marx maintained, then, that a successful political party of the working class must make itself the bearer of scientific socialist theory, and must preserve it, work it out and introduce it, and the practice of being guided by it, into the entire working-class movement. Thus it must become the vehicle for achieving what he maintained was the first essential for the victory of socialism—*the combination of scientific socialism with the mass working-class movement.*

Scientific inquiry always discloses *possibilities* for human action. For those interested, it tells how to do things they did not know how to do before. It makes possible practical achievements scarcely dreamed of, because it discloses the actual conditions for these things being brought about and how to bring them about.

Marxist science shows the working classes how it is possible to achieve emancipation. This was not known before social relations were in-vestigated scientifically and the laws of development of society disclosed. Marxist science shows the necessary conditions for emancipation—and one of the conditions is that the movement should base its practice on scientific theory and that "socialism should become a science".

Marxism shows further that the emancipation movement of the modern working classes is the final phase of a series of class struggles which began when the development of property first divided society into antagonistic classes. Summing up the conclusions of *The Communist Manifesto* in his Preface to the 1888 English edition, Engels wrote: "The history of class struggles forms a series of evolutions in which, today, the stage has been reached where the exploited and oppressed class—the proletariat—cannot attain its emancipation from the sway of the exploiting and ruling class—the bourgeoisie—without, at the same time, and once for all, emancipating society at large from all exploitation, oppression, class distinction and class struggles." Emancipation has its necessary conditions, and its practical possibility can only be realised if action, based on scientific appreciation of necessity, observes them. One such condition is the waging of class struggle. Another is to carry on the struggle to the point where "all exploitation, oppression, class distinction and class struggles" are deliberately removed.

Marxist science, then, applies in politics because it works out *how to win working-class emancipation and thereby emancipate the whole of society*.

Now of course, a scientific demonstration is—a demonstration. If it is valid it is valid not only for some people but for everyone, just as if a statement is true it is true, whether anyone chooses to believe it or not. Nevertheless, it is only for the working classes that Marxist science demonstrates how to win emancipation, because they are the people who need it and are interested in it. That does not mean that it true only for one class and not for another. It is true for anyone, but not everyone is interested in this truth. It shows the possibility to those interested in it and whose action is required to realise it. What Marxism says is as true for the ruling classes as for the working classes, as the former occasionally find to their cost. But while it shows the working classes how to do away with exploitation, far from showing the ruling classes how to perpetuate exploitation it shows that to do so is impossible—and this truth is not and cannot be acceptable to them. Naturally, therefore, *social science, with its applicability in politics, becomes a "class" science*. This is another and very important way in which, as Marx well understood, it differs in its methods and application from the natural sciences.

3. CONDUCT AND AIMS OF MARXIST POLITICAL PARTIES

According to Dr. Popper, Marxism applies (or claims to apply) in politics by demonstrating, not what it is possible to do, but what must inevitably take place. Dr. Popper's Marxists base politics on prophecy. They are a kind of political astronomers. For just as astronomers might say: "There is going to be an eclipse of the sun, so turn on the lights", Dr. Popper's Marxists say: "The revolution is coming, so close the ranks."

But in politics one has to reckon, first and foremost, with facts, with actual circumstances and their practicalities. The object of politics is to alter circumstances. What Marxists actually base politics on is a scientific analysis of the circumstances in modern society. Marx scientifically investigated the character of capitalist exploitation and its effects, thus demonstrating the issues of the class struggle in modern society and the real and practical possibilities and alternatives for the alteration of our circumstances which this poses. Either capitalism continues with all its consequences in the perpetuation of poverty, conflicts, oppressions and wars, or the working class carries on its class struggle to the point of overcoming capitalism and building socialism. Marxism scientifically demonstrates the necessary conditions for the latter. Emancipation from all exploitation and class struggles can be achieved, and can only be achieved, through the dictatorship of the proletariat. And so Marxism further works out the practical strategy and tactics of the struggle for working-class power and becomes the guiding theory of revolutionary political parties.

Dr. Popper regards as highly unscientific the Marxist way of understanding politics in terms of class struggle. Leaving the classes out of account, he presents politics instead in simple terms of "power" and control of power. Some people acquire power over others, so as to act as rulers; and politics is a matter of the acquisition of this power, and of its use and the control of its use. Men almost invariably abuse power unless their use of it is controlled. The most important thing in politics is therefore to control the use of power, for the ruled to find how to control the rulers so as to stop abuses of power. Democratic politics is, he says, the politics of the control of the rulers by the ruled.

From this point of view, he expatiates in scarifying terms about the political consequences of the Marxist error of basing politics on prophecy. Marxists believe themselves destined to come to power.

They therefore brush aside all questions of the democratic control of power and advocate dictatorship. If they succeed in their violent endeavours to achieve what they believe to be the decree of destiny, what happens is that a group of men, or perhaps a single "strong man", is put into power and all control over power collapses. But as Lord Acton warned: "All power corrupts, and absolute power corrupts absolutely." What we inevitably get is a violent dictatorship, or tyranny. There ensues "the rule of the strong man" (2–OS. 151), who proceeds forcibly "to control and stereotype interests and beliefs" (PH. 90), sets up "the Inquisition, the Secret Police" (1–OS. 200), and "civilisation disappears" (CR. 344).

I shall discuss in subsequent chapters, and in some detail, questions about democracy and dictatorship, and about the democratic principles concerning the conduct of popular organisations and their control over state power for the purposes of the dictatorship of the proletariat, which are implied by Marxism contrary to what Dr. Popper alleges. Here it may suffice to say that Dr. Popper talks of "power" and "control of power" *in abstraction* from the actual conditions of class interests and class struggles under which power is acquired, exercised and controlled. Marxism, on the other hand, in the discussion of political as of all other questions, undertakes "the concrete analysis of concrete conditions". Dr. Popper adopts a very abstract conception of political power, as the power of some individuals (the rulers) over other individuals (the ruled). He opposes this as "science" to Marx's political analysis of class struggles, which he calls "prophecy". Such a comparison only demonstrates Dr. Popper's own disregard for scientific method when it comes to discussing politics.

According to Marx, politics in class-divided society is class struggle. Political parties represent the interests of classes, and the control and acquisition of power by political parties serves class interests. A working-class party must seek to win political power, and to organise control over power and use power to reconstitute society on the basis of socialism. Working-class political parties can and must lead the masses of the people to the building of a new world, in struggle against the old. Their politics consists in giving political leadership in the struggle to end exploitation of man by man.

By and large, this is what political parties that base their policies on Marxism have done and are doing. Marxists have hammered out in practice guiding lines for the conduct of effective working-class parties. The party must not only educate people in socialist ideas, but campaign for socialist policies, agitating on the job and in the localities against every injustice, giving practical leadership in mass organisation; and when power is won, the party becomes itself the leading mass organisation through which power is both exercised and controlled. The party must train up the leading personnel, the individual leaders, whom the movement can trust in the fight against the exploiting classes, and whom it can entrust with office when the power of the exploiting classes is broken.

Dr. Popper expresses strong objections to the activities of Marxist political parties—though naturally enough, none of his objections is new. According to him, any political party that bases its policies on Marxism is outside the pale in a civilised community. The tolerance which democrats in principle extend to the expression of opinions should never be stretched to countenancing the subversive activities of Communists. For "in a democracy the full protection of minorities should not extend to those who violate the law, and especially not to those who incite others to the violent overthrow of the democracy" (2–OS. 161). Communists, believing that their own dictatorship is decreed by fate and will represent the consummation of mankind's historical destiny, care nothing for laws and proceed lawlessly and violently to attempt to fulfil what they consider to be their historical mission. Worse still, if such parties get into power they proceed to "stereotype interests and beliefs" and to introduce "the Inquisition, the Secret Police". They ought to be firmly put down.

We must, of course, plead guilty to opposing laws which protect exploiting classes. But as for lawlessness and violence, to establish socialism does not entail replacing law by lawless violence but the reform of laws. Again, in building a socialist society "interests" will certainly be "stereotyped" to the extent that the diversity of interests as between capitalists and wage-workers, and as between competing capitalists, will disappear and a greater community of interests will emerge. Through education and propaganda the authorities must certainly endeavour to propagate beliefs corresponding to socialist interests and to oppose beliefs counter to them. And a police force must certainly be maintained strong enough to defend the socialist regime against attempts to disrupt or overthrow it. The objections, however, are to fighting against exploitation, to laws which prohibit exploitation, to opposing cherished beliefs of the old order accustomed to the full protection of the establishment, and to taking police measures to protect the new.

But at the same time as he echoes all the customary execrations of anti-Communist propaganda, Dr. Popper still contrives to preserve an air of scientific objectivity. He does not say that Communists are evil-minded persons intent on getting power for themselves and injuring their fellow men. On the contrary, he stresses again and again that many Communists are sincere and mean well, and that their aim is universal happiness. The evil happens because the actual effects of acting on Communist principles are vastly different from Communist intentions. They intend to bring "heaven on earth", but "only succeed in making it a hell". The critique of Marxism is a case of "analysing the unintended repercussions of intentional human actions". Quite inevitably or, at all events, by the objective sequence of cause and effect, the effect of basing politics on Marxist theory is that the actions taken bring evil consequences.

The effect of Marx's alleged belief in historical destiny, Dr. Popper suggests, is to make Communists think themselves infallible, chosen by fate to fulfil a mission and destroy every opponent. Communists will therefore listen to no criticism, pity no suffering, and spare no violence to attain their ends. They scorn all methods of democracy which entail consultation, discussion and paying attention to what other people say, and instead favour and themselves fall victims to the open terrorist dictatorship of a Communist "strong man" or group of power-hungry leaders.

That, he evidently thinks, is what happened in the Soviet Union—an awful warning to the rest of mankind. There a "strong man" was placed in supreme power. Stalin's word was law, and any criticism of his policies, and even the least doubt, was treated as a hostile act. His secret police engaged in arbitrary arrests, imprisonment without trial or the rigging of trials, cruelties, tortures and executions.

That all was not well in the Soviet Union, and that evils were perpetrated by Communists, causing great and unnecessary suffering to thousands of individuals, is an established fact. Dr. Popper would give us to understand that such evils are *inevitable*. It is he himself, indeed, with his "unforeseen consequences", who tries to confound us with a doctrine of inevitability—the inevitability of the disappointment of revolutionary socialist hopes which, if they are not crushed by defeat, are even more completely frustrated by the tyranny which inevitably takes over after a revolutionary victory. But of course, Dr. Popper is no "historicist". He only makes a "conditional prediction": If you put a kettle on the fire it will boil, and if you let

Marxists get into the government they will turn it into a bloodthirsty tyranny.

What Marxists derive from the Marxist theory of social relations and of how social changes are brought about is, however, *a practical aim* for political action, and the strategy and tactics of political struggle, derived from knowledge of the necessary conditions for realising the aim. Socialism is presented by Marxism as a political programme. And Marxism is scientific socialism because it works out the socialist political programme on the basis of an objective review of facts, and not of any mythology about the destiny of mankind; and because it makes proposals for satisfying real interests rather than for realising a utopian ideal.

Marx and Engels said that "history is the history of class struggles". This statement, true of history ever since class divisions appeared in human society, is *incompatible* with any "historicist" doctrine about events moving with inexorable necessity in accordance with a pre-set pattern. For class struggles are waged by human individuals, in the conditions of the social relations in which they find themselves. As Marx and Engels recognised whenever they set themselves to describe any actual class struggle, the actual events proceed from the action of the personalities and passions of the individuals engaged in them, conditioned by and operating in the given circumstances of the time. As for the role of working-class parties in events, what they do is affected by their circumstances and stage of political development, including their illusions, mistakes, uncertainties, fears and fanaticisms, and not by decrees of destiny of which they have been vouchsafed infallible knowledge. How well they succeed in their aims, and what mistakes they commit and setbacks they experience in pursuit of them, is decided by a multitude of human causes, which historians can trace out if they look for them.

To win through to emancipation, people must *organise* and must *learn from experience*. From this element of political necessity comes the vital role of working-class political parties. First, the party must become *the well-organised leadership* of the whole movement. It must lead, not by continually disputing the right to exist of other parties and by establishing a political monopoly (for, as *The Communist Manifesto* declared, "the Communists do not form a separate party opposed to other working-class parties"), but by virtue (as the *Manifesto* expressed it) of "clearly understanding the line of march, the conditions, and the ultimate general results of the proletarian movement". Second, the party must concentrate in itself the lessons of the movement's *experience*, so that through it *the whole movement learns by experience and learns from mistakes*. Only in a political party does the movement create leadership and a leadership that learns systematically.

Marxists have always been at great pains to examine and to classify the various types of mistake to which working-class political parties may be prone. A party may sell out the workers' interests by compromising with exploiting classes, even to the extent of upholding their interests against those of the workers; on the other hand, it may be so "uncompromising" that, proclaiming mere revolutionary phrases, refusing to take circumstances into account, neglecting to build solid organisation and to find allies, it leads the workers to defeat. A party may give up or "revise" the theory of Marxism about the class struggle and the dictatorship of the proletariat; on the other hand, it may turn it into a mere dogma, into a mere set of formulas supposedly applicable in the same way at all times and in all circumstances. Again, a party may lead the workers of one nation into conflict with those of another by placing what are represented as national interests before those of the common interests of all working people; on the other hand, it may alienate itself from its own people by not recognising, or even despising, their national interests and sentiments. There are examples enough of all these sorts of mistakes. They arise from the difficulties and dilemmas of the actual conditions of practical struggle.

It is natural enough (and one might say, indeed, inevitable) that when Marxist parties make mistakes and get into difficulties their enemies are quick to proclaim that whatever evils ensue are all the fault of Marxism, and go on proclaiming it for years afterwards. More than that, when Marxist parties proceed to put right their mistakes, their enemies see the chance of scoring a further point and exclaim: Aha, you admit then that your Marxism did you no good and only led you into errors!

So it was with the abuses of power, accompanying some mistakes in economic policies, which took place in the Soviet Union under Stalin's leadership. No Communist and no Marxist is going to make excuses for the evils that then took place. There took place distortions of Marxist theory, mistakes in economic management, bureaucratic brutalities, arbitrariness and crimes in methods of government, which hindered not helped the building of socialism. They could not have taken place except as a result of abuses of power by individuals, violations of the rule of law, and violations of the democratic conduct of revolutionary organisations, including the leading one, the Communist Party. Dr. Popper censures them no more severely than was done subsequently at the Twentieth Congress of the Communist Party of the Soviet Union. But unlike the Marxists, he makes no attempt at analysing in what exactly these evils consisted, how they came about, or what was the remedy. He leaves out of account every consideration about how violence of every kind is instigated and organised on a mass scale by fascism and imperialism, and instead denounces violence as the inevitable consequence of the Marxist doctrine of "dictatorship". He then concludes that the universal remedy is "democracy" on the model of the frequently violent and dictatorial practice of the so-called "free world".

He may perhaps claim credit for denouncing bad practices for which Marxists were responsible at a time when Marxists failed to denounce or to remedy them. Let him! Marxists claim credit for the fact that, amid bitter struggle against both internal and external enemies, socialism was built in the Soviet Union and established on a firm foundation which completely confounds all the prognostications of anti-Marxists. Outside the Soviet Union we claim the credit that we gave the one socialist country unstinting support, opposed its enemies and refused to join them, and fought the injustices, oppressions and violence of capitalism even though this involved us in the guilt of injustices, oppressions and violence on our own side. Finally, Marxists claim credit for setting to work to get evils which took place under socialism put right—not by the method which many have advised as the remedy for "tyranny", namely, overthrowing socialist government, but by bringing the methods of socialist government into line with the teachings of Marxism. This reforming process is still going on in the Soviet Union, though not smoothly or without conflicts, setbacks, errors and injustices.

Dr. Popper apparently regarded malpractices in the Soviet Union, at the time he wrote *The Open Society and its Enemies* and *The Poverty of Historicism*, as verifications of his assertion that Marxism means tyranny. The exposure of these malpractices at the Twentieth Congress of the Communist Party of the Soviet Union might then be regarded as a final verification from evidence presented by Marxists themselves. But Dr. Popper has insisted that what counts is not verification but falsification. And what has actually happened has finally *falsified* his allegations. He could cite various facts as "confirmations" of his assertion that Communist government is tyrannical. The actual development of socialism and the struggle for socialism falsifies it. And the actual teachings of Marx likewise falsify his allegations that Marxism is a doctrine of historical destiny which advocates violence and tyranny.

A rational judgment on Marxist politics can only be reached by taking cognisance, among other things, of the history of Marxist parties—what they have done and are doing. Insisting on the fallacy of "the historical method", Dr. Popper seems to prefer to base his judgment rather on a sweeping assessment of what he takes to be the essence of Marxist teachings. Essentially, he says, Marxism is dogmatic and anti-democratic. As he himself has explained is usual with judgments about "essences", he then contrives to argue in a way to evade falsification. If a Marxist party is guilty of wrong doing, it is said to be acting in character; if it does well, then it is merely acting out of character.

Yet the way Marxist parties actually behave and develop gives the lie to what he says about Marxist politics. He in fact cites very little about what Marxist parties have actually done to prove his points. His chief citation is worthy of a passing remark, however. He deals at some length with the policies of Marxist parties towards fascism at the time of the rise of Hitler to power in Germany, and informs us that "the Communists did not fight when the fascists seized power" because they thought the fascist dictatorship "could only bring the revolution nearer . . . After all, since the revolution was bound to come, fascism could only be one of the means of bringing it about" (2–OS. 164–5).

Admittedly, a certain amount of "falsification of history" has on occasion been done by Marxists themselves, for polemical purposes (though such polemics do not advance the cause of Marxism). Bad as this was, it bears little comparison with the falsification of history by anti-Marxists, of which the above citation provides an example. The Marxist method of studying what happens puts the record straight, where it is falsified by anti-Communist propaganda.

The history of the international labour movement shows that the progress of Marxist parties is by no means the triumphal progress of the infallible "Party Line" which might be deduced from the doctrine of historical destiny Dr. Popper tries to foist onto us. There are many mistakes and many setbacks, as might be expected in real life. At the same time, the Marxist view that "history is on our side", or that

Marxist parties are indestructible and sure to win in the end, is justified by the actual conditions of class struggle in the modern world. For in general, *what is necessary to be done gets done in the end*. And in the conditions of capitalism, the development of revolutionary parties and the persistence of their activities up to the eventual abolition of exploitation of man by man *is a necessity*. To oppose exploitation, to oppose oppression, to oppose war, to oppose the threat of nuclear war today, and to carry on economic and political struggle until society is so ordered as to be able to use human resources for human welfare, is a necessity. We *must organise* for these purposes. If mistakes are made, they must be put right. If defeats are sustained, the struggle must still go on.

So it is that in the European labour movement the dominance of reformist policies has of necessity been countered by the rise of genuine revolutionary parties, the Communist Parties. The victory of the Russian Revolution was a decisive factor leading to the growth and consolidation of the international Communist movement, and to the development of the great movement for liberation from imperialism throughout the colonial world. Conditions are always changing with time, however. And they are not the same now as they were before the Second World War. We have to frame new policies accordingly. In this connection deep divisions and splits appear over policies—including, at the moment, a division within the world Communist movement, turning to a great extent on questions of peace and the coexistence of socialism and capitalism, on methods of transition to socialism and the strategy of the anti-imperialist national liberation movement.

There never was and there is not now a ready-made "doctrine" to cling to, nor a leadership appointed by destiny to lead us on a straight path and preserve us from error. What has to be relied on, now as always, is the development of clear-headed scientific thinking about policies, taking circumstances and changes of circumstances into account. From this we have to build up the unity in action of the left. On democratic counsel and organisation to build competent revolutionary parties chiefly depends the destiny of mankind— the overcoming of exploitation of man by man and, as Marx put it, the duration and severity of "the birth pangs" of a new world.

The point is that the capitalist mode of production, with capitalist economic and political power, cannot but engender a struggle against it by exploited classes; that this struggle has got to find leadership; that Marxism embodies scientific principles of leadership; and that therefore what has to be done is build Marxist parties and out of hard and often bitter experience develop Marxism in theory and practice.

3

THE CRITIQUE OF CAPITALISM

1. HAS CAPITALISM DISAPPEARED?

Marxism applies in the practice of the working-class movement as a practical policy for breaking the fetters capitalism puts on social production and developing production to the full to meet human needs. Dr. Popper, however, not only calls science prophecy and a practical political policy utopia, but adds that there is no longer any point in wanting to abolish capitalism because it has ceased to exist anyway. His criticism thus devastates at all points. Marx is shown to have been a singularly unfortunate prophet, because the evils whose destruction he prophesied have long since been quietly removed by means quite other than fire and brimstone.

"We must be on our guard", Dr. Popper writes, "against . . . the Marxist prejudice that socialism or communism is the only alternative and the only possible successor to capitalism. Neither Marx nor anyone else has ever shown that socialism . . . is the only possible alternative to the ruthless exploitation of that economic system which he first described a century ago and to which he gave the name 'capitalism'. And indeed, if anybody were attempting to prove that socialism is the only possible successor to Marx's unrestrained capitalism, then we could simply refute him by pointing to historical facts. For *laissez faire* has disappeared from the face of the earth, but it has not been replaced by a socialist or communist system as Marx understood it" (2–OS. 140). The "unrestrained capitalism" which Marx denounced has, says Dr. Popper, "given way . . . to our own period of political interventionism, of the economic interference of the state". For "all over the earth, organised political power has begun to perform far-reaching economic functions".

Marxists have for long maintained that in the normal course of economic development capitalism passes from an earlier condition of free competition to a stage of monopoly or state-monopoly capitalism, which was entered into by the older capitalist economies from the beginning of this century. This account of normal capitalist economic development is founded on Marx's own account of the processes of centralisation and concentration of capital, and of the development of the finance and credit system, under conditions of free competition, as a result of which free competition gives rise to monopoly. A marked feature of monopoly capitalism, according to Marxist views, is "the economic interference of the state", which Dr. Popper nevertheless tells us is now supplanting what Marx earlier described and denounced as capitalism.

Dr. Popper evidently thinks that all Marx achieved in *Capital* was to describe, fairly faithfully, the "unrestrained capitalism" of a century ago. Marx did indeed describe it. He described how men and women worked a twelve- or fourteen-hour day under unhealthy conditions in factories, while the owners engaged one another in cut-throat competition. Today the scene has changed. In many industries there is a forty-hour week (with plenty of bonus earnings and overtime at time-and-a-half or double time), health and safety regulations are enforced and, far from there being lots of competing individual masters, industries are dominated by a few great corporations. No longer do capitalists sit jingling their moneybags in dingy counting houses, where portraits of Grandfather Nathaniel and Great-uncle Ebenezer look down with grim approval upon the squalid scene, but members of a managerial élite play the power-game in spacious apartments decorated with works of abstract art. Hence, says, Dr. Popper, what Marx described no longer exists, and his entire analysis is of no more than historical interest. Marx takes his place with Charles Dickens as one of the great Victorians who, in their time, goaded the public conscience by exposing social evils, but now gladden the philistines with the sense of satisfaction that things are not like that with us.

But what Marx achieved in *Capital* was not simply a description of industrial conditions which soon became out of date as conditions changed. Marx laid bare *the social relations* which develop under capitalism, the capitalist *relations of production*, the mode of exploiting wage-labour on which the whole economic structure depends. He extracted *these* relations from the total mass of social activities in the midst of which individuals are related by them—extracted them not, as he put it, by means of chemical reagents or by fixing them under a microscope, but by "force of abstraction"—and showed what they are and what they lead to.

Marx made a most careful analysis of the production relations which develop when goods are produced as commodities. As Lenin pointed out in *What the Friends of the People Are*, "this analysis is strictly

confined to the relations of production between the members of
society. Without ever resorting to factors other than relations of
production to explain the matter, Marx makes it possible to discern
how the commodity organisation of society develops, how it becomes
transformed into capitalist economy . . ." and, we may add, how the
capitalist relations of production persist when *laissez faire* gives place
to "interventionism". "While explaining the structure and development of society exclusively in terms of relations of production,"
Lenin continued, Marx "went on to trace the superstructure corresponding to these relations of production . . . *Capital* exhibited the
whole capitalist social formation to the reader as a live thing."

   True, it has not so exhibited it to Dr. Popper, because Dr. Popper
prefers his own interpretation of what Marx was about. But Marx's
analysis of capitalist production relations shows how the economic
and political conditions of a century ago developed, and it also shows
how they have changed into the economic and political conditions of
contemporary capitalism. It shows that it is still capitalism. That in
the capitalist economies *laissez faire* has been largely replaced by
"interventionism", while "a socialist or communist system as Marx
understood it" has not yet everywhere succeeded capitalism, is a
very well-known fact. And something of the sort was predicted by
Marx himself in *Capital*—a prediction Dr. Popper has chosen to
overlook. In his mature years Marx recognised quite clearly that his
youthful hopes that "the ruthless exploitation of that economic system
which he first described" would be quickly overthrown were founded
on an underestimation of the staying powers of the exploiters—though
even so he might admittedly have been distressed to learn that they
would keep going for as long as they have done. The "interventionism"
of which Dr. Popper writes—economic interference by a state in
which the big capitalists retain pretty firm control—is one of the
principal means by which they have kept going, for they could
hardly have succeeded without it.

   But that in the development of capitalism *laissez faire* is replaced
by "economic interference of the state" does not imply either that
capitalism has disappeared or that socialism is not "the only possible
successor" to capitalism. On the contrary, as many Marxists, from
Marx onwards, have observed, the fact that the increasing socialisation
of the forces of production drives capitalists themselves to accept
forms of public control only shows how necessary it is to convert the
means of production into social property, and will, in the end, facilitate

that process. Thus Marx wrote in *Capital* (Vol. 3, Chapter 27) that capital becomes "directly endowed with the form of social capital as distinct from private capital, and its undertakings assume the form of social undertakings as distinct from private undertakings. It is the abolition of capital as private property within the framework of capitalist production itself". In this, he said, the functions of management become separated from ownership, and this in turn "is a necessary transitional phase" towards the conversion of capital "into the property of associated producers, as outright social property".

What does this change amount to? It was predicted and described with rather remarkable accuracy by Engels in *Anti-Duhring* (Part 3, Chapter 2).

The "pressure of the productive forces, in their mighty upgrowth, against their character as capital," he wrote, ". . . forces the capitalist class itself more and more to treat them as social productive forces, in so far as this is at all possible within the framework of capitalist relations". It brings about "that form of the socialisation of huge masses of means of production which we find in the various kinds of joint-stock companies . . . At a certain stage of development even this form no longer suffices; the official representative of capitalist society, the state, is constrained to take over their management." And increasingly, "the social functions of the capitalists are carried on by salaried employees".

But as Engels went on to say, this disappearance of *laissez faire* does not mean the disappearance of capitalism. "Conversion into either joint-stock companies or state property does not deprive the productive forces of their character as capital. In the case of joint-stock companies this is obvious. And the modern state, too, is only the organisation with which bourgeois society provides itself in order to maintain the general external conditions of the capitalist mode of production against encroachments either by the workers or by individual capitalists. The modern state, whatever its form, is essentially a capitalist machine . . . The more productive forces it takes over, the more it becomes the real collective body of all the capitalists, the more citizens it exploits. The workers remain wage workers . . . the capitalist relation is not abolished."

The point is that the capitalist mode of production is one in which investments of privately-owned capital in enterprises employing wage-labour yield a profit to the capitalists, from which ever greater accumulations of privately-owned capital accrue. In order to preserve the conditions in which the capitalist mode of production can continue to function, it is necessary that not only wage-workers but capitalists too should be subjected to various kinds of direction and constraint. It is this which is provided by "the economic interference of the state". But the fact that "organised political power has begun to perform far-reaching economic functions" does not mean that capitalism has disappeared but that, on the contrary, it is being preserved. And it is preserved for so long as the "interventionist" state remains "essentially a capitalist machine".

It is clear, then, that Dr. Popper's contention that the advent of "political interventionism" refutes "the Marxist prejudice that socialism or communism is the only alternative and the only possible successor to capitalism" is simply another case of his refuting Marxism by making it mean something other than what it says. Marx and Engels never said that "the only alternative" to *laissez faire* or "unrestrained capitalism" was "socialism or communism". They said very clearly indeed that it would have to be replaced as capitalism developed by "political interventionism" or "the economic interference of the state". This is exactly what has happened, so what has happened has confirmed and not refuted Marx's predictions about the development of capitalism.

2. THE LABOUR THEORY OF VALUE

Marx's account of capitalist production relations exhibits the relation which people enter into with one another when they produce and exchange *commodities*, and when, in a commodity-producing society, some, as wage-earners, are forced to sell their own labour-power as a commodity. This relation is defined in terms of the so-called "labour theory of value", which is thus fundamental in Marx's analysis of the nature and development of capitalist production relations.

Dr. Popper, having failed to grasp that in *Capital* Marx began with an abstract inquiry "strictly confined to the relations of production between the members of society", and having thus missed the whole point of the inquiry, fails to see the point of the labour theory of value. "Marx's theory of value, usually considered by Marxists as well as by anti-Marxists as a cornerstone of the Marxist creed, is in my opinion one of its rather unimportant points," he writes (2–OS. 170). As usual, he presents Marxist theory in terms which make its alleged meaning puerile; so no wonder he thinks it "rather unimportant".

On this question, however, the other "anti-Marxists" are right: the labour theory of value is indeed "a cornerstone" in Marx's theoretical model of capitalist production relations (called by Dr. Popper "the Marxist creed").

According to Dr. Popper, the labour theory of value was "introduced in order to explain the actual prices at which all commodities are exchanged". Thus "you have to pay for the job, or for any commodity you may buy, roughly in proportion to the amount of work in it, i.e. to the number of labour hours necessary for its production". Of course, "actual prices fluctuate. But there is, or so at least it appears, always something more stable behind these prices, a kind of average price about which the actual prices oscillate, christened the 'exchange value' or briefly, the 'value' of the thing. Using this general idea, Marx defined the value of a commodity as the average number of labour hours necessary for its production" (2–OS. 171).

Thus Marx is represented as a sort of careful shopper, who wants to know why this should cost more than that, and to find some standard by which a fair price can always be determined. He is represented as simple-minded almost to the point of imbecility. For of course, as Dr. Popper goes on to say, to understand why prices fluctuate you need "a more concrete theory; a theory which shows, in any particular case, how the laws of supply and demand bring about the effect which has to be explained" (2–OS. 175).

He therefore concludes: "But if these laws are sufficient to explain these effects, then we do not need the labour theory of value at all." The whole labour theory of value is therefore "unimportant" and "redundant". It is for this very reason, indeed, that all those sophisticated students of economic laws (whom Marx rather rudely called "vulgar") who are interested in formulating equations expressing how this economic variable is a function of that, find that they have no use whatever for the labour theory of value and have consequently expelled it from their economic science as a sheer irrelevancy.

Marx's primary interest, however, was not in the fluctuations of prices but in the formation, development and change of relations of production. He saw capitalism as an historically constituted system of relations of production brought into being in adaptation to a definite development of productive forces and then becoming an obstacle to their further development for the satisfaction of human needs. It was to define these relations of production and explain their formation and effects that he employed the labour theory of value.

As regards "actual prices" and their fluctuations, Dr. Popper is right in saying "that Marx realised" that a "concrete theory" must needs include an explanation of "how the laws of supply and demand bring about the effect which has to be explained". That does not imply that "the laws of supply and demand" constitute a complete explanation of the whole process of exchange of commodities, nor does it make the labour theory of value unimportant or redundant. The theory explains the formation and development of relations of production, and so is relevant to questions which Dr. Popper and the economists he thinks have superseded Marx do not even ask. They can explain to their own satisfaction the fluctuations of costs and prices (even though they cannot find how to control them). What they cannot explain, and ask no questions about, is the formation and character of the relations of production which give rise to the phenomena they seek to explain. They simply ignore, and bury out of sight, the character of the wages system and of the exploitation of labour in which capitalism consists.

Marx began his investigation of capitalist production relations by observing that in capitalist production "wealth . . . presents itself as an immense accumulation of commodities" (*Critique of Political Economy*, Chapter 1; *Capital*, Vol. 1, Chapter 1). Thus he started by defining capitalism as a mode of commodity production. He then inquired into what commodity production is in general, so as to demonstrate how it develops into that specific mode of production which constitutes capitalism. He thus arrived at the definition of the specific character of capitalist production relations.

In commodity production, individual producers or groups of producers do not simply produce things for their own use, but for exchange against other products for which they have a use. Commodities are products of labour which, firstly, have a use (people want them for one purpose or another), and secondly are exchangeable for other products. Hence they have both use-value and exchange-value. And the labour which produces them has a dual character, as producing objects for use, but not immediately for use but for exchange.

When people exchange commodities, what are they doing? What is the social relation they enter into with one another? This is the question to ask, in order to arrive at the definition of production relations. And, as usual with fundamental questions, the answer is pretty obvious. *They are exchanging products of definite quantities of labour*. In conditions where people share certain forces of production, a norm naturally gets established of how many man-hours of labour are socially necessary to produce each commodity. Therefore *in commodity production people enter into a relation with one another in which they exchange and acquire from one another products each of which embodies a definite quantity of socially necessary labour.* The labour theory of value consists simply in stating this fact—abstracting and stating this fundamental production relation which remains constant amid all the variable relations into which people enter with one another and with external nature in commodity production.

Besides its use-value, every commodity has an exchange-value independent of its particular use. Similarly, all labour, irrespective of its use—regardless of its materials and its instruments, and of the use to which people put its products, and the desirability of their use—has the common feature of producing goods and services for exchange. All the performances of social labour are alike in using up varying quantities of socially necessary labour for the production of goods and services for exchange, and all the products are alike in embodying varying quantities of labour socially necessary for their production.

In other words, *what all products have in common is that they embody a quantity of socially necessary labour. They can all be compared, therefore, in respect of how much socially necessary labour has gone into them.* This common feature of commodities, quantitatively determined and measured in terms of units of labour-time, is used in the labour theory of value to define "value".

The labour theory of value is therefore stated in the form of *a definition*, the definition of "value". But this definition is no mere "verbal" definition. It is no more merely verbal or conventional than are the definitions of basic concepts employed in any other sciences— for example, in mechanics. *It serves to abstract and define the common feature of all commodities, in respect of which they can all be compared.* There can, obviously, be no doubt whatever that commodities *do* have value, in the sense defined. If some economists prefer to use the word "value" in other ways, that does not affect the fundamental truth about production relations expressed in the labour theory of value. It only means that these economists prefer to overlook this fundamental truth.

Clearly, as so defined, the "value" of a commodity is not a property of an object (like its weight, for example) which it possesses independently of whatever people do, but appertains to commodities because people produce them by their labour and depends on how much labour they expend. And *the value relation between commodities* (i.e. that two or more commodities are of equal or unequal value) *holds between them because of the social production relations of men*, i.e. because men work to produce commodities and because in their work they have to devote varying amounts of socially necessary labour-time to producing various objects of use.

In supposing that the labour theory of value was "introduced in order to explain the actual prices at which commodities are exchanged" Dr. Popper absurdly misunderstands the *problem* the definition of "value" was used to solve. The problem is not simply one of explaining the actual prices of commodities but of explaining the social relations in commodity-producing societies. This explanation is achieved in the labour theory of value. Things people need or want are produced by labour; thanks to division of labour people have to exchange products of labour; hence products are produced as commodities; and in buying and selling them people are exchanging the embodiments of definite quantities of socially necessary labour-time.

Having defined the value relation of commodities in terms of the labour socially necessary for their production, or in other words, in terms of the social relations in commodity-producing society, Marx was then able to show quite cogently how value enters into the determination of price. In pricing commodities people are not just affixing price-tags but arranging the exchange of the products of labour. The quantity of labour that has gone into the production of each commodity is, when people are exchanging products of labour, a constant determining factor present in every act of exchange. Other things being equal, the products of a given quantity of labour would be exchanged for products of an equal quantity of labour. But in actual practice, commodities do *not* generally exchange at their value, but such factors as "supply and demand" affect the actual prices at which they exchange. Marx accordingly dealt with "actual prices" in *Capital* by the method of assuming, first of all, that goods do exchange at their value, and then, by examining in detail the actual concrete conditions of production and exchange, demonstrating the factors which make them exchange otherwise than at their values and the economic consequences which ensue.

Dr. Popper says that "the whole idea that there is something behind the prices, an objective or real or true value of which prices are only 'a form of appearance', shows clearly enough the influence of

Platonic Idealism" (2–OS. 177). It shows nothing of the sort; it shows simply that attention is paid to basic and empirically verifiable social relations of production. And having paid attention to these relations of production—having abstracted them, defined them and verified them—Marx was then able to show how actual prices are determined in commodity-producing societies. Far from being a "redundant" concept or an example of "the influence of Platonic Idealism", the concept of "value", as defined by Marx, first of all refers to empirically verifiable relations which men enter into in producing commodities, and is then used to state laws about the way men exchange commodities, and about the variations of the prices at which commodities are exchanged, which are likewise empirically verifiable.

Besides this, the labour theory of value throws a good deal of light on social relations in commodity-producing societies, which remain hidden and unremarked on so long as the exchange of commodities is regarded as no more than a matter of some people bringing goods to market and others buying them there at the market price. In any society people engage in social production, and the total social product is divided up, in the process of distribution, between the members of society. Each gets his share of the total product of social labour in a way depending on the production relations. The labour theory of value poses the question of how this division is effected in commodity-producing societies, through the process of production and exchange. It poses the question of how the values produced by labour are appropriated, how much goes to the labourers, how much goes to others, and how those others get it. So the labour theory of value has the merit of directing attention beyond questions of "explaining actual prices" to questions about social labour and the appropriation of its products which are ignored by those who simply want to study price fluctuations.

All this means developing political economy as a social science, that is, as *an investigation of social relations*. For Marxism, political economy is the investigation of the relations into which people enter in the production and distribution of their means of life.

In the section of *Capital* headed "the fetishism of commodities" Marx criticised the approach to economic science which treated it as an investigation of the properties and relations of the products of economic activity—as though commodities possessed properties of exchanging with one another, and so of selling at various prices, independently of the social relations of the people who produce,

exchange and consume such products. Like that, people's activity is
ruled by the economic relations between the things they produce and
exchange, whereas in fact such relations between things are not
inherent in things but are determined by the social relations of the
people who produce and exchange them. Marx called this approach
"fetishism" because of its resemblance to the attitude of savages who
suppose that their lives are ruled by properties inherent in the fetishes
they worship.

By criticising the fetishism of commodities in terms of the labour
theory of value Marx was able to direct attention to the production
relations in commodity-producing societies. He was able to show
under what conditions these develop into capitalist production
relations, and then that capitalist production relations are relations of
the exploitation of wage-labour by capital. Having shown that, he
was able to show how this form of exploitation can and must be
done away with.

3. SURPLUS VALUE AND EXPLOITATION OF
WAGE-LABOUR

In terms of the labour theory of value Marx could define the specific
new features of the production relations which distinguish capitalism
from earlier modes of commodity production.

In production, the labourer applies instruments of production to
the materials of labour in order to fashion the product. In commodity
production, this product is appropriated by whoever owns the materials
and instruments, that is, the means of production. He is the owner,
and it is he who is entitled to make a sale. In the simplest sort of
commodity production, goods are sold by the people who make
them. That is not so in capitalism. Capitalism arises only when the
labourer has been deprived of ownership of means of production
(Marx investigated in great detail how this happens historically).
What distinguishes capitalism is wage-labour. The means of production
are owned by the capitalist; the labourer has to work for wages with
means of production which belong to someone else; and the product,
together with the proceeds of its sale, is appropriated by the capitalist.
It is the capitalist who sells it, and he hopes to make a profit on the
sale.

The progressive feature of capitalism is that in these conditions
great numbers of workers are brought together to work under the

direction of a single capitalist management, so that the individual labour of individual commodity-producers is replaced by socialised labour—a far more effective force of production. But in contradiction to the new socialised character of production there remains from the older forms of commodity production the private appropriation of the product by the owner of the means of production.

Marx then demonstrated that in capitalism the worker who, not owning means of production, has no products of his labour to exchange for what else he needs to keep alive, has one thing of his own which he can sell—and that is his labour-power. The workers have to sell their labour-power to the capitalists. The capitalists, who own means of production, buy from the workers the use of their labour-power for a stipulated number of hours. The workers get wages, with which they can buy things they need; and the capitalists get the products of their work, which they can sell at a profit.

Where does the profit come from? Marx answered this question by the very simple demonstration that the total values the workers receive as wages are always less (much less) than the values they produce by their work and which are appropriated by the capitalists. Evidently, the value of the labour-power sold by the workers is equivalent to the quantity of labour necessary to produce all that the workers must consume in order to supply that labour-power. But the total quantity of work performed by the workers is considerably greater than the value of their own labour-power used up in producing it. This difference Marx called "surplus value". The capitalists get their profits and accumulate capital out of the surplus value they obtain by employing workers for wages.

Each capitalist does not, however, appropriate to himself the whole surplus value accruing from the employment of the labour he himself has hired. The capitalist has to borrow money from others, on which he must pay interest; he has to buy or hire things from others, and sell things to others—and the upshot of all these sorts of transactions is that the owners of capital are so linked together that what happens is not that each takes surplus value only from the workers in his own employ, and leaves the rest to other employers, but rather that the capitalist class as a whole appropriates surplus value from the labour force as a whole, and divides it up amongst the different capitalist claimants.

Marx devoted many chapters of *Capital* to demonstrating the various ways in which the total of surplus value extracted from the workers is divided up to be appropriated in the various forms of rent, interest and profit. If one considers contemporary capitalism, with its elaborate machinery of finance and credit, its shareholdings, its great corporations staffed by professional managements, and its "changing balance of public and private power", Marx's basic analysis continues to apply to it. For what is going on is still that wage-labour produces surplus value, out of which a wide variety of claims are met. Some of it is appropriated by public bodies for public purposes (by publicly-owned services and via taxation). It is a feature of contemporary capitalism that a great deal of this public appropriation goes to pay bondholders and property speculators, and to subsidise privately-owned concerns. The rest continues to be privately appropriated by the shrinking number of individuals who effectively remain the capitalist owners and masters of the means of social production. Some of it gets used for directors' fees and managerial salaries, some is paid out as interest, dividends, and so forth—and some is reinvested in production.

Capital accumulation is always made out of surplus value. The economic growth of the system depends on the continuous profitable investment and accumulation of capital. If capital is not growing and accumulating in this way, it is shrinking and values are being destroyed: it must expand or bust. The condition, therefore, for the conduct of production under capitalism is that the maximum of surplus value should be extracted out of the employment of wage-labour. "The aim of capitalist production", wrote Marx (*Capital*, Vol. 1, Chapter 13), "is to extract the greatest possible amount of surplus value, and consequently to exploit labour-power to the greatest possible extent."

What characterises the system is that in every productive process so much value in labour-power is used up, in fashioning so much value in material with the aid of so much value in wear and tear of machinery and other instruments of production; so much value in products is consequently produced; and so much surplus value is consequently extracted.

However, from the point of view of management (whether management of particular enterprises, or the sort of overall management which governments are now supposed to perform), the profitability of enterprise and the solvency of the economy as a whole depends on whether the sale of products does or does not cover costs, measured in money. In costs are included wages and salaries, materials, machinery, depreciation, costs of management, rent, interest on borrowed capital

—and also public works and social services. Management reckons and calculates, not in terms of quantities of socially necessary labour, but in terms of prices and costs—reckoning with indices of productivity, with borrowings and repayments, with finding sales outlets, with the division of income between personal expenditures and reinvestment, and so on. These are, naturally, the "concrete" things that concern it, and not such "abstract" matters as values, surplus value and the rate of surplus value. In general (as Marx showed), the wages-bill of a particular enterprise does not correspond to the value of the labour-power it buys, the sales income does not correspond to the value of the goods sold, and the profit does not correspond to the sum-total of surplus value extracted. Even if someone worked out the values, it would not assist the management in its practical calculations about costs and profits. Management, therefore, finds no employment for Marx's conception of value. This conception was not, indeed, worked out with a view to assisting capitalist management, and therefore appears to it unimportant, redundant, irrelevant, and even a relic of Platonic Idealism.

The majority of professional economists, who simply study indices of production, costs, prices, wages, investments, savings, national income, and so on, with a view to formulating equations which will cover their variations, can likewise find no employment for the labour theory of value. But evidently in this they are simply accommodating themselves to the point of view and interest of capitalist management, to which they are trying to sell professional advice. And while many of the equations may be accurate, and the advice practical and businesslike, nevertheless, considered as social science, the whole undertaking is strangely defective. For production costs, wages, prices, and all the rest, are only the results of people having entered into definite relations of production, in which all labour is productive of exchange-values, and labour-power itself and all its products are exchange-values and so have their variable production costs, prices, and so on.

When the economist has formulated his equations, he may claim to have explained that when this cost varies in one way that price varies in another way, and to advise the manager and legislator that if he can peg this variable he will be able thereby to keep another under control. However, he has neither defined nor explained the production relations into which people have entered. But it is only as a result of those production relations that the phenomena he studies occur at all.

Many economists object to talking about values defined in terms of socially necessary labour, and to talking about surplus value, on the grounds that it is a mere abstraction. It *is* an abstraction, but not an unimportant, redundant or irrelevant one. Abstraction is necessary, but the important thing is to assemble the information gained from different modes of abstraction so as to reveal the real connections, portray what is actually going on, and comprehend its law of motion. That is dialectics—and it was as a dialectician that Marx had the advantage as a social scientist.

As Lenin said, Marx abstracted for investigation "the relations of production between the members of society", and having done so was able to show what happens in the development of the process of production and exchange. Capitalist managers and their economists, on the other hand, also abstract—they abstract operations of producing and consuming, buying and selling, managing and being managed, from the relations of production by entering into which people come to do these things. They pride themselves on dealing with nothing but observable and measurable variables; but it is their portrayal of the economic movement of society as nothing but the process of these variables which is in truth a mere abstraction. What is actually going on is that people are producing, exchanging and consuming the products of social labour. To see only movements of costs, prices, productivity, national incomes, and so forth, is to represent the economic process simply in terms of a set of abstractions and then to say: these are the economic process.

Marx's analysis in terms of the labour theory of value portrays capitalism for what it is, a particular historically-constituted mode of production, and distinguishes it from pre-capitalist economic formations. It shows capitalism as a mode of production based on the exploitation of wage-labour, and clearly distinguishes this form of exploitation of labour from earlier forms. Thus it clearly defines capitalism in terms of basic social relations—a definition deplored as abstract and redundant by hard-headed managerial types, who do not like employees to be shown exactly how they are used for making profits for employers.

Whereas Marx demonstrated that capitalist production exploits wage-labour, many economists and sociologists today, who regard production relations as mere abstractions, deny that wage-labour is exploited. Nowadays they do sometimes agree that it used to be exploited; but they deny that it is exploited any longer, for they simply pay no attention to the capitalist production relations. Thus, as Dr. Popper has assured us, the exploitation of labour was an evil of the old *laissez faire* system which modern "interventionism" has almost got rid of.

According to this conception, the well-managed firm, which today enters into collective agreements with trade union officials, does not exploit its workers. A collective agreement is not exploitation; there is exploitation only if people are bullied and coerced. It is only the bad and selfish employer, who sacks shop stewards and undercuts the rate, who exploits labour—and he should be firmly dealt with by the interventionist authorities, though first it is necessary to deal with bad and selfish workers who persist in coming out on strike.

Exploitation, according to Dr. Popper's definition, consists of "long hours of work and low real wages" (2–OS. 169). And have not hours of work been reduced, and real wages raised? And would not real wages be raised still further if only workers would get rid of the idea that they must resist exploitation and instead devote themselves to increasing productivity by resisting restrictive practices? The fact is, however, that the modern well-managed firm probably extracts a higher rate of surplus value than does its less efficient rate-cutting competitor. As Marx quite conclusively showed, an increased rate of surplus value can be got by intensifying labour and rationalising production, at the same time as hours of labour are reduced and real wages raised.

Capitalist exploitation consists in the extraction of surplus-value, and this still goes on. It has not decreased but increased, for behind the façade of collective bargaining and modernisation it is conducted more efficiently and ruthlessly than ever. The capitalist, as Marx showed, always has a hard job to maintain his rate of profit, and to do so he has to scheme out how to intensify the exploitation of labour by rationalisation of every kind—which he duly does.

In demonstrating that capitalism is a system of exploitation of labour, Marx showed exactly how it is related to and differs from older forms of exploitation.

The essence (if I may be allowed the use of this word in its normally accepted sense, without being accused of "methodological essentialism") of exploitation consists in this: that *members of an owning and managing class contrive to appropriate to their own uses the products of the labour of productive workers, so that those workers are in effect working only in part for their own support and in the main for the support of the exploiters.*

It means that *a minority of exploiters appropriate to their own uses the labour of the working majority.*

The typical ancient forms of exploitation were, roughly speaking, slavery and serfdom. In slavery the slave is a mere chattel: he is the property of the master, who owns both him and all he produces. In serfdom the producers work a certain amount of time for themselves, but for the rest have to work to provide the requirements of their lords. The advent of capitalism depended on doing away with both slavery and serfdom, for only on that condition could the supply of free labour be available for employment in the factories. But the exploitation of labour remains, and has simply taken another (and more efficient) form. *For so much of the working day the wage-workers are doing that amount of work which has to be done to produce the value of their own requirements of life; for the rest of the day they are producing surplus value for their employers.*

3. THE GENERAL LAW OF CAPITALIST ACCUMULATION

In supposing that what he calls "interventionism" has actually *supplanted* capitalism, in the way Marx said that only socialism would supplant capitalism, Dr. Popper alleges that "economic interference of the state" has already brought those benefits which Marx said only socialism would bring. He goes so far as to say that "by social co-operation" monopoly capitalism has already gone a long way to abolish "the greatest evils which have hitherto beset the social life of man", namely, "Poverty, Unemployment and similar forms of social insecurity, Sickness and pain, Penal Cruelty, Slavery and other forms of Serfdom, Religious and Racial Discrimination, Lack of Educational Opportunities, Rigid Class Differences, War" (CR. 370). If that were true, one could not but agree with Dr. Popper that there would be no sense in following Marx—for if the *status quo* is satisfactory, why change it?

According to Dr. Popper, Marx based his entire "prophecy" that capitalism would inevitably be overthrown on the notion that under capitalism people's conditions of life would inevitably deteriorate until finally they became insupportable. According to this version, Marx predicted a century ago that the workers' standards in the industrial capitalist countries would not improve but grow steadily worse. But in fact, as we know, they have improved. Hence Marx's ideas about capitalism and its development have been proved to be entirely mistaken. And his idea that capitalism must be abolished and replaced by socialism, founded on these mistaken premises, is equally mistaken. Whereas Marx said that things would get worse and worse, they have, on the contrary, got better and better. Marxist theory, prophesying "absolute impoverishment", bears no relation to what has actually happened—and political policies based on it are therefore doomed to frustration. These circumstances, says Dr. Popper, force Marxists to "learn to believe blindly" and to become "hostile to reasonable arguments". And with withering sarcasm he concludes that "it is not only capitalism which is labouring under inner contradictions that threaten to bring its downfall" (2–OS. 192).

Like his refutation of the labour theory of value, this further refutation of Marxism so confidently presented by Dr. Popper is a hardy annual in the by now rather old-fashioned garden of refutations. What keeps it fresh and green is a single quotation from *Capital* (Vol. 1, Chapter 25, section 4): "To the degree to which capital accumulates, the workers' condition must deteriorate." This statement was called by Marx "the absolute general law of capitalist accumulation"—so this impressive title certainly justifies attaching to it some considerable importance in the body of Marxist theory. However, unless one proposes to be "hostile to reasonable argument", it is best to understand and interpret particular statements within the context of the whole theory to which they belong, rather than understand and interpret the whole theory as though it were summed up in one statement.

Immediately after stating in general terms "the absolute general law" Marx added the qualifying statement: "Like all other laws it is modified in its working by many circumstances." If words have meaning, these ones imply that, contrary to the interpretation put upon it by Dr. Popper and others, the "absolute general law" does *not* unconditionally predict that every accumulation of capital will be accompanied by a deterioration of the workers' conditions. On the contrary, "many circumstances" will prevent such a deterioration.

Whatever may be the case with others who have tried to refute Marx, it is rather extraordinary that an expert on scientific method like Dr. Popper should succumb to such a simple fallacy as to suppose that the scientific formulation of "a law" is the same thing as an unconditional prediction. Statements of laws are *not* predictions, but tools used in making predictions.

For instance, no one with any knowledge of science supposes that

the law of gravitation is a prediction that all bodies will always fall
to the earth. Some bodies rise and fly about in the air, and the use
of the law of gravitation is to assist us in calculating the conditions
under which they do so. Marx understood this perfectly well when he
wrote about "the general law of capitalist accumulation"—and so does
Dr. Popper understand it in any context save that of the refutation
of Marxism.

The point of "the absolute general law of capitalist accumulation"
is not that it enables us to predict that under no circumstances so long
as capitalism lasts will workers ever improve their conditions, which
will always deteriorate. And nowhere in *Capital* did Marx make any
such prediction. The point of the law is to state the "absolute general"
condition, existing so long as capital accumulates, under which
workers' standards either deteriorate or improve—just as gravitation
is the "absolute general" condition under which bodies fall or rise.
If you think a body can fly up and up not subject to the condition
of gravity, you are mistaken. And if you think workers' standards can
go up and up not subject to the condition of the absolute general
law of capitalist accumulation, you are mistaken too. Just as a body
exerts a gravitational attraction proportional to its mass, so does every
accumulation of capital, accumulated by extracting as much surplus
value as possible from the workers' labour, create a greater power and
urge to suck up out of labour an even greater accumulation—by
rationalising production, throwing redundant workers on the scrapheap, and encroaching in every possible way on the standards of
labour. That is the condition under which any battle to raise standards
has always to be fought.

When we consider, in the light of Marx's complete analysis of
capitalist production, the totality of actual circumstances created by
the accumulation of capital in the advanced capitalist countries, we
find that these circumstances are such that it would be surprising if
an improvement in the workers' condition had *not* taken place; and
that for several reasons.

In the first place, as Marx said very often and very clearly, the
actual level of workers' standards is determined, not by an "iron law
of wages" which decrees that they shall always be reduced to the bare
minimum for subsistence, but by the conditions of class struggle. The
growing strength of labour organisation succeeds in forcing standards *up*.

In the second place, the very great advances in technology which accompany the accumulation of capital have the result that all kinds of amenities become available on a mass scale, and consequently the consumption of these becomes a part of the material requirements and expectations of the worker. In other words, with an advanced technology the worker comes to require for his maintenance various goods and services his forefathers did without—and which his brothers in more backward regions still do without. In terms of the labour theory of value, the provision of these goods and services then enters into the determination of the value of labour-power in the advanced countries. This too was very clearly stated by Marx, who pointed out that in more developed regions the value of labour-power is considerably higher than in less developed ones—and he assigned this as a powerful motive for export of capital to regions of cheap labour, where the actual value of labour was much less than it had become at home.

In the third place, what Dr. Popper calls the performance of economic functions by organised political power, which Marx and Engels so clearly forecast, enables capitalist governments to mitigate to some extent the ravages of cyclical economic crises and sudden mass increases of unemployment. The effect is to lessen to some extent the consequent pressures against the improvement of workers' standards which these formerly exerted. Of course it is very advantageous for the capitalists to have managed to provide themselves with what they now call "economic levers" to control economic conditions in the interests of the profitable operations of capital. But at the same time it sets them a new problem. Accompanying the "far-reaching economic functions" which political power performs they have to include appropriate political measures to counteract labour's demand for rising standards.

These are circumstances which have made it possible in some favoured regions to work for and achieve the limited success in remedying social evils under capitalism which Dr. Popper celebrates. When we look at his list, quoted above, we cannot doubt that much benefit has been gained by social security legislation, health services, legal reform, the educational services, and opposition to religious and racial discrimination; while as for "slavery and serfdom", capitalism has *always* discouraged these forms of exploitation and sought to replace them by wage-labour.

It is hardly true, however, that the benefits listed have simply been bestowed on grateful humanity by a benevolently interventionist state. They have been won only by struggle in which the working-class movement has played the chief part. And we may well ask by how much *more* the various social evils could have been reduced had it not been for the obstinate resistance of the ruling class at every step to every measure proposed to raise the standards of common people. In fact, just as the development of *laissez faire* to "interventionism" has verified Marx's economic predictions, so have the benefits won in the process verified his prediction that *under capitalism the working people would never get any benefits without fighting for them*.

Coming to the last two items on Dr. Popper's list, one does perhaps wonder on what data he has concluded that "in Scandinavia, the United States, Canada, Australia and New Zealand, we have, in fact, something approaching classless societies" (CR. 371). Is there really no class distinction, in the countries mentioned, between people living by working for wages and by investments and capital gains? And is there none between the "organisation men" of the American corporations and the poverty-stricken masses in Latin America from whose labour such considerable revenue flows into the United States?

As regards war, Dr. Popper explains that what he means is that "the free world will only go to war . . . if faced with unambiguous aggression" (CR. 372). But whenever people in a territory under the special protection of a heavily armed power of "the free world" seek to dispense with that protection, this is called "aggression". That is why events since 1956 (which is when Dr. Popper delivered the lecture from which his eulogy of modern capitalism has been quoted) have continued to falsify his statement that "as far as the free world itself is concerned, war has been conquered" (CR. 372).

For all his claim to oppose "reasonable argument" to "blind" belief, Dr. Popper does not always trouble to inquire whether facts support his own assertions. This is evidenced by the opening sentence of *The Open Society and its Enemies*, in which he says that "our civilisation", by which he presumably means the civilisation whose economic basis is monopoly capitalism, "might be perhaps described as aiming at humaneness and reasonableness, at equality and freedom". It is true he does say "perhaps"; and perhaps so long as such methods as the spraying of defenceless women and children with napalm continue to be adopted for realising the aims, this should be accepted as the operative word.

Facts make it pretty clear that in the most advanced capitalist countries, for all the benefits won by their inhabitants, every other aim of policy is subordinated to the condition of preserving the relations of capitalist exploitation and safeguarding capitalist profits. But more than that, the facts make it even clearer that the political power established in these countries not only intervenes inside the countries themselves to preserve and foster capitalist exploitation. It intervenes very vigorously indeed outside their borders, in other territories, to conquer spheres of investment, markets and sources of raw materials, and to make the labour of people in economically more backward regions subject to imperialist exploitation. The aim of this is neither humaneness, freedom nor equality; nor is the conduct of the rivalry between imperialist powers, or the relations between them and their dependencies, especially noteworthy for reasonableness.

Dr. Popper assigned as Marx's reason for advocating a socialist revolution the alleged unconditional prophecy (said to be implied by "the absolute general law of capitalist accumulation") that, until that event, standards of life will from day to day and in every way go on getting lower and lower. So "increase of misery" will "force" the proletariat "to revolt against its exploiters" (2–OS. 137). The workers' economic and social demands will always be refused, and consequently they will become inspired "with a desperate knowledge that only revolution can help them in their misery" (2–OS. 191).

If that were true, the result would be discouragement and disorganisation rather than stronger organisation, and they would never make a revolution. The workers in fact organise because experience teaches them that that is the way to *improve* their condition—and they are forced to keep up an economic and political struggle against capital because only so can they hold on to their gains and gain more. That is what Marx teaches the labour movement, and not the doctrinaire and defeatist nonsense which Dr. Popper imagines. But Dr. Popper concludes that if the working class *can* improve its condition under capitalism there can be no reason for proposing to abolish capitalism. For if you can improve your condition why not improve it some more, instead of calling for the abolition of the system under which such improvements can be made?

Dr. Popper is right about one thing, and that is that for Marx "the absolute general law of capitalist accumulation" provided grounds for advising the abolition of capitalism and for predicting that it would eventually be abolished. Marx certainly did maintain that all those hopeful people (like Dr. Popper himself) who think that improvements in living standards can go on and on under capitalism, so that everything will get better and better and eventually all poverty, unemploy-

ment, class differences and war will simply disappear, are blind to the
operation of "the absolute general law". But the law is not an unconditional prediction of increasing impoverishment. And in general, as
Dr. Popper has rightly said, unconditional predictions are foreign to
science. What the law actually says can be summed up in three points.

First, capitalist accumulation is realised out of surplus value. To
obtain more surplus and accumulate more capital out of it, it is necessary to keep down the labourers' share of the values produced by
labour. Hence the accumulation of capital, essential for the continuation of the system, demands that in every way the pressure of the
wage-workers for a greater share of the values produced be opposed
and pushed back. Whatever makes for better living for the workers
is therefore always opposed by the steady pressure engendered by
capitalist accumulation to make living standards deteriorate.

Second, the drive for capitalist accumulation brings a continual
drive for rationalisation of production and the replacement of human
labour by machinery. Until it can be re-employed at a profit, capital
has no use for the labour displaced. The people concerned are thrown
temporarily or permanently on to the scrapheap. Hence, as Marx
stressed in the chapter of *Capital* devoted to the "general law",
capitalist accumulation continually generates an "industrial reserve" of
unemployed, and this is a continual and very powerful factor acting
against the raising of living standards.

Third, because capitalist accumulation thrives on maximum exploitation of labour, capital always seeks for spheres of investment where
greater profit can be got out of greater poverty. Hence such islands
of affluence as may be formed in particular places are surrounded by
a sea of poverty, out of the exploitation of which the affluence is
sustained. As Marx said, the more capital accumulates the greater, on
a world-wide scale, becomes the contrast between the wealth of a
few and the poverty of the many. As he said, the wealth accumulates
at one pole, the poverty at the other.

The "absolute general law" summed up in these three points continues to operate wherever capitalist accumulation goes on. We
continue to see it operating every day.

In the advanced capitalist countries experience to date contributes
little to suggest that the situation is a stable one which will permit the
steady uninterrupted improvement of conditions of employment and
standards of living. There is, as Marx and Engels predicted and Dr.
Popper has duly noted, a certain amount of planning and regulation

of the economy—but planning and regulation by whom and for whom? The condition of the whole thing is the securing of profits for the great capitalist corporations out of the employment of wage-labour. It is not planning for welfare but planning for profit; and so far as economic growth for the satisfaction of needs is concerned, there remains always a chronic waste and under-employment of resources both material and human. The anarchic character of the profit motive continually asserts itself against any schemes of planned growth, and at the same time the demands of labour that social production should be turned to the well-being of the producers are met by the owners' objection that we cannot afford it. As is happening in Britain at the time of writing (1966-7), the controllers know how to put the brakes on, and how to set about creating unemployment when "over-full employment" is giving the worker too much bargaining power. In affluent America there has always been a huge mass of permanent unemployment, and a vast and shameful accumulation of poverty.

These facts verify among other things Marx's theoretical conclusion that the process of circulation of capital, which is what capitalist management tries to manage, remains as a whole unmanageable.

The circulation of capital begins with an accumulation of capital in the form of money, which is used to buy materials, machinery and labour-power. Then labour-power is set to work, to produce both means of consumption and the machinery to be used for new production. Then the products are sold, so as to realise a new and greater sum of money with which to buy more labour-power, materials and machinery. This circular movement is the life process of capital. For it to flow on uninterrupted would suppose the continuous production by socialised labour of increasing quantities (in terms of value) of both means of consumption and means of production, and, at the same time, the continuous profitable sale of everything produced. Dr. Popper and others talk of "a communist utopia". However that may be, that this should happen is a capitalist utopia. It has never happened yet. And as a result of interruptions in the circulation, production keeps on being disrupted, poverty is perpetuated and resources are wasted or destroyed.

With capitalists competing for profit the whole circulation of capital cannot possibly be managed, since no management, not even the most well-advised capitalist state, has simultaneous control over all the factors involved. Breakdowns and disruptions keep occurring in one or another stage of the process; workers demand too much pay, or withhold their labour; investors don't invest enough in new capital equipment, or else invest too much; too much of something or other is produced, or else not enough; and so on. Management is for ever trying to repair the damage but never succeeds in preventing it, for while they are coping with one trouble another is breaking out.

However, the proclivity of capitalist circulation to suffer interruptions is not due simply to the difficulty of managing to adjust the simultaneous independent profit-seeking operations of competing blocks of capital. Neither the greatest luck nor the greatest judgment could solve the problem. For, as Marx showed, the necessity for capital to maximise its profit in order that capital should go on accumulating out of surplus value means that, on the one hand, the productive forces should go on being expanded without limit, while, on the other hand, the share in the product going to the producers should be restricted. "The last cause of all real crises", wrote Marx (*Capital*, Vol. 3, Chapter 30), "always remains the . . . restricted consumption of the masses compared to the tendency of capitalist production to develop the productive forces as if only the absolute power of consumption of the entire society would be their limit."

Formerly, interruptions in the circulation of capital took the regular form of the ten-year "trade cycle". But while the boom-bust rhythm has been interrupted, that has not let the circulation of capital go on without interruptions. It remains utopian to believe that it can ever possibly do so—either providentially, through the operation of the economic laws of the market, as earlier economists fondly believed, or by the brilliant contrivances of good management, as modern ones equally fondly incline to hope.

Meantime, although neither Dr. Popper nor the capitalist establishment is pleased about it, the fact is that approximately one-third of the people of the world have by now done away with capitalism (as Marx advised and predicted) before it had even the chance of proving to them the benefits it could confer. They are trying to build or have built a planned socialist economy instead. A very high proportion of the rest of the people, miserably poor, are in a state of revolt against imperialism, against colonialism and neo-colonialism. In these circumstances the major capitalist powers are spending a significant proportion of their national income on armaments—mainly for the purpose of stopping impoverished peoples from shaking free of the grip of foreign capital and to stop the socialist countries from helping them. These armaments, and the local wars and escalations of wars in which some of them are used, remain at once a threat to the peace of the world and to the very existence of civilisation, and a crushing burden on the people of the capitalist countries. We sustain them at our peril. And if we can force the capitalist governments to stop their wars and disarm, we can then hardly continue to save the capitalist interests the armaments, armed forces and wars are protecting.

Moreover, whatever capitalist powers do (short of world war, which would destroy them), the socialist powers will continue to develop, and that at an accelerating pace, their own technological resources. And the national liberation movements against imperialism and neo-colonialism will continue to grow, whatever their disunity and whatever setbacks they sustain in this or that place.

For how long can we suppose that such a situation, brought about by the operation of "the absolute general law of capitalist accumulation", can continue? For some time more, perhaps, but not for ever. The operation of the general law will, as Marx predicted, either bring general ruin or else be terminated by the removal of the capitalist relations which give rise to it.

And there is yet another factor of very great moment. The capitalist powers have now started on the road of a new technological revolution. If they slow the pace of technological advance they will cut away the foundations of their own affluence and be hopelessly outpaced by the socialist powers. They will then be totally unable to maintain their dominance over at present underdeveloped countries, their economies will stagnate, and very serious consequences in the way of unemployment and impoverishment will be upon them. On the other hand, if they carry on, and if they develop vast new resources of energy for powering fully automated production, how are they to secure the planned development of the economy, with full employment, if they insist that the key means of production should be privately owned and that the whole employed labour force should be wage-workers whose labour contributes to private profit? Unemployment on a huge scale would result, and not all the bread and circuses borrowed from the ancient Romans in the days of their decadence would be able to save the doomed system.

If, then, Dr. Popper and others demand why we should heed the advice of Marx that capitalism should be abolished, when some of us are doing so well out of it, the short answer is that we cannot afford not to. We are living in a fools' paradise if we remain blind to the operation of "the absolute general law of capitalist accumulation". It is overall true that as capital accumulates the workers' conditions must deteriorate.

In socialism, the accumulation of capital, in the sense of accumulation of resources out of which social production can be expanded, has no tendency to lead to the deterioration of the conditions of workers. On the contrary, the more social capital accumulates the higher can standards of life be raised. The accumulation of resources is then the condition for raising the standards of all workers (*all*, not some) up to a high level, for lightening labour, making hours of necessary work shorter and the means for enjoyment of leisure greater. This, Marxism concludes, is the condition of affairs which we must organise to achieve—or else perish.

As we have seen, Marx expounded as the basic law of all social development the law that relations of production must always be brought into conformity with the development of forces of production. When, from being forms of development of production, relations of production become fetters on it, a social revolution is needed to change the social system. The need to get rid of capitalism and replace it by socialism is the need to get rid of production relations which have become fetters on the growing forces of production. The *"absolute general law of capitalist accumulation" is the concise statement of the way in which capitalist relations act as fetters on production*. Instead of productive resources being accumulated for the purpose of raising the general standards of life of the producers, capitalist accumulation takes place at the expense of general welfare, is accompanied by wastage of material resources and human capacities, and improverishes producers at the same time as it enriches owners of capital.

It may be added that, as Lenin said, Marx dealt not only with relations of production but "went on to trace the superstructure corresponding to these relations of production". He demonstrated the consequences in the encouragement of individual selfishness and greed, in conflicts and grabs, in speculation and corruption, in frustration, waste and needless suffering, in political chicanery and political oppression and wars. Thus his economic analysis, "strictly confined to the relations of production between the members of society", succeeds in explaining and interpreting the hateful experience of the members of society caught up in the economic system. The same theme which is explored by poets, painters, musicians and novelists in bourgeois society is given its scientific exposition by Marxism.

4

SOCIAL REVOLUTION AND SOCIAL ENGINEERING

1. THE SOCIALIST REVOLUTION

A basic change in relations of production would mean drastic interference with the rights of property—at the present time, the ownership
of capital—and this would constitute a social revolution. It is this
which is so widely regarded as unthinkable or, at any rate, as not to
be proposed in works of science which might qualify for research
grants. Dr. Popper undoubtedly speaks for the whole establishment
in stating that a revolution is one of the very worst things that could
possibly happen to us.

A revolution, he says, involves "the prolonged use of violence"
which "may lead in the end to the loss of freedom, since it is liable to
bring about not the dispassionate rule of reason but the rule of the
strong man" (2–OS. 151). Nay more, it "destroys the institutional
and traditional framework of society . . . once they destroy tradition,
civilisation disappears with it . . . they have returned to the beasts"
(CR. 343–4). And in a more dispassionate vein he argues that "it is not
reasonable to assume that a complete reconstruction of our social
world would lead at once to a workable system. Rather we should
expect that, owing to lack of experience, many mistakes would be
made. . . ." (1–OS. 167).

But not only would "revolutionary methods . . . increase unnecessary suffering" and "lead to more and more violence" (CR. 343), but
the "humanitarian aims" which revolutionaries pursue can be achieved
without any revolution. Once it is admitted that, as experience proves,
social benefits can be won under capitalism, there is no reason "why
the workers, who have learned by experience that they can improve
their lot by gradual reform, should not prefer to stick to this method
. . . why they should not compromise with the bourgeoisie and leave
it in possession of the means of production rather than risk all their
gains by making demands liable to lead to violent clashes". Gradual
reform can continue, and "there is no logical necessity why gradual
reform, achieved by compromise, should lead to the complete destruction of the capitalist system" (2–OS. 155). Anyway, Dr. Popper argues,
those who believe in smashing everything up would have to undertake

gradual reconstruction afterwards, so it would be far more sensible to get on with gradual construction in the first place and forget the smash-up (1–OS. 168).

Dr. Popper takes a rather apocalyptic view of revolution. He assumes that if once capitalist ownership of means of production were abolished everything would crash, that if private capital were prevented from making profits out of exploiting wage-labour civilisation would end. So he cries: "They destroy tradition!" "Civilisation disappears!" "They have returned to the beasts!" and (a bit of an anti-climax) "Many mistakes would be made!" He is, of course, justified in his last apprehension—for people always do make mistakes, whatever they do. But as for "tradition" and "civilisation", it would seem that Dr. Popper's sweeping statements were made under some sort of emotional stress, for they are certainly "not reasonable".

Do "tradition" and "civilisation", in the senses in which these may be regarded as something to be preserved, mean specifically capitalist tradition or capitalist civilisation? No, for tradition and civilisation are more permanent, more lasting, than particular production relations; civilisation and norms of civilised living are developed by men through the ages, so that advances made within certain production relations are not lost but carried further under new production relations, which are "higher" in the sense that they correspond to a higher development of forces of production. To develop civilisation and civilised living, people have to go on developing their forces of production; and when production relations are acting as a fetter upon the utilisation of new forces of production they have to be changed, or else civilisation and its traditions may suffer degeneration instead of renewal.

Of course, if one considers only particular local traditions or pieces of tradition, or particular local or specialised amenities of civilisation, it would have to be admitted that they are frequently destroyed or disappear—and a good thing too. For example, there is a parliamentary tradition in Britain that the Chamber of the House of Commons should not contain seats for all the members. This tradition was successfully upheld by both Sir Winston Churchill and Lord Attlee when the House was rebuilt after the Second World War; but no doubt a socialist revolution in Britain would destroy this particular tradition. Again, the kind of civilised or gracious living associated with the ownership of town and country mansions, with grouse moors and large staffs of servants, is already disappearing, and would completely disappear if there were a socialist revolution. But are such destructions of traditions and disappearances of civilisation a bad thing? Only a few would regret them, and their loss would scarcely return the rest of mankind "to the beasts". But if by "civilisation" and "tradition" is meant, more generally, the ever-developing production by and distribution to the members of society of the necessities and comforts of life, with the development of the sciences and the arts, and of social freedom and justice, then there is no reason at all to conclude that a change in the relations of production, calculated to promote the development of social production for social welfare, would destroy tradition or cause civilisation to disappear. Indeed, a far more pressing danger arises from the growth and continuation of certain traditions of commercialism, corrupt politics and militarism fostered by the existing capitalist set up, and the greatest danger of all from the stock-piling of nuclear weapons. If mankind should ever be "returned to the beasts" by the destruction of civilisation, it will be as a result of nuclear war unleashed by mad imperialists (and all this claptrap about "the institutional and traditional framework of society" is a part of the phraseology of such madness).

Dr. Popper's apocalyptic visions arise simply and solely from his obsession with the idea that revolution involves "the prolonged use of violence" and "more and more violence". It is this violence which he sees as doing the damage. And he represents Marxism as in part a fatalistic prediction of violence, in part a conspiracy to incite violence.

For Marxism, though not for Dr. Popper, the word "revolution" has a precise significance defined in terms of Marx's theory of social development and class struggle.

Hitherto, the development of relations of production, that is to say, of forms of ownership of means of production and appropriation of the products of labour, has divided society into antagonistic classes. In any particular social formation, a particular dominant class maintains its existence by exploiting the masses of producers in a particular way, and preventing other exploiting classes from developing as rivals their own methods of exploitation. The political system is the means by which this is managed and a particular form of ownership and appropriation of products of labour is imposed upon the whole of society. A revolution, then, is a change in the political system of such an order that another class comes to power and deprives the former ruling class of its opportunities to maintain itself by its former methods of exploitation. A revolution thus effects a change in the relations of production. And it is a phenomenon peculiar to and typical of class-divided society, where there are exploiting and exploited classes.

There have been many revolutions recorded by history, and all of them have been violent (involving, indeed, "the prolonged use of violence"). The cause of this universal violence is clear. Ruling classes have maintained their rule only by aggression and violent repression of their subjects, and the only way to get rid of them has been by violently opposing them. Revolutions in the past have, however, by no means been distinguished as regrettable outbreaks of violence interrupting periods of calm and peaceful progress and putting in jeopardy the gains of civilisation. There has always been violence and war, revolutions have been conducted by violence and war, and in them violence and war have been made the vehicles by which men have managed to get rid of old forms of property which fettered social production, the material basis of civilisation.

Marxist analysis claims to demonstrate that what is on the agenda now is socialist (or "proletarian") revolution, and to demonstrate, too, the ways in which this must *differ* from all previous revolutions.

In previous revolutions ruling exploiting classes succumbed to the hostility not only of masses who were exploited but of other classes of exploiters or would-be exploiters. The working masses had to do most of the slogging, but new exploiters reaped the reward and came to power.

In the past, slave revolts or peasant revolts weakened the ruling classes, but the invariable upshot was the defeat and dispersal of slave or peasant insurgents and the reconsolidation of exploitation by either the old or new exploiters. In modern history it has been typical of bourgeois revolutions that at a certain point the bourgeoisie rounded upon and disarmed the insurgent masses who had been making the pace at the start, and entered into a compromise with the defeated counter-revolution. In bourgeois revolutions there has always been an incipient democratic revolution, with demands going far beyond what the bourgeoisie was disposed to grant. (This is illustrated by the English, American and French revolutions, and by the European revolutionary movements of 1848; when it came to the Russian revolution in 1905 and 1917 there was already in existence a well-organised industrial working class with revolutionary socialist leadership, and the result was the socialist revolution of 1917.)

But wherever the bourgeoisie comes to power and a fully capitalist economy is created, the ruling bourgeoisie no longer faces any other rival group of exploiters. There emerges a direct confrontation of exploiters and exploited, uncomplicated by any issues of substituting some new form of exploitation for the existing form. Thus the single issue becomes that of either continuing capitalist exploitation or ending it by depriving the capitalist class of political power and instituting social ownership of the principal means of production. Thus whereas previous revolutions substituted new forms of exploitation for old, the issue now is to end exploitation once for all.

This confrontation of classes, with the issue it poses, exists in all developed capitalist countries today. Dr. Popper, incidentally, raises some rather irrelevant objections to the recognition of this fact. "We must be prepared to find," he says, "that a very considerable middle class exists (or that a new middle class has arisen) and that it may co-operate with the other non-proletarian classes against a bid for power by the workers; and nobody can say for certain what the outcome of such a contest would be. Indeed, statistics no longer show any tendency for the number of industrial workers to increase in relation to the other classes of the population" (2–OS. 156).

By a "middle class" and "a new middle class" he presumably means all kinds of workers on their own account, and professional workers; and by "the other non-proletarian classes" he means chiefly working farmers and peasants. What he says about these classes is quite true, but it does not in the last alter the fact that the only alternative to continuing *capitalist* exploitation is now to end *all* exploitation: there is no question of any of these classes ousting the big capitalists and setting up some new sort of exploitation of their own, but only, as he quite rightly says, of whether or not they will support "a bid for power by the workers". Clearly, therefore, and as Marxists have always said, it is an important element in contemporary socialist tactics to seek to win the support of these classes for socialism, and not to antagonise them by a narrow sectarian concern with the interests of industrial workers alone. As for the decreasing proportion of "industrial workers", by that he means, presumably, the relative increase in the number of technicians, "white collar" workers, and "brain workers" of one kind and another. True, there is such an increase; and these are exactly the sorts of people who will be needed in large numbers to build a modern socialist economy. Dr. Popper, in fact, has understood the Marxist theory of socialist revolution so little, that he cites circumstances which confirm it as insuperable objections.

In the socialist revolution the exploited classes play an altogether new role. They are not the unruly rank and file of the revolution, but its organisers and leaders.

This difference is illustrated by the difference between the role of the organised working-class movement in the modern class struggle and that of the so-called "mob" in certain phases of bourgeois revolutions. The "mob" would come together in a spontaneous way, driven usually by anger at some sudden deterioration of conditions that made the already miserable condition of the poor desperate (often a rise in food prices, as demonstrated by G. Rudé in *The Crowd in the French Revolution*). It was a very formidable force, but without permanent organisation or aims, or its own permanent leadership. Its swift and sometimes destructive activities could pave the way for other classes gaining their ends, and then the mob itself could be dispersed. This "mob" has become transformed into the organised democratic labour movement, a far more formidable force when it unites to exert its strength, its aims clearly delineated, and neither destructive nor riotous but disciplined and not easily dispersed, and fully capable of staffing from its own ranks the entire legislative and executive apparatus of modern society.

The modern working class is able to play this new role because the conditions of modern industry lead to its becoming organised and educated, and to the formation of competent groups of socialist intellectuals and political leaders of the labour movement. Thus it is an exploited class able not only to kick against exploitation, as the exploited have always done, but to manage affairs when the rule of its exploiters is ended.

Another feature of socialist revolution is its world-wide international character.

The local development of capitalism in only a few countries had the effect (the inevitable effect, if Dr. Popper will forgive the expression) of bringing the entire world into the orbit of capitalist exploitation. The world became divided up into spheres of exploitation of a comparatively few capitalist powers. With them, capital has developed to the monopoly phase, with the merging of industrial and finance capital, and the export of capital; capitalism developed into the phase of imperialism. This meant that throughout the world the struggle of exploited people against their being exploited involved, beyond issues of kicking free from whatever local feudal or proto-feudal forms of exploitation they suffered, the final struggle for emancipation from the exploitation of capital. Besides, comparatively "primitive" people, whose tribal way of life still retained many communal features, found themselves suddenly subjected to capitalist forms of exploitation totally foreign to their own phase of social development, and were flung into the struggle against it. Thus the impingement of capitalist exploitation stirred up the whole world, and forced on the working masses everywhere, whatever their own prior stage of economic and social development, the issue of resisting capitalist exploitation and, therefore, the issue that if they were ever to be rid of it they must take the road of socialism.

There has thus begun, and continues to go on, a world-wide process of socialist revolution, in which particular local movements are contributory parts; a world-wide process of emancipation from the exploitation of capital, and therefore from all exploitation. This is something quite new in the history of revolutions. Hitherto there have been only local revolutions, in which local people upset the rule of local exploiters and other local exploiters took their place. But now every revolutionary movement is up against the same opponents, and all the local movements, whether their members fully understand it or not, add up to a world-wide movement which cannot relent until the exploitation of man by man is ended throughout the world. It cannot relent because, although particular groups of people may suffer defeat or turn their coats, the same world-wide circumstances which drove *them* into action will continue to operate, and drive others into action.

The words "socialist revolution" denote, therefore, not particular local revolutionary events (a "bid for power" or "desperate uprising", as Dr. Popper puts it) which are repeated, or which Communists predict will be repeated, in much the same way at different places and times, but rather a whole epoch, a whole process of disturbance of social relations and institutions, continuing over a long period of time (perhaps a century, perhaps longer) and involving the whole world. To say, as Marxists say, that this is the epoch of the socialist revolution, and that socialist revolution is inevitable, is not to prophesy that a particular sort of armed uprising is fated to occur in each particular place (in Britain, for example, where far from predicting an armed uprising the Communist Party's programme includes no such thing, and regards it as not only unpractical but undesirable); it is to say that mankind is now unavoidably involved throughout the world in a struggle against capitalist forms of exploitation, that the removal of exploitation has already begun, and that the struggle against it cannot but go on until it is done away with everywhere.

2. SOCIAL ENGINEERING

According to Dr. Popper, the rational alternative to the revolutionary overthrow of the entire "institutional and traditional framework of society", which he says Marxists think inevitable, is piecemeal "social engineering". By "social engineering" he means "the planning and construction of institutions, with the aim, perhaps, of arresting or of controlling or of quickening impending social developments" (PH. 45).

Social engineering must be, he says, "piecemeal". That is to say, it starts with institutions as they are, examines in what ways they work badly, either by causing preventable human inconvenience or suffering, or failing to alleviate it, and then introduces reforms to make them work better. "Blueprints for piecemeal engineering are comparatively simple," he informs us. "They are blueprints for single institutions, for health and unemployment insurance, for instance, or arbitration courts, or anti-depression budgeting, or educational reform." And he continues: "If they go wrong, the damage is not very great, and a readjustment not very difficult" (1–OS. 159).

This sort of social engineering advances by trial and error, it becomes ever more effective and successful as practical experience accumulates, and in this way it can bid fair "to be supported by the approval and agreement of a great number of people" (1–OS. 158), rather than causing people to fall out with one another, as is likely to result from more ambitious and far-reaching projects of social reconstruction. It goes hand in hand with the development of the social sciences. For, says Dr. Popper, "the social sciences have developed very largely through the criticism of proposals for social improvements or, more precisely, through attempts to find out whether or not some particular economic or political action is likely to produce an expected, or desired, result" (PH. 58).

In one of his more eloquent passages, Dr. Popper states the *credo* of the social engineer: "Work for the elimination of concrete evils rather than for the realisation of abstract goods. Do not aim at establishing happiness by political means. Rather aim at the elimination of concrete miseries. Or, in more practical terms: fight for the elimination of poverty by direct means—for example, by making sure everybody has a minimum income. Or fight against epidemics and disease by erecting hospitals and schools of medicine. Fight illiteracy as you fight criminality. But do all this by direct means. Choose what you consider the most urgent evil of the society in which you live, and try patiently to convince people that we can get rid of it." That, he informs us, provides "a simple formula or recipe for distinguishing between what I consider to be admissible plans for social reform and inadmissible utopian blueprints" (CR. 361).

In opposition to genuine or "piecemeal" social engineering, Dr. Popper castigates what he calls "utopian social engineering". According to this, it is of no use "tinkering" with this or that institution; what has to be done is to reconstruct the entire fabric of society. First "we must determine our ultimate political aim, or the Ideal State; . . . only then can we begin to consider the best ways and means for its realisation, and to draw up a plan for practical action" (1–OS. 157).

Dr. Popper criticises projects for "utopian social engineering" on several grounds. First, to reconstruct society as a whole there must needs be a dictatorship, which would have to be imposed on society by violence and would create a state of affairs much worse than any it was proposed to remedy. Second, it is not true that only by a complete reconstruction of society could social evils be remedied, for experience shows that much can be achieved piecemeal, by tackling them little by little and one by one. Third, in his enthusiasm for "abstract goods" the utopian actually disregards concrete evils which are under his very nose. "Do not allow your dreams of a beautiful world to lure you away from the claims of men who suffer here and now", Dr. Popper implores. "Our fellow men have a claim to our help" (CR. 361). To help them effectively we must tackle the immediate evils they are suffering, whereas the utopian condemns this as mere "tinkering", believing that what is needed is nothing less than complete reconstruction of the whole society.

Marx may have argued against "utopian socialism", Dr. Popper continues, but nevertheless Marxism embraces the chief error of "utopianism". This is the belief "that nothing short of a complete eradication of the offending social system will do". What distinguishes Marxism from other utopian creeds is the "historicist" theory that eradication of the social system is fated to happen by the laws of history. According to Dr. Popper, what Marxists call "scientific" as opposed to "utopian socialism" does not consist in working out what to do in order to free mankind from exploitation on the basis of understanding how causes may be set in motion in order to produce effects (which is what in other spheres engineers trained in science normally do). On the contrary, it consists in "blindly" believing that socialism will be brought about by inexorable historical necessity. Therefore, says Dr. Popper, "Marx condemns in fact *all* social engineering. . . . He denounces the faith in a rational planning of social institutions as altogether unrealistic, since society must grow according to the laws of history and not according to our rational plans. All we can do, he asserts, is to lessen the birthpangs of the historical process" (1–OS. 164).

So Dr. Popper presents us with an alternative: to choose between "utopian" and "piecemeal" social engineering. On the one hand, we may choose to believe that nothing short of the complete eradication of the present social system will benefit humanity, and that therefore it is of no use working out rational plans for improving our institutions because the only practical thing to do is to speed the fateful day when they will all be smashed up. On the other hand, we may reject any idea of a radical change in the social system and choose to keep on tinkering with single institutions, so as to satisfy bit by bit, so far as the present system allows, the various claims of our fellow men.

This choice, as we might indeed expect when it is presented by Dr. Popper, is the choice of Wonderland. "In *that* direction lives a Hatter; and in *that* direction lives a March Hare. Visit either you like; they're both mad." "But I don't want to go among mad people", Alice remarked. "Oh, you can't help that: we're all mad here." Let us see if we cannot, in this predicament, fare better than Alice.

A practical socialist policy does not, as Marx made perfectly clear in his criticism of "utopian socialism", take off from the enunciation of an "ultimate political aim, or the Ideal State". As for "the Ideal State", it is equally a utopia whether it is supposed to be realised, as the utopian socialists believed, by everyone becoming convinced of its rationality, or, as Dr. Popper says Marxists believe, by inexorable processes of historical necessity. A practical socialist policy takes off from the scientific analysis of the mode of exploitation in modern society, the consequences of this exploitation, and the practical long-term possibilities of removing it and instituting relations of production which will permit the utilisation and development of modern forces of production for purposes of the general welfare. It then takes into account what sort of political organisation and policy will be necessary to this end, and what sort of opposition it may expect to encounter.

As for "our ultimate political aim", this is not presented as "the Ideal State", but as the aim which follows from the scientific analysis of the actual human situation. It is presented as demonstrably practicable, and as demonstrably necessary, in view of the actual human situation.

Thus the question posed is not one of choosing between, on the one hand, the utopian aim of an "Ideal State", to realise which requires the violent suppression of the existing order, and on the other hand, the rational practice of "piecemeal social engineering", tinkering with existing institutions so as to alleviate hardships by trying to meet the claims of everyone concerned in them. The question is one of whether, on the one hand, to accept the existing mode of exploitation, or on the other hand, to examine what is wrong with it, what can be done to remove it, and what issues to tackle and what constructive proposals to make, step by step, in order to do so.

It is totally untrue, as stated in the *credo* of "social engineering", that revolutionary socialists aim only at "the realisation of abstract goods", whereas the "piecemeal" social engineers "rather aim at the elimination of concrete miseries". Communists "aim at the elimination of concrete miseries", and it is their consciousness of these "miseries" and of their roots in the existing system of exploitation, that makes them revolutionary socialists. We do not oppose capitalism in order to realise "abstract goods", but in order to "fight for the elimination of poverty by direct means". That which Dr. Popper misnames "social engineering", on the other hand, will allow "concrete miseries" to be eliminated only in so far as their elimination is compatible with maintaining capitalist exploitation. There is no occasion at all for Dr. Popper to admonish us: "Our fellow men have a claim to our help." We know they have. That is why we are in favour, for instance, of "erecting hospitals and schools of medicine" to the full extent necessary "to fight against epidemics and disease", and are not impressed by the admonitions of social engineers who tell us that the programme can be only a limited one because, meantime, we have to pay for the costs of fighting communism.

Dr. Popper advises us: "Do not aim at establishing happiness by political means." For, he goes on to explain, "it is my thesis that human misery is the most urgent problem of a rational public policy and that happiness is not such a problem. The attainment of happiness should be left to our private endeavours" (CR. 361).

It is possible "by political means" to remove the causes of poverty and war, and to provide everyone with the material means for useful work, education, leisure, comfort and the protection of health. Even that, of course, would still not suffice to "establish happiness"; for whether individuals are happy or not will still depend on how they treat each other, and how each behaves, in personal life. But all the same, it is pretty ridiculous (or possibly cold-blooded) to pose "human misery" as "the most urgent problem of a rational public policy", in opposition to "happiness". A politics which really tackles "the problem of human misery" is not indifferent to fostering the pursuit of happiness, and can certainly go further towards "establishing" it than one which is content simply to leave it "to our private endeavours". The social engineer clears a slum, builds a council estate, dumps people in it, and tells them: "Your happiness now depends on your private endeavours". Could not more be done to remove the frustrations and help establish the happiness of the council tenants?

Revolutionary change of the social system is not opposed to "reform". No politically serious socialist, and certainly no Communist, ever says: Either eradicate the social system, or else reform existing institutions—you cannot do both. We always propose and we always support such reforms as will benefit the people. We do this because "our fellow men have a claim to our help". It is not Communists who look on with indifference at preventable human miseries. Nor do we tolerate miseries because we believe that the more miserable people are the more likely they are to support our plan for a violent revolution. That is just one of Dr. Popper's smears. On the contrary, it is certain "social engineers" of the ruling classes who look on with indifference, believing that if these people can be kept down they can be kept out, and that it will be good for profits. Every Communist is a social reformer. And practical ardour for social reform is not in the least incompatible with seeking to eradicate the social system, but is rather a necessary quality of effective revolutionary leadership.

It was Lenin (in *What is to be Done*) who said that Communists should always be "the tribunes of the people". Those who hope to mobilise a great movement to transform society must know how to respond to every grievance and every demand of every section and, indeed, of every individual that composes the movement. A movement that will be able to unite and organise to achieve a new order of society must be composed of persons and organisations who will never take any imposition lying down, but who know how to better their condition and not let others worsen it. And those whom people will trust as leaders are those who have shown that both heart and mind are involved in protest against every deprivation and every injustice suffered by even the most insignificant or undeserving individual.

3. REFORM AND REVOLUTION

Revolutionary change of the social system is the alternative, not to reform, but to the policy of allowing only such reform as can be accomplished without jeopardising the profits of the ruling class.

According to Dr. Popper, "it is not so very difficult to reach agreement by discussion on what are the most urgent social reforms". So it is not difficult to get agreed the measures of "piecemeal social engineering". That is one of its great virtues, he says, for in this way "we can get somewhere by arguing . . . we can profit here from the attitude of reasonableness. We can learn by listening to concrete claims, by patiently trying to assess them as impartially as we can, and by considering ways of meeting them without creating worse evils" (CR. 361).

This, says Dr. Popper, "is a fact, and not a very strange fact". Certainly, it is "not a very strange fact" that agreement on some "urgent social reform" should sometimes be "not so very difficult", when, on the one hand, there would be a great deal of protest if the urgent need for reform were ignored and, on the other hand, the agreed reform impartially but generously acknowledges the "concrete claims" of capitalist vested interests. Thus, for example, there is general agreement in Britain today that something must be done to meet the housing situation. And although some disagreement is expressed as to the proportionate parts that private enterprise and public authorities should play in the housing programme, no very serious disagreements break out so long as rent, interest and profit are duly upheld. Housing may be, with a considerable measure of agreement, subsidised out of public funds, so long as the subsidy guarantees that the moneylenders shall be paid in full. So isn't that "reasonable"? Surely the rehousing of homeless families removes a positive evil, and creates no "worse evil", even if the condition for it is that vested interests shall get their rake off? And even though the job is done very slowly, and is interrupted whenever the government declares a "crisis", it is still claimed that this way of doing it is the best way. For the removal of the vested interests which obstruct an all-out effort to solve the housing problem could well prove a "worse evil", because they would object, government would have to suppress their objections, and that would be "dictatorship"; at all events, it would put an end to the desirable but "not very strange fact" of agreement.

In actual fact in capitalist society—and this, too, is "not very strange" —all "agreements", whether they concern such matters as social services or wages, hours, working conditions and holidays, are arrived at as accommodations between opposed interests—for instance, those of people wanting cheap and good houses, and those of moneylenders and landlords who want interest and rent; or those of workers wanting more real wages, and those of employers wanting more profits.

It may then be said—and, indeed, Dr. Popper does say so—that the fact that affairs get arranged through these sorts of accommodations means that the class struggle has been abated and is on the way to disappearance. But, on the contrary, *these accommodations demonstrate the continued existence of the class struggle, and are its outcome.*

First of all, it was the conduct of class struggle which led to the position where they could be made at all. If there were no class organisations of the working class, which have grown strong enough and fight hard enough to gain recognition, the ruling class would not be so accommodating. And secondly, what can be got depends on the complex balance of effective pressures behind the competing claims of competing class interests. If the working people want to gain more benefits, and stop vested interests from robbing them of them, they must fight more determinedly and harder.

Persons in ministries and offices drafting blueprints for making this or that improvement in this or that institution or service, and other persons sitting critically commenting on them in the London School of Economics, or getting on their hind legs in parliament, may imagine that they are, like wise and impartial legislators, performing judicious operations of piecemeal social engineering. But they are not in fact like engineers working out designs for a new bridge or, maybe, for strengthening one which is failing to stand up under the load of heavier traffic. They are seeking *to control people* and shape their social relations, and dealing not with mechanical but with social stresses; and what they can plan, and what actually happens to their plans, depends on the actual power that is exerted in the social institutions by conflicting class interests.

The occurrence of so-called "piecemeal social engineering" is only a particular contemporary manifestation of the class struggle between capital and labour, and its laws of operation are not those of engineering but of class struggle.

The fact is not very strange that, so long as the situation remains such that accommodations *can* be reached which do not vitally impair the accumulation of capital and which, at the same time, bestow benefits on labour, such accommodations will go on being reached. It has never happened, and is not likely to happen now, that an exploiting class will be removed from power so long as it is able to make substantial concessions to the interests of other classes. What goes on in the meantime is the pressure of the one class for those concessions, and the resistance of the other class to every infringement of its interests. The outcome is the expression of this immensely complex social interaction. It cannot be decided simply by reference to the blueprints of "social engineers". They delude themselves when they fancy that the backrooms where they have set up their drawing-boards have been miraculously transformed into engineering workshops strategically placed in the corridors of power, and that everyone outside is just waiting patiently for claims to be met.

The necessity for the eventual socialist solution of the contradictions of capitalism arises from the fact that capital cannot indefinitely go on in the same way exploiting labour whose forces of production are being continually revolutionised, and cannot indefinitely go on drawing raw materials and tribute from industrially underdeveloped dependencies. Social strains are unavoidable, and cannot but issue in revolutionary crises, when the ruling class can no longer go on ruling in the old way and is divided as to what to do, and the popular organisations are determined on a change which the rulers cannot concede. It is at such moments that the actual organisation and influence gained by revolutionary scientific socialism in the preceding years becomes decisive; and that the illusions of "social engineering" become manifest. They are revealed as no more than what Marx (analysing earlier class struggles in *The Eighteenth Brumaire of Louis Bonaparte*) called the "imbecility which holds those infected by it fast in an imaginary world and robs them of all sense, all memory, all understanding of the rude external world".

In "the rude external world" the fact which escapes the notice of all who dream of engineering a perpetual motion machine of reform by agreement is the fact (about which we shall have a lot more to say presently) that *control of political power* is in the hands of the big capitalist interests. *They* keep the power; and though they may discreetly keep it in reserve most of the time, it is there to be unmasked when occasion arises and exercised with authoritarian violence, both in foreign wars for the defence of capitalist profit and in repression at home. No schemes of social engineering can get round the fact that at some time or another this power will have to be challenged and overcome.

Marx is rather severely reproached by Dr. Popper for having written, in the Preface to *Capital*, that "when a society has discovered the natural law that determines its own movement, even then it can neither overleap the natural phases of its own evolution, nor shuffle them out of the world by a stroke of the pen. But this much it can do: it can shorten and lessen the birthpangs". He interprets this as meaning that Communists lack any policy based on working out on scientific principles what can be done for social betterment. For they believe that a violent revolution is historically inevitable and that therefore it is useless to attempt reforms and the only thing to do is by revolutionary propaganda and conspiracy to hasten the day of reckoning. This is "a peculiar variety of fatalism", he says, and as such scientifically untenable and unacceptable to "social engineers" (PH. 51).

But the scientific sense of Marx's statement is quite clear, and so is its truth.

Marx's fundamental discovery of "the natural law" governing social changes was the discovery of the universal limiting conditions of men's conduct of their social relations—much as fundamental discoveries of thermodynamics, for example, were discoveries of limiting conditions for the exchange of energy in physical systems, namely, that energy is conserved and entropy increases. Marx's fundamental discovery was that relations of production have to be adapted to forces of production. So what was he saying in the Preface to *Capital*? He was saying that to discover this law is not to discover how to abrogate it, how to "overleap" its limitations—any more than to discover the laws of thermodynamics is to discover how to abrogate them by constructing perpetual motion machines. But it *is* to discover what to expect to happen and how to act in concrete situations governed by the law—just as discoveries of thermodynamics are discoveries about how to make engines more efficient. Hence Marx said that when we have discovered that relations of production have to be adapted to forces of production, that does *not* enable us to contract out of the painful business of involvement in the processes of this adaptation, but it *does* enable us to work out ways of speeding them up and making them less painful.

The social circumstances we are in (so Marxism explains to us) are governed by universal laws of social development, and so valid expectations must be limited. Some things are possible, and other things are not. The indefinite and prosperous continuance of capitalism, free from revolutionary crises, is one of those that are not possible. On the other hand, if we are to develop and utilise the forces of production we have already got for social welfare, we must find how to bring into being relations of production within which production can be organised for welfare. It is up to us how long it takes and how much we suffer: by militant organisation and wise policy we can "lessen the birthpangs", but by no possible means can we dodge the issues, the crises and conflicts which the existing situation entails.

This concept that we cannot "overleap" the consequences of the law that production relations must be adapted to productive forces, but that we can "lessen the birthpangs" occasioned by their becoming adapted, makes both scientific and political good sense. For example, capitalism could be let develop into the final crisis of World War Three—but this is not inevitable, and we can work to prevent it. Again, capitalism could be let develop the automation of production under private enterprise to the point where it creates vast unemployment. It is possible that things will be let develop in the U.S.A., for example, to the point where there are millions of desperate displaced people without support and without hope, making chaos and bloodshed a certainty; but this need not happen if in good time organised labour, in an orderly way, takes over control of the situation.

The phrase "social engineering" is, all things considered, a pretty inept one. Those to whom Dr. Popper applies it are, if they can be called "engineers" at all, at all events remarkably innocent of scientific theory, like engineers who, when a few wheels start turning, think they have become masters of a perpetual motion machine. But if any sense is to be given to the expression, it is the policy of a united labour movement engaged in bringing into being and lessening the birth-pangs of a new social order, which deserves to be called "social engineering".

5

THE INSTITUTION OF POLITICAL POWER

I. INSTITUTIONS

Social engineering, according to Dr. Popper's conception, is concerned with institutions and their management. The social engineer does not directly deal with individuals, but he is both maintenance and construction engineer for institutions.

Institutions (says Dr. Popper) become amenable to rational scientifically directed social engineering operations when they are democratic. Non-democratic institutions cannot be engineered. For instance, social engineers entering the court of the Khalif Harun al-Rashid would have been liable to summary expulsion as unbelieving dogs, if no worse; their field of operation is in the democratic institutions of modern capitalist society, where they are not merely tolerated but rewarded. Social engineering is thus the product of democracy. It was the development of democratic institutions that made possible the rational practices of social engineering, instead of the crude methods of violence which prevailed in earlier times; and their continued development not only requires the services of social engineering, but will be wrecked if violent methods of smashing up institutions are chosen in their place.

Dr. Popper thus sees social engineering as the democratic method of conducting human affairs, in opposition to violence. "There are only two kinds of government institutions," he explains, "those which provide for a change of the government without bloodshed, and those which do not" (CR. 344). The former he calls democratic. If undemocratic types of institutions prevail, then, obviously, violence is the only means available for righting wrongs. "The use of violence", he concludes, "is justified only under a tyranny which makes reforms without violence impossible, and it should have only one aim, that is, to bring about a state of affairs which makes reforms without violence possible" (2–OS. 151).

These simple truths about democratic institutions are not, he charges, understood by Marxists. For, as we have already learned from him, "Marx . . . denounces the faith in a rational planning of social institutions as altogether unrealistic, since society must grow according to the laws of history and not according to our rational plans". The laws of history are those of the development of class struggles. Consequently "Marxists have been taught to think in terms not of institutions but of classes". But whereas "Marxists nowadays do not think in terms of institutions . . . rationalists, on the contrary, are more inclined to rely on institutions for controlling men. This is the main difference" (CR. 345).

Since, then, Dr. Popper says that Marxists are taught not to "think in terms of institutions", let us see how he himself teaches us to think in terms of them. For in this matter of teaching us how to "think in terms of institutions", he would have been well advised to attend to several large chunks of opaque matter in his own eye before concerning himself with motes in the eyes of his Marxist neighbours.

Human progress, says Dr. Popper, depends on the design and working of *institutions*. "For institutions, like levers, are needed if we want to achieve anything which goes beyond the power of our muscles. Like machines, institutions multiply our powers for good and evil. Like machines, they need intelligent supervision by someone who understands their way of functioning and, most of all, their purpose . . ." (1–OS. 67).

At the same time, the social engineer must remain cautiously aware of what is called "the human element" in institutions. He "cannot construct foolproof institutions, that is to say, institutions whose functioning does not very largely depend on persons: institutions, at best, can reduce the uncertainty of the personal element, by assisting those who work for the aims for which the institutions are designed, and on whose personal initiative and knowledge success largely depends" (PH. 66–7).

Democratic institutions are not only the means we can use for engineering social achievements, they also provide "checks" on what would otherwise be the irresponsible power of certain individuals or groups of individuals. "This leads to a new approach to the problem of politics," says Dr. Popper, "for it forces us to replace the question: Who should rule? by the new question: How can we so organise political institutions that bad and incompetent rulers can be prevented from doing too much damage?" (1–OS. 121).

Thus he concludes: "Just as the task of the physical engineer is to design machines and to remodel and service them, the task of the piecemeal social engineer is to design social institutions and to reconstruct and run those already in existence. . . . The piecemeal technologist or engineer recognises that only a minority of social institutions are consciously designed, while the vast majority have just 'grown', as the undesigned results of human actions. But however strongly he may be impressed by this important fact, as a technologist or engineer he will look upon them from a 'functional' or 'instrumental' point of view. He will see them as means to certain ends, or as convertible to the service of certain ends; as machines rather than as organisms" (PH. 64–5).

Although he admits that in the past "the vast majority have just grown", Dr. Popper asserts that institutions can be increasingly engineered once the practice of engineering them has been instituted. "Marx was quite right when he insisted that 'history' cannot be planned on paper," he assures us. "But *institutions* can be planned; and they are being planned" (2–OS. 143).

In the course of this instruction on how to "think in terms of institutions", Dr. Popper remarks, with justice, that "their construction needs some knowledge of social regularities which impose limitations upon what can be achieved by institutions. These limitations are somewhat analogous, for instance, to the law of conservation of energy, which amounts to the statement that we cannot build a perpetual motion machine" (1–OS. 67). He has very little to say, however, on this all-important topic of just what these "social regularities" are and in what way they "impose limitations". Surely, to "think in terms of institutions", this question needs looking into with care. That is exactly what Marxists have done. And if only Dr. Popper had done so, he too might have gained "some knowledge" of the "limitations upon what can be achieved by institutions". He says that, for Marxists, "society must grow according to the laws of history and not according to our rational plans". But what Marxists actually maintain is that "our rational plans" must take account of "the laws of history"—that is to say, of "social regularities which impose limitations upon what can be achieved by institutions". Marxists do not believe that plans for a democratic perpetual motion machine are rational.

Dr. Popper has very rightly observed that no social life can be carried on except through institutions of one sort and another. But when he teaches us to "think in terms of institutions" his lessons include no instruction about how institutions are instituted, under what conditions and limitations, or how one influences or limits another. The term itself is never clearly defined by him. "The term 'social institution' ", he tells us, "is used here in a very wide sense, to include bodies of a private as well as of a public character. Thus I shall use it to describe a business, whether it is a small shop or an insurance company, and likewise a school, or an 'educational system', or a police force, or a church, or a law court" (PH. 65). He then goes on to point out that the term bears an even "wider" sense than these examples would suggest, and tells us: "Language is a social institution. . . . Writing is a social institution. . . ." (PH. 154). Thus any product of men's getting together in society, which regulates social activity, from language to a small shop, is an institution. He attempts no sort of analysis of institutions, as to their different kinds and their inter-connections. And that being so, the best we may expect from him is the best he gives us—the solemn assurance that, while institutions "just grow" in some unspecified manner, and are never "foolproof", nevertheless some of them can be "planned", subject always to un-stated "limitations". If that is to "think in terms of institutions", then by all means let us try to "think in terms of classes" and find out what the limitations are.

We need not dispute that both languages and small shops are institutions—for, of course, if the term is used in a wide enough sense it can be made to cover both. But since the term is such a very "wide" one, how are we to "think in terms of institutions" without getting hopelessly muddled in the use of words? We must draw distinctions between institutions, in terms of their social functions, and examine how one set of institutions is conditioned by and grows out of another. That is what Marx did (although he seldom used the word "insti-tutions", which was not so much in vogue when he was writing). Here in Britain today the English language, the capitalist system, the Marylebone Cricket Club, the Oxford and Cambridge Boat Race, Harrods, British Railways, the Prices and Incomes Board, Parliament, the Board of Trade, the trade unions, political parties and the Secret Police are all social institutions. If we want to know how we can use our institutions, and what to do about them, distinctions must be drawn and connections traced. Dr. Popper has stressed, for example, the importance of making our institutions democratic. But the term "democratic" applies only to some institutions, and makes no sense at all in relation to others. For example, how could the English language be democratic? Or a small shop, for that matter?

As I have said, institutions, in the widest sense, are products of our getting together in society, and they regulate social activity. An institution is anything socially instituted. The sense of the verb "instituted" can best be demonstrated by examples. Thus for communication we use language, and also telephones. Both are social products, but a telephone is a material implement, whereas a language is not. The telephone is manufactured, and the language instituted. The material object, a telephone, is not an institution—but the language we use when we communicate by telephone is an institution; and so is the Post Office (or in the U.S.A. the private company) which instals and controls telephones. Institutions are not material things: they cannot be seen or touched or pointed at, like material things.

This non-material character of institutions is illustrated by the sort of explanations we have to offer when someone does not know what it is we are referring to when we refer to some given institution, and we explain it to him. Take the Oxford and Cambridge Boat Race, for example. To explain what "a boat" is, one must explain that it is a manufactured object which people can sit in and propel through the water. To explain what "the Boat Race" is, as an institution, is much more complicated. One must say: "Every year, at approximately the same date, two sets of eight young men, one set from Oxford and one from Cambridge, get into boats on the River Thames and propel themselves from Putney to Mortlake; they start when someone gives the signal, and the ones who arrive at Mortlake first are the winners." One can of course (in this instance) "see" the Boat Race—but not in the same sense as one can "see" the boats. The Boat Race itself is "seen" only in the sense that one sees particular crews engaging in activity regulated in accordance with the institution. The Boat Race is like a Platonic Idea manifesting itself in time—and so is language, the Post Office, and any other institution. But yet institutions are not "eternal objects" which manifest themselves in the material world, but social products, instituted by men.

The universal distinguishing feature of institutions is, that they have *rules*—conventional rules, definitive of each institution. People institute institutions when, for carrying out their various activities, they come to adopt certain rules of procedure—like the vocabulary and syntax of a language, or the rules of the Boat Race, or the multifarious conventions which govern the conduct of small shops or the Secret Police. Such rules generally get established by custom, as the activity develops, though they may also be, in certain cases, consciously formulated, agreed and promulgated. Very often, to begin with, they "just grow", then at a certain stage of growth they are formulated and promulgated (language itself is a case in point). That is why our social activities may be said to be "regulated" by our institutions.

In our social actions we use various material objects and material products for our purposes, in a way regulated by our institutions. Institutions with their rules of social behaviour are essential for social activities and the realisation of their purposes, for without this kind of regulation the activities could neither be conducted nor succeed. Indeed, all social activities are, and must be, institutionalised. There is not first an activity and then, later, an institution—but social activities only develop by developing the appropriate institutional regulation. Hence while one can, in words, distinguish a social activity and the institution for performing it, each is an abstraction apart from the other, and the concrete reality is the institutionalised activity.

Of course, separate individual activities are not always fully institutionalised. For example, a man enjoying himself in a boat on the Thames is not engaged in institutionalised activity like the crews in the Boat Race; though even *his* activity is institutionalised to some extent, since he probably has to hire the boat and return it within a stated time, and the motions he performs are those which have been instituted in the development of boating, and have to be learned by him in the school of Thames boating—different in many respects from that of, say, the Yangtse. It is *social* activity that is institutionalised; but so social is man that institutional rules are often obeyed in solitude, as when an Englishman exploring the jungle dresses for dinner.

Clearly, it is important to distinguish between, on the one hand, the rules enjoined by institutions and, on the other hand, the objective laws characteristic of material processes and the objective requirements for dealing with them. This is a distinction which, historically, people have found it hard to draw. Thus, on the one hand, we imagine ourselves to be bound by the rules of our institutions as by natural laws, and on the other hand, we imagine natural laws to have been instituted somehow or other (by God) for the regulation of natural processes. There is, however, a pretty close connection between the rules of institutions and objective laws. The institutional rules of an activity have to accord with the laws which limit the activity, so that we cannot simply make up and alter the rules in any way we like. The purely conventional rules of a language, for example, have to accord with the objective requirements of communication which govern speaking. Again, such an institution as the Board of Trade, in Britain, has to be conducted in accordance with the objective requirements of the economy. We could neither institute rules for language just as we please, nor regulate trade just as we please. Moreover, in so far as activities deal with material objects, they have to be regulated in accordance with the natural properties of the objects.

Institutions, then, are characterised by rules—rules which are themselves limited by the laws of the activities they regulate. In the second place, most institutions (but not all—languages, for example, are exceptions) require the construction of some sort of permanent material equipment for the purpose of carrying on the regulated activity. Thus, for example, many institutions are housed in buildings; others possess moveable equipment, such as the locomotives of British Railways or the cloaks and daggers of the Secret Police.

This sometimes leads to verbal confusion in talking about institutions, when the material equipment is identified with the institution itself. Thus the words "The Board of Trade" may be used to denote the building in which the Board of Trade operates, or "British Railways" to denote the totality of railway lines and rolling stock. Again, the so-called social engineer is often very much concerned with material equipment—as when the educational reformer calls for the building of new schools, and for their architectural design in accordance with his recommendations about how the education inside them should be conducted. Again, he may call for "the taking over" of material equipment, as when he calls for his own nominees to be installed in positions where they will manage its use in different ways from that in which it was managed before.

This general definition of institutions makes clear, then, a point in which Dr. Popper is interested, from the point of view of "social engineering", when he asks how institutions can change, or be changed. In general, institutions are changed when the rules are changed—including cases where new material equipment is introduced, necessitating change of rules, and where change of rules necessitates provision of new equipment. It also makes clear that there are, as Dr. Popper recognises but abstains from too much inquiry into, definite limitations both to how existing institutions can be changed and to what new or changed institutions can, in given circumstances, be introduced.

In considering the development of institutions, as means and regulators of human social activity, and what can and cannot be done by way of purposively developing them in the future, it is evidently of great importance to consider both the character and objective laws of interconnection and development of human social activities, and the modes of interconnection and interdependence of institutions in regulation of social activities. This is dialectics: fitting abstractions together in the concrete picture of how a process actually proceeds. It is in fact what Marx did, and Dr. Popper does not do—although Dr. Popper says that Marx teaches us not "to think in terms of institutions" and that he himself is overthrowing Marx by performing an "institutional analysis". From a very exact analysis of the laws of development of institutions Marx arrived at a practical political programme for changing them. It is from trite and empty phrases about "institutions" that Dr. Popper arrives at equally vapid generalisations about "social engineering".

Marx examined the connections and interdependence of institutions as they are formed for socially necessary purposes of human activity. He did not just talk about "institutions" in general, drawing no distinction between languages and small shops, or between boat races and police forces. His analysis showed that the condition for all other human activities is the performance of social production, so that the techniques of production have to be instituted and, as an essential requisite first for social labour and then for everything else people do together, languages. To carry out production with the given techniques, with the given forces of production, men have to enter into corresponding relations of production—which therefore have also to be instituted, so that an economic structure and property relations are instituted. Then follows the institution of all the common activities of everyday life, from the acquisition and exchange of products to sports and the pursuit of arts and sciences. Lastly, to hold society together, there must be institutions of education, propaganda and management —schools, churches, legal institutions, government and political institutions, equipped where necessary with means of material coercion.

2. INSTITUTIONS AND CLASSES

The all-important "social regularity" which Dr. Popper overlooks when he lectures us about social engineering and institutions, and to which opacities in his intellectual retina render him quite blind, is the fundamental one which Marx discovered, namely, that to maintain and continue our social existence we have to enter into relations of production corresponding to our forces of production.

Unless we instituted arrangements to carry on social production we could have no social life at all. In other words, the whole of social life is lived on the basis of having entered into and instituted definite relations of production. The production relations are the basis or "foundation" of all the institutions for regulating how we use or enjoy the various material means and mental abilities which we derive from having engaged in social production. As Marx said (in the Preface to the *Critique of Political Economy*): "The sum total of relations of production constitutes the economic structure of society, the real foundation on which rises a legal and political superstructure and to which correspond definite forms of social consciousness. The mode of production of material life conditions the social, political and intellectual life process in general."

Relations of production include, as Marx went on to say, "property relations". To enter into relations of production is to enter into regulative arrangements of production and distribution such that both means of production and products are treated as the property of definite persons or groups of persons. The institution of production relations is thus the institution of property—and so Marx called the institution of property "but a legal expression of the same thing".

Incidentally, property and all other institutional arrangements of society are dependent, not only on the development of techniques of social production, but on language. People had to speak, because social techniques of production involve this sort of communication. The institution of language then supplies the necessary means of communication for instituting everything else, including property. Indeed, every human attribute is dependent on language—labour, thought, property, religion, the sciences and arts, the whole development of social life and of the individual personality which is the product of social life.

As Dr. Popper has said, many institutions "just grow". That is to say, they are not begun, nor thereafter are they changed, as a result of anyone thinking up the rules and inventing the equipment, and everyone else then agreeing to do as he proposes. Rather do people enter into certain arrangements, and modify them, from the necessities of their social life, in accordance with what is possible and what is necessary for them to do in view of their productive forces. Marx devoted a great deal of attention to the question of how relations of production, and property relations, "grow". People have entered into them, as he said, "independent of their will". And so these institutions have appeared to the people who have regulated their lives by them as either natural or God-given laws of life, since they themselves never deliberately instituted them.

Property, Marx showed, is derivative from division of labour in social production. With the very primitive techniques of small groups engaged in hunting and food-gathering everyone had much the same things to do, and such division of labour as there was came from the natural differences of the two sexes. The development of production techniques, such as began first of all with agriculture, the domestication of animals, and the development of various crafts, brought increasing division of labour; and this division of labour led to means of production and products becoming allocated as the property of this or that person or group of persons. "The various stages of development in the division of labour", wrote Marx and Engels in *The German Ideology* (I, 1), "are just so many different forms of ownership; i.e. the existing stage in the division of labour determines also the relations of individuals to one another with reference to the materials, instruments and products of labour."

Property relations have been, in their development, *class* relations. The division of labour has given rise to property, and the development of property to the division of society into classes. Classes are distinguished by "the place they occupy in social production and, consequently, the relation in which they stand to the means of production". Lenin, to whom we owe this brief definition of class distinctions, also elaborated the definition of "social class" at more length: "Classes are large groups of people which differ from each other by the place they occupy in an historically definite system of social production, by their relation (in most cases fixed and formulated in laws) to the means of production, by their role in the social organisation of labour, and, consequently, by the dimensions of the social wealth that they obtain and their method of acquiring their share in it. Classes are groups of people one of which may appropriate the labour of another, owing to the different places they occupy in the definite system of social economy" (*A Great Beginning*).

The development of property divides society into classes when some acquire monopoly-ownership of means of production of such a kind as enables them to exploit the labour of others in definite ways. In the total social process of division of labour in production and distribution each class fulfils its role, whether of labour or of management. But the relations of classes do not constitute a harmonious system in which the function of one requires and complements the function of another (as in Plato's ideal Republic, where "justice" consisted in each class being content to perform its proper role, or in the fable of Menenius Agrippa in Shakespeare's *Coriolanus*). On the contrary, these relations are antagonistic. Exploiters and exploited continually dispute their share of the social wealth as well as the method of acquiring it, and so do exploiters with rival methods of exploitation.

Classes are not institutions, but groups of people who have become differentiated as a result of the institution of property and of class relations. Thus the regulation and management of production in accordance with the institutional development of property relations—which have developed in a definite way because of the necessities imposed upon the regulation of production by definite developments of the forces of production—has divided society into social classes, with some exploiting others. As a result of the division into classes, distinct and antagonistic "class interests" have arisen. For institutions of property, with resulting class divisions, which have brought material benefits to one class have brought the opposite to another. Hence one class has had an interest in carrying on institutions in one way, and another class in carrying them on in another way, or in doing away with them and substituting different institutions.

Institutions of all kinds are instituted, carried on and changed by people—and so, in a society divided into classes, *the instituting, carrying on and change of the social institutions is done by people with divergent antagonistic class interests*. Some classes are interested in preserving the existing class relations, and in setting up and managing other institutions (for example, for government, for enjoyment of leisure and, in general, for all kinds of social purposes) on the basis of preserving the property relations; whereas other classes have contrary interests.

What happens to institutions, and what is done with their aid, is decided, naturally enough, by the aggregate of interactions of all the persons concerned. Hence naturally enough (indeed, inevitably) *what happens to institutions in class-divided society, and what is done with their aid, is decided as the outcome of class struggles*. And this is equally true whether, in given circumstances, class struggles result in fundamental changes in institutions, or whether their temporary issue proves to be some sort of accommodation or compromise. The basic issue of class struggle is always that of preserving or changing property relations. The classes dispute their share of the social wealth and the method of acquiring it. In this dispute *they form specific class-institutions of their own*, *and likewise dispute over the management and character of all sorts of other institutions.*

Classes are formed by the divisions introduced by property relations. They develop and consolidate their existence as classes by the development of institutions to preserve and push forward their interests in opposition to other classes, and of definite modes of consciousness or "ideologies" in which their collective determination to do so, and belief in the rightness of so doing, is expressed. Thus the modern working class, for example, was formed as a result of the divisions introduced by the relations of capital and wage-labour; it developed and consolidated its existence as a class by setting up working-class organisations and developing corresponding modes of consciousness.

These are the conclusions scientifically drawn by Marx. We can now judge, therefore, whether it is true to say, as Dr. Popper has said, that "Marxists have been taught to think in terms not of institutions but of classes". The implied disjunction is false. To think of social activities, as one is bound to do, and as Marx did, "in terms of institutions", is to think of them "in terms of classes", since the people who set up institutions, and keep them going, are divided into classes. To think of any institutions connected with property and its administration otherwise than "in terms of classes" is to think of them in abstraction from the people who institute and use them, and from the actual social circumstances in which they institute and use them. Dr. Popper may favour that kind of metaphysical abstraction, and make out that when people are divided into classes they can nevertheless regulate their social activities through institutions as if they were not divided into classes; but we who have paid some attention to what Marx had to teach about dialectics are able to spot this false abstraction, and recognise how the categories of "class" and "institution" are *connected* in the actual concrete development of social activity.

Classes are, we may note, and as Marx demonstrated, *derivative* from the development of relations of production, or the institution of property. Having, as a result of the division of labour consequent upon development of productive forces, instituted property relations which divide society into classes, people have thereafter been engaged in class struggles, and have changed their institutions only in the course of and as the outcome of class struggles. To listen to Dr. Popper on "the class struggle" one would be led to imagine, however, that for Marx the class struggle was some sort of fundamental law of society— so that one must "think in terms not of institutions but of classes".

But on the contrary, classes and class struggles are merely derivative from certain temporary historically-constituted types of social institutions. Let us find how to get rid of these types of institutions and we shall have got rid of the class struggle. As a result of his paying no attention to the scientific analysis of class struggles as actually derivative from the institution of property, Dr. Popper's own exposition is most inconsistently and curiously divided between imagining that classes have already disappeared, so that capitalist institutions can be managed as though there were no class struggle at all, and imagining that class-division is so necessary a feature of all human society that "a classless society" is "a utopia".

Revolutionary changes in institutions, that is to say, the ousting of one form of exploitation by another or, in socialist revolution, of all exploitation, are made necessary, as Marx showed, by the development of productive forces. It is evident enough that, in Europe for example, the sorts of improvements in agricultural techniques which took place under feudalism not only were not but could not have been effected on the slave estates of the ancient Roman Empire, and that the later developments of industrial techniques which took place under capitalism could not have been effected so long as feudal relations hampered them. To make these things possible great institutional changes had to be effected. And these changes were effected as a result of long and, indeed, bloody struggles, in which one interest in the acquiring of wealth overcame another. Ruling classes succumbed, and institutions became radically altered, only when the former had been sufficiently weakened and divided as a result of their inability successfully to manage the existing economy through the existing institutions. Revolutions, necessary for the development of the social forces of production, are brought about as a consequence of clashes between people interested in different ways of acquiring their share of the social wealth.

Today *the necessity of socialist revolution is deduced from the fact that the full development of modern forces of production, including the full employment of all human, technological and scientific resources, and the full enjoyment of the possible benefits, is not possible so long as capitalist property relations prevail. Once again the institutional changes that are necessary cannot be engineered except through the sort of "engineering" effected by class struggles.* Dr. Popper (echoing the spurious wisdom of other bourgeois sages of greater antiquity) maintains that "a revolution" is a sort of unnecessary catastrophe, brought about as an interruption in orderly progress by some explosion of passions or conspiracy of bloody-minded agitators, which could have been avoided had the rulers been wiser. After the destructive anarchy of a revolution, order has eventually to be restored again and affairs brought back to normal —and such progress as may then be achieved could have been achieved just as well, and probably much better, without a revolution. This is to overlook the fact that the institutional changes effected by revolution were necessary, and could only be effected by class struggle and the decisive overcoming of one interest by another. Opposing "social engineering" to revolution, Dr. Popper tells us that "only by planning, step by step, for institutions to safeguard freedom, especially freedom from exploitation, can we hope to achieve a better world" (2–OS. 143). But to "safeguard freedom from exploitation" it would first be necessary to have instituted freedom from exploitation, that is to say, to have instituted socialist relations of production, that is to say, to have "engineered" a socialist revolution.

3. CLASSES AND POLITICAL POWER

Human social activity is, one need hardly stress, a very complex thing, and has got more complex as civilisation has developed. This complexity is due not simply to the multiplication of activities but to the corresponding multiplication of institutions. For every social activity is regulated in one way or another and so has its institutions. As activities have multiplied, so there has developed activity the object of which is to direct, organise and control activities, to administer and to manage, and so also institutions of direction, organisation, control, administration and management.

It is always as well to bear in mind, when talking about institutions, that they are of many distinct types and that what may sensibly be predicated of one type makes no sense if predicated of another. Statements about "all institutions" or "institutions in general" are, therefore, often merely nonsensical. When Dr. Popper lectures us about "social engineering" he is evidently specially concerned with *institutions of management*. The special character of such institutions is expressed in the fact that certain persons are "in charge" of them, "hold office" in them, and so on—statements which make no sense at all applied to other types of institution. With these institutions there enters into social life the element known as "authority" and "power". And with this we must be concerned if we are to talk practical sense about "social engineering" to "plan step by step institutions to achieve a better world".

Authority or power has sometimes been understood by some rather simple-minded sociologists (including Duhring, whom Engels criticised, but not, of course, including Dr. Popper) as consisting simply in the possession by some persons of material means for intimidating and bossing others. Thus the man with the big stick is the man of power, and the origin of power is explained in a very simple way by the theory that one day long ago some people armed themselves with big sticks while the others weren't looking. Power, however, is developed in society by the development of institutions of management, and is exercised through those institutions and in accordance with their rules. This fact is expressed in our language by the virtual equivalence of "power" with "authority". Even tyrants, against whom Dr. Popper inveighs so much, are not able to seize power simply by beating other people over the head, but only by achieving authority in social institutions and "planning and constructing" special institutions of their own for the exercise of their power.

An important feature of the relation of institutions of management and government to other institutions is that changes in the latter are often effected through the agency and by the authority of the former. Thus, for example, changes in instituted propery arrangements may be made through the agency of legislation adopted and executed by government institutions. On a lesser scale, changes in the rules of cricket may be made through the agency of such a governing body as the Marylebone Cricket Club. On the other hand, the power of such agencies is not unlimited. They cannot effect any changes they like, but only those which conditions permit and which they can get people to accept. And at the same time, changes taking place in the sum of social activities, and particularly the development of class struggles, often demand and lead to considerable changes in the constitution and operation of power.

The limitations of instituted power take the form that there are not only some things those in power cannot do but other things they are obliged to do. This applies to the power of tyrants and dictators equally with that of democratically instituted authorities. And it applies equally whether the powers concerned be the supreme powers of government or the lesser powers exercised in, say, women's institutes or village cricket clubs. Every office is subject to obligations and restrictions. In a cricket club, for example, the pitch must be kept in condition, the games organised, and funds raised. The club committee is obliged to attend to such matters, since they are objective conditions for playing cricket. Somewhat similar considerations apply to governments. And, in either case, if those in authority neglect obligations or seek to exceed their mandate, their power is either lost at once or begins to decrease. Thus Engels observed that, even in the case of "despotic" governments, "the exercise of a social function was everywhere the basis of political supremacy . . . political supremacy has existed for any length of time only when it fulfilled its social functions. However great the number of despotic governments which rose and fell in India and Persia, each was fully aware that its first duty was the general maintenance of irrigation throughout the valleys, without which no agriculture was possible" (*Anti-Duhring*, Part II, Chapter 4).

According to the scientific way Marx thought about institutions, a government or a state is a highly specialised type of institution (or rather a complex of specialised institutions), evolved subject to the requirements set by the mode of production. The specialised function of governing, performed through governments or state institutions, is, clearly, a case of division of labour, a product of the social development of division of labour. In primitive conditions, where the institution of tribal meetings and the leading role of headmen and suchlike suffices for directing and organising the simple communal life, specialised institutions of government are unknown. It is where division of labour has led not merely to a multiplicity of specialised individual activities which need co-ordination but to the institution of private property in means of production, and consequently to class divisions and antagonism of class interests, that the specialised kind of overall social management which is done by government institutions becomes necessary. At that stage these institutions are established, with certain individuals becoming governors, office-holders and rulers. The multiplication of diverse and interdependent social activities and functions, each regulated and directed by its appropriate institutions, makes necessary the institution of a supreme power which will make as secure as possible the general conditions within which they can all develop; and at the same time the antagonisms entailed by property relations and class divisions make necessary the institution of a power strong enough to hold conflicts in check and prevent them from disrupting the social order.

It is obvious that when the instituted relations of production are such that a comparatively few men of property are able to exploit the toiling majority, such a social order could not (human nature being what it is, as Thucydides used to say) last very long unless the state institutions served to uphold the property relations and hold back or punish any who might combine to resist exploitation. *Whenever and wherever a social order has been instituted based on the exploitation of man by man, it has included state institutions which serve to maintain that exploitation and, therefore, the interests of the principal exploiting class.* It has endured only so long as such institutions endured, and has fallen only when its state institutions have succumbed either to internal revolution or external attack or a combination of both.

Such, in its most general terms, is the Marxist theory of the origin of the state. Dr. Popper protests, with his customary vigour, that one cannot deduce conclusions about what can or cannot be done with something *now* from a theory of origins. States may have *originated* to uphold exploitation; but that does not necessarily imply that the social engineer *today*, who wishes to "plan institutions to safeguard freedom from exploitation", must lead a revolutionary attack on the existing institutions of government—for whatever the origin of these institutions in ancient society, they may have changed fundamentally in the interim period. That is, of course, quite true. Nor are Marxists quite so stupid as to deduce conclusions about "the essence" of government institutions housed today on the banks of the Thames from hypotheses about the origins of those set up thousands of years ago on the Tigris and Euphrates.

The point of inquiring into origins is that such inquiries throw light on functions. To propound a theory about how government activity and its state institutions originated out of the multiplication and diversification of human activities and relations consequent upon the development of social production (which is what Marx did) is to demonstrate *the social functions which state power has fulfilled and to which its institutions have been adapted.* So far as the present day is concerned, the question to settle is the factual question of whether or not state power is still required to fulfil, and still fulfils, analogous functions. Since capitalism continues to be based on the exploitation of man by man, and class struggle of exploited with exploiters continues, Marx concluded (and his conclusion continues to be verified) that in capitalist society *state power continues to exercise the function of preserving the social order with its relations of exploitation.* He therefore concluded that those who wish to get rid of exploitation, and to "plan institutions to safeguard freedom from exploitation", should carefully examine the existing state institutions in order to ascertain just how they function to preserve exploitation. Having ascertained that, they can work out what to do in order to stop this function from being exercised.

As for Dr. Popper's "social engineers", if they really want to "plan a better world" they ought at least to make some inquiry into what can be done about those institutions which confer powers to preserve a worse world. But that inquiry would upset Dr. Popper's utopian hopes of "agreement", for the powers in question are not likely to agree to abdicate without a struggle. He prefers to stick to his airy-fairy generalisations about "institutions in general".

According to Dr. Popper, the great superiority of a democratic system of government over a tyranny or dictatorship lies in the elaboration of institutional mechanisms for *controlling* office-holders and getting rid of them if they fail to give satisfaction. A bad tyrant like a bad prime minister can be ejected—but only by violence, whereas there are institutional provisions for changing the prime minister by constitutional means without violence. We may wholeheartedly agree that democratic government does possess this advantage, and that accordingly the evolution of democratic institutions is progress in the arts of civilised living. All the same, we should qualify our assent to Dr. Popper's jubilation over the perfection of our government institutions by asking what particular class interests these institutions have been evolved to promote, and what safeguards they include for the promotion of class interests. If "to achieve a better world" requires other interests to be promoted in opposition to those chiefly promoted by the existing institutions of government, our concern must be not so much to preserve our institutions as to change them—to remove safeguards for one set of interests and institute safeguards for another, to remove provisions to ensure that one set of interests are always satisfied and institute provisions to satisfy another. Precisely that is the political programme of the Communist Party.

One complaint of Dr. Popper against the Communist Party is that Marx has taught it to "think in terms not of institutions but of classes". But the great contribution of Marx to scientific thinking about institutions lay in his demonstration of the ways in which *classes secure and promote their interests through the agency of institutions, and particularly of government institutions.*

It is a commonly held view, amongst those who do not go so far as to deny that class interests have an important influence in government (and, to do him justice, Dr. Popper should perhaps be included amongst them), that the function of government is to hold a kind of balance between class interests—to ensure that each interest is satisfied so far as is possible without injuring others. This view appears to receive confirmation in the custom of contemporary governments in the case, for example, of industrial disputes, when they generally invite each side to the Ministry of Labour in an effort to achieve a compromise. A less pleasing version of this theory of government is the view that governments retain power by playing off one interest against another (according to Charles II this was the secret of royal power in his own merry reign). The essential tenet of all such theories is that the government is not itself the instrument of any sectional interest (or if it is, it is a "bad" government), but that its function is to maintain law and order in the general interest of everyone—of "the people", "the community" or "the nation". Dr. Popper's view is evidently that, although in the bad old days governments were often far from disinterested, democracy as instituted in Great Britain and the United States of America has today actually achieved, or very nearly achieved, this object.

The falsification of such theories in the case of every social order based on the exploitation of man by man, which includes contemporary capitalism, is ensured by the fact that, *to preserve the basic property relations and to direct affairs within the framework they provide, the government has always got to uphold the essential interest of the exploiting against the exploited classes.* This function of contemporary capitalist governments is, indeed, demonstrated clearly enough in the case of industrial disputes, cited above. If the workers won't accept a compromise acceptable to the employers, the government always proceeds to assist the employers in coercing them to accept it. Otherwise, as the spokesmen of the government always tell us, the very fabric of society, and the essential welfare of the community as a whole, would suffer. This function of governments is ensured by the fact that powerful well-established institutions exist to ensure that governments *do* function in that way.

In general, authority, with the exercise of power, is instituted to serve a social function, to direct, organise and control certain social activities for certain purposes. Office-holders and persons of authority possess power on the condition that they fulfil their social function. The power they exert is the power socially instituted for preserving certain social relations and organising social activity within them, in which not only the office-holders but numerous other people, over whom the office-holders exert authority, have a direct interest.

Even a tyrant must, if his power is to survive, take care of the obligations which his office entails to definite social interests. The successful tyrant is always, in certain matters of key social importance, a very conscientious person: he looks after irrigation works, for example, or he promotes trade and industry. Unconscientious tyrants (like several Roman emperors) have usually come to a sticky end. Today, in democratic capitalist countries, there have been evolved elaborate systems of institutional checks and counterchecks which ensure not only that office-holders carry out their functions to the satisfaction of capitalist interests, but that only persons of requisite social outlook and allegiance shall be selected for office, while the unreliable are weeded out. In the democratic government of Britain, for example, this is provided for not (as is often suggested) simply by periodic elections, but by the party system, and the elaborate processes of behind-the-scenes jockeying by which civil servants influence ministers and industrial and financial interests influence civil servants and party executives.

Of great importance, therefore, are the institutional mechanisms whereby, in the case of any exercise of power (whether it be that of a club committee, an oriental despotism, or a democratic government), the persons of authority are selected, kept in line, restricted in their exercise of power, and made to fulfil their functions and carry out their obligations to those whose interest is served by their activity.

Class interests are asserted through institutions. This does not mean that all institutions promote exclusively class interests, for obviously they do not: it means that *wherever there is a class interest there are institutions to promote it.* It is quite true that the numerous individuals who compose a class do not one and all devote themselves to furthering the common class interest, since many individual causes lead individuals to pursue aims irrelevant to or conflicting with their class interests. But *in the aggregate of social activities* class interests get affirmed. The existence of a common class interest leads to institutions being formed to promote it, and these exert much greater power than belongs to institutions which serve only the eccentric aims of other groups of individuals. Thus in Britain today the Conservative Party is a far more powerful institution than, say, the Anti-vaccination League or the Lord's Day Observance Society, and the Federation of British Industries than, say, the Canine Defence League.

I have already observed that classes are developed and consolidated by the development of institutions to preserve and push forward their interests, in opposition to other classes. A class may be said to be powerful to the extent to which there has been established a system of institutions through which its interests are effectively promoted. When these include key institutions of government, the class concerned may be accurately described as "the ruling class". Under such circumstances, *state or political power effectively belongs to that class*—as it effectively belongs to the capitalist class in capitalist countries today, democratic as some of them may be.

"Classes never rule," says Dr. Popper. "The rulers are always certain persons" (CR. 345). It would be difficult to imagine a more flagrant example of Dr. Popper's illogical habit of posing false antitheses. Of course "rulers are always persons". If I am asked, for example, who is the prime minister of Britain today (1967), I answer: Mr. Harold Wilson. Because as a Marxist I am of opinion that the capitalist class is the ruling class, I would not suggest that the capitalist class is the prime minister, but only that the prime minister is under the thumb of the capitalist class. Clearly, the sense in which a class rules is different from that in which an individual rules by virtue of his holding high office. The prime minister in Britain holds the highest office. But the government institutions of Britain are so contrived (not as a result of anyone's plot but of a long process of historical growth and class struggle) that there are hundreds of institutional links whereby the capitalist class is able to prevent the appointment to high office of persons unreliable from the point of view of its class interest, and to ensure that those who wield power shall exert it in one way and not in another. That is how the capitalist class rules. If and when this complex institutional mechanism is broken, the capitalist class will no longer be the ruling class. Mr. Wilson, although he sometimes calls himself a socialist, does not even want to break it—nor could he, just on his own. For that there is required the concerted efforts of a great many people, united in institutions which promote other class interests.

Instituted power is always tied up with the preservation and promotion of definite interests. This is as true of many lesser institutions (societies, clubs and such-like) as it is of state power and governments. Those who want to make a change are always up against a dead weight of traditional resistance. They often put this down to the obstinacy and thick-headedness of individuals—but it is more than that, it is the resistance of institutions geared to one interest to the promotion of another. In face of this, individuals, even those in office, may well feel helpless: "I would so much like to do something else, but I'm not allowed to." *To make a change another interest has got to organise effectively enough to break the links of power with the former interest.*

Marx's class approach, teaching us to think of government institutions concretely in terms of classes, and not to think of them in the abstract, abstracted from the promotion of aggregate class interest, teaches us that the capitalist order of society survives, and can only survive, thanks to the established institutional arrangements whereby the capitalist interest is served and preserved through the power of the state. To break the fetters which capitalist relationships impose on social production for social welfare it is necessary to develop working-class organisation in resistance to the instituted power, to the point where power passes into the hands of the working class. This means that not only must persons be put into power who are persons of socialist allegiance and with the will to execute a socialist programme, but that the institutions of power must themselves be altered and replaced, to the extent that the entire machinery of government is geared to instituting socialist relations instead of preserving capitalist ones, and its former links with capitalist class organisations are broken and different links consolidated.

4.   THE EXECUTIVE POWER OF THE STATE

In his book *The Origin of the Family, Private Property and the State* (Chapter 9), Engels described a "state" as a "power, arisen out of society, but placing itself above it". Its first "distinguishing characteristic", he continued, is that "the state is distinguished by the grouping of its members on a territorial basis"; a state holds sway over a definite territory. Its second characteristic is "the institution of a public force" which "consists not merely of armed men, but also of material appendages, prisons and coercive institutions of all kinds". Within the territory of the state, therefore, the officers of the state, who are "in possession of the public power", act as "officials of society standing above society".

Marxism recognises very clearly, therefore, that a state, as an instituted system of management and government, has to include not only an organisation of *administration* but an organisation of *coercion*. Of course, with the growing complexity of social activity and social relations, modern states have come to provide a number of social services, to undertake a number of specifically economic functions, and to employ a very large number of officials for these purposes only. However, what remains essential for the existence of the state and of its power is the same as what has always been essential for any state— "the institution of a public force", a coercive apparatus, with its command and administration. As Engels said in the chapter quoted, this public force first became necessary, and has been necessary ever since, on account of the appearance of class antagonisms within society. "In order that these antagonisms, classes with conflicting economic interests, shall not consume themselves and society in fruitless struggle, a power, apparently standing above society, has become necessary to moderate the conflict and keep it within the bounds of 'order'." There must be corps of armed men, prisons, effective material means to intimidate, coerce and punish, and a group of persons in command of these, so as to preserve the social order from any individuals or body of individuals whose activities threaten to disrupt it.

In a number of studies of what were then contemporary or fairly recent events, Marx showed how in the course of the bourgeois revolution (by which is meant that series of events in which capitalist relations of production and democratic rights were instituted) the administrative, judicial and coercive apparatus of the state was immensely strengthened. The building of such a strong centralised apparatus was already beginning under the Absolute Monarchy. Today it is obvious that, compared with anything at the disposal of ancient despotisms or feudal states, the modern civil service, judiciary, army and police is an immensely powerful force. This tightly-knit, centralised, well armed and seemingly permanent force has become attached to the service of capital by thousands of ties of sentiment and interest; and it has acquired a permanence, stability and continuity independent of the comings and goings of ministries and governments.

Marx was, of course, not the only observer to have noted this phenomenon. Balzac, that close student of the bourgeois revolution to whose acumen Marx owed a good deal, observed it before him. At the end of his novel *Les Petits Bourgeois* the hero joins the Secret Police (but do not ask for it at the library in the expectation of reading the adventures of a prototype James Bond); and the Chief of Police then congratulates him as a new recruit to that force "whose influence the last half-century has daily increased . . . to whom all governments, as they fall one on top of the other like houses of cards, come to ask for safety and for the power to rebuild their future . . . Governments pass, societies perish or dwindle, but we—*we* dominate all things; the police is eternal."

I dare say those responsible for "security" in the British State today are not personally gifted with such powers of clear expression; but they could well talk in exactly the same way as they watch the rise and fall of successive Conservative and Labour governments.

In *The Eighteenth Brumaire of Louis Bonaparte* (Chapter 7) Marx remarked on the growth of an "executive power with its enormous bureaucratic and military organisation" which, at every stage in its efforts to establish or preserve security for capital investment, the bourgeoisie has "found itself compelled to strengthen". In times of weakness or danger this organisation is there to take command, independent of any democratic forms, for the purpose of preserving law and order. And ministers holding temporary elected office, while nominally the masters of the whole organisation, have left it intact to work on, administering and protecting the social system based on exploitation of labour; or, if they interfered too much, they have been thrown out of office. The machine works on while its masters come and go. And to change over to a Biblical metaphor, if they don't suit it, it spews them forth.

Marx pointed out, and what he then observed has continued to happen, that throughout a series of economic developments and of changes in the institutions of political power, the increasing activity and organisation of the working people, though playing a great part in all the events, did not prevent the growth of the "enormous bureaucratic and military organisation" which sustains capitalism. Indeed, protests and demands made it strengthen itself in order to cope with them; and of late years, as labour organisations have been consolidated, it has been further strengthened and perfected by including machinery for labour consultation and conciliation. Marx concluded: "All revolutions perfected this machine instead of smashing it." But if the exploitation of labour is ever to be ended, then instead of allowing this organisation of executive power to be strengthened and perfected *the working class must use the power of its own organisation to smash it up, and institute a differently constituted and oriented executive power.*

In a modern capitalist society there is an immense complex of interlocked institutions through which affairs are conducted and managed. To mention only the most indispensable ones, there are the institutions of industry, of finance, of education and other social services, all of them with their own commands, and with control working on them both from "above" and from "below". There are elected assemblies, councils and committees, and manifold arrangements for consultation. And the preservation and working of this entire institutional complex depends on the activity and vigilance of the central state institutions of administration and compulsion. Here is the apex of the power structure. Controls of power work from lower bodies to higher, and from higher to lower. From this centralised top organisation control is exerted from above over all the rest of the structure. The power so instituted is used both to direct and to protect the whole.

How is this top organisation of power itself controlled? The whole institutional structure has developed on the basis of the development of capitalist relations of production, and in this development there are instituted close ties between the "bureaucratic and military organisation" of the state and the top ranks of industry and finance in control of "economic power". As capital has become concentrated in fewer and bigger organisations, so has this tie-up become more firm.

In such a country as Britain, for example, the commands of the civil service and the armed forces, together with the police and judiciary, have grown up over long years as protectors and executive officers of capital. It is not the case, of course, that certain tycoons in the City of London give the orders and these commands simply obey them. It is not as simple as that. And often it is the other way round. The system represents in fact a system of checks and balances, where those who occupy the corridors of power in Whitehall and those in the City both consult each other and manoeuvre against each other as individuals. But the institutional tie-up is complete, and is far stronger than any agreement or disagreement between individuals who hold office either in the state machine or in the organisation of big business. It is an immensely strong impersonal force working for the preservation and profit of monopoly capital, which thus appears as an impersonal power far greater than any individual tycoon or government official.

To break this tie-up, to take the bureaucratic and military organisation into democratic control, under the leadership of labour organisations, and use it to administer the change-over from capitalist to socialist relations of production, would amount to "smashing" the existing organisation. Dr. Popper and others, including the leaders of the present

(1967) Labour Government in Britain, say the organisation is efficient, so the sensible course is to work democratically to make it more efficient in the service of the common welfare—not to "smash" it. But a bureaucratic and military organisation, though often called "a machine" (and Marx himself used this word for it), is not something which, like a conventional machine, is built as a complex of parts subject to a motivation and control applied externally, so that anyone who can get his hands on to the controls can set it working on any job he chooses. The organisation has grown and been perfected as an organisation of capitalism, and of the capitalist tie-up of economic and political power.

A lot is said nowadays about the struggle for power within democratic institutions of government. This is not a struggle to make any great change in the power-institutions and the ways they are controlled and work, but a struggle of individuals, political factions and political parties for particular coveted offices within them. Its premise is acceptance of power-institutions more or less as they are, and its aim to get oneself and one's friends into office and not be left in the cold outside. Those who engage in this sort of politics must watch their step, or instead of being able to use the power they have won to operate the policy of their choice they find that the machine which they have sought to control operates against them and throws them out. This point was well illustrated in C. P. Snow's recent novel *The Corridors of Power*, where a minister, moved by his concern over the nuclear arms race to make proposals which business organisations, influential men of both parties and the top ranks of the civil service felt to be going too far, is forced to resign and is relegated to the position of an ineffectual back-bencher. (I say nothing of this novelist's literary merits, though to mirror so clearly how affairs are conducted is perhaps itself an item of literary merit.)

It should be added that as democratic institutions have developed, making ministers responsible to the electors (a development which has proceeded apace since Marx wrote), so have the means of propaganda, "mass media" and highly-organised party machines been perfected—financed by big business and controlled by it. Hence this powerful apparatus is there to serve big business, to influence the electors, to manipulate votes and stampede public opinion as required.

6

THE BATTLE OF DEMOCRACY

I. DEFINITION OF DEMOCRACY

The central political issue posed in capitalist society is to deprive the capitalist class of state power and vest it in the working class, so that this power can be employed to get rid of capitalism and construct a socialist society. This was the conclusion Karl Marx drew from his analysis of institutions, and particularly institutions of management and government, in terms of classes and class struggles. Dr. Popper, on the other hand, is of opinion that the central political issue is that of extending and strengthening democracy. The issue is not between one set of rulers and another, but between democracy and dictatorship. In posing the issue in this way Dr. Popper denies that democracy is (as Marx maintained) an institutional form within which class-power is exerted, and maintains that it is, on the contrary, something which renders any issues of class-power irrelevant and obsolete.

Dr. Popper traces back to Plato what he takes to be Marx's confused and antidemocratic way of thinking about political power. "It is my conviction," he says, "that by expressing the problem of politics in the form 'Who should rule?' . . . Plato created a lasting confusion in political philosophy" (1-OS. 120). The political issue then seems to be one of what persons or what groups or what classes should seize and hold on to power. But experience shows that whoever gets power is always under a strong temptation to misuse it. Of greater political importance, therefore, than the question of who holds power is the question of how to *control* their use of it. The key political question is not that of who should be entrusted with power, but rather the question (since none are really trustworthy with all power in their hands) of how to organise, through political institutions, the most effective checks on power. Democracy is the answer to this question.

In *The Communist Manifesto* Marx and Engels said that to "raise the proletariat to the position of ruling class" was to "win the battle of democracy". They said this, Dr. Popper suggests, because they thought that "democracy" means "the rule of the people" or "the rule of the majority"—and the proletariat *is* the majority. But on the contrary, he tells us, democracy does not consist in "the rule" of anyone in particular, but in "institutional control" of those who hold office by those who do not hold office. Thus the Marxist "theory that the only alternative to the dictatorship of one class is that of another class" (1–OS. 122) is refuted by pointing out that the alternative to any dictatorship, whether of a class or of an individual, is the democratic organisation of effective "institutional control of the rulers". But as for "the dictatorship of one class", Dr. Popper has already contended that it is in any case an absurd idea, since "classes never rule. The rulers are always persons." The so-called "dictatorship of the proletariat" is in reality nothing but the tyranny of a small clique masquerading as "the rule of the people".

The greatest advantage of democracy, Dr. Popper explains, is that it enables checks to be exerted upon the actions of the rulers or office-holders, whoever they are; and for the rulers to be changed, if necessary, without violence. If there are no democratic institutions, or if these institutions are undeveloped or weak, the only way of checking the rulers, or of changing them, is to oppose some form of violence to the violence of the rulers. It is, of course, historically from opposition to the actions of tyrannical rulers that democratic institutions have been established. And Dr. Popper is accordingly able to state a definition of "democracy" in these terms: "By a democracy I do not mean something as vague as 'the rule of the people' or 'the rule of the majority', but a set of institutions (among them especially general elections, i.e. the right of the people to dismiss their government) which permit public control of the rulers and their dismissal by the ruled, and which make it possible for the ruled to obtain reforms without using violence, even against the will of the rulers" (2–OS. 151).

With this definition go two conclusions, with the first of which we are already familiar.

The first conclusion is that "we may distinguish two main types of government", namely, democracies and dictatorships or tyrannies. "The first type consists of governments of which we can get rid without bloodshed—for example, by way of general elections. . . . The second type consists of governments which the ruled cannot get rid of except by way of a successful revolution" (1–OS. 124).

The other is that "the principle of a democratic policy" is "to create, develop and protect political institutions for the avoidance of tyranny. This principle does not imply that we can ever develop institutions of this kind which are faultless or foolproof, or which ensure that the policies adopted by a democratic government will be right or good or wise—or even necessarily better or wiser than the policies adopted by a benevolent tyrant. . . . What may be said, however, to be implied in the adoption of the democratic principle is the conviction that the acceptance of even a bad policy in a democracy (as long as we can work for a peaceful change) is preferable to the submission to a tyranny, however wise and benevolent" (1–OS. 125).

As a Marxist, I cannot but agree with Dr. Popper that "by a democracy I do not mean something as vague as 'the rule of the people' or 'the rule of the majority'". Marx and Engels may perhaps be reproached because they often used the word "democracy" without defining it. But at all events it was not Marx but Abraham Lincoln who defined democracy as "rule of the people for the people by the people". And it was not any Marxist but the late John Strachey, after he had stopped being a Marxist, who defined it as the wide dissemination of power amongst the members of the community. This is the type of definition of "democracy" which, as H. G. Wells relates, so much puzzled the immensely intelligent supreme ruler of the moon when the first man on the moon "gave him an outline of the democratic method", explaining that on the earth "*all* rule". On hearing this, the Grand Lunar is reported to have "ordered cooling sprays upon his brow". Democracy certainly cannot be defined as a political system in which everyone, or even the majority, takes his share of "ruling". Nor can it be defined in terms of what particular persons or classes hold power. That much is very clearly implied in Marx's insistence that there can be both capitalist and socialist democracies, or in other words, that the capitalist class, a small exploiting minority, can and often does exercise effective power in governing the lives of the majority through the operation of democratic institutions of government. To define "democracy" as "the rule of the people" would imply one or other of two conclusions, both of which Marxists would dispute: either there is no democracy in capitalist countries, or else political power in those countries does not effectively belong to the capitalist class.

Whatever Dr. Popper may say we mean, Marxists cannot define "democracy" in terms of "who rules" or "who has the power". On the contrary, we may agree with Dr. Popper in understanding it as a characteristic or form of power-institutions, or of institutions of management, defined in terms of *the institutional control over office-holders or governors*, including their dismissal and replacement, which is exerted by those whom they govern.

For us, therefore, as for Dr. Popper, the practical test of whether an institution through which affairs are managed and people are governed is democratic, or of how far it is democratic, lies in determining whether, or how far, it includes institutional provisions by which *those who do not hold office can question, check and control the policies of office-holders, and confirm them in, or dismiss them from office.* This test suffices for us to criticise undemocratic procedures, and to propose or support democratic ones, whether in the management of a cricket club, a trade union or the national economy. We are in favour of democracy. And we are in favour of it for very much the same reasons as Dr. Popper declares himself in favour of it: it is a bulwark against tyranny, a means of getting rid of bad rulers, a means of getting policies discussed and criticised, and a means of securing reforms without violence.

But Dr. Popper, apparently without noticing it, or at any rate without being too scrupulous about it, jumps from defining democracy as that characteristic of institutions of management whereby office-holders are made answerable to other people, to defining "a democracy" as a complete political system, or as "a set of institutions" which, all together, "permit public control of the rulers . . . and make it possible to obtain reforms without violence". Yet it is a far cry from establishing particular democratic institutions and enjoying through them certain democratic rights, to establishing a complete "set of institutions" to do all the work of government, and which is a democracy and nothing but a democracy. It cannot be too much emphasised that *democracy is a characteristic of institutions of management, or a form of such institutions,* and not itself either an institution or a set of institutions. While there are many democratic institutions through which government is carried on, there is nowhere any complete set of institutions of government in which democratic methods are not countered by, and often at war with, undemocratic methods. There is no such thing as "a democracy" pure and simple, but only various kinds of democratic institutions. All of these are historically formed out of the exigencies of particular circumstances, in particular conditions of class relations and class struggles.

When Dr. Popper divides all governments into democracies and tyrannies he is adopting a principle of classification which will not fit the facts, as is obvious if one considers cases. Were the Tudor governments in England tyrannies or democracies, for example? One can hardly call them either without qualification, though to call them "democracies" would perhaps require more qualification than to call them "tyrannies". This proposed classification of all governments is far from accurate. And its chief failing becomes evident when one considers how particular governments have actually been constituted and what they have done. Thus, for example, the ancient tyranny of Peisistratos in Athens was in its social basis and functions very different from the modern tyranny exercised by Hitler in Germany, inasmuch as what Peisistratos did was to break the power of the former ruling class, whereas what Hitler did was to ensure that the ruling class could rule without restraint. Again, the admittedly high-handed and often violent policies of the Tudor monarchs effectively checked the former rampages of feudal lords and so provided conditions for the subsequent growth of industry and commerce, whereas the conquests of tyrants of the type of Ghenghiz Khan in Asia plundered and broke up the civilisations on which they imposed themselves. Evidently there are important distinctions even between tyrannies. As for democracies, the democracy of ancient Greece (the road to which in Athens was in fact prepared by the former tyranny) provided methods of institutional control for carrying on the exploitation of peasant proprietors and slaves, whereas the democracy we at present enjoy in Britain or the U.S.A. provides institutional methods for carrying on capitalist exploitation.

There is, of course, a clear distinction between democratic and tyrannical methods in government, inasmuch as one can distinguish democratic and tyrannical elements in particular governments and, in some cases, describe governments as wholly tyrannical. But that does not mean that simply by distinguishing tyrannical and democratic methods all governments may be neatly divided into democracies and tyrannies, and still less that the distinction suffices to sum up the part which any particular government has played in the progress or otherwise of society, including in the political advance to "democracy and freedom".

Of primary importance in the assessment of governments is the distinction which Marx has the merit of stressing (he was not himself the first to recognise it)—the distinction between governments in terms of the class relations they foster and the classes whose interests they promote. When Dr. Popper says that "we need only distinguish between two forms of government . . . i.e. democracies and tyrannies" (2–OS. 161) he ignores the fact that there are also to be distinguished (amongst others) slave-owners' governments, feudal governments, capitalist governments and socialist governments. If governments are considered in these terms, it is possible not only to distinguish but also to explain the varying democratic and undemocratic elements in their modes of operation, whereas if they are all lumped into the two exclusive categories of "democracy" and tyranny" not only are these important differences between governments obscured but a great many governments refuse to fit into either category. Dr. Popper rather pointedly suggests that Marx's ideas about government were highly doctrinaire. But if by "doctrinaire" one means introducing hard-and-fast distinctions which do not fit the facts and cover up important features of the facts, it is Dr. Popper himself who is doctrinaire in his ideas about government.

Thus Dr. Popper says roundly that in "a democracy", as distinct from a tyranny, there is "public control of the rulers". But how far and in what sense is this true in such a democracy as Britain or the U.S.A., for example? Such institutions as general elections establish public control inasmuch as rulers (meaning office-holders) have periodically to submit themselves to election. But "the public" are a very heterogeneous bunch in our class-divided society, including not only wage and salary workers and professional people, but bankers, industrialists and financiers. The institutions which in their totality permit a certain amount of generalised "public control of the rulers", permit a more continuous and stringent control over them by that section of "the ruled" who constitute the capitalist class—who for this very reason are described by Marxists as "the ruling class", even though they do not count for much in terms of their votes. And furthermore, while the rest of "the public" are deciding how to vote, their sources of information, and the propaganda agencies which influence their ideas, are very little controlled by them. *Democracy includes powerful institutions for controlling the majority of the nominal controllers, as well as for ensuring continuously effective control by a minority. So long as the capitalist class within a democracy can hold onto these types of control it remains effectively the ruling class.*

Further, these characteristics of the actual methods of control in practice qualify that other property which Dr. Popper praises in democratic institutions—that they "make it possible" to secure "reforms without violence".

True, in Britain the institutional rules of the democratic electoral system "permit the ruled" to vote into office a parliamentary majority to introduce any reforms they wish. But it does not follow from this that the British political system does not include institutions which might well not permit certain reforms to be operated. Thus while the financial institutions, under present control, can do a great deal to sabotage many intended economic reforms, the judiciary, the civil service, the police and the armed forces are so controlled, despite their obligations to parliament, that at a pinch they could act not only to sabotage reform but even to nullify it by violence. Thus independent action by the military has often been known in very recent times in democracies— for example, the action of the military in Ulster to prevent the operation of the then British Government's Irish policy, to say nothing of more recent examples in Africa, Asia and Latin America, and in Europe too. Are we quite sure that the present system of command in Britain and the United States could permit no similar actions in any circumstances?

Indeed, the management institutions of Britain and the United States in their totality are so constituted that even far less radical reforms than, say, socialising capitalist property have not been permitted without violence. The violent scenes often enacted when any considerable number of "the ruled" have attempted to exercise their democratic right to demand such reforms as the abandonment of nuclear weapons, or the ending of racial discrimination, or (in time of unemployment) work or full maintenance for the unemployed, bear witness to this. So how democratic is democracy? What some institutions permit and make possible, other institutions do not permit or make, if not impossible, at least difficult and dangerous.

Perhaps it is because he is so well aware of these features of our democratic system that Dr. Popper so earnestly advocates that no reforms should ever be attempted except very little ones. One must be as careful not to go too far in a democracy as under a tyranny, lest the powers that be are provoked to violence.

Dr. Popper, who accuses Marxists of such dismal confusion of thought on the question of democracy, is not altogether clear himself. Thus he tells us that "the various equalitarian methods of democratic control, such as general elections and representative government, are to be considered as no more than well-tried and . . . reasonably effective institutional safeguards against tyranny, always open to improvement" (1–OS. 125). This statement has the undoubted merit of bringing out two important truths. One is that democratic institutions are evolved historically in the struggle against various forms of oppression—that they are not set up in accordance with some perfect model of "democracy" but in accordance with the conditions and needs of particular class struggles. The other is that democracy is not an "all or none" characteristic of political systems, but that particular political systems provide a variety of methods of institutional control over rulers, some more and some less democratic, and that the measure of control which may be exerted through one institution in the interests of one class may be counteracted by the greater measure of control exerted through another institution in the interests of another class. But yet in writing about democracy Dr. Popper postulates the existence of "a set of institutions which permit public control", without taking into account the fact *that society is divided into classes and that there are powerful institutions for pushing the interests of classes—institutions for assuring that effective control, the last word, shall belong to one class and not to another.*

True, democratic institutions do provide "institutional safeguards against tyranny". But that is not the same thing as providing "equalitarian methods of control". When he speaks of "equalitarian methods" Dr. Popper implies that no one class has more weight in the exercise of control than any other. But this could never happen, and certainly has never been known to happen, in a class-divided society in which an exploiting class, owning means of production, can exist only by maintaining its general management of the processes of production. In the system of control of the office-holders in such a society the institutions of control allow to some groups among "the public" far more controlling influence than others, and their influence is measured not by their abilities or their devotion to the public welfare, but by their property.

2.   PUBLIC CONTROL AND CLASS CONTROL

The fallacy in Dr. Popper's account of democracy (and not of his account alone) lies in his defining it simply as "public control of the rulers" without asking how, in a society divided into classes, such control is divided between the classes.

It is because he ignores the existence of classes, and ignores the ways in which people in the aggregate work for and protect class interests through institutions, including democratic institutions, that Dr. Popper can counterpose as he does the issue of extending and strengthening democracy and the issue of class-power. It is only another example of the fallacious posing of antitheses. If we think concretely about the real social relations and social processes which confront us, instead of engaging in merely abstract phrases, it becomes evident that *the question of extending and strengthening democracy raises the question of class power,* and does not supersede it. Similarly *the question of class power raises that of extending and strengthening democracy.* These questions mutually involve and do not exclude one another. This is what Marx discovered with his dialectical approach to the study of social questions.

Dr. Popper counterposes to the issue of one class or another exercising power through the government institutions the issue of instituting checks on the power of individual office-holders. He sees as all-important the question of whether such checks, or such control, can be exercised without violence or only by the use of violence. In the first case there is democracy, in the second tyranny. But the institution of non-violent methods of checking and controlling office-holders, including dismissing them, does not remove the issue of class power. For the issue remains of whether the political system permits or does not permit an exploiting class effectively to protect, through the institutions of government, its property rights and its mode of exploitation. Marxists entirely agree about the desirability of instituting forms of democratic control over office-holders. But that does not prevent us from advocating effective measures to put an end to exploitation, including government institutions which will effectively enable those who were exploited to ensure that they shall be exploited no more. We agree with Dr. Popper in not wanting to be ruled by tyrants—whom he has defined as office-holders who cannot be removed from office except by armed force. But we do not want to be ruled by servants of the capitalist class either.

Arguments about democracy are always deceptive when they ignore the existence of classes, class struggles and class power. This is what Dr. Popper ignores when he classifies all governments as democracies or tyrannies, and says that democracy is simply a system of institutional control over office-holders which permits them to be shifted without violence. And he goes on ignoring it when he holds forth about "the democratic principle" or "the principle of a democratic policy". He represents democracy as the institution of "safeguards against tyranny", paying no attention to the safeguards which continue to be required, and are always instituted, for class interests.

When Dr. Popper says that "the principle of a democratic policy" is to develop and protect "political institutions for the avoidance of tyranny", his "democratic principle" is so conveniently vague and abstract, in relation to contemporary problems, that it can be, and regularly is, appealed to in justification of political institutions to avoid *damage to capitalist interests.* This is represented as avoiding the tyranny of *prohibiting* one class from exploiting another. Of course a democratic policy is opposed to tyranny, and will not permit rulers to rule without a measure of democratic control. But to establish political institutions to safeguard the majority from being exploited by the minority demands establishing a greater degree of democratic control than is permissible with political institutions that ensure that the majority shall go on being exploited. Marxism poses the issue of a policy to establish and build the former institutions, and to disestablish and destroy the latter. That is not opposed to any genuine democratic principle of public control over office-holders.

Dr. Popper tells us that the policy advocated by Marx "amounts to doing the work of the enemies of the open society ... And against the *Manifesto* which says ambiguously: 'The first step in the revolution of the working class is to raise the proletariat to the position of the ruling class—to win the battle of democracy', I assert that if this is accepted as the first step, then the battle of democracy will be lost". Where Marx went wrong was in telling the working class "that there is only one way to improve things, that of the *complete conquest of power*. But this neglects the one really important thing about democracy, that it checks and balances power" (2–OS. 162). If ever a single person, group or class achieves "the complete conquest of power" there is an end to democracy, and tyranny holds sway. Democracy is a matter of "checks and balances". Rather than one person, one group or one class exercising unchecked and unbalanced power, different persons, groups and classes check and balance each other.

However, there is a contradiction here, and Marxists see it quite clearly. On the one side is the demand in a capitalist society that the capitalist class shall always have its say in the control of government, and that government, while it may be got to do something to check the rapacity of individual capitalists and make them compromise their interests, will never suppress them. On the other side, in contradiction to this, is the demand that institutional progress shall continue towards "equal democratic rights" and "freedom from exploitation". We cannot have both. If institutions are democratic in so far as all persons concerned have rights of control over the office-holders, it is these specific rights which are presumably to be classified as "democratic rights". They are not equal so long as membership of a propertied class confers a power of control not possessed by other classes, any more than there is "freedom from exploitation" so long as the exploiting class retains the right and the power to go on exploiting. So if we are going to satisfy the demand of the capitalist class to retain its stake in society and the rights that go with it we must set strict limits to institutional progress towards "equal democratic rights" and "freedom from exploitation".

The establishment of democratic institutions has always been a matter of the fight for them against opposition; and Dr. Popper himself speaks of "the battle for democracy" (2–OS. 161). What he does not see is that *this battle is always a class battle*. Democratic institutions guaranteeing democratic rights have been fought for and introduced by exploiting classes only when they were concerned to protect themselves and others from the oppression of some other form of exploitation than their own, and to secure at least their own control over the activities of persons placed in office. No more than this has ever been secured without organised pressure from the exploited, while the exploiters for their part contrive to limit the democratic features of government institutions and to rig them in their favour. The history of the working-class movement has been a history of organised class struggle, not only to secure better conditions in the face of capitalist exploitation, but to win democratic rights and to have them embodied in law. Traditionally, the working-class movement has been democratic. It has fought for democratic rights because these are the political means to its economic emancipation. Its own organisations have been democratic too—so that for all their defects they have set the model for democratic methods of conducting business. The advice of Marxists to the working-class movement is, and has always been, to organise democratically, to fight for democratic rights, and to fight against every attack and restriction on these rights. But rights are won in order to be used. And Marxists advise the working class never to be kicked around by those who consider the interests of capital and profit paramount, and never to be duped into accepting their policies, but to use its organisation to defend and improve its standards and, by defeating the policies and overcoming the opposition of the capitalist class, to lay the foundations of a co-operative socialist commonwealth.

Dr. Popper says that there is "ambiguity" in the statement of *The Communist Manifesto* that "to raise the proletariat to the position of the ruling class" is "to win the battle of democracy". There is considerable ambiguity in his own dispositions for winning that battle. On the one hand he is for "equal democratic rights" and "freedom from exploitation"; on the other hand he is for perpetuating capitalist control over government and capitalist exploitation of labour. There is no ambiguity at all in the programme of *The Communist Manifesto*. It is *to continue the struggle of working people for democratic rights to protect themselves from exploitation and its consequences up to the point of abolishing exploitation and the power of exploiting classes.*

From his "democratic principle" Dr. Popper deduces the consequence that it is better to accept a bad policy in a democracy than to submit to a wise and benevolent tyranny. Why should we do either? And the choice is in any case a somewhat unreal one—for whereas we suffer much from bad policies in a democracy; the prospect of relief through a "wise and benevolent tyranny" is remote. Dr. Popper is evidently merely counselling patience in putting up with bad policies. "You may not think much of the established parties but don't be kidded by the Communists who invite you to submit to a wise and benevolent tyranny administered by themselves. Democracy is always better than tyranny." But it is Dr. Popper who is kidding us. Communists do not invite you to submit to a tyranny, whether benevolent or otherwise. They simply urge you not to accept bad policies. They point out that in a democracy we have democratic mass organisations, which we can use to compel a better policy, and to counteract the influence of those whose interests have dictated a bad policy. The working class should use its democratic rights to enforce its interests when these are threatened by policies dictated by capitalist interests.

Dr. Popper condemns the policy "of Marxist parties" because it "can be characterised as one of *making the workers suspicious of democracy*" (2–OS. 161). But Marxism does not make the workers "suspicious of democracy". It makes them suspicious of the capitalist class. It makes them suspicious of the ways in which institutions are managed and governments engineered in the capitalist interest. It makes them suspicious of the ways in which the agencies of information and propaganda are actually controlled, of the ways in which education is actually conducted, of the ways in which the judiciary actually functions. It makes them suspicious of the ways in which, whenever a crisis threatens the profit system, governments invariably launch attacks on the standards of the working class. It makes them suspicious of the ways in which the police break up peaceful protests against social injustices and preparations for war and spy upon and intimidate their organisers, and of the ways in which the armed forces are sent all over the world to protect the investment of capital. It explains how and why these things happen, and says that they had better be opposed and stopped, and that the only way to oppose and stop them is by demo-cratic mass organisation.

Dr. Popper has told us himself, and with truth, that no democratic institutions are "foolproof". The policies operated through them are not, he tells us, necessarily "right or good or wise". It is up to us to try to make them so, he suggests, through the public control over policies which democratic institutions permit. But he might have added that there is another way in which democratic institutions are not foolproof —they can always be rigged.

Everybody who has anything to do with any democratic organisa-tion knows very well that conferences, for example, can be rigged, if the organisers have decided beforehand what they want to put across and have managed to deceive the delegates either by lies or by with-holding information. Similarly governments are rigged when the electors return members to parliament who have promised to protect their interests, and then the majority party sets up a cabinet which works all the time in the closest consultation with a small gang of monopolists and uses all the powers of force and persuasion vested in the state machinery to put across the measures which they have agreed upon behind the scenes. If the people whose interests are at stake in the policies operated through democratic institutions are thus deceived into accepting policies contrary to their interests, they may be said to have been made fools of, if no worse. The value of Marxism to the working-class movement is that it teaches the workers not to be made fools of by those adept at rigging democracy against the workers, and to work for a democratic policy to defend the interests of working people against capital, and ultimately to emancipate society altogether from all forms of the exploitation of man by man.

"We must learn", says Dr. Popper, "that in the long run all political problems are institutional problems, problems of the legal framework rather than persons, and that progress towards more equality can be safeguarded only by the institutional control of power" (2–OS. 162). How very true that is! With institutions as they are in Britain at the time of writing, if we vote out Mr. Wilson we will only get Mr. Heath instead—and a lot of good that will do us! The real political problems for us are certainly not merely those of one person rather than another, but of "institutional control of power". The same applies to Americans when it comes to a presidential election. That is exactly what Marxism teaches. But where Dr. Popper's arguments, and all arguments like them, deceive us about democracy is in their assumption that the democratic "institutional control of power" operates independently of classes, class interests and class struggles.

This assumption is not true, and could not be true so long as antagonistic class interests continue to exist. The "institutional control of power" presents a battle for control between different classes, each of which has its organisations and other institutional means for pushing its interests and aims. At the present time, in capitalist countries like Britain and the U.S.A., institutional control, as operated through the entire "legal framework", is rigged in favour of the capitalist class, which through its organisations and institutional facilities maintains a pretty firm control over the conduct of affairs. This means that the institutions of government, in their totality, confer effective power upon the capitalist class. That class still virtually exercises, as Marx said, "a dictatorship". Marxism poses the question of how to alter this state of affairs—of how to build a democracy in which the "institutional control of power" will ensure the advance from capitalism to socialism.

3. POLITICAL AND ECONOMIC POWER

One thing that stops Dr. Popper's objections to Marxism from becoming boring is that they are full of surprises. And perhaps one of the chief surprises is that, when he comes to explain the basic errors of Marx's theory of "the dictatorship of the proletariat", and to show how these led Marx to advocate replacing democracy by dictatorship, he informs us that Marx made the mistake of adopting a "disparaging attitude towards political power" (2–OS. 126), and that Marxism is a "doctrine of the impotence of political power" (2–OS. 129).

This, he explains, was the result of Marx misunderstanding the distinction between "political" and "economic" power. Marx thought that economics ruled politics, so that political power was always secondary to economic power and impotent in face of it. Dr. Popper even has a kind word to say in excuse of this error. For Marx "discovered the significance of economic power; and it is understandable that he exaggerated its status. He and the Marxists see economic power everywhere" (2–OS. 127). It was this that led him to "the dogmatic doctrine that economic power is more fundamental than physical power, or the power of the state" (2–OS. 128).

But on the contrary, says Dr. Popper, "it is only the active intervention of the state—the protection of property by laws backed by physical sanctions—which makes wealth a potential source of power;

for without this intervention a man would soon be without his wealth. Economic power is therefore entirely dependent on political and physical power" (2–OS. 128).

If it were not that I hesitate to describe Dr. Karl Marx as Dr. Karl Popper's grandmother, I would say that the latter is singularly unsuccessful in this attempt to teach his grandmother to suck eggs. It will perhaps be remembered that in contradiction to what he here tells us, Dr. Popper told us elsewhere that to say the state protects property is nothing but an "historicist" dogma about "the functions of the state". Marx, on the other hand, always consistently maintained that the state protects property and that, without this role of the state, property, together with the wealth and economic power that accrues from it, could not be preserved. It was of course for this very reason that Marx concluded that we cannot make any fundamental change in institutions of property, or end the evil effects of the exercise of economic power by men of property, without the political power to make the change.

It is not Marx but Dr. Popper himself who creates confusions by introducing the notion of "economic power" as a power separated from political power, and asking which is dependent on which. Marx never did so. He never wrote about "economic power" in this way. It is like asking which came first, the chicken or the egg. A dialectical approach to understanding human institutions in their real connections in processes of development saves Marxists from the puzzles resulting from such questions. Marx showed how from the formation of property and the ensuing conflicts of class interests there have resulted forms and operations of state power to protect property and to promote class interests. If a class is interested in furthering its economic power by either preserving or changing property relations, then it has to seek ways and means of doing so through the instrumentality of the state, that is, by controlling the operations of political power. And no political power has yet been known which did not serve, in one way or another, the furtherance of economic power.

"Of course," Dr. Popper continues, "in practice Marxists never fully relied on the doctrine of the impotence of political power. So far as they had an opportunity to act, or to plan action, they usually assumed, like everybody else, that political power can be used to control economic power. But their plans and action were never based on a clear refutation of their orginal theory, nor upon any well-considered view of that most fundamental problem of politics: the control of the controller, of the dangerous accumulation of power represented in the state. They never realised the full significance of democracy as the only known means to achieve this control" (2–OS. 129).

Marxists never in fact needed any "clear refutation of their original theory", because they never believed in any "doctrine of the impotence of political power". And it is Dr. Popper himself who lacks "any well-considered view of that most fundamental problem of all politics: the control of the controller". According to the way he sees it, "we" or "the public" must "control the controller". We must do this by electing office-holders and controlling what they do. And the elected office-holders will then, on behalf of the electors, use their political power "to control economic power". Marx (or so Dr. Popper says) could never grasp the significance of this democratic process because he believed that political power was impotent in face of economic power. Political power could not control economic power, but on the contrary, economic power controlled political power. The thing to do, therefore, was not to secure democratic control of political power, but to make a direct assault on economic power by a revolutionary uprising which would put paid to economic power by chasing away those who possessed it, locking them up, or hanging them on lamp-posts. Such a "doctrine" may well be considered hardly "well-considered". But Dr. Popper's simple scheme of double control, where the public controls political power and political power controls economic power, is hardly well-considered either.

What concerns us today in the matter of "economic power" is the power of capital. The economic power inseparable from ownership of capital is the power to accumulate surplus value from the exploitation of labour. In this process one capital swallows another, and an ever greater and more dangerous accumulation of economic power results in the hands of a few industrialists and financiers. To preserve and control it, there is the capitalist control of political power. For, as we discovered when we began to discuss democracy, what has actually happened is that the class which owns the means of production, and exercises the economic power which that ownership confers, has found its own ways and means to secure for itself effective "control of the controller". One class is effectively in political control. And that is why that class continues to possess and control economic power. So "the fundamental problem of the control of the controller" is in fact the problem of which class is going to have political power.

Marx therefore concluded, not that we must immediately attack economic power because so long as it exists political power is impotent, but that before any effective change can be made in economic management the "dangerous accumulation of power represented in the state" must be taken out of the control of the present possessors and beneficiaries of economic power, namely, the capitalist class. And so far was he from believing that "political power is impotent" in face of economic power, that his whole "doctrine" rested on the belief that a sufficient accumulation of political power in the hands of a revolutionary political movement could stop the nation's economic resources being used for capitalist profit and use them instead for the people's welfare. Such economic power as might still be left in the hands of private capital could then, he thought, be effectively controlled.

4. SOCIALIST DEMOCRACY

What is necessary, if it is proposed to do away with capitalism, is to break up the institutional ties of big business with the executive machinery of the state, and likewise with the organs of opinion formation. It is necessary to smash the whole organisation of control by big business, a control which is built into the entire machine. No elected administration, whatever its socialist aims, and no aspirants to political power, can end the domination of capital unless the organisation of this domination is smashed. That means that the strings of control must be cut, the channels of influence destroyed, the key personnel removed from their offices. The whole state organisation of administration and compulsion must be adapted, under a new command, to serve new purposes, dictated by working-class socialist organisations and not by big business. To accomplish this, however it is done, whether by armed workers storming government offices or by more constitutional means, is to establish "the dictatorship of the proletariat".

It is not only Dr. Popper who warns us that, whatever Marxist parties may say about their programmes and aims, whenever they are in the government they always try to turn it into a tyranny. Dr. Popper's contribution is to demonstrate from first principles why this must always be so. It is because, following the alleged teachings of Marx, Communists insist on having "complete" and uncontrolled power, and to this end employ violence against democratic institutions so as to dismantle the controls of power and the "checks and balances" which such institutions impose. What Marxism teaches, however, is that we should dismantle the control of power by the capitalist class in order to build socialism, and to this end conduct a struggle for democratic rights and use them when we have got them.

Organisation is needed both to smash the capitalist control of power and to control the exercise of power that replaces it. But in Dr. Popper's account of democratic control it is never admitted that *it is only organisation that can exert an effective control of power.* Democratic control by unorganised individuals is a myth. They may express opinions and vote, but it is *organisations* that do the real controlling. And while individuals express individual opinions, it is through organisation that influential bodies of public opinion are formed. Without revolutionary labour organisations, then, majority public opinion will always be moulded by the great mass media whose propaganda serves the ruling class. People in the mass will only learn to turn a deaf ear to this propaganda when they have themselves in the mass entered upon an organised struggle. And without such organisation it is impossible to break and replace the highly organised control of the state machine by the ruling class.

Dr. Popper says that militant mass organisation violates the principles of democracy and leads to dictatorship. On the contrary, it is the means to tear control of out the hands of a minority ruling class and exercise it on behalf of the majority. It means *that working people have the democratic organisation to exert effective and continuous control over how affairs are run for them.*

In capitalist parliamentary democracy the mass of working people have the right to vote for members of parliament. But having done so, they exert practically no further control themselves until there is another general election—though of course they do have democratic rights to lobby their representatives and to protest against unpopular policies through mass meetings. It is this lack of organised popular control over the executive that allows, despite the democracy of parliamentary elections, effective continuous control over the executive by highly organised big business. Because it is this latter control that has to be abolished if we are to get socialism, the method of effective control which socialism demands is that of *continuous control by mass democratic organisation.* In socialist revolution *the organisations which led the struggle against capital take over from the organisations of the exploiters both the offices of power and the control of power.* It is from this that socialist democracy emerges as a system of government distinct from capitalist democracy.

The central democratic achievement of the bourgeois revolution has been the institution of forms of representative government, in which the key institutions are parliaments or similar elected legislative assemblies. Such an assembly is distinct from the executive, from the "bureaucratic and military organisation" of the state. But by making laws, by holding ministers and permanent officials answerable to it, by setting up committees and commissions, and prosecuting inquiries, it exerts powers of control over the executive. Of course, the individual electors do not exert such control directly: their representatives exert it.

The fact that in the power structure of capitalist democracies the place of legislative assemblies is as instruments of control is clearly indicated in the history of the so-called "mother of parliaments" in Britain. The English Parliament began as a far from democratic institution by which the feudal barons sought to exercise a measure of control over the arbitrary power of the king. In the course of time the burgesses obtained entry into parliament, and its power increased especially by way of controlling the royal finances. Eventually it became the sole authority for making and unmaking laws, and assumed powers of control over every aspect of government without exception. This is the "sovereignty" of parliament, and such is the position in Britain today. But at the same time as universal suffrage gave members of all classes the right to vote, and all classes the right to form their political organisations, the system of parliamentary control became, for the time being, a pretty effective system of control of government by big business. As we have seen, this took place as a result of the institutional links established between business interests and party machines, and of both with the entire "bureaucratic and military organisation" of the state. In the U.S.A. the constitutional relations between Congress and Senate, on the one hand, and the President, as chief executive, on the other show up even more clearly the controlling function of elected assemblies, just as political practice in the U.S.A. shows up even more clearly how big business controls government.

The object of socialist revolution is not to destroy the democratic achievements of the preceding bourgeois revolution but, on the contrary, to make use of them. Hence socialist revolution does not imply, as Dr. Popper seems to think, smashing up elected assemblies and parliaments and instituting a tyrannical rule not subject to any such form of control. Responsibility of the executive to a representative assembly, and its control by such an assembly, is necessary for the democratic government of a large modern community—for without it, as Dr. Popper absolutely correctly says, power could become uncontrolled and the executive could do what it liked and trample on people's rights. Hence the policy of socialists must always be—and this is what Marxism quite unambiguously advises—to *make use of the controlling functions of representative assemblies where they already exist, and to carry out a fight to get them instituted where they do not exist.*

The point is not to get rid of representative assemblies and rule without them, but to *turn them into effective instruments of popular democratic control.* And that means defeating and putting out of business the old political party machines, and making the assemblies they dominated into institutions of control wherein *the political representatives of the organised majority of working people carry out the business of control in the interests of and under the instructions of the members of the organisations that sent them there.* It is in this way that the organised masses can control government. They do it through the controlling power of a democratically elected assembly which their own organisations dominate—while at the same time their organisations can play a direct part in various functions of economic management, local government, the administration of the social services, control of the mass media, and so on.

For Marxism, in all circumstances and all stages of "the battle of democracy", *democracy is not a matter of merely allowing individuals to vote while organisations of the exploiting classes take control of the executive organs of power, but of the activity of popular democratic organisations and the control of power through them alone.*

PART THREE

TOWARDS AN OPEN SOCIETY

EQUALITY

I. EQUALITY OF RIGHTS

Like everyone who is in favour of democracy, Dr. Popper brackets it with equality and freedom. He speaks of "general elections and representative government" as "equalitarian methods of democratic control", and of "the institutional control of power" as "progress towards equality". According to his account of it, democratic institutions, with the provision of representation and a voice in the control of affairs to all persons of all classes, bring equality; equality is lost, just as freedom is lost, without democratic institutions; and democratic progress towards equality is at the same time enhancement of individual freedom.

What is this "equality" which is somehow bound up with democracy, and towards which democracy progresses?

It is evident enough that people are in fact unequal in respect of abilities, characters, bodily attributes, desires and needs; and that not only would it be impossible by any measures taken by democratic (or any other) institutions to remove such inequalities, but such removal would even be undesirable since, as Dr. Popper says (expressing agreement on this point with the philosopher Kant), "the variety and individuality of human characters and opinions" is "one of the main conditions of moral as well as material progress" (2–OS. 357).

Equality is realised through the removal of inequalities. And the sort of inequalities we are concerned with in democratic progress towards equality are those inequalities which result from social institutions, as distinct from what may be called "natural" inequalities. Inequalities which result from social institutions may be removed, and equality instituted instead, by changing or reforming social institutions. So Dr. Popper very logically and properly concludes that, although there can be no question of removing the inequalities exemplified in the physical and mental make-up of human individuals, "this has no bearing upon the question whether or not we decide to treat men, especially in political issues, as equals, or as much like equals as possible; that is to say, as possessing equal rights, and equal claims to equal treatment" (2–OS. 234).

The inequalities which democracy removes are inequalities of *rights*, and the equality it brings is, Dr. Popper maintains, that of "equal rights" and "equality before the law". "Equalitarianism proper," he says, "is the demand that the citizens of the state should be treated impartially. It is the demand that birth, family, connection, or wealth must not influence those who administer the law to the citizens" (1–OS. 95). "Men are not equal," he concludes; "but we can decide to fight for equal rights" (2–OS. 278).

These explanations make it clear that democracy is indeed bound up with equality. For the democratic principle of establishing measures of institutional "control over the rulers by the ruled" implies that "the ruled" should possess equal rights of participation in this control: to the extent that that is not so, the instituted control is defective in respect to democracy.

Understanding "equality" in this way, it is evident that "general elections and representative government" are indeed "equalitarian methods of democratic control", and that universal suffrage is not merely "progress towards equality" but the establishment of a very important measure of equality. It means that everyone, irrespective of "birth, family, connection, or wealth", and irrespective likewise of ability and personality (provided he is not a lunatic), has the equal right to vote, to make representations to his representative, and to seek nomination himself, and that no class is excluded from taking part in this democratic business of institutional control (as the slaves were, for example, in the imperfect and far from equalitarian democracy of ancient Athens). Similarly, the laws which the elected legislature enacts apply to everyone in the same way, so that everyone is entitled to the same legal protection for his person and property, and liable to the same penalties for breaking the law.

Even when everyone has the right to vote, and a system of the impartial rule of law is well established, there is likely still to remain plenty of room for democratic reform, continuing the progress towards equality. For example, the electoral system can be made more democratic, and the equality of electors more equal, by rearrangement of constituencies, by devising systems of proportional representation, and so on. Loopholes in the law and in the administration of the law can be stopped up. Progress towards equality means removing inequalities, and we must always look out for the sorts of defects in organisation and administration which might make one vote count for more than another, or enable some people to evade the law or to use it unfairly for their own gain and to the detriment of others. Dr. Popper therefore holds before us an invigorating prospect of continued democratic progress.

But there still remains a question about equality of rights which Dr. Popper never asks, and this is the question pressed by Marxists. Even when everyone has the equal right to vote and join in political organisation, and when everyone is equally amenable to the laws (and Marxists have never doubted that these equalities are worth fighting for, and worth fighting to preserve), do there not remain other inequalities which it would be desirable to remove, quite apart from those individual inequalities which we all agree are characteristic of human nature and have "no bearing" on the political struggle for equality?

Rights in general are not (as Dr. Popper would presumably agree, in view of his objections to "essentialism") inherent in men as men, by virtue of their common human essence. They correspond rather to definite social requirements of definite people situated in definite circumstances. Thus, for example, the right to own property in means of production and to hire labour is not an "inalienable human right" but a specific right applicable only in certain definite conditions of development of a commodity-producing economy. Such a right is unheard of in a primitive tribe, and is precluded by socialist relations of production. In general, when new relations of production supplant old, rights associated with old forms of property are lost. They are abolished, along with the old forms of property. Thus the rights of feudal lords, from "the right of the first night" to the right to levy private armies, were lost and, indeed, forcibly suppressed when capitalism was developed; and similarly, capitalists must lose their rights to own capital and exploit labour when socialism is introduced. Rights may be claimed to exact service from others and command their actions, or to live free from oppression and exploitation by others. Clearly, the first sort of claims are claims for *unequal rights*, and the second for *equalisation of rights*. And as clearly, these sorts of claims are contradictory.

To discuss questions of equalisation of rights, as Dr. Popper proposes, it would be as well, therefore, to inquire into the source of removeable inequalities in social institutions.

Marx undertook this enquiry, and reached very definite conclusions. There is a common source of inequalities, and they have all sprung from the institution of private property in means of production, class divisions, and the exploitation of man by man. Dr. Popper may have failed to take account of this because, although he begins by giving the word "institutions" a very wide reference, he most of the time confines his intention exclusively to institutions of management and government, and completely overlooks the institutional connections between these and such institutions as the institutions of property, class division and exploitation.

No person of sense can object to one man's possessing greater natural abilities than another, for this is due to no defect in social institutions but, on the contrary, with good institutions, encouraging the employment of all abilities for improving the human condition, we could all gain advantage from this sort of inequality. What we can reasonably object to is that one man should be provided with opportunities to develop his abilities denied to another, and still more than one man should be compelled to sell the use of his abilities for the profit of another. These are inequalities resulting from social institutions and the way they work, and could be removed by changing the institutions. Again, that people should receive unequal rewards for unequal contributions to social life may seem fair enough, but it represents a gross inequality in the distribution of the means of life when some receive a superfluity provided from the labour of others because they own property in means of production, while others receive much less because they can only work and own no such property.

These inequalities are not removed simply by instituting general elections, representative government, equal political rights and equality before the law. But their source is the same as that of all inequalities of rights, namely, in the institution of property relations within which one class exploits another.

If throughout the centuries until quite recently every political system was a system of unequal political rights, it was because exploiting classes preserved rights for themselves which they denied to others, as slaveowners denied rights to the slaves, or feudal lords denied rights to the serfs. Many political philosophers have tried to make out that political inequalities have natural causes. Aristotle, for example, tried to make out that the political institutions which denied political rights to slaves were a consequence of some people being natural slaves unfitted by nature to exercise the rights of free men. Similarly some theoreticians of racism today try to make out that the natural differences in the colour of men's skins are differences which render persons without pigmentation alone capable of exercising political rights. These sorts of natural disabilities on the part of whole classes and races do not in fact exist. What has happened is that the social institutions attached political rights to certain forms of property, and that is why rights were unequal. Similarly, certain forms of property carried with them their own law and exemptions from laws applicable to those without such property, so that men were not equal before the law.

In democratic capitalist countries today the democratic process has at last removed most of these political inequalities. Such as remain are merely anomalies, hangovers from earlier times before democratic demands began to be won, but removeable without thereby altering the capitalist property relations—such as the double vote for business-men and members of universities, which was only a few years ago abolished in Britain; or such as the legal exemptions which peers still enjoy in Britain. Dr. Popper very rightly calls this "progress towards equality". *But the causes of inequalities in property relations and class relations remain.* So long as the system of exploitation of man by man remains there remain gross inequalities between men, which are only glossed over, but not alleviated, by the existence of certain "equalities" of political rights and "equality before the law".

There are rights necessarily associated with property, so that the inequalities of private property entail inequalities of rights. When there is private property in means of production it confers upon the owner the right of appropriating the products, and therefore the right of appropriating the products of the labour of other people who work for him with those means of production. The capitalist class and the working class may all be "equal before the law" as citizens, and each individual may have a vote irrespective of his class, but they do not possess equal rights—for the one has the right to appropriate the products of labour, and the other has not. And this is inequality. It is impossible for there to be equality of rights as between exploiters and the exploited, whatever rights of voting, bargaining, striking, organising, protection of working conditions and provisions of services and holidays the exploited may have won.

Dr. Popper and others may say that this sort of inequality does not matter, so long as wages, working conditions and social services are good. If that were true, we had best stop talking about institutional "progress towards equality", since instituted inequality does not matter. But it *does* matter, because so long as it exists wages, conditions and social services are under threat, and can only be made good and kept good by a fight; and because this system of inequality has always been and still is inseparable from underemployment of resources, crises, poverty and wars.

One may justly protest that the phrase "equality of rights", as used by Dr. Popper as well as by many other people, is extremely vague and loose. Dr. Popper himself keeps on talking only of certain political and legal rights, and notably of the right by voting, and by political organisation, to elect, control and dismiss the "rulers". These are rights which we in the democratic countries have won and value (though working-class organisations could still use them to considerably more effect, and though some democratic states still use all their power, including armed force, to prevent their being exercised in some other countries in which some of their citizens have invested their capital). But besides the right to vote and to organise, and "equality before the law", there are other rights which people have sought to win through democratic institutions, namely, rights to education, health, social security, enjoyment of leisure, and free speech. How equal are these?

In Britain, at all events, everyone not only nominally possesses but actually enjoys basic minimum rights of this kind. At the same time, there can be no doubt at all that the ownership of property, and the income accruing from it, confers the right to very substantial advantages in all these respects, quite irrespective of personal merit. The mere possession of enough money guarantees better opportunities for education, protection of health, security and enjoyment of leisure—while as to free speech, it is a well-known fact that wealth confers on its possessors very considerable privileges in the way of ownership and control of organs of propaganda and opinion-formation. Effectively, these rights are not equal, and cannot be so long as property relations remain unchanged.

Dr. Popper has pointed out, and Marxists agree, because we knew it before, that there can be no question of removing all "natural" inequalities between persons in respect of characters, physical strength and abilities. But in this context it should also be said that even this is not true without qualification. What of the inequality between a well-nourished person and an under-nourished one, one who is crippled or suffers from congenital disease and a healthy man, the sound in mind and body and the sick? Much can be done to remove these inequalities. Even the inequality between clever and not so clever people might be reduced by provision of equally good conditions of upbringing and education from conception onwards. Again, the disabilities which women naturally suffer as a result of the constitution of their bodies and of their bearing children can readily be compensated by providing special consideration, special services, special compensating advantages, for women. But effectively the right of those without money for assistance in these respects is not equal to that of those with command over money, social services or no social services.

Money, the universal medium of exchange in commodity-producing society, is in one way a great equaliser—for everyone is equally entitled to receive money for whatever he has to sell, and to buy whatever he wishes with the money he has received. This entitlement has nothing to do with birth or rank, and applies to the beggar as much as to the millionaire, and to the peasant as much as to the lord. Former rigid divisions of rank broke down before the equalising power of money. At the same time commodity-production inevitably breeds inequalities, since when both means of production and labour-power are commodities, some acquire means of production and appropriate the products, while others have only their labour-power to sell. These inequalities may then make no difference to either the right to vote or to "equality before the law". They make a great deal of difference to other rights. In these there is still inequality. Everyone possesses certain basic and essential rights, but the institutions at the same time impose inequality, because they confer on the class that appropriates the products of the labour of the other the right to substantial advantages.

Dr. Popper and others may justly praise such British institutions as universal free education, the national health service, and social security legislation, and point out what an advance they are over conditions that prevailed not long ago. Very good! These institutions do indeed represent victories in the struggle for people's rights. But only in a socialist Britain will we be able to cite them as examples of equality of rights.

2. EQUALITY AND THE ABOLITION OF CLASSES

But what of political equality itself? Is it true that the equal right to vote and to take part in political organisation amounts, within a capitalist organisation of society, to equal political rights in exercising control over the rulers? It is not true. As was already remarked in a previous chapter, the organisation for protecting and pushing the interests of the capitalist class exerts an overwhelming controlling influence over government, even though this control is that of a very small minority in terms of the numbers of electors. This control may be, and sometimes is, counteracted by the results of general elections; but it is reinforced and works through the operation of a whole complex of institutions, such as the party system and system of cabinet government, the entire system of backstage political intrigue, the entire layout of the so-called "corridors of power", the organisation of the civil service, the judiciary, the police and the military, and, not least, the system of ownership and control of organs of mass information and propaganda, and the management of the educational system. All these institutions in their totality effectively institute inequality of control over government by the different classes, and make the capitalist class the ruling class. And, as Marxists have continually insisted, this inequality cannot be removed simply by counting votes, but only by radical reforms in the entire working institutions of government, or in other words in the structure of the democratic state.

Similar considerations apply to so-called "equality before the law". Law is founded on rights, and exists to protect rights and ensure their exercise—so that if certain rights are to be abolished the corresponding law is changed or falls into disuse, if certain rights are to be established the law defining and protecting them is adopted, and unless there is a comprehensive and well-enforced system of law the "rights" people may exercise depend solely on their own strength in getting their way, and not on social institutions. So integral is this connection of law and rights that in some languages the same word does service for both. Unequal rights are therefore embodied in and protected by law, and when persons with unequal rights stand before the law they stand as unequals: they are "equal" only in the formal sense that each is equally amenable to the law which decrees their inequality. Dr. Popper lays it down that "birth, family, connection, or wealth must not influence those who administer the law to the citizens". These are fine words, but how are judges to obey them when administering laws which concern precisely the rights of birth, family, connection and wealth?

Of course, if someone commits a theft, or an assault or murder, or creates a public disturbance, his birth, family, connection or wealth must not influence the magistrate or judge (at least, the law says it must not, although it often does, especially in cases of public disturbance and in minor cases of theft or assault). This is because the citizens' rights of property and of personal security demand protection irrespective of the social status of offenders. And of course, through the development of class struggle in capitalist society, the law comes to protect not only the rights of capital but also rights of labour. This is because that protection can be afforded as an item of the protection of unequal rights based on capitalist property relations. The law protects the right of the owner of means of production to buy labour power and direct its employment, of the worker to sell labour power, and of each to organise to get the best terms he can in the bargain. That is the protection of unequal rights, and in affording it the law upholds the rights to services and respect, and to appropriate the products of labour, which accrue from birth, family, connection and wealth.

There is no doubt that it is a great gain to have won and established in capitalist society a system of law within which all persons in authority have to act, which allows no exemptions, which allows not only the right of capital to make profits but of labour to organise, and which protects everyone's personal property and personal security at least against assaults by individuals if not against the economic effects of the profit system. Marxists thoroughly agree with Dr. Popper that these are gains worth defending from persons misguided enough to wish to destroy them in favour of a lawless tyranny. He is mistaken in including us among such misguided persons. But we shall not boast that all this, good as it is, yet represents full "equality before the law", so long as the law upholds the inequalities inseparable from capitalist property. Progress towards equality demands not only that the law shall apply universally and equally to everyone, but that laws which uphold inequalities shall give place to new laws which abolish inequalities.

Progress towards equality has always been effected by the institutional removal of instituted inequalities. And the policies of revolutionary socialism which Marxists advocate are policies to continue this progress. If Dr. Popper denies it, it is because he supposes that "general elections and representative government" have done far more to remove inequalities than is actually the case—and he can suppose that only because he is blind to all inequalities except those which either deny rights to political representation, organisation and ownership of personal property to some classes or bestow on others exemptions from the law. Workers do vote, they are represented, they are allowed to organise, they have all legal rights to acquire and dispose of personal property, and no one is exempted from the law—but that does not bring equality between exploited and exploiters, nor make the classes equal either in the exercise of political control over government or in economic and cultural opportunities. There cannot be equality between exploiters and exploited, and exploiting and exploited classes cannot possibly be equal.

For this reason Engels said that "equality must not be merely apparent, must not apply merely in the sphere of the state, but must also be real, must be extended to the social and economic sphere . . . the real content of the proletarian demand for equality is the demand for *the abolition of classes*" (*Anti-Duhring*, Part 1, Chapter 10).

Dr. Popper fears that to abolish classes would be so undemocratic a proceeding as to plunge us from the heights of democracy into the abyss of tyranny. But why should that be so? To abolish classes involves suppressing and abolishing all those institutional means by which the exploiting class maintains its control over government, establishing institutional means by which social production can be taken into social ownership and planned for social welfare, and instituting laws which prohibit the exploitation of man by man. Where is the departure from democracy? Such institutional changes could not possibly be effected without the support of at least the majority of the population, and there is nothing in them which requires the rule of any persons, or of any "strong man", independent of popular democratic control through democratic institutions. The inequalities consequent on private property in means of production, including over-riding control of government by a small minority for its own profit, would be removed. But to remove these sorts of privileges for a minority at the expense of the majority, and even to take very firm steps to prevent the possibility of anyone ever being able to restore them, would not abolish democratic control of the rulers by the ruled but rather provide a basis for strengthening it.

When Dr. Popper, like other supporters of the capitalist democratic establishment, speaks of "equality" and of "democracy" he speaks as though society consisted simply of an aggregation of individuals whose affairs are directed by certain persons holding government office and regulated by a set of laws. He says nothing about the property relations and consequent class relations which define the economic structure of society, as an organisation of individuals based on the social production of the means of life. He is content to consider each individual, singly and individually, and to say that there is democracy and that each of them has equal rights when they each have the right to vote, to make representations to their representatives, to a fair trial if they commit an offence against other people and to legal protection if anyone else commits an offence against them. But just as it is deceptive to describe institutions in general as democratic without taking into account the class-controlled institutions which enable one class to exert an over-riding control of government in its own interest, so it is deceptive to describe rights in general as equal without taking into account the class relations which entail inequalities of rights. The institution of "equalitarian methods of democratic control" demands ending the unequalitarian control by an exploiting class, and "progress toward equality" demands ending the inequality of exploiting and exploited classes. Yet Dr. Popper and others not only ask us to accept inequality as equality, but warn us that to abolish it would be to destroy democracy.

2

FREEDOM

1. FREEDOM AND RESTRICTION OF FREEDOM

Passing in the discussion of democracy from the provision of equality to the provision of freedom, Dr. Popper reminds us of "the well-known paradox of freedom", namely, that "the free man . . . may exercise his freedom, first by defying the law and ultimately by defying freedom itself and clamouring for a tyrant" (1–OS. 123). He concludes that "freedom defeats itself if it is unlimited . . . This is why we demand that the state should limit freedom to a certain extent, so that everyone's freedom is protected by law" (2–OS. 124). As for Marx, he "never grasped the paradox of freedom, and . . . never understood the function which state power could and should perform, in the service of freedom and humanity" (2–OS. 126).

But Marxists would agree with Dr. Popper that "freedom defeats itself if it is unlimited". For, as he goes on to say, if everyone is free to do whatever he likes "a strong man is free to bully one who is weak and to rob him of his freedom" (2–OS. 124). So if people together are to enjoy freedom, what they do must be limited by restrictions and rules. No man should be free to get hold of a club and beat other people over the head. Nor, Marx adds, should any man be free to acquire capital and exploit the labour of others. Marxists agree that there should be laws to stop strong men from bullying the weak, and they also conclude that there should be laws to stop exploiters from exploiting labour. To protect freedom, the law must take his club away from the bully, and also take his private capital away from the capitalist. Marx in fact grasped "the paradox of freedom" ("freedom defeats itself if it is unlimited") with a rather more sure grasp than Dr. Popper.

It is as obvious to Marxists as it is to Dr. Popper (indeed, one may think, rather more obvious) that the promotion of human freedom does not consist in establishing "unlimited freedom" for anyone to do anything, but consists in establishing the specific freedoms of specific people to do or not do specific things, and simultaneously in preventing anyone from hindering them. If freedoms are to be effectively provided that must be protected. Therefore the assertion of some freedoms entails the denial of others, since protection entails prohibition. There is therefore no practical sense in talking about "freedom" unless one specifies freedom for whom to do what, and unless one is also prepared to accept prohibition of actions which would hinder these freedoms. In other words, freedom consists in the provision and protection of specific freedoms of individuals—in the provision of freedom of individuals to do or not do certain things, and in the prohibition of their doing things to hinder each other's freedoms.

Marxists are sometimes accused of proposing to deny freedom to individuals in order to dragoon them into courses of action which will somehow represent collective but not individual freedom. For instance, individuals will be conscripted to work, each as no more than a cog in the machine, so that social production of social needs can go freely forward. But just as collective action which is not the action of individuals is an absurdity, so is collective freedom which is not the freedom of individuals—and it is a mockery of individuals too. A free society is nothing but an association of free individuals, for, as Engels remarked (*Anti-Duhring*, Part 3, Chapter 3), "it goes without saying that society cannot be free unless every individual is free". Although Dr. Popper says that Marxism regards individuals as "pawns" and advocates the subordination of the individual to the collective, he parenthetically admits that, nevertheless, "Marx was ultimately an individualist" (2–OS. 126). This does Marx no more than justice. Marxism is concerned to promote specific freedoms of individuals, which can only be won and protected by collective action and by the prohibition of whatever hinders them.

The provision of freedom to individuals depends on their social institutions: so says Dr. Popper, and so also says Marx.

Marxism advocates practical ways and means for establishing institutions which will ensure that social production will be carried on with the highest techniques and minimum expenditure of labour, so as to provide amply for material needs. With these, we need institutions for education and research, for the sciences and arts, for individual and group enjoyment of leisure, and institutions of management and administration. Such institutions can do the most to make people free—free from want, so that they can freely enjoy material necessities and comforts, which is the essential basis for every other freedom; free to amuse themselves in a variety of ways; free to take every advantage and benefit they can from the social development of technology, knowledge and culture, and to contribute to it personally in every way they are able.

Marxism advocates establishing institutions to provide these freedoms, not for some people only, but for everyone. Free institutions provide freedoms equally for all citizens, and not just for a privileged few. Indeed, if institutions provided certain freedoms for some and denied them to others, it is evident that for the latter these would be institutions not to provide for their freedom but to deny it to them. It is very obvious, therefore, why demands for the maximum provision of freedoms should always be demands for equality. Marxism therefore links freedom with equality.

The institutions through which human freedom may be secured (or, on the other hand, through which individuals are deprived of freedoms they might otherwise enjoy) include economic, sports, scientific, artistic, literary, educational and a host of other types of institution. But there can be no doubt, and Marxists certainly have never doubted, that the key institutions are those of government and law, the state institutions. The state can allow and assist the fullest development of institutions for freedom, or it can hinder or forbid it; and the government policies, the laws and the actions of the enforcers of the law can either uphold the conditions for individual freedom or can deny them. From this follows what Dr. Popper calls "the function which state power could or should perform, in the service of freedom and humanity", and which he says Marx never understood.

So in this connection Dr. Popper asks "What do we demand from the state?" And he says that "the reply of the humanitarian will be . . . I demand protection for my own freedom and for other people's . . . I am perfectly ready to see my own freedon of action somewhat curtailed by the state, provided I can obtain protection of that freedom which remains, since I know that some limitations of my freedom are necessary . . . But I demand that the fundamental purpose of the state should not be lost sight of; I mean, the protection of that freedom which does not harm other citizens. Thus I demand that the state must limit the freedom of citizens as equally as possible, and not beyond what is necessary for achieving an equal limitation of freedom. Something like this", Dr. Popper concludes, "will be the demand of the humanitarian, of the equalitarian, of the individualist. It is a demand which permits the social technologist to approach political problems rationally, i.e. from the point of view of a fairly clear and definite aim" (1–OS. 109–10).

We too are humanitarians, equalitarians and individualists, we try to approach political problems rationally, and we make demands upon the state for the furtherance and protection of freedom. Yet, for some reason or other, Dr. Popper thinks that his rational political question, "What do we demand from the state?" is posed as an alternative to such rational sociological questions as "What is the state, what is its true nature, how did it originate?" He says that Marxism asks such "historicist" questions instead of asking "What do we demand from the state?" (1–OS. 190). But the fact that, as Marxism claims to demonstrate, the state originated out of the protection of class interests, and the capitalist state protects capitalist interests, does not preclude our asking ourselves "What do we demand from the state?" and concluding that one thing we demand is the protection of certain freedoms. To have asked and answered the other factual or so-called "historicist" questions does not prevent us asking "What do we demand from the state?", but what it does do is to show us what we are up against in fighting to win our demand.

Indeed, it is merely hot air to proclaim "We demand that the state should protect freedom", unless we are prepared to make what Dr. Popper is pleased to call an "historicist" inquiry into the state in its actual developments up to the present day, to examine in what ways it falls short of protecting freedom, or hinders people from winning their freedom by protecting the freedom of others to exploit them, and to work out what can be done to get a state which will in the fullest sense protect freedom because it provides the necessary conditions for it.

Dr. Popper further contends that if the state is to protect freedom, democratic institutions are necessary. Even without the benefit of Dr. Popper's advice, this was Marx's contention too. For those who want to ensure that their freedom is protected must see to it themselves, and not rely on protectors over whom they themselves have no control. If the masses of humanity are to live free from exploitation and free from want, they must see to it that those in charge of management and administration manage and administer accordingly—and that requires "equalitarian methods of democratic control". To help demonstrate that this is so, Dr. Popper adds a good deal of useful argument to the effect that while uncontrolled power in the hands of exceptionally benevolent despots may occasionally be exerted to protect certain limited freedoms, the protection is at best extremely insecure except to the extent controls are instituted to ensure that it continues.

But while Marxists agree with Dr. Popper that democratic institutions are necessary to protect freedom, Dr. Popper does not agree with Marxism. For Marxism, he says, belittles the role of democracy even while claiming to be in favour of it—and from belittling democracy Marxism goes on in practice to try to overthrow it altogether. It calls the exercise of democratic rights "mere formal freedom", and from this goes on to propose supplanting it with "real" freedom. But without this "mere formal freedom" whatever other freedom Marxism proposes cannot be freedom at all.

"What Marxists describe disparagingly as 'mere formal freedom'," says Dr. Popper, is in fact "the basis of everything else. This 'mere formal freedom', i.e. democracy, the right of the people to judge and dismiss their government, is the only known device by which we can try to protect ourselves against the misuse of political power; it is the control of the rulers by the ruled. And since political power can control economic power, political democracy is also the only means for the control of economic power by the ruled. Without democratic control, there can be no earthly reason why any government should not use its political and economic power for purposes very different from the protection of the freedom of its citizens" (2–OS. 127).

But where and when did Marxists say that democratic control was not necessary for the protection of freedom? "It is the fundamental role of 'formal freedom' which is overlooked by Marxists", Dr. Popper continues to fulminate, "who think that formal democracy is not enough and wish to supplement it by what they usually call 'economic democracy', a vague and utterly superficial phrase . . .". But stop, Dr. Popper has been carried a bit too far by the exuberance of his verbosity. For it is not Marxists who usually talk vaguely and superficially about "economic democracy", but Fabians and such-like "vague and utterly superficial" persons.

By "economic democracy" is presumably meant measures of public control (or sometimes it means more narrowly "workers' control") over the management of economic enterprises, just as by "political democracy" is meant measures of public control over government. So far as freedom is concerned, both are self-evidently in the same sense "forms" or "mere forms". And to call them "forms" is only to call them by their right name, not to "disparage" them. The freedom to vote, and to take part in instituted control, whether in general concerns of government or in particular items of economic management, appertains to the form of democratic control of institutions, which is necessary, as the form of control, in order that through the operation of those institutions people may enjoy the freedom associated with the exercise of their faculties and abilities, and the satisfaction of their needs.

Dr. Popper himself continually talks about such freedoms as "freedom from want" and "freedom from exploitation", and says that these are the freedoms which democratic institutions should be designed to protect. In the context of freedom there is nothing "vague and superficial" in the use of such antithetical terms as "form" and "substance", or "formal" and "real"; and it is a perfectly proper and precise use of language to say that formal freedoms, such as freedom to vote, appertain to the form of control of the working of institutions within which such real or substantial freedoms as "freedom from want" and "freedom from exploitation" may be realised. Marxism does not "disparage" mere "formal freedom". But what it does say is that we must not let ourselves be tricked into accepting the form without the substance.

It is perfectly true that "formal democracy is not enough", whether it is "political democracy" alone or is supplemented by a measure of "economic democracy". Marxism tells the workers that to have the right to vote and trade union rights is not enough; these rights must be protected; but it is not enough to protect them, we should also use them; we should also seek to win, and then to protect, all that substantial freedom which goes with "freedom from want" and "freedom from exploitation". It is not Marxists who "overlook the fundamental role of 'formal freedom'" but Dr. Popper who overlooks it—for he overlooks that the role of "formal freedom" is to enable us to establish and protect real freedom.

Dr. Popper says that "the view of the state which I have sketched here may be called 'protectionism'", and proceeds to explain that "the protectionist theory of the state" is not a theory about the origin of the state, nor about "the essential nature" of the state, "nor does it say anything about the way states actually function. It formulates a political *demand*, a *proposal* for the adoption of a certain policy"—and that demand and that proposal is that the state should protect freedom, and that everything it does to this end should be democratically controlled. It may perhaps be thought an odd use of words to call a demand or proposal "a theory", since for most people a theory is something on which demands and proposals may be based. However, Dr. Popper goes on to say that theories of the state must always "be translated, as it were, into the language of demands or proposals for political action before they can be seriously discussed. Otherwise, endless discussions of a merely verbal character are unavoidable" (1-OS. 111-12).

We can certainly agree that theories of the state should be "translated into the language of demands or proposals for political action before they can be seriously discussed", and that unless such a translation can be done theories are not worth serious discussion anyway. But if we are going to put forward the demand that the state should protect something, as a serious proposal for political action, we should at least have some idea as to whether the state is protecting it already, if so how effectively, or whether it is protecting something else. For political action has to start from an existing situation, and a proposal for it can hardly be serious unless it includes an estimate of the situation. The Marxist theory of the state can be and has been "translated into the language of political action". What Dr. Popper deplores as its "elements of historicism or essentialism" is that it not merely proposes political action but proposes it on the basis of an analysis of how things are and how they have come to be like it. Yet if political action aims at remedying an evil, it is as well to understand something of the evil it is proposed to remedy.

So far as "protectionism" is concerned, Marxists agree that the state does fulfil a protective role, and we put forward political demands and proposals which concern its protective role. In that sense we are "protectionists" too, only we differ from Dr. Popper in that we think it necessary to examine "the way states actually function" in order to discuss seriously the way we propose to get them to function.

According to the way Marxism interprets the historical evidence, states came into being as a result of the development of private property and of classes, and have always fulfilled a primary function of protecting property and property relations. Exploiting classes have made themselves ruling classes by means of the forms of institutional control they have exerted. This remains true of the ruling class in capitalist countries today. As I have already pointed out more than once, the "equalitarian methods of democratic control" which have been won in some capitalist countries are still strictly limited. The right to vote, the right to take part in political organisations, the trade union rights, and the rights of free speech and assembly, are limited and counteracted by the over-riding control which the capitalist class institutionally exerts over the organs of government, including not only the legislature and executive, but also the organs of information, education and propaganda. This control is exerted to protect capitalist property and the freedom of capital to accumulate surplus-value and seek profitable investment.

As a result, it is the same with the state today as it always has been: *it protects property*. There are various freedoms which individuals seek— freedoms to take part in the institutions of democratic control, and freedoms to dispose of their property and to develop their physical and mental capacities. The capitalist state actually allows and protects, and at the same time curtails and disallows these individual freedoms in so far as it accords with the preservation and development of the capitalist forms of property it protects. These are all facts, highly relevant to any "protectionist theory of the state", which Dr. Popper overlooks.

2. FREEDOM, RIGHTS AND SECURITY

Recognising "that freedom must be limited", Dr. Popper says that "it is certainly difficult to determine exactly the degree of freedom that can be left to the citizen without endangering that freedom whose protection is the task of the state. But," he continues "that something like an approximate determination of that degree is possible is proved by experience, i.e. by the existence of democratic states" (1–OS. 110). For this purpose he concludes that "the state should be considered as a society for the prevention of crime, i.e. of aggression". For when the state is considered in that light, "the approximate degree of freedom that can be left to the citizens" is readily determined as a result of experience. To illustrate the practical principle on which such "approximate determination" is made, he quotes "the famous story of the hooligan who protested that, being a free citizen, he could move his fist in any direction he liked; whereupon the judge wisely replied: 'The freedom of movement of your fists is limited by the position of your neighbour's nose'" (1–OS. 111).

No doubt. But even so it may be doubted whether the existence of democratic states has yet proved that they can always readily learn from experience how exactly to determine the limits of freedom. Experience has not yet taught the democratic American state that the freedom of its pilots to drop bombs should be limited by the position of its neighbour's women and children. As "a society for the prevention of aggression" this democratic state may be deemed a failure. Experience has not even taught some of the state legislatures that the right of their own children to education should not be limited by the colour of their skins.

Furthermore, there is a difficulty in determining exactly what "that freedom" is "whose protection is the task of the state". The American state, for example, considers that it must at all costs protect the freedom to invest capital—and that is why, far from considering itself guilty of aggression against some of its neighbours, it considers *them* guilty of aggression. Again, is the democratic state to protect the freedom of managements of private enterprises to declare workers redundant when they cannot make a profit out of them? If so, then this automatically curtails the freedom of workers to earn their living and contribute their working capacity to the social production of the means of life. For this right of private capital contradicts what in socialist countries is considered a fundamental right, the right to work.

Dr. Popper's view about freedom and its limitations, and the role of the state, is summed up in his demand that the state should protect "that freedom which does not harm other citizens". This is recognisably the same liberal view as was put forward by J. S. Mill *On Liberty*, when he said that the state should not interfere with the freedom of individuals to conduct their affairs and dispose of their property as they please except in so far as experience showed was necessary to stop them from harming one another. But the fact is that the general concept of "harm" is by itself, in Dr. Popper's phrase, far "too vague and utterly superficial" to serve as the key concept for deciding in what ways a democratic state should protect and should restrict freedom.

A practical difficulty in the interpretation of Mill's practical principle has always arisen over the decision of what sort of harm, and what degree or quantity of harm, should be done before the state is justified in interfering. People can and do harm one another in a variety of ways, so that if the liberal principle were taken literally it would suggest an intolerable amount of interference by the state in the private lives of citizens. This very point was touched on by W. S. Gilbert in *The Mikado:* in Gilbertian Japan flirting was made an indictable offence, since it was judged to lead to harm being done to innocent maidens. As we have seen, Dr. Popper maintains that "experience" will always show democratic states where to draw the line; and long before Dr. Popper began his elucidations, liberals, being commonsensical folk, were trying to draw some distinction between "public" and "private" life, with the proviso that the state should let the latter alone except in extreme cases. They likewise tried to draw some sort of balance between, on the one hand, the harm which could be done by permitting certain sorts of activity and, on the other hand, the harm done by interfering. For the liberal principle contains the implicit assumption that state interference, being a restriction of liberty, is in itself harmful, and so should be practised only when a demonstrably greater harm would result from not interfering. Thus in a television discussion got up by the B.B.C. in the summer of 1966 the question was debated whether pornographic literature (prevalent in floods in England) ought to be banned—with one rather diffident and academic gentleman from Oxford arguing that it ought to be banned because of the harm it does, and all the other representatives of a free culture that it ought not to be banned because of the harm done by any form of censorship of publications. In political and economic debate, J. S. Mill's principle was used to argue the case for *laissez faire;* but is is now generally agreed, and J. S. Mill himself was one of the first to argue the case, that a limited amount of state interference is desirable in economic affairs. But if socialists try to argue that any form of exploitation of man by man does harm, the counter-argument is that the state interference needed to stop it would do much more harm.

The hidden reason why Dr. Popper and others think that neverthe-less experience in democratic states shows quite clearly what to allow and not to allow, in the light of their formula, is that they take it for granted that there should always be private ownership of means of production, buying and selling of labour power, and private appropria-tion of the products of socialised labour. On that assumption, experi-ence does indeed indicate the advisability of imposing certain restraints and not imposing others. But this is not at all the same thing as restraining people from harming one another.

To determine the limits of freedom to be allowed by a democratic state is therefore not so easy nor so uncontroversial a task as Dr. Popper tries to make out. For what limits freedom is not simply the decision, wise or otherwise, of the legislature, which decides to allow or disallow individuals the freedom to do this or that. The laws must allow or disallow freedoms in accordance with the *rights* which go with different forms of property, so that what finally decides the limits of freedom is *the institutions of property*. The question is, shall the state legislate for the existing forms of property and continue to protect them, or shall it, on the contrary, legislate against them, promote the institution of other forms of property, and protect these other forms instead? This is the difficult question which has to be decided in order to determine the limits of freedom. And its decision invitably involves *a struggle of classes for control of the state, and to preserve or change state institutions.*

Dr. Popper has correctly stressed the necessary connection between provision of freedom and limitation of freedom. And it is not difficult to see that this implies also, in practical discussion, a necessary connection between the uses of the terms "freedom," "rights", "law" and "security". The *freedoms* to be provided correspond with *rights*—everyone is to be free to exercise and enjoy his rights; rights are embodied in *law;* and the enforcement of law brings *security* for the free exercise and enjoyment of rights. Thomas Hobbes was quite correct when he said that unless men's actions were governed by social rules effectively enforced, the lives of men would be "nasty, brutish and short"; it would not be a condition of freedom. As Dr. Popper's wise judge recognised, a hooligan or thief is the enemy of men's freedom, for he attacks their security. Similarly with military or economic aggression by states, in international affairs. And this, of course, is why Dr. Popper says that a democratic state should work "for the prevention of crime, i.e. of aggression". Marxists entirely agree with that precept. But what Dr. Popper overlooks when defining "the function which state power could and should perform, in the service of freedom and humanity", and the recognition of which made Marx understand this function rather better than Dr. Popper subsequently understood it, is that *states always have to protect property rights and the security of property*. It is therefore important to decide what sort of property rights are to be protected, and what sort of *security* is thereby to be provided.

There are certain basic sorts of security which Marxism demands, voicing in these demands the immediate interest of the working class in modern society and at the same time stating the necessary condition for the unimpeded further development of social production. We demand for everyone the security of being able to find work to do, so as to contribute to social production and, as Marx put it in *Capital* (Vol 3, Chapter 48), "achieving this with the least expenditure of energy and under conditions most favourable to, and worthy of, their human nature". We demand for everyone the security of the use and enjoyment of personal property. And we demand for everyone security in conditions that will enable him to develop his capacities for life and happiness, both in his own person and in his personal relations with others.

This, it may be said, is a rather tall order, human nature being what it is. Many argue that it is of no use demanding institutions which would provide such social security, because people as individuals are by nature far too bad or stupid ever to make them work. However,

Marxism opposes this kind of cynicism about human nature so long as there actually exist institutions which by their nature as institutions *prevent* such social security, whether individuals are by nature bad or stupid or not. And such are the institutions of capitalism.

So long as the state protects capitalist property relations it must be concerned, whatever democratic demands are placed upon it, to provide as much security as it can for the accumulation and investment of capital, and for individuals, whether individually or through corporate organisations, to enjoy freedom to accumulate and invest capital and to live on the surplus values accruing to them from the exploitation of the labour of others.

This demonstrably goes counter to providing security of work. For employment depends on the vagaries of the crisis-ridden process of the circulation of capital; and so far as concerns working with "the least expenditure of energy and under conditions most worthy of their human nature", the workers find progress in this respect impeded.

Equally it goes counter to security of personal property. Although the state and the law protect personal property, one's security of personal property remains contingent on the insecurity of one's job or one's shares. The worker who has managed to acquire various personal possessions, and even to buy a few shares, is in danger of losing the lot through inflation or unemployment.

As for the more intangible goods of life and happiness and personal relations, it is a well-known fact, extensively demonstrated in sociological writings and explored in art and literature, that their sources are poisoned by the free-for-all competition and the monopolising of resources, the "I'm all right, Jack" and "dog eats dog" ethic, of capitalist society.

By instituting social ownership of means of production we can institute social planning of production to employ available resources and labour to meet human needs. And the state which abolishes the rights of private capital and sets out to protect public property in means of production can then protect everyone's right to benefit from social production and, by the social planning of production, can seek to establish and protect social security for everyone for work, personal property, and the pursuit of happiness.

The freedom and equality which socialism can thus secure can be secured only be restricting and denying certain freedoms, as well as removing inequalities. Marxists have always said so, demonstrating therein a perfectly sound grasp of the so-called "paradox of freedom" and of "the function which state power could and should perform, in the service of freedom and humanity".

The sort of restriction of freedom which is exemplified by preventing fists from coming into contact with noses goes without saying—Dr. Popper himself agrees that that is "wise". To secure freedom and equality based on social ownership of means of production demands also prohibiting private enterprises which make profits out of buying the use of labour-power and selling the products. It demands taking away the freedom of individuals, singly or in corporate organisation, to own such enterprises, or to buy and gamble with shares in them, or to display their initiative and competitive spirit by directing them. It demands taking away the freedom of one man to exploit another's labour. It likewise demands the removal of all those institutional means, and the blocking up of all those corridors of power, through which a minority exploiting class can contrive to maintain its influence and control over government. All the rights claimed by representatives of that class to positions of influence and power are forfeited. And this forfeiture includes the rights to own and dictate the policies of newspapers and other means of propaganda, to control radio and television networks, to own and run publishing businesses and art galleries, to direct the organisation of science, and to exert censorship over what is taught in the schools.

In such an undertaking of restricting freedom to secure freedom there is no doubt that, as Dr. Popper warns us, "many mistakes will be made". And in fact many mistakes have been made already, and are still being made, by socialist states—hampered as they have been both by lack of democratic traditions and by an initially backward economy. But whatever mistakes have been made, or will be made in the future, they have at least got rid of property relations which block the road to security and freedom and established basic institutional forms of property and government within which the road ahead is *open*. And experience will show, and is showing, how to correct the mistakes.

3. FREEDOM FROM EXPLOITATION

When "freedom" is reckoned a social and political good, and preserving and winning it set as a social and political aim, what do we mean by it? To explain what we mean it is necessary, not (as Dr. Popper has already explained in another context) to dig for and uncover the hidden "essence" of what the word stands for, but simply to state the implications of the uses of the word. If that is understood, then it is evident that when people say they want to be "free" they imply that they want either to cast off some constraint from which they are suffering or else to prevent some constraint from being imposed on them. Thus *to be free implies to be free from constraint.*

Accordingly, Dr. Popper considers that the object of political action to promote freedom is to free people, so far as it can be done, from the constraints imposed upon them when they are ordered about and coerced by representatives of instituted power over which they have little or no control. So the political objective of freedom is realised by instituting democracy and self-government.

There can be no doubt that this objective does correspond to most people's actually expressed aspirations for freedom. For most people, to be "free" includes to enjoy democracy and self-government; and so long as they remain deprived of their own democratic institutions people do generally mean by winning "freedom" very little else than winning these institutions for themselves. As Dr. Popper has said, it is recognised that once democracy and self-government are won people may fail to make good use of them. But *the first consideration in fighting for freedom is to win democracy and self-government.*

As against this it is sometimes argued that, according to Marxism, it is a mere "bourgeois" or "liberal" illusion to suppose that "freedom" implies freedom from constraint. But the concept of freedom, as understood by everyone who aspires to freedom and refrains from using the word in tricky senses designed to cheat people by foisting on them something they do not want by denoting it by the word they customarily use for something they do want, does bear the implication that to gain freedom is always to throw off some constraint imposed on us. And if Marxism disagrees with "bourgeois liberalism" it is not because we advocate imposing all sorts of constraints on people which liberalism urges them to throw off, but because we advocate getting rid of constraints which liberalism is quite content to accept.

Dr. Popper's idea that "we demand that the state protects that freedom which does not harm other citizens" leads him, like other liberals, frequently to argue as though the constraints placed on freedom were only political, that is, only impositions by the state. You have your freedom curtailed when the police come after you—and Dr. Popper insists that that should be done only to stop you harming anyone else. Apart from what the state, or officers of the state, may do to curtail our freedom, we are free.

But quite apart from such constraints on freedom as may be imposed by the state and the police, is not our freedom to do as we please, and to enjoy and cultivate the advantages which individuals can gain from the amenities of civilisation, very severely constrained by long hours of work, arduous, dull and unrewarding jobs, lack of good food and living conditions—and even more constrained when the individual cannot find work? Is it not limited, too, by lack of education, and by people being subjected to a multitude of propaganda influences which stultify their minds, condition them to believe what they are told, and lead them to believe they are living well when in fact they are only grabbing what they can get in a competitive scramble with their fellows? All these limitations exist. But because they, or even worse ones, have always existed they are taken for granted, as natural features of the human condition. So long as techniques were comparatively primitive such conditions were unavoidable, and to do away with them was not within the range of practical politics. But it is within the range now—and Marxism is the working out of the theory and practice of of such politics.

For that matter, it is equally true that institutions of democratic control, in which the whole population to some extent participates, and not merely those privileged by owning property, were not within the range of practical politics in earlier times. Such institutions of freedom have fairly recently begun to be established. Liberals, enthusiastic as they rightly are about the gains of freedom made by democracy, and prepared, as they say, to fight to the death to preserve even such limited items of democracy as we have so far got (and Marxists join them in this), make the mistake of thinking that because controlling the power of rulers to dictate to citizens is a necessary condition for the citizens' freedom it is the whole of their freedom. It is nothing of the sort. For even when we have gained a measure of control over how far we may be dictated to by the decrees of rulers, that is to say, have gained political freedom, we may still be relatively unfree, and under heavy constraint, on account of our production relations and of the whole way in which we organise social production and the distribution of the means of life and enjoyment of life. Liberals accept this constraint and this unfreedom. Marxists seek the ways of ending it.

Marx and Engels were of opinion that, as a result of socialist ownership and management of social means of production, and the restrictions which that would imply on the freedom of individuals to own means of production and buy and sell labour-power and its products, an organisation of social production could be achieved on the basis of which all individuals could enjoy a freedom they cannot enjoy in any society based on the exploitation of labour. And in *Anti-Duhring* (Part 3, Chapter 3) Engels proceeded to spell out the conditions for such individual freedom, and in what it consists.

The main thing, he explained, is that "in making itself the master of all the means of production, in order to use them in accordance with a social plan, society puts an end to the former subjection of men to their own means of production". Thus "productive labour" is no longer "a means to the subjection of men".

In order that the human race should exist at all, and that anyone should be able to live, let alone live freely, productive labour has got to be done. The ways in which it has become "a means to the subjection of men" are all, so Engels gives us to understand, consequences of the social division of labour. First, individuals have become tied to particular jobs in such a way that all opportunities for development of abilities and personality, and for enjoyment of goods, have been conditioned and restricted by the job to which each individual is tied: thus the peasant is tied to the land, the worker to the bench, and the managing director to the board room, all being equally in a state of "subjection to their own means of production". Second, some individuals live by exploiting the labour of others, so that the latter are tied down by having to work for the benefit and under the direction of the former. Third, individuals are compelled to devote the greater part of their energies to socially necessary labour, with little time or energy left to devote to avocations freely chosen by themselves.

Engels argued that "the present development of productive forces is already adequate" for us to do away with all this subjection. Starting with the third item, he pointed out that the social development of modern productive forces can now "reduce the time required for labour, with every individual taking his share, to what on our present conceptions would be a small amount". So everyone can be given plenty of time and opportunity to live a good life as he chooses. Second, all exploitation of man by man can be abolished. And third, it is possible with modern productive forces to do away altogether with the former crippling effects on individuals of the division of labour. "Modern industry, indeed, compels society," Marx had written in *Capital* (Vol 1, Chapter 14, section 9), "under penalty of death, to replace the detail worker of today, crippled by life-long repetition of one and the same operation and thus reduced to the mere fragment of a man, by the fully developed individual, fit for a variety of labours, ready to face any change of production, and to whom the different social functions he performs are but so many modes of giving free scope to his own natural and acquired powers." In particular, the development of techniques and of people's mastery of them can end the two greatest divisions which impose restrictions and inequalities upon individuals—the divisions between mental and manual labour, and between town and countryside.

So, said Engels, the individual freedom which people can get as a result of socialist ownership of means of production is the correlative of the removal of these forms of subjection. What it amounts to, he said, is "giving each individual the opportunity to develop and exercise all his faculties, physical and mental, in all directions".

Marx explained the same point, but perhaps with greater eloquence and less attention to detail, at the end of the third volume of *Capital* (Chapter 48).

"The realm of freedom actually begins," he wrote, "only where labour which is determined by necessity and mundane considerations ceases; thus in the very nature of things it lies beyond the sphere of actual material production. Just as the savage must wrestle with nature to satisfy his wants, to maintain and reproduce life, so must civilised man, and he must do so in all social formations and under all possible modes of production. With his development this realm of physical necessity expands as a result of his wants; but, at the same time, the forces of production which satisfy these wants also increase. Freedom in this field can only consist in socialised man, the associated producers, rationally regulating their interchange with nature, bringing it under their common control, instead of being ruled by it as by the blind forces of nature; and achieving this with the least expenditure of energy and under conditions most favourable to, and worthy of, their human nature. But it nonetheless remains a realm of necessity. Beyond it begins that development of human energy which is an end in itself, the true realm of freedom, which, however, can blossom forth only with this realm of necessity as its basis. The shortening of the working-day is its basic prerequisite."

Thus Marx and Engels both made very clear that what they regarded as freedom—a goal worth striving for, and which could be realised only on the basis of social ownership of means of production—consisted in each individual enjoying equally the possibility "to develop and exercise all his faculties", and to engage in "that development of human energy which is an end in itself" and which is done, not because one *has* to, but because one *chooses* to. The necessary condition for this, they explained, was something which could only be realised by social action—the fullest development of social production on the basis of social ownership of means of production and planning, overcoming the crippling effects of division of labour, abolishing all exploitation of man by man, and reducing to the minimum the hours of necessary labour for each individual and the individual energy expended in them.

As Marx suggested in his *Critique of the Gotha Programme*, individuals would then hardly begrudge the time spent in social labour, under orders within a social production plan, for they could recognise that work is "the prime necessity of life". Moreover, as Engels pointed out, with the fullest use and development of techniques "labour will become a pleasure instead of a burden".

It is for these reasons that Marxists maintain that it is only by the institution of socialism that men can make a real beginning to the achievement of a free society. For as Engels said, it is only after "the seizure of the means of production by society" that "in a sense man finally cuts himself off from the animal world, leaves the conditions of animal existence behind him and enters conditions which are really human. The conditions of existence forming man's environment, which up to now have dominated man, at this point pass under the dominion and control of man,who now for the first time becomes the real conscious master of nature, because and in so far as he has become master of his own social organisation. . . . It is only from this point that men, with full consciousness, will fashion their own history; it is only from this point that the social causes set in motion by men will have, predominantly and in constantly increasing measure, the effects willed by men. It is humanity's leap from the realm of necessity into the realm of freedom" (*Anti-Duhring*, Part 3, Chapter 2).

To achieve such freedom as this, *not only must more effective forms of democratic control of rulers be introduced but social relations must be changed.* Denying this, the liberals not only justify political constraints associated with the existing capitalist relations as necessary to prevent harm, but also accept the powers and privileges of the existing ruling class, and the subjection of the majority of people to the cramping conditions of exploited labour, as normal features of the working of a democratic political system. So far as freedom is concerned, their horizons are extremely limited.

It is, indeed, always important to remember that what is called "liberalism" is in fact often far from liberal. Liberalism in social and political theory is often as hidebound and stuffy as the great Liberal Party itself.

Liberal myosis as regards the bounds of freedom is due to their accepting capitalist relations as those within which human freedom must be confined. Dr. Popper talks, indeed, of "freedom from exploitation". But, for him, it is only unorganised workers, who lack bargaining power against unscrupulous employers, who get themselves exploited; when there is organisation, and wages and hours are settled by collective bargaining (or, perhaps we should now say, by the incomes policy decided on by a democratically elected government), there is already an end to exploitation. On such a view, freedom does indeed seem to be in the main a matter only of political and economic democracy. The essential freedoms are seen as freedom of individual enterprise, freedom for individuals with a common interest to organise for the promotion of their interest and to bargain with other interests, freedom both by individual initiative and by collective organisation to better one's condition. But yet within the capitalist relations the utmost betterment that can be hoped for is only a little easing of the constraints of economic necessity and the demands of one's job. And in these conditions people naturally see as objectives of all their efforts only the grabbing for themselves of such satisfactions as they can get amid the free-for-all, and grab and consume these the more greedily because their possession of them is constantly being thwarted and threatened by the economic crises, and crises in political and international relations, which capitalism engenders and the onset of which no-one can control. Such, for liberalism, is the inescapable human lot.

Marx, as Dr. Popper admits, saw all these evils of capitalism clearly enough—but he saw beyond them, towards how to overcome them. He did not disparage the political freedoms associated with democracy. On the contrary, he advocated enlarging them be removing the political and economic controls of the ruling class. But he saw clearly *that political power must be used to change social relations in order to set men free*—that is to say, to make men individually free on the basis of their co-operation in social techniques to produce the means for satisfaction, and collectively secure by their control over their means of livelihood and their own social organisation.

The account rendered by Marx of freedom, and of the constraints which must be removed to win it, is of profound importance because it sets before us an aim of political action. Dr. Popper is very scornful about aims and ideals because, he says, the object of political action should not be to realise ideals but to remove evils. However, Marxists fight harder than most to remove evils because that is the practical way of fighting to realise ideals. One's idea of what is an evil to be removed can never be dissociated from one's idea of what good is to be got by removing it. For if one lacks the conception of what good is to be got by removing evils one may well think it not worth the trouble of removing them, or even fail to see them as evils at all. By demonstrating something of the full potential scope of human freedom Marxism urges us to go on removing what blocks our freedom. And while it urges that we value and defend the freedoms already won, it does not teach us that in winning them we have won all the freedom we want or could get.

In capitalist conditions, therefore, Marxism urges that we should organise to protect the democratic freedoms already won, or to win them if they are still lacking; that we should organise to defend our standards of life and to improve them; and that we should organise to deprive the ruling class of its powers to protect its own privileges at the expense of the freedoms of the majority, and, having done so, institute socialist relations of production. And when socialism is won, Marxism urges that *we should go on working for the conditions of individual freedom*, defined not simply in terms of democratic rights, though those must be established where they are lacking, but defined also in terms of conditions of work "worthy of human nature", and of the production of plenty "with the least expenditure of energy", so that "that development of human energy which is an end in itself . . . can blossom forth".

It is a very well-known fact today that under socialist governments, in the first fifty years since the first was established, people have lacked many conditions of freedom, even some which they have got in capitalist countries, not only because of unavoidable economic and political difficulties, but because of misconceived policies of socialist governments. But whether all who hold office in socialist countries are as yet aware of it or not, Marxism presents to the whole great movement of peoples in revolt against exploitation their goal of freedom, their conception of freedom in terms of which they can continue to judge *what has still to be done* to establish free institutions.

4.   FREEDOM AND NECESSITY

Dr. Popper quotes some parts of the observations by Marx and Engels about individual freedom and a free society quoted in the last section. And he then comments that "as far as I am able to see" Marx "followed Hegel's famous equation of freedom with spirit, in so far as he believed that we can be free only as spiritual beings" (2–OS. 103).

This seems a surprising interpretation of Marx's view, even for Wonderland. But, continues Dr. Popper, Marx described all that pertains to material life, material conditions, and the production of the material means of life, as "a realm of necessity", and said that "true freedom" only begins "beyond it". So Marx evidently supposed that true freedom can come only in so far as we "emancipate ourselves entirely from the necessities of our metabolism", For Marx, in fact, just as for "any Christian dualist", freedom consists in "the emancipation from the flesh". And Engels expressed the same concept when he wrote that, to win freedom, man must "cut himself off from the animal world".

Of course, Dr. Popper adds, Marx and Engels knew well enough that we could never achieve one hundred per cent "emancipation from the flesh". So what they advocated was simply that we should spend as little time and energy as possible on fleshly concerns, so as to leave all the rest for "true freedom" (2–OS. 103-5). He supposes that Marx regarded human metabolism, our material existence, "the flesh", as unavoidable limitations on our freedom from which we should try to emancipate ourselves. Alas, we can never emancipate ourselves entirely, and so we are always forced to devote a certain amount of attention to material necessities.

The view which Dr. Popper tries to foist onto Marx that "we can be free only as spiritual beings", can justifiably be regarded, as Dr. Popper regards it, as not merely nonsense but pernicious nonsense. He tends to call any such nonsense "Hegelian", regardless of whether Hegel actually propounded it or not. But this view is in fact considerably older than Hegel, since it is to be found rather forcibly expressed in writings attributed to Saint Paul. The pernicious practical implication hidden behind its high-sounding spiritualistic phraseology is that because the body limits and fetters the freedom of the spirit it is as well to chasten the body in order to free the spirit. Thus the view that "true freedom" is "spiritual" can be (and often has been) used to justify all kinds of oppression and cruelty in the name of "true freedom".

Dr. Popper has already warned us that the practical outcome of the Marxist advocacy of revolution as the means for securing freedom from exploitation can only be tyranny. But now he has shown how Marx and Engels tried to cover up this unpleasant fact with a load of non-sense about "true freedom".

The idea that only "spirit" is free, whereas "the flesh" is unfree, which Dr. Popper rather arbitrarily ascribes to Hegel and still more arbitrarily to Marx, has become associated in modern times with certain philosophical arguments about freedom and causality.

Put in its simplest terms, the argument that "we can be free only as spiritual beings" goes like this. Material events have causes and take place in accordance with causal laws. In so far as we are material organisms, therefore, we are subject to causal laws, so that if the cause of an action is present the action necessarily follows as the effect, and if the cause is not present the action does not follow. If the cause is present there is therefore nothing we, as mere material organisms existing in a material environment, can do to stop the effect from following; and if the cause is not present, there is nothing we can do to bring the effect about. In either case we have no choice, no freedom in the matter. Hence if we are in any way free in what we do, it can only be as spiritual beings, because there is some spiritual principle in us which acts independently of the chain of causation in material processes.

The answer to this argument is pretty obvious, to such an extent that it has today become even a commonplace in philosophy. So far from causality and causal law precluding our being able to choose to do something and then to do it, it is the necessary condition for such free action on our part. It is only because causes produce effects, and in so far as we know what effects given causes will produce, that we can decide on a course of action and carry it out. For if we could never know what causes produced what effects, how could we possibly deliberate on any course of action, or embark on any undertaking whatever? Men are material organisms and, as such, our activities and the effects of our activities are subject to causal laws. But that does not imply that we can only be free in our choice of activities if there exists some part of us which is free from the chain of material causality On the contrary, when we know what causes will produce what effects, that is the cause of our freely producing such effects as we choose.

Professor Ryle, of Oxford, has illustrated this line of argument by examples from the free play of games. He pointed out (in *The Concept of Mind*) that the fact that both billiard balls and billiard players are subject to the laws of mechanics does not prohibit the free play of billiards but is its necessary condition. "The billiard player asks for no special indulgence from the laws of physics any more than he does from the rules of billiards. Why should he? They do not force his hand." That players exercise freedom in pushing billiard balls where they want them to go does not imply that the players are "spiritual beings", nor that to play billiards well "we must emancipate ourselves from the necessities of our metabolism". With that admirable facility for stating the obvious which is characteristic of the school of philosophy to which he belongs, Professor Ryle further pointed out how baseless is the assumption that "a golfer cannot at once conform to the laws of ballistics *and* obey the rules of golf *and* play with elegance and skill".

It is the same in more serious affairs as in these examples of games. In so far as an effect follows from our own deliberate action, rather than from external causes independent of our deliberations, we may be said to be responsible for it—it was our own choice of action that brought it about. And in so far as we have learned from experience what to do in order to bring about one effect rather than another, we have made ourselves free to act upon and realise our own purposes, and so "emancipated ourselves" from conditions in which what happens to us, and what happens as the effect of causes we have set in motion, depends not on ourselves but on external forces beyond our control.

Understanding all this, Marx and Engels did not regard material existence and its necessities as limitations on what, without them, would be our freedom as "spiritual beings". Obviously, since man is a material and not a spiritual being, his freedom is that of a material and not of a spiritual being. His material existence is not a limitation on his freedom, but its condition. For example, breathing and having air to breathe is not a limitation on our freedom, but is is a condition for its exercise. According to Marx and Engels, therefore, man makes himself free by his control and use of material conditions for his own purposes, to satisfy his own needs. The achievement of freedom depends on understanding and mastering the necessities of material existence.

A word in time here about this use of the word "necessity" may save some misunderstanding. It is, of course, a word which may be used in several different senses in different contexts. Neither Marx nor Engels ever went to the trouble of splitting hairs in the distinction between these different senses—an omission for which they may perhaps be reproached by contemporary philosophers, and which affords ample scope for much lively nonsense at mad tea parties. The sense given to the word "necessity" is quite clearly the sense of "necessary condition" or "necessary conditions". Thus if we say that eating is a necessity of life, that does not mean that we necessarily eat, but that unless we eat we do not stay alive. Again, if we say that to construct aircraft we must understand and master the natural necessities expressed in the laws of aerodynamics, that does not mean that those laws are "necessities" in any more abstruse sense than simply that they express the conditions for controlled flight of bodies through the air.

So when Engels said that "man leaves the conditions of animal existence behind him" he did not mean that man achieves "the emancipation from the flesh" by freeing himself from the necessities of his material existence, but he meant exactly what he said, namely, that "the conditions of existence forming man's environment, which up to now have dominated man, pass under the dominion and control of man". Leaving "the conditions of animal existence" behind us is not a matter of our spiritual being overcoming our material being and escaping from its limitations, but of our learning, as animals which live by satisfying their needs and creating new needs for themselves by social production, how to develop our social and personal relations and activities so as to satisfy our needs.

As Marx explained, when men learn rationally to regulate the "interchange with nature" which is necessary to support human existence they thereby make themselves free to engage in many pursuits which they undertake, not because they are forced to do so in order to support life, but because their success in producing material necessities leaves them free to devote energies to other pursuits of their own choosing. So when Marx said that "the shortening of the working day" is a condition for "true freedom" he meant simply that it would allow more time in which to do things, not because we have to do them whether we like it or not, but because we like doing them and choose to do them. This is a point which most industrial workers can readily grasp, even if it is beyond the compass of Dr. Popper's understanding.

Dr. Popper's statement that Marx "followed Hegel's famous equation of freedom with spirit", and believed that we are truly free only in so far as we somehow cut ourselves off from the necessities of material existence and emancipate ourselves from them, is the more surprising because in *Anti-Duhring* (Part 1, Chapter 11) Engels had already succinctly and explicitly explained that exactly the opposite is true. Dr. Popper perhaps failed to notice the significance of what Engels had to say in *Anti-Duhring* because he dismisses that work as mere "apologetics", and also because, believing correctly that in certain respects Marx and Engels "followed Hegel", his own lack of understanding of Hegel precludes him from all possibility of understanding what following Hegel meant.

"Hegel was the first to state correctly the relation between freedom and necessity. To him, freedom is the appreciation of necessity," Engels wrote. He then continued: "Freedom does not consist in an imaginary independence of natural laws, but in the knowledge of these laws, and in the possibility this gives of systematically making them work towards definite aims . . . . Freedom therefore consists in the control over ourselves and over external nature which is founded on knowledge of natural necessity."

In talking about freedom Dr. Popper follows the well-worn liberal tradition of dealing exclusively with *political* questions about how far the state should prevent anyone doing just as he pleases, and demanding that people should be forbidden to do some things only to protect their freedom to do others. As a result, and as I have already noted, he fails to take into account the very fundamental fact of human life that, quite apart from any notices the state posts up about what is permitted or prohibited, people's freedom is restricted by their relationship to their own means of production, so that each enjoys only that unequal area of freedom which is allowed him by his ownership of property and position within the social division of labour. Now it may further be noted that in talking about freedom Dr. Popper fails to take into account an even more fundamental consideration, namely, that before anyone is free to do anything, the means must be available to enable it to be done, and also the knowledge of how to do it.

To make ourselves free to carry out activities we must get control over the necessary means for activities. People must have done this collectively before individuals can be free to engage in those activities.

This consideration underlines and explains the fact that men can be said to seek and to exercise a freedom in their activities of a kind not attainable by other animals. This fact is misunderstood by Dr. Popper when he assumes that the creation and extension of human freedom is entirely a matter of politics, an activity in which other animals do not engage, quite as much as it is misunderstood by those who say our freedom is "spiritual", whereas other animals are not "spiritual beings". Men are animals. But the species *Homo sapiens*, with upright stance and human hands and brain, distinguished itself from all others by the method of social production of the means of life. To do this men learned how to make tools and construct the means to bring about various effects, and to represent to themselves (a first indispensable means to this was the institution of language) effects which they wished to produce and the actions necessary to bring them about. Thus they developed the ways of purposive action in which human freedom resides, whether in the production process itself, the management of public affairs, or the pursuit of personal desires and aims. This consists in making means available and knowing how they can be used to produce various effects, so that one can choose whether to produce those effects or not.

In the passage in *Anti-Duhring* quoted above, Engels said that human freedom is people's own creation, and we create it by learning to master and control material causes so as to set them to work for our own purposes. To the extent that we learn how to use objects for our own purposes our freedom of action is expanded. There is more we can do. And this expanded freedom depends on our having acquired, as Engels put it, "the capacity to make decisions with real knowledge of the subject"—so that instead of being compelled to act all the time simply in response to external stimuli, in which case our activity "is controlled by the very object it should itself control", we are able to select practicable purposes and set causes in motion and control their effects so as to realise our purposes.

This freedom, Engels continued, "is a product of historical development. The first men who separated themselves from the animal kingdom were in all essentials as unfree as the animals themselves, but each step forward in civilisation was a step towards freedom." The "first men" were "unfree" simply because in all their activity they remained, like other animals, tied to their natural environment. They lived a free life in the sense that they could roam around as they chose, and no one oppressed them. But there was nevertheless very little they had made themselves free to do, and as a result their lives were confined within a very restricted round of tribal activities.

Material objects are the objects of our activity, and their laws are the laws on the operations of which we rely in deciding how to act. It would therefore be absurd to say (as Dr. Popper seems to suppose Marx to have been saying) that the material world and its laws constitute a restriction on our freedom—as though we could enjoy "true freedom" only if there were no material world or if we ourselves were not part of it and subject to its laws. But what *is* true is that material objects and their laws are obstacles to our freedom of action, and their presence ties down our action, except in so far as we can find out how to use them and master them.

This, no doubt, is one reason why the more people become conscious of themselves as free agents the more imperative becomes their urge to explore and master the environment. Thus quite apart from considerations of economic or political advantage people form expeditions to climb a mountain "because it is there": there it is, an obstacle to men going wherever they wish on our planet, so they feel determined to find the way to get to the top of it. Similarly, we feel it to be worth while in itself to get to the moon, and then to other planets, and then maybe outside the solar system. Apart from any other considerations, it is a matter of demonstrating that the ruggedness of mountains and the vacuity of space will not be allowed to prevent men's freedom of movement.

But to find out how thus to master the environment is not a matter of finding out how to cancel or evade the laws of material existence, nor is it a matter of simply pitting our own will and endurance against the resistance of natural forces. It is a matter of finding out how to construct the means.

In general, the basic condition for the expansion of human freedom has been the advance of technology and the sciences. As Engels pointed out: "On the threshold of human history stands the discovery that mechanical motion can be transformed into heat: the production of fire by friction. And at the close of the development so far gone through stands the discovery that heat can be transformed into mechanical motion: the steam engine." The discovery of how to produce fire, he continued, "gave man for the first time control over one of the forces of nature, and thereby separated him for ever from the animal kingdom". And so he concluded: "All past history can be characterised as the history of the epoch from the practical discovery of the transformation of mechanical motion into heat up to that of the transformation of heat into mechanical motion" (*Anti-Duhring*, Part 1, Chapter 11).

Thus, according to this account of it, the freedoms won by men up to the latter part of the last century were those made possible by men's initial conquest of "control over one of the forces of nature", developed from transforming mechanical motion into heat to transforming heat into mechanical motion. This is what made men free to do all the things they could do up to the time Engels was writing. And this, he added, "shows how young the whole of human history still is".

Since Engels' time the next great technological revolution has begun with the discovery of how to generate and control nuclear energy, coupled with the discovery of techniques of automation. This is fully comparable with the initial discovery of fire. And its implications for the expansion of human freedom are even greater. The development of this technology is what can give substance to Marx's idea of men "regulating their interchange with nature with the least expenditure of energy and under conditions most favourable to, and worthy of, their human nature". If Marx and Engels themselves could talk of the future "realm of freedom" only in rather general terms, not readily understood by Dr. Popper, that was because they died before the present technological revolution began. The freedom which can be achieved on the basis of future socialist production surpasses anything that could have been made possible by even the most rational employment of steam and internal combustion engines, and comprises all that is made possible by the employment of nuclear energy and computers. This means that men can draw on almost limitless sources of energy, and apply them, not to powering machines which have all the time to be arduously fed, repaired and controlled by human labour, but in processes which are made self-feeding, self-repairing and self controlling in the service of human purposes and needs.

5.   THE MEANS AND OPPORTUNITIES FOR INDIVIDUAL FREEDOM

All the freedom which people win, and can win, is not won by each individual for himself, but it is, as Engels stressed, a social product of the combined efforts of many individuals over a long period of time. This does not imply, however, that the freedom won consists of anything else than a variety of specific freedoms enjoyed by individuals. On the contrary, it is human individuals, and only human individuals, who enjoy and exercise human freedom. But they enjoy and exercise it thanks only to their living within, and their lives being regulated by, social institutions.

The freedom which we want and strive for is the freedom of individuals: there is no other human freedom. But if individuals are to get all, or even any part of, the freedom which could be theirs, it is essential to recognise that the freedom of each individual depends on what has been and will be done by all individuals taken together, associated in society. It depends on the opportunities for activities and choices of activity which the individual enjoys. And in turn the opportunities and choices open to each individual depend on what means for activities and satisfactions have been created in the society to which he belongs, and on what other members of that society permit and do not permit him freely to do.

There is no doubt that individual freedom implies freedom of choice for the individual. Thus to claim freedom is to claim individual freedom of choice, that is, freedom to choose what to do without being externally constrained to do one thing and not to do another. Hence to be free also implies personal responsibility. The free person chooses and decides for himself, and does not merely do what he has been ordered to do.

This is a point heavily and, we must agree, rightly stressed by Dr. Popper when he writes about "the open society". There must be "personal responsibility" in a free society, he says, rather than individuals being instructed in all they should do (1-OS. 113). Such a society, he insists, is one "in which individuals are confronted with personal decisions" (1-OS. 173).

However, for the very reason that freedom implies personal responsibility, though freedom is proclaimed as a fine thing it often appears as something of a burden. It is, indeed, a hard fate to have to choose what to do and bear responsibility for it, under circumstances when one is beset with all sorts of personal problems and lacks means and opportunities to solve them, and also, very likely, is so deprived of education that one does not even know what the problems are, let alone how they might be solved. For this reason, people are sometimes apt to welcome lack of freedom as a sort of refuge, and to advocate depriving others of freedom for their own good. As Tolstoy wrote of the army: "Here in the regiment all was clear and simple . . . there was nothing to think out or decide" (*War and Peace*, V.15).

Dr. Popper himself recognises this difficulty when he goes on to talk about "the strain of civilisation" consequent upon our having as individuals "to look after ourselves and to accept responsibilities" (1-OS. 176). It would seem, therefore, that when individuals take upon themselves the onus of personal responsibility they would be well advised at the same time to do all they can to assist one another by socially providing all possible means and opportunities for each individual to benefit from it rather than harm himself and others.

Evidently, then, if social institutions are to promote and support individual freedom, we must demand more of them than only that individuals should be left free to act as they choose, on their own responsibility, and not be pressed or constrained to perform various actions whether they choose to or not—with the proviso (on which Dr. Popper and other liberals strongly insist) that if, nevertheless, they act so as to harm others the police will be after them. We must demand that all individuals should have access to the means and opportunities for a variety of activities in which they can "develop and exercise all faculties, physical and mental", in co-operation and not to each other's detriment; and we must demand that they should be afforded that education which will enable them to "make decisions with real knowledge of the subject", and not be forced to make their decisions in a random way, or on impulse or relying on the prejudiced advice of others, uncontrolled by knowledge.

Recognising all this, what Marxism is therefore concerned about in the matter of freedom is not only to decrease the number of constraints imposed on individuals, but also to increase the opportunities and choices available to each individual. This implies deploying the technical resources of society and organising education so as to provide all with the means to a full life, and arranging social relations so that each individual is able to take the fullest advantage of his opportunities.

To work this out, the first question to tackle is the question why the opportunities for individuals have in fact remained so very restricted, and why people, whose freedom depends on each other, have done so much more to hamper and restrict each other's freedom than to enlarge it. The Marxist theory of "the laws of social development" (in Dr. Popper's view so irrelevant on account of its "historicism" to any questions of what is to be done to create a free society) not only supplies the scientific answer to the question of why we have not yet a free society, but also answers the question of what we must now do to get one.

In brief, during the whole period of social development from men's first discovery of how to turn mechanical motion into heat up to the discovery of how to turn heat into mechanical motion, the condition for the social production of the means of life and enjoyment for individuals was that the great majority of people should be continuously engaged in arduous labour. Hence whereas on the one hand people were learning how to control forces of nature so as to produce what they wanted for themselves, on the other hand the condition for this production was that the great majority became tied to their own means of production by bonds which condemned them to unremitting toil. As

Marx and Engels showed, the necessary division of labour consequent upon the development of social production led to private property in means of production, a separation of functions of ownership and management from those of productive labour, and the division of society into exploiting and exploited classes. The exploiters and masters then appropriated to themselves the opportunities for free activities and enjoyments accruing from production, together with access to culture and education, and the labouring classes, from whose labour these opportunities were created, necessarily went without. Thus the condition for the freedom of the few was the unfreedom of the many. The many were driven to toil, whether by the physical force which oppressed slaves and serfs or by the economic compulsion which compels free wage-workers to sell their labour-power. They had no choice but to toil for most of their lives.

It is in this that the unfreedom of the labourers has essentially consisted. Superimposed on it have been the various political forms of bondage, consisting of deprivations of rights, and oppressions and coercions of various kinds, imposed on them within the social institutions.

Throughout this period of history the class struggle has always taken the form of struggles for freedom, or rather for specific freedoms which people fought to retain or saw the possibility of winning. Such freedoms can always be characterised in two ways, negative and positive, "freedom from" and "freedom for". People seek to free themselves from specific impositions and restrictions on their activity, and to win (or retain) conditions in which they are free to do specific things which they want to do and in which they see advantage. Thus in class struggles people have managed to free themselves from specific forms of political oppression, and at the same time to win specific rights. The winning of rights for some has always and necessarily meant the cancelling of rights for others—for instance, the rights won when slavery was ended cancelled the rights of slaveowners, the rights won in connection with the establishment of capitalism cancelled feudal rights, and so on. But whatever impositions and restrictions were shaken off, and whatever rights were won, the fact remained that the exploited classes never won freedom from exploitation, and the rights of the exploiters continued. Hence whatever freedoms the exploited classes won (and in some countries they have won a lot) were always limited by their being driven to work for the greater part of their lives for the benefit and under the orders of others, and the most cherished freedom of the exploiting classes has always been their freedom to direct and appropriate the labour of others.

The great contribution of the social researches of Marx was not simply that he expounded these facts about freedom and lack of freedom in the historical development of the past, but that he showed that private property in means of production, and exploitation, originally necessary consequences of the division of labour, and necessary conditions for the development of social production, have now become so far from being necessary that they act as fetters on the further development of social production. He recognised the fact (which none who take into account the potentialities of modern technology can deny) that with the modern development of forces of production it is no longer necessary that the majority of the human race should devote the greater part of their lives to labour, nor that the opportunity of education and leisure to enjoy most of the advantage accruing from it should belong to only a few. The conditions are present for the human race finally to free itself from the age-old bondage of labour. And what Marx did (Dr. Popper mistakes this for an historicist unconditional prophecy of a violent revolution) was to work out the foundations of the theory of how to win this freedom.

On the basis of his scientific social and historical analysis, Marx demonstrated the necessary condition for it. This is that the modern working classes must carry through what, when it is done, will be the last act of the class struggle—to bring an end to private property in means of production and the exploitation of labour, and establish social ownership of means of production and planning of production to satisfy human needs.

Then it will be possible (but not, of course, without considerable collective efforts over a long period of time, nor without "many mistakes" being made) to bring about the organisation of a free society, in which collective management of the production of all the necessary means to free activities is done and controlled with no other object than the provision of those means to individuals. Then every individual can enjoy for the greater part of his life all the opportunities for unconstrained free human activity afforded by "the associated producers rationally regulating their interchange with nature, bringing it under their common control instead of being ruled by it as by the blind forces of nature, and achieving this with the least expenditure of energy and under conditions most favourable to, and worthy of, their human nature".

This freedom which individuals can then enjoy comes from their togetherness. It is the product of their working together. And only by working together, obeying the rules of communal life, educating themselves, and each contributing all he can to producing the satisfaction of the needs of others, can they enjoy that freedom.

As regards work, or social production, Marx emphasised that in this matter men do not have and cannot have a free choice as to whether to engage in it or not. In this sphere, as he said, the only freedom that can be won is the freedom of being able to work in the best obtainable conditions, and of being able to contribute to the best of one's abilities. This is the point which Dr. Popper finds so incomprehensible that he can only interpret it as meaning that "true freedom" consists in "the emancipation from the flesh". But the point is simply that we are not free to choose whether or not to engage in social production, because if we are to enjoy any social life, and the freedoms obtainable in social life, we have got to work for it. The means must be supplied, the work has got to be done. So as human freedom springs from appreciation of necessity, and not from any imaginary emancipation of any of our activities from their necessary conditions, men and women in a free society will regard work as a necessary condition for all their freedom. Consequently, if they follow Marx's advice, they will arrange for it to be done as expeditiously, efficiently and effortlessly as possible, and to this end will share it out on equalitarian principles according to a rational plan.

3

THE OPEN SOCIETY

"We can return to the beasts", so Dr. Popper tells us. "But if we wish to remain human, then there is only one way, the way into the open society" (1–OS. 201).

According to him, "the open society" is something we find our way into by getting out of "the closed society". So its characteristics are defined in opposition to those of the closed society. A "closed" society is, he explains, a "primitive tribal society" which "lives in a charmed circle of unchanging taboos, of laws and customs which are felt to be as inevitable as the rising of the sun, or the cycle of the seasons, or similar obvious regularities of nature". It is characterised by a "magical attitude", as opposed to a scientific one. Its members think that the rules current in their tribe which "forbid or demand certain modes of conduct" are as fixed and inviolable as natural laws (1–OS. 57). So they never think of altering them, and anyone who disobeys them is strongly disapproved of and punished for his audacity.

The attitude of the closed society, Dr. Popper next explains, is continued in societies in which the state undertakes to regulate more or less the whole of the citizens' lives. This, he warns, is to "replace personal responsibility by tribalistic taboos and by the totalitarian irresponsibility of the individual" (1–OS. 113). In the closed society all the "norms" of conduct are laid down and strictly enforced, so that individuals are not allowed to exercise their personal judgment as to what is right. The results are generally bad. In the open society, on the other hand, individuals exercise their own judgment, and so far from their having to renounce personal judgment in subordination to the state, the state is answerable to *their* judgment.

This contrast between the principles of operation of an open and a closed society is pointed by Dr. Popper (1–OS. 7) in two quotations from the ancient Greeks. One is a statement by Pericles: "Although only a few may originate a policy, we are all able to judge it." The other is taken from Plato: "The greatest principle of all is that nobody ... should be without a leader. Nor should the mind of anybody be habituated to letting him do anything at all on his own initiative ...

even in the smallest matter he should stand under leadership. For example, he should get up, or move, or wash, or take his meals . . . only if he has been told to do so. In a word, he should teach his soul, by long habit, never to dream of acting independently, and to become utterly incapable of it."

In contrast to "the magical or tribal or collectivist" closed society, then, the open society is "the society in which individuals are confronted with personal decisions" (1–OS. 173).

"In the light of what has been said," Dr. Popper continues, "it will be clear that the transition from the closed to the open society can be described as one of the deepest revolutions through which mankind has passed" (1–OS. 175). According to his reading of history, this revolution got under way in ancient Greece in the great days of Athenian democracy. For it was there and then that "there rose a new faith in reason, freedom and the brotherhood of all men—the new faith and, as I believe, the only possible faith of the open society" (1–OS. 184).

But the breakdown of the closed society, that is to say, the breaking of its "charmed circle of unchanging taboos, of laws and customs" within which everything individuals had to do was settled for them, leads to individuals feeling a "strain" due to difficulties encountered in trying to use their own judgment (1–OS. 176–7). Hence the continued urge is expressed to get back again somehow to the security of a closed society, and to reimpose its fixed rules of life. This is expressed in doctrines of "totalitarianism", which echo the creed of the closed society "that the tribe is everything and the individual nothing" (1–OS. 190). It is likewise expressed in "nationalism", which "appeals to our tribal instincts, to passion and to prejudice, and to our nostalgic desire to be relieved from the strain of individual responsibility which it attempts to replace by collective or group responsibility" (2–OS. 49).

That is the sum-total of what Dr. Popper has positively to tell us about the open in contrast to the closed society. What it amounts to is that society is "open" when individual members of society are constrained by no externally imposed laws and customs in forming judgments, and when not only is each individually responsible for his own actions but exercises his independent judgment in approving or disapproving public policies. To make such a society work, reliance is not placed on inviolable law or custom or on the dictates of traditional or any other authority, but on "faith in reason, freedom and the brotherhood of all men". For it can flourish only when the members of society try to form judgments by the exercise of reason, value the freedom of each and all, and agree to live in brotherhood. On that condition they can not only each exercise his individual judgment but together preserve conditions of security for enjoying their freedom.

From this premise Dr. Popper concludes that, firm in "the faith of the open society" we "must go on into the unknown, the uncertain and insecure, using what reason we may have to plan as well as we can for both security *and* freedom" (1–OS. 201).

Always anxious to be fair to Marx, even while exposing his errors as sins against the open society, Dr. Popper allows that "he admitted his love for freedom . . . Marx's faith, I believe, was fundamentally a faith in the open society" (2–OS. 200). But, he warns, "in spite of his merits, Marx was . . . a false prophet . . . responsible for the devastating influence of the historicist method of thought within the ranks of those who wish to advance the cause of the open society" (2–OS. 82). Just as the "historicist" doctrine that society progresses from stage to stage by inexorable necessity teaches individuals that their personal decisions can count for nothing and they cannot be responsible for what happens, so the dictatorship which Marx advocated would actually deprive them of all responsibility. "The prophetic element in Marx's creed was dominant in the minds of his followers", Dr. Popper concludes. "It swept everything else aside, banishing the power of cool and critical judgment and destroying the belief that by the use of reason we may change the world." Marx left us with "an oracular philosophy" which "threatens to paralyse the struggle for the open society" (2–OS. 198).

We have seen, however, that Marxism in fact investigates the conditions for obtaining security and freedom for individuals, and advocates the conquest of political power in order to plan the bringing of these conditions into existence. Dr. Popper makes a great point of emphasising "security *and* freedom" when he holds forth about what we must plan for. Quite so. And a merit of Marx which Dr. Popper does not share is that Marx did work out the necessary conditions for planning for just that.

We may perhaps detect in Dr. Popper's statement about "the way into the open society" a certain vagueness, and even a combination of big words with little meaning. For if we are to use "what reason we may have", not simply to protect our security and freedom when they are in danger, but "to plan as well as we can" how to advance them, then surely we must work out what conditions are required for maximising both security and freedom and strive to bring them about. And if that is a practical objective, then what we are heading towards cannot be so entirely "unknown" as Dr. Popper says. True, it cannot but remain "uncertain" because we cannot know how well we shall succeed, and "insecure" because of the unexpected difficulties we may encounter. But if Dr. Popper is right in saying that "the way into the open society" leads "into the unknown", his advice that "we should plan as well as we can" how to take it is mere hot air. For how well can we plan the way to go when we do not know where we are going? Although Dr. Popper says that the route mapped out by Marxism is to be avoided, because by taking it we shall only "return to the beasts", Marx's views are still perhaps worth more serious consideration than his own, because Marx did at least try to use such reason as he possessed to work out what were the practical conditions for security and freedom which we can now try to bring into existence.

Dr. Popper has written two volumes on "the open society and its enemies", comprising 481 pages of text plus 221 pages of notes. But if one searches in them for information about how to go forward into the open society and get rid of some of the deprivations of material necessities, education and opportunity which individuals continue to suffer on a large scale, one is left with nothing but generalities about "individual responsibility". One may well be tempted to echo Prince Hal's exclamation when he examined the record of his mentor's proceedings: "O monstrous! but one half-pennyworth of bread to this intolerable deal of sack!"

2.   THE WAY INTO THE OPEN SOCIETY

Dr. Popper assures us that "the transition from the closed to the open society can be described as one of the deepest revolutions through which mankind has passed", but has little to say about how it happened. In one of his luminous and voluminous notes, however, he supplies us with a "criterion". "It seems to be possible to give some useful criterion of the transition from the closed society to the open. The transition takes place when social institutions are first consciously recognised as man-made, and when their conscious alteration is discussed in terms of their suitability for the achievement of human aims or purposes. Or, putting the matter in a less abstract way, the closed society breaks down when the supernatural awe with which the social order is considered gives way to active interference, and to the conscious pursuit of personal or group interests" (1–OS. 294).

As he told us at the start, in the closed society institutions are not recognised as man-made, but are regarded as fixed and inviolable parts of the order of the universe. So they cannot be interfered with, and their alteration cannot be discussed. When there enters into men's heads the consciousness that their institutions are man-made, they can start discussing how to alter them. After that, Dr. Popper concludes, the chief thing that has continued to obstruct our going foward with the conscious and rational alteration of institutions "for the achievement of human aims or purposes" has been the dead weight of prehistoric beliefs left over from tribalism and elaborated by enemies of the open society as doctrines treating institutions as other than manmade.

Dr. Popper's statement that people came to recognise their institutions as man-made and advanced out of the closed society by altering them to suit the various purposes suggested by personal or group interests is not very illuminating as a description of what happened, and even less as an explanation. Marxists may perhaps be excused for suspecting in this account of what happened in history, if not an "historicist" doctrine about the "pattern" of historical development, at least a considerable oversimplification. But that Dr. Popper does not himself altogether share the idealist doctrine that great changes in human social behaviour can be described and explained simply as the spontaneous generation in some men's minds of new ideas about their social institutions is shown by his own statement in the text, that "perhaps the most powerful cause of the breakdown of the closed society was the development of sea-communications and commerce" (1–OS. 177).

The point was made a long time ago by Marx, and is now generally agreed (including, it seems, by Dr. Popper), that what makes "tribal society" break down and other more "open" forms of society emerge is the development of technology. Sea-communications and commerce are, of course, a part of this, and have had a very disturbing effect on societies in which they were developed—though tribalism in fact began to break down before sea-faring commerce got under way. Anyway, where technology has not been developed, there tribalism with its "charmed circle of unchanging taboos" has not been disturbed. Marx showed, and subsequent researches have continued to show, that technological innovations proved incompatible with many of the laws and customs previously held inviolable in tribal society, as a result of which the laws and customs were violated. This circumstance broke into the "superstitious awe" with which the tribal order was surrounded. And because the use of new technology, with division of labour, set up personal and group interests as distinct from the single tribal interest, it led to "the conscious pursuit of personal or group interests".

The consciousness that social institutions are man-made is indeed, as Dr. Popper says, of vital importance for human progress, because of the implication that what man made man can improve on. But if we are to understand the real issues and problems men have faced since the breakdown of tribalism, and still more what it is possible to do now to alter institutions to suit human purposes, and what is necessary in order to do it, it is hardly sufficient simply to be conscious that institutions are man-made. As I have said before, we need to know the laws and conditions of their making.

Dr. Popper says with truth that when tribal society breaks down there ensues "the conscious pursuit of personal or group interests"—though this statement could be qualified by remarking, with Marx, that consciousness of interests often takes a disguised form. If in primitive tribal society there was as yet no attempt made to alter institutions to suit personal or group interests, that was not so much because the tyranny of tribal custom forbade it as because there were no separate personal or group interests to be suited. Obviously, once separate interests had arisen, to get institutions altered to suit them was an example of "the achievement of human aims or purposes", because the interests were human ones. But as obviously, it is a far cry from "the pursuit of group interests" to "the achievement of human purposes" in the sense that the achievement suits the interests of all human beings and not only of one group of them in opposition to another. In fact the "pursuit of personal or group interests" which ensues upon the breakdown of tribal society led invariably, and quite inevitably, to the forcible subordination of the interests of persons to the interests of groups, and of the interests of one group to those of another. So far as most persons were concerned, the kind of class-divided society which succeeded tribalism was very far from "open", not because their opportunities for "personal decision" in the conduct of life were thwarted by tribal taboos, but because they were thwarted by the subjection of their personal and group interests to those of the ruling class.

Marx demonstrated clearly enough how it was that "personal or group interests" came to be pursued, and what were (and still are) the overall results of this pursuit. The cause was the development of the social forces of production. And Marx pointed out that this development was not simply a process of invention of new techniques but a change in the sum-total of activity of human beings in obtaining and distributing the means of life.

The primitive tribe, living by food-gathering and hunting, constituted a single group of people banded together to produce and appropriate their own product for their own use. Its unchanging taboos, laws and customs represented no tyranny practised against individuals but rather the means of maintaining the tribal solidarity on which the very existence of every individual in such conditions depended. The invention of techniques of cultivating the land, domesticating animals, handicrafts and metalworking broke up the closed society of the tribe, because they entailed the division of labour. This differentiated people from one another in their ways of obtaining the requirements of life. It brought property in means of production and in products, exchange of products, and the production of a surplus out of which owners and managers could be supported.

This in turn meant that while social wealth increased, and consequently the scope of the activities and enjoyments possible for individuals, the producers collectively lost control over their product. For it was no longer a collective product but a sum of individual products passing into the process of exchange. And those who owned property acquired separate interests in augmenting it. Some persons could acquire property in means of production to the exclusion of others, and in that way command the labour of others and appropriate its surplus for themselves. The labourers were then placed in a position where they had to work to supply products to owners and managers, as directed by the latter. Their working capacities were no longer exerted by them after the tribal custom as part of the collective effort to supply the collective need, but were appropriated by an owning and managing class for its own enrichment.

Thus the antagonisms of classes were created, and the history of society became the history of class struggles. With this, the whole business of social management changed. The state came into existence, as an institution through which some men rule over the rest.

With the capitalist economic formation, the changes which were set up by the breakdown of tribal society eventually come to a head.

All products are produced as commodities for exchange, which means that the entire social product passes out of the control of the producers. The producers' own labour-power becomes a commodity, so that the direction and control of their personal abilities to produce what each needs is entirely lost to them. People cannot now decide to work to produce what they want, since they have to work for whoever will buy their labour-power; and the increase or decrease of the total product, the proportions of different branches of production, and the eventual destination of products are all outside the producers' control and settled by economic laws of the market which operate independently of the voluntary actions of men. The class struggle is polarised into a single antagonism between the class which sells its labour-power and the class which buys it. And finally, the state, as a power which men have set up over themselves to rule them, becomes greatly strengthened and centralised; and the more it intervenes in economic production and distribution, the more does it stand over the producers as an organisation which rules them but which they do not control.

In all these respects, the social relations which obtain under capitalism are *the complete negation* of those which originally obtained under tribalism or primitive communism. In moving away from the tribal order, the social formation has gone as far as it can go, into the direct antithesis. In men's social development, *capitalism stands at the furthest remove from tribalism.* Where before nothing was produced as a commodity, now everything is produced as a commodity. Where people appropriated and consumed their social product as they produced it, now it has gone out of their control. Where people banded together to try to produce what they wanted, now each worker has to do what work he is told. Where there was no division of class interest, now there is a deep class division cutting right through society. And where people decided their common affairs for themselves according to their own tribal laws and customs, now they are subject to the rule of an all-powerful state.

Since, then, Dr. Popper identifies "the closed society" with tribalism, it is natural that he should see in the antithetical conditions obtaining under capitalism the realisation of "the open society". For him, indeed, "the open society" is only another name for capitalism.

But he never sees that the development of forces of production and of relations of production, which led from the breakdown of primitive communism to the establishment of capitalism, was a development of different methods of exploiting labour. He only remarks superficially on some of their effects in institutions of social management, in ideologies and in the lives of individuals. Hence he sees the antithesis between tribalism and capitalism only as the antithesis between a society which "lives in a charmed circle of unchanging taboos, of laws and customs which are felt to be as inevitable as the rising of .the sun", and one where institutions can be regarded as "man-made" and people can discuss their alteration to suit their personal or group interests. For him, capitalism is "the open society" because there are separate personal and group interests inside it and people can organise to press them; and because no human institutions are any longer regarded as sacrosanct but everyone can discuss whether it is best to keep them as they are or alter them. In that sense, it *is* "open". But yet the way the institutions of the production and distribution of the means of life are fixed *prevent* people from being able to take personal decisions and to accept individual responsibility for *working together for the production of their needs.*

In the light of these considerations we cannot but view with scepticism Dr. Popper's contention that all those institutions and ideologies which have oppressed individuals since the demise of tribalism are at bottom hangovers from the tribe, dragging mankind backwards to the tribal closed society. One may freely admit the obvious fact, which Dr. Popper vigorously affirms, that ideologies and institutions imposing beliefs, taboos, laws and customs to be accepted and obeyed without criticism are incompatible with individual responsibility, personal decision and rational judgment. One may agree that such were the ideologies and institutions in tribal societies. And one may agree, too, that subsequent exemplars have often and regrettably appealed to the same irrational fear and hatred directed against taboo-breakers and outsiders which tribesmen sometimes evince. But that does not mean that all subsequent repressive ideologies and institutions have been hangovers from tribalism. On the contrary, the shut-down they impose on individuals has had no tendency towards restoring the primitive communal way of life. The state of affairs which the hymn "All Things Bright and Beautiful" finds so admirable

> "The rich man in his castle, the poor man at his gate,
>   God made them high or lowly, and ordered their estate"

is absolutely foreign and unknown to tribesmen. The ideas and institutions of tribalism were those of the solidarity of small groups in which no one pursued personal or group interests in antagonism to his fellows. These subsequent ideas and institutions were consequent upon the destruction of that primitive human solidarity and the dominance in society of acquisitive class interests.

Dr. Popper tries to make out that such modern phenomena as "totalitarianism" are a return to tribalism, induced by people feeling "the strain of civilisation" in an open society. But the facts make it clear that the repression of individuals under modern totalitarianism has little in common with primitive tribal solidarity but represents *the violent assertion of the interests of an aggressive group of exploiters.*

Having identified "the struggle for the open society" as the attempt to alter institutions to suit personal or group interests, and "the closed society" with the suppression of separate interests, which in turn is identified with tribalism, Dr. Popper then goes on to contend that the policies of a militant labour movement are another sort of totalitarianism which will likewise lead us back to tribal conditions. For these policies will suppress certain interests, and subordinate personal and group interests to a common interest. It would seem that a delegate conference is like a tribal jamboree, and that in every militant mass demonstration civilisation is threatened by the primitive horde run riot. So by representing "the struggle for the open society" as the struggle finally to overcome tribal hangovers, consummated in the capitalist antithesis to primitive communism, Dr. Popper ignores and obscures completely *the struggle to overcome the forms of class domination* which superseded tribalism, and the resistance it meets with from the forces which organise to maintain class domination.

In capitalist society the "open" conditions have been created where people can organise to change their social institutions in a way consciously decided to suit their interests. And the class struggle has reached a stage where the working class emerges as an organised force equipped with a scientific theory of how social changes can be brought about. So the issue which insistently arises in this society is that of organised action by the working class to throw off the fetters of capitalism, take control of the state into the hands of its own democratic organisations, and institute social measures to bring social production under the control of the organised producers. The very "openness" of capitalist society provides the conditions for ending the exploitation of man by man which supervened on the break-up of the "closed society" of tribalism. The issue therefore posed by "the open society" as it actually exists at the present day is not that of defending it from

reversion to tribalism but of going forward to socialism and communism.

The progress of mankind from the animal condition from which
we sprang is progress in the human activity of socially producing the
means of life, and of increasing the scope of human activity and
achievement as we get further from the animal condition by mastering
the materials and forces of the natural environment for human purposes. It is in this progress that there is made possible the individuality
of the human person, as distinct from the animal as a member of the
species conditioned to the unchanging habits of the species. Human
individuality is the product of the increase of men's collective powers
and of the increased supply of the means to a more varied life. Dr.
Popper says that "if we wish to remain human" we must go forward
"into the open society". If we wish to remain human we must go on
producing our needs, and we shall go forward with this the better if we
manage by human co-operation to control the product so as to supply
everyone's needs and thus allow to the development of everyone's
individuality full scope. That means *we must overcome the exploitation
of man by man, and the divisions of class-society*.

The poor life of primitive communities, when all individuals had to
be much the same as one another and cling together in a common
observance of taboos and customs, was overcome by the development
of new forces of production, which in turn led to the negation of the
tribal solidarity of primitive man by class divisions. The poverty-
stricken subsistence economy was negated by commodity production.
The close ties of kinship between individuals within the tribal organisation were negated by making all individuals living and working
in a territory the subjects of a state. But these negations must be
negated by the working people of today asserting their control as
producers over the socialised production of modern industry, equipped
as it is with techniques capable of producing plenty, thus instituting
once more the social appropriation of the social product, and taking
over organised democratic control of state power. Then the future
conditions for the freedom of human individuals, with their individual
responsibilities and personal decisions, will be secure.

This is what Dr. Popper, with his abstract description of "the open
society" as the antithesis of the tribal or "closed" society, entirely fails
to understand. He simply fails to comprehend what Marx demonstrated, namely, that the negation of the "closed society" of tribalism only
led to class divisions and exploitation, and that the way forward

"into the open society" now demands *the negation of this negation.*
Shocked by such Hegelian horrors, Dr. Popper protests vociferously
that this is nothing but an "historicist" doctrine cooked up by dogmatically applying to human development the arbitrary pattern of
"thesis-antithesis-synthesis". To end the conditions of the pursuit of
antagonistic personal and group interests which superseded tribalism
will,.according to him, only land us back into a worse sort of tribalism.
But it is in these capitalist apologetics of Dr. Popper that an uncom-
prehending dogmatic attitude is to be found, not in the scientific
socialist theory of Marx. Marx did not deduce the course of history
from any Hegelian formula. *He examined how men actually made their
institutions, and saw that the time had come when the exploitation of man by
man could and should be ended.*

This being so, to go forward "into the open society" is not to go,
as Dr. Popper says, "into the unknown". On the contrary, there are
definite issues to face, a definite job to do, and an organisation to be
built to do it.

3. RESPONSIBILITY, INDIVIDUAL AND COLLECTIVE

In Dr. Popper's conception, the essential feature of "the open society"
is that individuals in it bear personal responsibility and make personal
decisions. With him, this suffices to define "the open society": a
society is "open" when it allows enough scope for personal responsibility and personal decisions. His objection to Marxism is so strong
because he says Marxists hatch plots to take personal responsibility
away from individuals, and to prevent their making personal decisions,
by enforcing on them a tyranny similar to that which he says existed
in tribes—the tyranny of collective taboos, laws and customs. But let
us agree with him in calling society "open" when it allows scope for
responsibility and decisions; then far from objecting to society being
made "open" in that sense, Marxists agree with him that the more
"open" it can be made the better. Apologists for capitalism have no
monopoly in wishing society to be "open". Still less have they a
monopoly in policies of how to make it so.

"Our own ways of life", Dr. Popper freely admits (meaning the
ways of life in capitalist democracies), "are still beset with taboos. . . .
And yet . . . there is between the laws of the state on the one hand and
the taboos we habitually observe on the other, an ever-widening field
of personal decisions, with its problems and responsibilities." This field

of personal decisions and responsibilities is not just the field of private life, for "many of us make rational decisions concerning the desirability or otherwise of new legislation, and of other institutional changes; that is to say, decisions based upon an estimate of possible consequences, and upon a conscious preference for some of them. We recognise rational personal responsibility" (1–OS. 173). The great point which we have won is that we recognise that institutions are man-made and that it is open to us to alter them, so that there exists, as Dr. Popper goes on to point out, "the possibility of rational reflection on these matters"—rational reflection consisting of estimating possible consequences and formulating conscious preferences. So although we "are still beset with taboos", everyone can judge for himself as to what is best in the way of "new legislation and other institutional changes", and is not bound to submit his judgment to that of anyone placed in authority over him.

This personal responsibility and freedom of personal decision in our open society is opposed by Dr. Popper to "the totalitarian irresponsibility of the individual" where individuals are not allowed to judge or decide anything for themselves. In the open society choices are open to individuals as to what they shall do and what they shall make of their lives, as individuals, and also as to what they shall think and what public policies they shall support or oppose, so that in deciding all these matters for themselves there is also open to them "the possibility of rational reflection".

That being so, he opposes "collective" to "individual responsibility". He sees the collective as a tyranny, or at all events a potential tyranny, over the individual, which would force the individual to abandon his personal judgment to a collective judgment, his individual responsibility to a collective responsibility, and his personal choice as to what he should do to a collective instruction as to what he should do. To call for "collective responsibility" is, he implies, a case of reintroducing "the totalitarian irresponsibility of the individual".

It is of course perfectly true that in "our own ways of life" there is, exactly as Dr. Popper says, "an ever-widening field of personal decisions, with its problems and responsibilities". How much this field has widened in the case of working people in particular can be readily appreciated by comparing the conditions of contemporary wage-workers with former serfs. When in the year 1381 the English King, Richard II, told the defeated remnants of the peasants' revolt "serfs ye are, and serfs ye shall remain" he meant, among other things, that they should make no personal decisions as to whom they worked for or where they worked. The serf was in fact allowed very little personal responsibility for anything. The contemporary wage-worker is, by comparison, a very responsible person with scope for a large number of personal decisions on matters ranging from where to apply for a job to whom to vote for in parliamentary elections.

If Marxists now sought to deprive workers of the individual responsibilities and scope for personal decisions they have won it would be a strange inconsistency, considering that Marxists have always fought to help win them and in that sense have been among the foremost champions of "the open society". But Marxists do say that for individuals to have individual responsibilities and make individual decisions is not enough. We want to institute forms of the exercise of *collective* responsibility and *collective* decision. The reason why we want this is that individuals live, and can only live, within a framework of the social production of the means of life. And this reason also defines the sphere within which we think that collective responsibility should be exercised. But this is what causes Dr. Popper to conclude that we are heading straight back to tribalism. For according to him, individual and collective responsibility are incompatibles. He sets them in antithesis, so that anyone who calls for collective responsibility is in effect calling for an end to individual responsibility and its replacement by "the totalitarian irresponsibility of the individual". It is also the end of rationality. For it puts an end to "the possibility of rational reflection" which resides in the making of personal decisions.

One ought to ask what exactly can be meant by "collective responsibility". Dr. Popper cites "nationalism" as a case where it takes over. Though he is far from explicit as to his meaning, it seems a fair guess that his reference is to cases where a large number of persons constitute themselves into a mob, activated by a common sentiment. It is true that in such cases the individuals concerned can hardly be credited with "rational responsibility" for what they are doing, and that together they bully, intimidate and coerce any other individuals who try to think for themselves and oppose themselves in any way to the clamour of the mob. It is also true that when such a tyranny of the mob occurs it can provide the opportunity for a "strong man" to step into the leadership and exert his own personal tyranny, so that the tyranny of the mob leads to "the rule of the strong man" and "the strong man" makes use of mob sentiments in order to enforce his own rule. But while it may be true that this type of social behaviour "appeals to our tribal instincts, to passion and to prejudice, and to our nostalgic desire to be relieved from the strain of individual responsibility which it attempts to replace by collective or group responsibility", it is hardly true that it presents an example of anything that could reasonably be called "collective responsibility". Indeed, one of the chief objections to letting ourselves forgo our "individual responsibility" and be carried away by mob sentiments is that the result is not "collective responsibility" but collective irresponsibility.

Collective responsibility is created where and only where people are united in democratic organisation. In that case they can engage in rational discussion and debate as to what to do as an organised body. And when they do it, it is done as a result of a collective decision arrived at as the product of the organised accumulation of a number of individual decisions. Clearly, *collective responsibility exercised through democratic organisation is not incompatible with individual responsibility.* On the contrary, *it follows from the exercise of responsibility by individuals united in an organisation.* And it is not incompatible either with "the possibility of rational reflection", but furthers it.

Marxists, therefore, who favour the development of democratic organisation, are not, as Dr. Popper alleges, seeking to replace "individual responsibility" and "personal decision" by a fictitious "collective responsibility" which only masks the tyranny of the mob or "the rule of the strong man". On the other hand, to set the one against the other, as Dr. Popper does, is in effect to seek to limit the sphere of responsibility. For the truth is that there exists a large sphere of matters of public concern for the continuous control of which no one can be held responsible unless there is organised collective responsibility.

Dr. Popper sees responsibility and decision exclusively as individual matters. Thus in public affairs certain persons, namely, those who hold offices of power, make decisions and are responsible for making them; and other persons, when there are democratic institutions, control them by casting their votes in accordance with individual "decisions concerning the desirability or otherwise of new legislation and of other institutional changes". And that is "the open society". But, we may ask, *who is responsible for the forms taken by our social relations of production?* In our present capitalist way of life, where it is open to individuals to make so many "rational decisions", no one is responsible. Of course, decisions taken by numerous individuals in the pursuit of their personal or group interests resulted in these social relations being instituted. But no individual or collective decision was ever taken to institute these kinds of social relations, in which social production is fettered by the private appropriation of the social product by owners of capital. The fact is that, as Marx pointed out, men have entered into relations of production independent of their will. The way people conduct themselves to produce and distribute their means of life has not been and in capitalist countries still is not decided upon in the light of any rational estimation of consequences. Marxism is concerned with ways and means of remedying this deplorable situation of irresponsibility in the most basic affairs of social life. Marxists work *to build organisation by means of which the conduct of social production can be collectively decided and its management collectively controlled. Only within such organisation can it become open for individuals to discuss and take rational collective decisions as to how the common social resources are to be used to meet individual needs.*

Once again, it is not liberals and individualists like Dr. Popper who advocate the extension of "rational responsibility" for all members of the human race, while Marxists oppose it. It is exactly the other way round.

When writing about institutions, Dr. Popper himself clearly recognised that, because institutions are man-made, it does not follow that anyone is responsible for the decision to make them or for decisions as to how they are altered. As he said, many "just grow". But when it comes to writing about the "open" and "closed" societies, and contrasting capitalist society as "open" with tribal society as "closed", he forgets this simple truth. For he fails to notice that a similar condition of irresponsibility as regards the most important institutions—those concerned with relations of production—continues throughout the development of social formations from tribalism or primitive communism to capitalism. In tribal society the "taboos and customs" were certainly "man-made", but because no one was consciously responsible for making or altering them the tribesmen thought of them as inescapable conditions of human life which men were bound to accept. Thus they were closed in by rules of their own making which nevertheless ruled them like an external power determining their personalities, their relations with each other and their conduct of life. When tribal society broke up as a result of the development of the forces of production people made for themselves the rules of property, of exploitation of man by man and of the division of classes. And these have ruled them just the same, and closed them in, even though (for some people at any rate) there is greater scope for personal decisions and personal responsibility.

In our capitalist society we are still ruled and closed in in the same way. Thus in social production people have to sell their labour-power, so that they have to work on tasks set for them and not on producing what they have decided to produce to meet their needs. Everyone concerned, whether worker or manager, is driven to work for the accumulation of capital. The product of labour is put into the market, so that neither whose who make it nor those who need it have overall control to ensure that what is made shall get to those who need it and that what is needed shall be made. Again, the relations which people have entered into in producing the means of life create divisions between them so that they find themselves in dispute and at enmity, and are driven to injure one another, for reasons for which they are in no way personally responsible.

In all this, where is the rational responsibility, open to all individuals to accept and exercise, for arranging social relations so as to make the most rational use of social resources? It is not open to us, and cannot be until we organise to assume it collectively.

In our society these conditions are what we accept and are used to and adapt ourselves to, as to the weather or the constitution of our bodies. So they generally seem to us "as inevitable as the rising of the sun, or the cycle of the seasons, or similar obvious regularities of nature", and as much an unalterable element of "human nature" as having a head, two arms and two legs. Hence doctors of philosophy and of science are judged to advise us wisely when they say that any radical alterations are out of the question, just as were doctors of magic in more primitive communities. They exclude human relations from the sphere of human responsibility.

The fact is that in these and other ways we are now, as men were originally in tribal society, in the grip of man-made conditions which men made for themselves independent of their will. These man-made conditions are to us like an external power for which no one can be held responsible. And this external power rules us with laws of its own, imposing on us our relations with one another, compelling us to do what we do and treat one another as we do, and determining the consequences of social actions irrespective of intentions or desires.

To talk about increasing the scope for responsibility and decision in making and altering social institutions, and in the activity of in-dividuals within these institutions, therefore, leads us to the fundamental question of how to organise "rational responsibility" for our institutions, and especially for the basic institutions of relations of production, so that rational decisions about them can be made and carried out. Great as may be the scope for the pursuit of "personal and group interests" in existing capitalist society, and for "personal decisions" and "individual responsibility" in their pursuit, our society remains *closed* in the sense that there is no organisation through which rational responsibility can be accepted and exercised for conducting the basic business of social production for satisfying human needs.

Part of Marx's great achievement was that he devoted to the conditions of "the closed society", and to their historical development, an analytical investigation more penetrating than that now deemed convenient and sufficient by Dr. Popper. He studied how men have come to make for themselves these conditions which have always closed us in, and still do. And this led to the conclusion that mankind is at last in a position where they can be overcome.

The issue posed by Marx was that of the organised working-class movement, in conscious pursuit of an interest scientifically defined and understood, taking control of political power so as to plan social production. That would mean that at last people would begin collectively to *take responsibility* for arranging the basic relations of property in means of production so as to get control over the whole process of social production and direct it to meet human needs. As Engels said in *Socialism, Utopian and Scientific*, "men's own social organisation, which has hitherto stood in opposition to them as if arbitrarily decreed by nature and history, will then become the voluntary act of men themselves". And if we adopt Dr. Popper's quite suggestive terminology, we shall conclude that this is the great step to be taken out of the "closed" into the "open" society. The production of the means of life is then controlled by collective decisions, in the making and carrying out of which individuals bear personal responsibility, as responsible members of the organisations that see to it. And the overcoming of want, of exploitation and of enmity, with the sharing and lightening of labour, brings to everyone far greater opportunities and choices for personal activity than heretofore, and therefore more personal responsibility and more freedom in personal decisions.

COMMUNISM

I. THE RATIONALITY AND PRACTICALITY OF COMMUNISM

I shall now return to the question of whether, to "plan as well as we can for security and freedom", we have to "go into the unknown".

Marx quite clearly defined where we have to go in terms of *communism*, explaining that the socialist organisation of social production which must immediately replace capitalism is only a transitional stage towards a communist society. His advice about the socialist planning of production and distribution was therefore based on the idea that this should be planned with the end in view of creating communism. The transition from socialism to communism is explained in the simplest terms by stating that it is the transition from a society ruled by the maxim "from each according to his ability, to each according to his work" to one ruled by the maxim "from each according to his ability, to each according to his need". When by the rational planned development and use of techniques there is being produced an abundance of everthing people need, the communist maxim becomes the one to adopt.

Dr. Popper's objections to communism are based on saying that it is "utopian". A communist society sounds attractive as Marx describes it but, says Dr. Popper, the thing is impossible. It is only a dream. It is the dream of returning to the primitive tribal condition of everyone working together and sharing—but with the whole human race engaged instead of only a few kinsmen, and with mechanised production to produce plenty instead of crude implements to eke out a bare living in the bush. If we try to realise such a dream, he informs us, we are in for a rude awakening. For it would involve forcibly suppressing all that "pursuit of personal or group interests" which has now become the chief engagement of citizens of "the open society". We would be back into "the closed society", but under a tyranny much worse than the old tribal "taboos, laws and customs". There would take place, "the most brutal and violent destruction of all that is human" at the hands of "the Inquisition, the Secret Police and a romanticised gangsterism" (1–OS. 200).

Dr. Popper's grounds for saying that the goal of communism is utopian are entirely political. He says that the concentration of political power required as a preliminary would necessarily be uncontrolled, and seeks to portray, in the customary language of anti-communist politics, the inevitable consequences of any such uncontrolled concentration of political power in the hands of the working-class movement. I think I have already written enough in rebuttal of his deposition that communist politics is the politics of violence and tyranny, suppressing all rights, all freedom, all democratic control, all individual responsibility and personal decision. He is mistaken in supposing that Marxism advocates or communism requires such politics. He is additionally mistaken in supposing that the argument as to whether or not communism is a practical goal is or could be primarily a political argument. Marx's reasons for putting forward the communist programme were economic. They were, in brief, that with socialised production carried on with techniques eventually capable of producing abundance of all we need, the form of social organisation eventually required will be one which permits everyone to contribute to social production to the best of his ability and derive from it the satisfaction of his needs.

Dr. Popper blames Marx for holding that economics rules politics. But yet the problems which political policy has to solve are derived from the state of the economy. Marx worked out the politics based on recognising the economic facts of our time, the politics for instituting that control and that planning of social production which is required to make the fullest social use of it. He clearly recognised the economic fact that modern production techniques are capable of development to produce abundance to satisfy human needs. That being so, what is there utopian in proposing the social aim of actually producing abundance and satisfying needs out of it? The proposal is to engineer institutions through which we can work together to satisfy needs in the way we know well they can be satisfied, instead of institutions which leave us to "go into the unknown" and accept "personal responsibility" for the inconveniences which ensue when one does not know where one is going.

The opinion that communism is nevertheless a utopia boils down to the opinion that the "pursuit of personal and group interests" which has predominated since the establishment of "the open society" precludes the practical possibility of our working together for the common benefit. It is a poor advertisement for "the open society" if that is so, and if we cannot accept "individual responsibility" and make "personal decisions" without mismanaging our economic affairs in the way they are mismanaged under capitalism. This opinion fails to take account of the issues of the class struggle under capitalism. Marx pointed out that so long as control is exercised by competing interest-groups, each bent on its own power and profit, it is indeed not only unlikely but impossible that production should be developed as it is capable of being developed to satisfy needs—but that the democratic class struggle and democratic control of power by working-class organisations, under scientific socialist political leadership, could manage it.

The fact that the working class exists as a social force opposed to capitalism, and willy-nilly pursues a class struggle disruptive of capitalism, is what makes the ending of capitalism and social advance towards communism a practical proposition in our society. For if no interest were interested in it, such an advance could not take place in a society where "pursuit of personal or group interests" predominates. The working-class interest is the class interest in capitalist society which demands the use of social production to meet social needs, whereas the other class interests interpose considerations of their own preservation against such a demand. Anyone who proposes to work for communism today must therefore join in with the working-class movement.

But so far as the goal is concerned, and the contention that the foundation of a communist order of society is the known objective to be gained in order to establish security and freedom, the case for communism is based on considerations about technology, and the communist programme is a programme for making use of modern technology. To appreciate the case for communism, and to appreciate that the revolutionary movement which aims at communism is the one which knows how to solve the problems and realise the possibilities now presented by the economic development of the forces of production, it is only necessary to employ, quite disinterestedly, "what reason we may have".

2. SOCIAL IMPLICATIONS OF MODERN TECHNIQUES

Marx based his conclusions on examining the techniques of the industrial revolution of the eighteenth and nineteenth centuries. Two definitions which he gave are of especial importance. One is that of "an instrument of labour", as "a thing, or a complex of things, which the labourer interposes between himself and the subject of his labour, and which serves as the conductor of his activity" (*Capital*, I, 7, 1). The other is the definition of "a machine": "All fully developed machinery consists of three essentially different parts, the motor mechanism, the transmitting mechanism, and finally the tool or working machine . . . The machine proper is therefore a mechanism that, after being set in motion, performs with its tools the same operations that were formerly done by the workman with similar tools" (*Capital*, I 15, 1).

In the industrial revolution machinery replaced hand tools. And while the motive power for the simplest machines is supplied by human or animal muscle-power, once machinery began to be widely introduced in industry men began to look for other motive power to drive it—and discovered it in such inventions as the steam engine, the internal combustion engine and the generation of electricity.

Marx observed that at first a manufactory contained a number of separate machines set side by side, as in a weaving factory or a sewing factory. But in various branches of industry there was soon built up "a real machinery system . . . to take the place of these independent machines". In this "the subject of labour goes through a connected series of detail processes, that are carried out by a chain of machines of various kinds, the one supplementing the other". Finally, "as soon as a machine executes, without man's help, all the movements requisite to elaborate the raw material, needing only attendance from him, we have an automatic system of machinery, and one that is susceptible of constant improvement in its details" (*ibid*). Marx concluded, in language perhaps slightly reminiscent of William Blake, that "an organised system of machines, in which motion is communicated by the transmitting mechanism from a central automation, is the most developed form of production by machinery. Here we have, in the place of the isolated machine, a mechanical monster whose body fills whole factories, and whose demon power, at first veiled under the slow and measured motions of his giant limbs, at length breaks out into the fast and furious whirl of his countless working organs."

In the machine system the role of the individual worker becomes more and more reduced to that of "attendance" on the machine. He has lost the freedom of the independent craftsman, and his own life of personal decision and responsibility is lived only outside his working hours. Even the serf who was forced to toil from dawn to dusk for the whole of his life on the same piece of land was the owner and master of his own implements of labour and did his own job in his own way. But the worker who is employed to work in a machine system is forced to match his own motions to those of the machine whose servant he has become during his working hours.

Meantime someone has to take responsibility for management and take decisions about production, and this function is separated from that of attendance on machines. The subjection of the worker to the machine, denial to the worker of all responsibility of management, and separation of management from labour have been inescapable consequences of machine production.

When the machine system began, the responsibility of management was vested in the individual capitalist who purchased machines, hired labour to work with them as he directed, and sold the product with a view to realising a profit on his capital investment. Subsequently the means of production owned by individual capitalists were taken over (as Marx saw beginning and predicted would continue) by larger and larger companies. These are, of course, purely corporate individuals—not persons of flesh and blood, and born of women, but *institutions* which people set up over themselves to regulate the social activities of producing and distributing the means of life. These corporations own and control blocks of capital and invest it, thereby increasingly monopolising whole branches of production.

As a result, individual responsibility for directing labour and managing the disposal of products is separated from individual owners of means of production just as it is from individual workmen. It falls on those who hold controlling positions in the corporate capitalist institutions, and those whom they appoint. The situation that results is one in which management of machine production remains distinct from and antagonistic to labour, and the aim of management remains that of realising the maximum profit for the corporate owner out of the sale of the product. But if the owner is a fleshless corporation, the men in control still receive the wherewithal to put on plenty of flesh.

A further and immensely far-reaching consequence of the development of machine industry was noted by Marx. This is the development of the sciences. And in this development, as he noticed, a change takes place in the role of science in relation to industry. Initially, the sciences studied the processes—mechanical, physical and chemical—employed in industry, with a view to understanding them better and formulating their laws. Inventions were rather due to the ingenuity of men engaged in industry than introduced into industry by the creative intervention of specialised scientists. But this situation changes into one in which science becomes the pacemaker, the leading agency in the development of techniques, rather than an auxiliary. This change is also a change in the structure of institutions. From independent individuals interested in studying the constitution of nature and the laws of operation of natural forces, scientists become enrolled as members and employees of great research institutions feeding know-how into social production, and these in turn are ever more closely linked with the great corporations which own the means of production and direct the processes of industry.

Marx designated scientific research as itself one of the modern forces of production, and one that makes itself more and more into the leading revolutionising force. While others were regarding (and still regard) the sciences, in abstraction from their social function, in the light of a methodology for framing hypotheses which it is interesting to verify or falsify, Marx appreciated from the outset the revolutionising role of science in relation to social production. This led him to conclude that the further development of the social forces of production, begun under capitalism, would be such as to end the need for either arduous or mindless labour, end the subjection of the worker to the machine and the separation of the tasks of labour from managerial responsibilities, and finally achieve the planned social production of abundance to satisfy human needs. These consequences, as he saw clearly enough even though not able to specify the exact forms which technological development would take, must follow from science taking the leading place among the forces of production. They are incompatible with the survival of capitalist relations of production.

The character of the scientific-technological revolution which has got under way in the second half of the twentieth century confirms Marx's forecasts and conclusions in the nineteenth century.

The principal feature of the contemporary technological revolution is the leading role of science in relation to industry. This accounts for the very rapid pace of technological progress today compared with anything experienced before throughout the whole history of mankind. Of course, though the change has been so marked during the past twenty years, this is a situation which has been developing for some time—for instance, radio technology and a lot of electrical technology, or again medical techniques, were introduced as direct results of scientific research. But now the long sequence of scientific discoveries has rather suddenly culminated in a situation where the dominant pattern is that of new techniques being fed into industry by science rather than being evolved in industry with science undertaking investigations attendant on them. This sudden change is dated, and recorded in quantitative terms, as a sharp and accelerating increase in the rate of introduction of technological innovations.

The innovations now introduced can be classified under three headings. First, there is the introduction of new types of tools, for use both in production and in research—including not only extremely ingenious and adaptable implements and gadgets of one sort and another, but new agencies (lasars, for example). Second, there is the tapping of new power sources, namely nuclear energy. Third, there is the introduction of techniques of automation and computation.

It is evident that, *provided the forms of organisation and co-operation can be established through which it can be done*, the combined use of these innovations would enable mankind as a whole to do a lot more than could be done hitherto, and to know a lot more. All these means are useful, moreover, not only for production but for research, which itself will contribute new means to production and to the activities of human beings—so that the prospect is not that of an advance followed by settling down at a new level, but of continuous sustained advance. Already, for example, people are building vehicles to take off into surrounding space and expect soon to make themselves at home on the moon. Possibly of greater practical consequence, new instrumentalities of research are penetrating the secrets of the constitution of living matter and of the formation of organisms on the earth. Evidently, there has already been created the possibility of a vastly increased production of things people need for far less expenditure of human labour-power and physical wear and tear of human bodies, which would bring to all individuals the material requisites, the time and the opportunities for indulgence in free activities on their own responsibility and decision. The age-old condition of poverty of human resources is *already* ended which made it necessary for anyone, let alone the majority of the human race, to earn a mere pittance by the sweat of his brow, or to live in an environment not thoroughly reshaped by human agency to suit his needs and tastes, or to suffer the ravages of disease or premature old age.

So far as the opening up of real possibilities is concerned, all this is what Marx predicted would happen; and it has happened. But to understand the problems of social reconstruction inherent in the process of realisation of these possibilities, we must look more closely at certain features of the contemporary technological revolution.

This revolution is not only a further development of the design and use of machines, though that is included in it. It really is *a revolution* in technology in as much as it introduces into the process of social production something new to supersede machines, just as the machines of the industrial revolution introduced something new to supersede hand-labour. This gives us grounds to conclude that it requires as great, if not greater, changes in the relations of men in the social use of the new forces of production. To think otherwise is indeed to remain blind to the implications of the technological changes going on under our eyes.

To appreciate how revolutionary the technological revolution is we must go back to definitions. The innovations comprise new or improved tools, new and greater sources of motive power, and techniques of automation. A machine, as we saw, consists of a motor transmitting motion to a tool or set of tools. Bearing this in mind, it is clear that a new element is added by the techniques of automation. These have been defined (for instance by Sir Leo Bagrit in his 1964 Reith lectures, *The Age of Automation*) as techniques of "communication, computation and control".

Of course, no social production of any sort is possible without employment of these three interrelated functions. In social production a number of people work to try to produce a product decided upon at the start of the operation. For this purpose there must be *communication* from one phase of the operation to another—so that, for example, a new job can be started when the preceding job is done, or when something goes wrong steps can be taken accordingly. There must be *computation*, so that the operations of the job can be fitted together. And there must be *control* sufficient to carry through all the motions required for the work from beginning to end.

These functions have always been performed by human agency; and they are so performed in machine production, since machines do not include any apparatus to perform them for themselves, automatically throughout, without the need for human intervention. But the techniques of automation add these functions to the performance of the material structures which men design and build for purposes of social production.

In automated production the motive force employed sets in motion a process of communication, computation and control guiding the motions of the tools to which the motion is transmitted. This is a system which replaces a machinery system, even of the most automatic kind, just as a machinery system replaced a gang of hand-labourers.

An automated system contains a fourth component added to the machine. And just as the machine system frees the productive worker from having to transmit motion to the tool by his own bodily exertions and to guide it with his hand, so does the automated system free him from the burdens of "attendance".

The very revolutionary character of the automated system, as compared with all previous material means men have constructed for the purposes of social production, is revealed by the fact that the relationship which has always been the basic one within the social forces of production, between men and their instruments of production, is changed.

According to Marx's definition, an *instrument of labour* is "a thing or complex of things which the labourer interposes between himself and the subject of his labour as the conductor of his activity". Marx stressed that the distinguishing feature of human actvity in social production is that men formulate a plan of what they want to do to the subject of their activity. Having formed a plan in their heads, men use instruments of labour for the purpose of altering the subject of labour in accordance with their plan. It is in this sense that instruments are interposed as conductors of human purposive activity. Men *set themselves a task* (or some men are set a task by others), and then *use the instruments of labour to carry it out*, as the conductors of the human activity of carrying out alterations of the environment corresponding to the tasks we set ourselves. It is in this way that men have used first very crude tools and subsequently elaborate machine systems as instruments of labour. But with a complete automated system we do not thus set *ourselves* a task and then use instruments of labour for our carrying out of the task. No, *we set a task to the system which we have designed and built to perform such a task for us, and it carries it out for us.* Automated systems are instruments of production designed to carry out the tasks we set them. And such "instruments of production" are different from the "instruments of labour" which were formerly the only known instruments of production. They supersede the instruments of labour the operative use of which entails a task set to the labourer, which the labourer must perform by his own exertions, the expenditure of his labour-power.

What we have to realise, therefore, is that the scientific-technological revolution now being begun by men is altering the part which men themselves have to play in the process of social production. Men have always been both designers and artificers of instruments of production and *labourers* who use them as instruments of labour. Now men's part is to design, build and supervise the operations of instruments of production which can operate effectively without the intervention of men as labourers equipped with instruments of labour.

3. THE COMMUNIST PROGRAMME

Hitherto mankind has been split into two antagonistic parts in the production process. On the one hand there have been the people (the majority) who had to wear themselves out wielding the tools or attending the machines. On the other hand there have been the owners and bosses who governed their fellow men and appropriated a large part of their labour. The communist programme follows from the fact that this is becoming an anchronism. For if the technological revolution is pushed on to embrace more and more of social production, there will be a new sort of work, consisting of people co-operating to design, build and supervise material systems to produce for them what they have agreed they want; and a new sort of management consisting of the co-operative arrangements people make to build these material systems and keep them in motion. The labourer who is set a task to perform with instruments of labour will become redundant, and the boss at whose behest the task is set will become redundant too.

What therefore becomes necessary is for men to agree amongst themselves on the purpose to be served by production, and co-operate to design, build and supervise the instruments which will carry out our purpose. This purpose can only be the satisfaction of human needs. To achieve it, everyone must work to the best of his ability to help with the design and maintenance of the productive system.

The guiding principle of a communist society thus turns out to be no unworldly ideal, but the statement of how human relations will have to be arranged to adapt to the uses of a very highly automated system of production. To build such a system is not a problem of building utopia, but a problem of engineering.

If, then, we care to follow Dr. Popper in importing the same word, "engineering", into the definition of problems of managing social institutions, we can conclude that the engineering involved in building a fully automated system of production sets engineering problems as regards social institutions, namely, to adapt these to the requirements of people getting on with production engineering and using the instruments of production. The problems of "social engineering" are formulated inadequately if we pose them only abstractly, as problems

of changing institutions so as to allow people "security and freedom".
For what is necessary for this security and freedom? It is to adapt the
social institutions to the system of material production. Dr. Popper and
other objectors to communism have failed to notice the fundamental
fact, that it is impossible to solve the problems of production engineering which will enable us to produce abundance for human needs
without breaking up those institutions through which one class of
men exploits the labour of another. For there is a formal contradiction
between some men setting others to work on tasks of labour to produce goods which they appropriate and sell for profit, and a production
system in which the tasks of labour are transferred to the material
instruments of production.

The fact is, that a society in which full use is made of modern
methods of production can only be a communist society. Conversely,
the full use of the productive techniques which are now being evolved
and introduced can never be achieved unless we succeed in changing
our relations of production into communist relations, unless classes
are abolished and all men co-operate on the communist principle "from
each according to his ability, to each according to his need". Hence, on
the one hand, the development of the full *economic* potential of productive techniques now depends on the *political* struggle to overcome the
capitalist rule which upholds capitalist relations of production. We shall
never succeed in carrying those techniques forward *unless* we take up
and win the political struggle for communism, with all its difficulties
and dangers. On the other hand, the *economic* fact that the greed for
capitalist profit and the competition of capitalism with socialism, as
well as of rival blocks of capital with one another, drives capitalist
managements forward to improve productive techniques will face the
masses of people more and more urgently with the necessity of *political*
action to defend themselves from the consequences of capitalist free
enterprise.

That communism is the social form necessary for the full use of
modern techniques does not imply that communism will be achieved
imply as the result of modern techniques being introduced. Far from
it, for communism can come, if it does come, only as a result of prolonged political struggles. And while the introduction of new techniques may stimulate and aid that struggle, at the same time lack of
resolution and defeat in the struggle may inhibit and in the end entirely
prevent the introduction and full use of techniques. The point is that
the goal of communism, and the ideas we can already project of how a

communist society would be practically arranged, are not dreamed up as ideals of utopia but are strictly deducible from the actual character of technological progress and the requirements for continuing it. A communist society is not utopia, but one in which relations of production and methods of distributing the social product have become adapted to the productive forces created by the contemporary scientific and technological revolution.

We can proceed to examine in more detail consequences of an advanced technology, which further define the character of a communist society (which is nothing but a society employing such technology) and differentiate it from earlier modes of production.

Products will no longer be produced as commodities for exchange. For the production complexes from which different products issue cannot exchange these products as men do, as values embodying labour, but must rather be programmed to put them into distribution according to a plan. And this plan of supply of needs will be computed like everything else in the production process in accordance with the purpose for which men have designed the production process and set it in motion. Commodity-production will therefore be entirely superseded. The mode of production in which men or groups of men produced goods by their labour and exchanged the products of labour will be superseded by a mode of production in which the products are distributed amongst men according to their needs. One rather striking consequence is, of course, that there will be no such thing as money, as the measure of value and medium of exchange.

Advanced technology likewise supersedes the division of labour amongst human beings which every invention of new instruments of labour has hitherto entailed—and of which commodity production and private property in means of production were consequences. New instruments of labour mean new jobs, and since the instrument is specially constructed for the job so must the labourer specialise in the use of that instrument. The multiplication of instruments of labour gives rise to the division of labour amongst the human beings who make and use them. In the fully automated system, on the other hand, the division of detailed and specialised functions in the operations of social production is transferred in its entirety from human beings to the material instruments of production, the various parts of which each specialises in its particular job without requiring any man to specialise in the same way. As for men, one man will not be required to specialise in turning a screw or tightening a bolt, another in adding up figures and another in the work of overall management of a production complex, but all will share the common human function of being designers, masters and beneficiaries of the instruments of social production. This does not mean, of course, that all will have to do the same things or be exactly like each other. On the contrary, the differentiation of human abilities, pursuits and enjoyments is not the same thing as division of labour in social production, and its condition is that individuals should be freed from the stultifying effects of the division of labour.

Ending the division of labour implies two specially important consequences, on which Marx laid considerable emphasis. One is the abolition of the division between town and countryside. This does not mean that all land will be covered with streets and buildings—though with new techniques of food production it may well happen that agriculture as we know it will disappear and the earth be turned into a sort of park (those who find it tame will perhaps go mountaineering on Mars or swimming in a sea of ammonia on Jupiter). It implies that the division between rural communities labouring on producing food-stuffs and raw materials, and urban ones consuming their produce, with the superior amenities concentrated in the latter, will be ended. This raises an issue among the most pressing we face in the contemporary world. It means ending the division between "underdeveloped" and "developed" nations, where the former are kept down as suppliers of food and raw materials to the latter. It means raising the productivity and welfare of all human groups to a common level. It also implies, as has often been pointed out lately, instituting rational measures of population control.

The other consequence Marx stressed is the abolition of the division between mental and manual labour. Once again, this does not mean that there will be no difference between mental and manual skills—for obviously this difference is inherent in the circumstance that people have brains and hands, and no doubt some people will always take more delight in the one than in the other. For example, there will no doubt always be a difference between, say, people who especially like doing higher mathematics and use their hands mostly to scribble symbols on bits of paper, and people who especially like painting pictures or making sculptures and use use their brains to guide their hands in producing the effects they want—though perhaps the latter will not remain ignorant of the uses of the calculus and the former be well capable of doing jobs about the house. At the risk of labouring the point, I repeat that such differences in individual pursuits and skills are not the same thing as division of labour as it has been forced on people hitherto by the development of the forces of production. What the abolition of the division of mental and manual labour means is the abolition of the division between people who act as managers and others whom they manage, and of the division between the common herd who labour with their hands and are educated for not much else, and the élite who are educated to other pursuits.

Finally, all these changes imply what Marx and Engels described as "the withering away of the state". In Engels' words, "the government of persons is replaced by the administration of things, and by the conduct of processes of production" (*Socialism, Utopian and Scientific*, Chapter 3). Managing the general affairs of society will no longer entail any exercise of coercion, to force one set of people to perform a task of labour under the orders of another, or more generally to force one set of people to compromise or subordinate their interests in what they obtain from social production in deference to the interests of another. Hence no "public force" will be required to exercise and enforce its authority over individuals and, as Engels said in *The Origin of the Family, Private Property and the State* (Chapter 9), the "whole state machinery" will be put "where it will then belong—into the museum of antiquities, next to the spinning-wheel and the bronze axe".

Naturally, there will still be social management. It will be a co-operative management, in which everyone has a say or vote, and in which what is set in train will be done in the light of thorough computation of requirements and consequences, and not blindly as at present, according to the will of one interest against another. The concurrence of individuals in what is decided will be secured by education, habit and argument, by each recognising his responsibility as a member of society, and without holding a big stick over anyone or depriving anyone of his opportunities for cultivating his individual bent. This means, incidentally, that individual responsibility will indeed become the general rule of an open society. Not only will the social organisation grant to individuals responsibility rather than making them do whatever they are told, but this individual responsibility will be the main thing on which the whole co-operative social organisation depends.

The idea that communism is a mere utopia is attributable to the fact that for a very long time there were imaginative thinkers who dreamed

of a communist society although there existed no practical possibility
of realising it. Conscious of the irrationality and brutality of people
oppressing and exploiting one another instead of co-operating for the
common welfare, they dreamed of a society in which all would
co-operate to produce social wealth, and wealth would be owned in
common and shared out according to individual needs. These imaginings have been rightly regarded as mere utopias because there was no
technological basis in prospect for the communist organisation of
society, and so nothing could be done to organise for it politically.
Communism was not a practical proposition, only an impractical
ideal. But in modern conditions it has become not only practically
possible but *necessary*. It is a practical possibility because we know how
to set about building the technological basis, and know what political
moves to make to start changing social institutions in the communist
direction. And it is necessary because *unless* we start moving towards
communism we shall be hindered from developing and using modern
technology.

But even so, many remain of opinion that communism is something
to be realised, if realised at all, so far in the future that it is unpractical
to start seriously organising for it at present. One reason for this opinion
is to be found in the contrast between the selfish modes of behaviour at
present in vogue and the socially responsible behaviour which would
have to become universal if a communist society was ever to work.
It is thought that if "human nature" is to change so much it will take a
very long time to change, and meantime we had best accept unchanging human nature for what it is and always has been.

These opinions, which those who hold them regard as realistic
facing of facts, are really based on nothing but a refusal to face facts.

As regards "human nature", it may be stated at once that we posit no
such extraordinary change as is imagined. We do not suggest that
people must change from caring only for themselves to caring for
others, for in fact most people have always cared for both. We are only
of opinion that if there is interesting work to be done people will like
doing it and want to do it if they get the chance; and that if needs can
be satisfied without people having to compete with one another to
get their satisfactions they will not go out of their way to grab things
from each other.

It is not Communists who ignore the facts of human nature, but
sceptics about communism who *ignore the fact of the very rapid pace of the
contemporary scientific-technological revolution*. This fact demands that at

our peril we do something *now* to cope with its consequences. The need for organisation for that purpose is *urgent*. And in face of this urgency, the bungling and complacency of politicians and business managers as they practise "social engineering" in the capitalist world is alarming.

If technology could be developed and put straight into full use without check, it would probably not be unrealistic to say that a condition of world communism could be established within fifty years. Allowing for plenty of time for necessary social readjustments, it would perhaps be more realistic to put the period of change-over at, say, a hundred and fifty years—which is not long on the scale of historical change, though occupying the energies of several generations. So political organisation to carry through these readjustments is not utopian politics oriented to a far-distant ideal goal, but *the practical politics of the century we live in*. The fact we have to face is not that communism is such a long-term goal as not to be worth bothering about at present, but that the actual and accelerating rate of technological change is already so impetuous that we will face the most serious social consequences if we do *not* commence the practical organisation of communism.

Technological change cannot be halted without (as Dr. Popper so eloquently puts it) destroying our civilisation. So our civilisation must be adapted to technological change. The technological revolution will within a few decades render most of the old equipment, the current layout of services, and the current ways of training, directing and deploying labour completely obsolete. Their retention will not stop the advance of technology, but it will inevitably cause greater and greater difficulty and conflict in the management of social production and distribution. Increasing mismanagement is the prospect if the bosses of corporations competing for private profit try to manage in their own way an economy which requires integration in a single plan of social production. If it is left to them we are in for worse and worse conflicts as it becomes more and more evident to the masses of working people that their affairs are being mismanaged. Worse still, there will inevitably be continuous international conflict as people in the "underdeveloped" countries grow more and more intolerant of the contrast between their poverty and the affluence and greed of those who, pretending to aid them, forcibly intervene in their affairs to hold them down. What is desperately urgent is to establish right away that measure of democratic control by informed working-class organisations which can begin the planning of production in the industrially developed countries and offer real aid to the underdeveloped.

Nearly everyone recognises that the present is a time of transition. The claim of Marxism is to have demonstrated scientifically where we are heading, and to have set out the real problems of the transition. The communist programme is the imaginative forecast of the road we must take, not because it is our inexorable fate, but because the means we are creating to produce our needs demand it. The modern working-class movement, able on the basis of scientific information to see the road clearly in imagination so as to take it in practice, can by its mass democratic organisation sweep out of office the fumbling administrators of the old order, and bring into actual existence the rational and open society which was only a dream for so many who have gone before.

5

THE TRANSITION TO COMMUNISM

I. DEMOCRATIC SOCIALIST PLANNING

If we discount his more phrenetic utterances about returning to tribalism and thence "to the beasts", Dr. Popper's chief misgivings about the communist programme arise over two points: the dangers inherent in economic planning and in attempting to control thoughts. But on these contentious points, too, his arguments can scarcely pass muster as "rational".

He objects to "planning on a very large scale", such as Communists advocate, because it "must cause considerable inconvenience to many people" (PH. 89). If this were a rational argument he must say why it must; but he does not, and merely asserts it with all the perseverance of a Conservative backbencher.

He then goes on to say that to get a plan operated the planner "must suppress unreasonable objections"—which is true enough. "But with them he must invariably suppress reasonable criticism too." In the name of reason, why should one invariably have to overrule reasonable criticism whenever unreasonable objections are overruled? It is only by entering into critical discussion, and making it as reasonable as one can, that it is possible to decide which objections are in fact unreasonable. Dr. Popper lays it down that the planner can never allow any discussion at all about the plan. In that case it is only too probable that he will "cause considerable inconvenience to many people" and his plan will come to grief. But those who seek to operate "planning on a very large scale" will, if they know their business, do exactly what Dr. Popper says they cannot do (because he says only "social engineers" who operate planning on a very small scale can do it): they will make it their business "to look out for mistakes, to find them, to bring them into the open, to analyse them, and to learn from them" (PH. 88). And to this end they will encourage "reasonable criticism" in every way they can.

Dr. Popper does, it is true, attempt to assign a reason why learning from mistakes is possible only in small-scale or "piecemeal" planning, and not in "holistic" planning "on a very large scale". He says there is a "technical" reason: "Since so much is done at a time, it is impossible to say which particular measure is responsible for any of the results" (PH. 88–9). This "technical" reason is on a par with saying that productive apparatus must never be let grow too large and complicated, for if so it will become impossible to find the cause of a breakdown. Dr. Popper should certainly have known better than that, for it is the reasoning of a man unacquainted with scientific technology. Just as very large-scale production engineering has to master the intricacies of how the many different parts of an apparatus fit together in their operations to produce the desired results, so must competent planners master the intricacies of how the many different things done at a time fit together to produce results. Indeed, the science of planning as it is being successfully developed now in socialist countries is concerned with precisely that problem. The result is not "considerable inconvenience" but lightening of labour and increase of articles of consumption.

From these very insufficient objections to "planning on a very large scale" Dr. Popper deduces what he takes to be the worst and most fatal consequences of indulgence in such planning. For this purpose he introduces a premise with which one can hardly disagree. It is "impossible", he says, "to centralise all that knowledge which is distributed over many individual minds" (PH. 89–90). So what follows? The "holistic planner", who will not listen to anyone else's advice and supresses all criticism, reasonable as well as unreasonable, denies himself access to accumulated knowledge. Therefore "he must try to simplify his problems". And refusing to let other people express themselves, he must take energetic steps to shut them up and "to control and stereotype interests and beliefs by education and propaganda. But this attempt to exercise power over minds must destroy the last possibility of finding out what people really think, for it is clearly incompatible with the free expression of thought, especially of critical thought. Ultimately, it must destroy knowledge" (PH. 90). So "planning on a very large scale" leads first to tyrannical measures of thought-control and suppression of all freedom of thought, and then to the destruction of all the human knowledge on which successful management must rely.

A less reasonable argument than this would be hard to put together. For since it is plainly impossible for a single "holistic planner" to know everything relevant to the operation of a successful plan, planning demands the widest consultation amongst all those people in whose minds relevant knowledge resides. A person responsible for planning will therefore not "simplify his problems" by shutting everyone else up, but will do his utmost to draw in the maximum number of people to help. The idea that planning on a very large scale should ever be done by a single "holistic planner", or plans be made up and dictated without consultation by an institute of "centralised power", is merely one of Dr. Popper's fantasies, with the aid of which he works himself up into a state of alarm and indignation about communism. It is obvious that large-scale planning demands a very far-flung apparatus of consultation at all levels, between economists, administrators, scientists, technicians, works managers and ordinary workers.

The fact that mistakes of over-centralisation were made in planning in the Soviet Union is no excuse for Dr. Popper's nonsense, even though he did not know at the time he was writing that these mistakes would soon be remedied. Right from the start in the Soviet Union planning was done on the basis of wide and elaborate consultation. This was the basis for a real science of planning being instituted there, and for earlier mistakes being later corrected.

But even though Dr. Popper's charges against planning must be ruled out of court (except, indeed, in the Wonderland court of his own book, where he is not only the prosecutor but the judge and jury too) there are *real* problems connected with planning, and related problems connected with the control of thoughts, which are worthy of attention.

Planning on a very large scale has become necessary because of the socialised character of modern industrial production. The fact is that Marxists are not doctrinaire busybodies who want to make everyone do as we say instead of letting them do as they please. We advocate planning because it is necessary, as a condition for managing modern production to meet human needs. But how can planning be made effective and at the same time not encroach on democratic rights and the freedom of the individual?

The reason why planning on a large scale has become necessary for the use of modern forces of production can be appreciated by comparing modern conditions of production with those that have gone before.

In primitive conditions of subsistence economy, for example, questions of planning hardly arose. People produced what they could with their primitive equipment and consumed it as they went along. Planning only came in by way of trying to preserve as much stock as possible, so as to have a chance of survival when the next season came round. Again, there could not be much planning in the commodity production of peasants and handicraftsmen, since these people could only go to the market and sell their product for whatever price was offered. Individual merchants planned to buy cheap and sell dear, but there could be no overall planning. Feudal lords planned busily but their plans took the form of conspiracies to grab each other's lands and possessions. When capitalist production appeared on the scene, large numbers of workers were collected together and set to work in industrial enterprises, and within these enterprises a great deal of planning was at once required—aimed at keeping production going, increasing it and increasing the rate of exploitation. The product was all taken to the market, just as with pre-capitalist commodity production. And it was from this circumstance that the need for some kind of overall planning of production and distribution became apparent. As Engels pointed out in *Socialism, Utopian and Scientific*, a contradiction now became manifest between the planning of production in each individual enterprise and the anarchy of production within the sphere of production and distribution as a whole.

The necessity for overall planning of modern production arises from two related conditions, both of which Marx analysed in the three volumes of *Capital*. First, production is now divided into two great departments, producing respectively means of production and goods for consumption. Unless due proportions (which are calculable mathematically) are maintained between the production of these two departments, production as a whole must suffer dislocations and interruptions. For instance, the production of consumer goods cannot be maintained or increased unless sufficient means of production are produced for the purpose. And again, if the effective demand for consumer goods is not sufficient to use up all the means of production that are being produced, then production in the department producing means of production will be interrupted because its products are not for the time being wanted. Therefore, secondly, production will suffer interruptions unless arrangements are also made so that the members of society are actually able to buy and consume all the consumer goods that are produced. Clearly, neither of these necessary conditions can be satisfied if every independent enterprise is left to plan its own production entirely at the will of its own management. There must be some sort of overall economic plan.

Throughout that phase of capitalist production known as *laissez faire* this need for overall planning was denied by capitalist managements. Their idea (worked out for them by professional economists) was that the conditions of the market would automatically bring about the necessary adjustments. For instance, if relatively too much or too little of something was being produced, the market conditions would automatically cause capital in search of profit to flow from one branch of production to another. This sort of adjustment proved in practice extremely painful and injurious, and took place only through a series of economic crises with wastage of productive equipment and unemployment. Today, when whole branches of production have come to be monopolised by very big capitalist corporations which plan their own production and marketing arrangements in a big way, the corporation managements have come to recognise the need for at least a certain amount of overall economic planning (and professional economists have duly criticised old-fashioned economic theories and worked out new ones). At the same time, the corporations consider that they can do whatever is necessary themselves, with the aid of the state over which they exercise so considerable a measure of control.

Recent experience is making plain the limitations of monopoly-capitalist economic planning. This so-called "indicative planning" is not so much planning as forecasting. On the basis of data about past and present resources forecasts are made of what would have to be produced in all the main branches of production, and how it would have to be marketed, in order to bring about a given rate of increase of total production. Government then takes various measures by way of offering incentives such as credits and tax relief to encourage the enterprises concerned to behave according to the forecast, and at the same time to gear nationalised industries and services to it. But there is no overall control to ensure that what is forecasted is done. Experience to date has shown that in no case are the forecasts of a capitalist national plan ever realised. Something always goes wrong—even though not always so rapidly as was the case with the national plan announced in 1966 by the Labour Government in Britain, which collapsed within a few months.

It might be thought, incidentally, from his strictures about "planning on a large scale", that Dr. Popper would disapprove of all such planning as altogether too "holistic". However, he professes to disapprove of *laissez faire* and to approve of capitalist overall planning on the good grounds that it is still "piecemeal social engineering" and contains so little of the element of *compulsion*. But it is in these very qualities which meet with his approval that its limitations show themselves. In the fierce market competition of so many profit-seeking enterprises it is not possible for them all to keep to plan, even if their managements intended it, and the same types of maladjustment as have always shown up in capitalist production continue to take place. Meantime the organised workers who demand that conditions of work, wages and social services shall be improved are subjected to a restraint and compulsion not applied to their employers, on the grounds that their demands will divert resources from production to consumption, render industries uncompetitive especially on export markets and prevent the national economy from paying its way. If capitalist planning increases employment it increases the incidence of industrial disputes, so that some begin to think a dose of planned unemployment would be advisable as a means of bringing industrial workers to heel.

By one of those twists of the meaning of words which are the stock-in-trade of capitalist apologetics, capitalist planning has been called "democratic". As well as never working, it suffers from the drawback of being undemocratic. For it is most emphatically not under democratic control. The job of drawing up the plan is done by experts of the corporations and the government, and its operation is left to the managements of the corporations and nationalised industries, without any exercise of democratic control apart from drawing in a few trade union officials. To say that this represents a measure of democratic control over the managements of corporations, or that it is democratic because permanent civil servants constitute key personnel, is to accept a very meagre and remote form of popular control as sufficient to qualify as "democracy". Many advocates of capitalist planning (for example, Professor Galbraith in his B.B.C. Reith lectures of 1966) now recognise this fact, and are saying that "democratic planning" is nonsense because planning is an expert business and experts should be controlled only by their fellow experts. Others, however, continue to maintain that capitalist planning is democratic because economic decisions remain voluntary, and the plan only offers guidance to the corporations and not instructions; it is thought democratic to allow individual decision of this voluntary kind and undemocratic to use compulsion. But why it is democratic to allow decisions affecting the livelihood of millions to be taken by a handful of managers exempt from democratic control, and undemocratic to ensure that what is planned for the public welfare is actually done, are two questions never answered by the champions of capitalist democracy.

The need for socialist planning is the need for planning which includes provisions to ensure the carrying out of plans, and which operates under democratic control. These things are connected. Measures to secure the democratisation of economic decisions are at the same time measures to ensure that the decisions are well planned and are carried out.

The abstract definition of "socialism" as "public ownership of the means of production and exchange" requires completion by defining the object of public ownership as *bringing the management of social production under the control of democratic organisations and planning it for the satisfaction of human needs.* On the other hand, the fear of socialist planning is the fear that if ownership of all major enterprises is taken over by the state, the state will dictate a plan to the nation and arbitrarily compel everyone to accept it and work for it, so that there will be even less democratic control than is the case under capitalist private ownership.

The spectacle of Soviet people not only bearing up under the rigours of socialist planning, but holding discussions to improve its methods and doing very well for themselves, has led many who expressed these fears to admit it has not turned out so badly as they expected. Some now try to account for this by saying there is not after all much difference between having production managed by private corporations and having it managed by state trusts. Such an assurance is calculated to have a calming effect on those who believe we must at all costs hold out in a last-ditch struggle against socialist planning, and at the same time supplies a new argument against socialists who advocate a struggle to advance from capitalism to socialism. For it is argued that if capitalism now equals management by large corporations it amounts to very much the same thing as socialism, which equals management by large state trusts.

These points were urged strongly by Professor Galbraith in his Reith Lectures. He said that the methods adopted by state trusts to plan production in the Soviet Union and by corporations to plan production in other industrial countries are becoming more and more alike. It is not true, however. The methods of planning production in the Soviet Union differ from those in capitalist countries in at least two important respects. First, *the plan is decided upon on the basis of very wide consultation amongst democratic organisations, and the managements responsible at all levels have to operate within the framework of democratically decided objectives.* Second, *there is democratic control over the carrying out of the plan*, to ensure that measures are taken to carry it out. As a result, the objective of planning in the Soviet Union is the supply of what people need and its delivery to its destination. And what is planned is actually achieved. The basis of socialist planning is democratic control by popular organisation over the production and distribution of what people need, and "public ownership" is the form within which this democratic control is effected.

Socialist planning for social welfare requires the building of a very elaborate institutional framework within which the plan is formulated and carried out. This is, of course, something entirely unlike Dr. Popper's "brave new world" fantasy of a single "holistic planner" issuing orders. There are required institutions of research and teaching, institutions of economic science, working out the theory of planning as an "exact science" employing mathematical techniques. There are required interlocked institutions for the central and regional formulation of plans, closely tied up with instituted consultation with public organisations, trade unions, works managements and so on. And institutions are required to supervise and check up on the carrying out of plans, tied up with the production institutions (factories, farms, railways, local government services, and so on) which carry out the plan. When such an institutional framework is built for planning, as it has been in the Soviet Union, it becomes evident that the idea that expert management is incompatible with democratic control is only one of the latest illusions of capitalist ideology. For in this framework are combined, on the one hand expertise, the making of economic planning into an expert business employing highly trained technicians, and on the other hand democratic control.

These considerations show what has to be done to progress from capitalist to socialist institutions in the advanced industrial countries. There can be no question of smashing up all the institutions, as Dr. Popper imagines would be done by a revolution which transfers political power to the working class. There already exists in the institutions of research and technology, in the managerial apparatus of the great corporations, and in the organisations of nationalised industries and municipal and social services the basis of the apparatus of socialist planning. The great step that has to be taken is that of *the institution of democratic control by popular organisation*, which is lacking at present. To "raise the proletariat to the position of ruling class" is, exactly as *The Communist Manifesto* said, "to win the battle of democracy".

TOWARDS AN OPEN SOCIETY

2. FROM SOCIALISM TO COMMUNISM

A major part of socialist planning must always be concerned, not directly with the production of consumer goods and services, but with the production of means of production. And where these are insufficient that department of production must take high priority if later on a greater part of consumers' needs are to be satisfied. The controlling aim is to plan the increase of production so as to meet all individual needs from it. This controlling aim implies that *all socialist planning is planning alomg the road to communism*, when such absolute abundance will be produced that "to each according to his need" will become the maxim governing the social organisation.

This, of course, is why Marxist parties generally call themselves "Communist Parties". Communism is the controlling aim of all their politics. And, incidentally, it demonstrates another big difference, and perhaps the biggest difference of all, between socialist democratic planning and the planning which already goes on in capitalist countries. The latter has certainly no aim of advancing towards communism, but presupposes the retention of social relations entirely incompatible with it, and is therefore likely to get into the worse confusion the higher the level of technological advance. At present the name "Communist" is not widely understood; but it will have to be made better understood if we are to cope with the problems which technology is setting.

Marx described socialism, in the *Critique of the Gotha Programme*, as "the first phase of communist society". It is this because already, when means of production are taken into social ownership and socialist planning is instituted, production ceases to be controlled by the profit obtainable by private owners from selling the products, and begins to be planned instead for the satisfaction of human needs. Communism is the organisation of social production to satisfy human needs. In its first imperfect or socialist phase production is not yet sufficient to satisfy all needs, and a fully communist society emerges only when this limitation has been overcome.

At the same time, socialism can be described as a transition phase between capitalism and communism, because when capitalist ownership and control is first abolished many conditions remain, carried over from capitalism, which will also have to be abolished before communism is fully instituted. As Marx put it, "what we have to deal with here is a communist society, not as if *it had developed on a basis of its own*, but on the contrary as *it emerges from capitalist society*, which is thus in every respect tainted economically, morally and intellectually with the hereditary diseases of the old society from whose womb it is emerging . . . these deficiencies are unavoidable in the first phase of communist society when it is just emerging after prolonged birthpangs from capitalist society."

The chief of "these unavoidable deficiencies" is the retention of the wages system. People enter into agreements with employing organisations (state trusts and the like) to work for so many hours for so much pay. What they receive to satisfy their needs depends therefore chiefly on their work. So far as the worker is concerned, he gets paid for his work, and receives as much as he can earn by enhancing his skills, finding jobs and working diligently—just as in capitalist society. The retention of the wages system is a social necessity because, so long as the social product is not yet sufficient to satisfy all needs as of right, the distribution of the social product cannot but be controlled by the socialist principle "from each according to his ability, to each according to his work".

Of course, this principle is never applied with full consistency and rigour. That would mean that children, old people and the sick would all have to be maintained out of individual earnings and savings; wheareas socialist governments always do their best to apply the communist principle by doing all that can be done to meet their needs out of public funds. And numerous other social services are provided, of which the enjoyment does not depend on earnings and the benefits supplement earnings. Indeed, a good deal on these lines is already done under capitalism, where social necessity reinforced by working-class demands already compels the ruling class to concur with the intro-duction of these first instalments of communism. Capitalists have, how-ever, always been grudging of social services, which they think both cost too much and sap the moral fibre of the recipients. They administer them so far as possible on a contributory insurance basis and make the wage-earners pay as much as possible of the cost. In a socialist society, on the other hand, social services are continually expanded and it is not thought desirable to run any of them as an insurance business.

The wages system, reinforced by social services, is, then, and must be carried over from capitalism to socialism. With it there are inevitably carried over many old habits and ways of thinking—habits of grabbing whatever one can for oneself at the expense of others, of caring pri-marily for one's livelihood and letting others look after their own if they can, and ways of thinking which go with these habits. Such phenomena of individual consciousness would in any case be likely to persist through inertia, since it always takes a long time for new modes of consciousness to spread amongst all individuals. But they are encouraged by the retention of the wages system. It is therefore not surprising, though disturbing, to find that in a socialist society many of the most hateful phenomena of capitalism persist, including ambitious people climbing up over the backs of their fellows, people in jobs commanding status despising those below them and expecting deference from them, and so on. A good Communist cannot lose confidence in the advance of humanity towards communism because of this, for it is only to be expected. But because it is only to be expected, he will not therefore take up an attitude of accepting and concurring in it, and still less behave like that himself.

At the same time, the wages system in socialist society differs fundamentally from that under capitalism. The chief difference does not show itself on the surface, in the make-up of the wages packet or in the procedure of passing it from the wages-clerk to the wage-earner, but only in the overall mode of development of social production. It consists in the fact that wages are no longer the price paid by the employer for the purchase of the worker's labour-power, but are the worker's entitlement, paid over to him in the form of money from the employing organisation, to receive so much in value out of the total social product in proportion to the work he has contributed. Labour-power is no longer bought and sold. And its value, that is to say, the value of the goods and services required to maintain fitness for work, no longer enters into the determination of wages. For labour-power is no longer a commodity, and wages no longer the price of that commodity. Exploitation, in the technical sense of the worker contributing unpaid labour-time as surplus value to the employer, has been ended.

It may be objected that such theoretical considerations are meaningless in human terms, since the worker will feel just as much exploited so long as he has to work too hard and gets too little for it. They are far from meaningless; for what they mean is that under socialism the amount the worker receives is not determined by a bargain with an employer who buys his labour-power at so much an hour, but by a calculation of how much of the social product is currently available to distribute as goods and services for consumption. As the social product increases, so must the workers' welfare improve. The settlement of wages is no longer an issue of class struggle. Quite literally, the workers are working for themselves, not for the profit af an employer.

It is sometimes objected too that in socialist society exploitation continues, just as under capitalism, because the workers by their labour contribute to the upkeep of a large "class of officials and bureaucrats". These are described as exploiters who direct the workers' labour and appropriate the surplus value just as capitalist exploiters do. While it is true that any system of management permits individual peculation unless something is done to stop it, it is nevertheless absurd to allege that payment of officials, administrators and managers represents a form of exploitation of the workers. Of course these people have to be paid, because they do necessary work. If some types of work are paid more than others, that may or may not be unjust, but it is not exploitation. Supporting an apparatus of management out of the values produced by productive labour is no more exploitation of labour than it is exploitation to reinvest a proportion of the values produced in the production of fresh means of production instead of distributing the entire product in consumer goods and services.

Naturally, to keep socialist production going, and to expand it, it is necessary that social labour should continually produce a surplus over and above what is currently paid out in wages, for investment in future production, for costs of management, and for provision of social services. This shows, incidentally, that the insistence in current Soviet planning methods on enterprises showing "a profit" does not represent the reintroduction of capitalism, but is an item in the efficient planning of production for welfare, which is heading straight for communism.

That socialist planning is heading for communism means that this planning progresses towards *planning the full satisfaction of needs*. Communism grows out of socialism in the course of a period of planning, the length of which must depend on the level of social production from which it started. The transition is made by gradually transferring supplies from the sphere of goods to be bought out of earnings to the sphere of free services. When social production is producing sufficient resources for the completion of that process, we have arrived. Thereafter there can be no question of paying people for their work, but only of the provision of needs as a social service to the benefits of which everyone is entitled. The wages system disappears, and with it all production of goods as commodities. Naturally, so long as people are paid wages they use their wages to buy what they can get for them

—so that all the things they need to buy are still produced as commodities. If needs are supplied and distributed as a social service, there is no more buying and selling and no more commodity production.

That does not mean, however, that there is no more personal property—that no one possess anything of his own but everything is shared. Everyone will possess a great deal *more* personal property than most people possess at present. But he *acquires it as of right* (the human right to appropriate the things one needs for personal use and enjoyment) and does not have to *buy* it. The effective enjoyment by everyone of this right depends on their having co-operated and continuing to co-operate in producing the means necessary for its enjoyment.

6

THE OPEN SOCIETY AND ITS ENEMIES

I. COMMUNISM AND ANTI-COMMUNISM

From our discussion it seems that progress towards the open society must be progress towards communism.

The way of the open society is the way of *democratic control of social management*. And whether we like it or not, *this entails class struggle*. For the class interests of exploiting classes do not harmonise with freedom and security for the rest of society. We cannot move into the open society while respecting the rights of exploiting classes, but only by infringing on them and finally doing away with them. What is necessary is for popular democratic organisations to unite in practical policies in opposition to the ruling classes. They must, in the apt phrase of the British national anthem, "confound their politics, frustrate their knavish tricks". This is the fight for the open society.

But this is the very opposite of what Dr. Popper says about the open society and its enemies. Believing that capitalism has fundamentally changed recently in such a way that exploitation, classes and class struggles are disappearing, he says that capitalism is itself the open society. So he says that the friends of the open society, who are organising to get rid of capitalism, are its enemies; and the enemies of the open society, who are organising to preserve capitalism, are its friends.

This topsy-turvy way of looking at contemporary issues is justified by Dr. Popper in *The Open Society and its Enemies* by his making out that the great fight for the open society against its enemies is a fight against certain ideas and teachings. And these ideologies at enmity with the open society are, he says, those which regard human institutions as other than man-made. They teach that institutions are not made by men to suit their purposes but decreed by God or evolved through the operations of inexorable necessity. With them go authoritarian or totalitarian views to the effect that both in public affairs and in private life everything men do should be directed by authorities placed over them, and no one should challenge authority by thinking for himself.

As typical of such ideologies he selects the views of Plato, Hegel and

Marx. But whatever may be urged on behalf of Plato and Hegel by Platonists and Hegelians (of whom not many survive), our discussion of the views of Marx has shown that Dr. Popper is much mistaken in selecting Marxism as such an ideology opposed to the open society. That beliefs of the kind he describes are indeed incompatible with progress is not in doubt. But as well as being mistaken in including the scientific ideas of Marxism among them, he is mistaken in supposing that these sorts of beliefs are the main barrier today to our advancing into the open society. If they were there would not be much to worry about, for they have long since been exploded in the minds of most thinking people.

The real ideological enemy of the open society today is everything that is included under the expression "anti-communism". And the fight for the open society is the fight against everything being done to enforce and preserve the exploitation of man by man under the cover of anti-communism. It is not so much a set theory as a passion and a prejudice entering into and perverting every expression of theory. Views may be "progressive", adopting a critical attitude towards the establishment, urging democracy, equality and freedom, and seeking ways of improving conditions for the majority of the human race—but at the same time the element of anti-communism turns them into support of the capitalist *status quo* and hostility to practical proposals to get rid of it. In that they agree with the most "reactionary" views, which are opposed to scientific ways of thinking and uphold traditional dogmas and the sanctity of old-established oppressive institutions. Nowadays there are few in authority who do not profess themselves convinced of the values of democracy and of freedom; but they profess to protect these values from the threat of communism, and for this purpose use force, tell lies, put people under orders and stamp on democratic organisation as vigorously as if they were convinced by Plato's *Laws* that democracy and freedom were evils to be suppressed.

In no doubt sincere anti-communist indignation Dr. Popper dedicated his tirade *The Poverty of Historicism* "in memory of the countless men and women of all creeds or nations or races who fell victims to the fascist and communist belief in Inexorable Laws of Historical Destiny". He couples communism with fascism, and the victims of Hitler's gaschambers with the victims of Stalin's misrule while socialism was building in the Soviet Union. Yet it was the Soviet people, advancing to communism, who dealt the death-blow to Hitler and subsequently by democratic methods put to rights the abuses of power which happened under Stalin. We should remember all those who have since fallen victims in Vietnam, in Greece, in Spain and Portugal, in many parts of Africa, Asia and Latin America to the violence and cruelty of imperialist aggression done in the name of anti-communism.

Dr. Popper denounces "tyranny". And his principle of political science, that "we need only distinguish between two forms of government, democracies and tyrannies", seems to have been formulated less as a guide to sociologists and historians in their study of the forms of state (for which purpose it is very inadequate) than as a guide for practical politics, to lead us to distinguish between capitalist democracies and communist tyrannies, and to exhort and entreat the guardians of "the free world" to oppose and ward off the latter with all their power. This principle is a rallying-cry of the defence of imperialism. Dr. Popper can, indeed, justifiably rebut any suggestion that his arguments are mere echoes of anti-communist propaganda, since *The Open Society and its Enemies* announced the strategy of the cold war even before Churchill's Fulton Speech. But for working people the issue of power is not the issue of democracy versus tyranny, but of control of power by *us* versus control of power by *them*. To take the road of the open society the latter control of power has to be overcome, and with it the deceptive use of the ideology of anti-communism.

Seen in this light, Dr. Popper's mistakes in *The Open Society and its Enemies* are indeed serious ones. What he has done is to propagate systematically and in detail the arguments of anti-communism. For this he deserves thanks (and he has in fact received them) from the enemies of the open society. But not from its friends.

2. AGAINST VIOLENCE, FOR JUST LAWS, FOR INDIVIDUAL RIGHTS

Communism is a tyranny, communism will smash up democratic institutions, communism will destroy individual freedom, communism will forbid you to think for yourself, it will place you under orders, destroy all opportunities for criticism, impose a reinforced dogmatism, turn back the advance of science, destroy culture, destroy civilisation, return us to the beasts—all this is the theory of anti-communism. It is the enemy of the open society, because on the one hand it prevents the coming together in mutual respect and understanding, and in common action, of those who want to advance out of the closed society of exploitation, violence, wasted resources, want and insecurity; and on the other hand it provides the propaganda and the justification for everything done, however tyrannical, however violent, to preserve the rule of capital. In accordance with it, Dr. Popper rests his main case that communism is the enemy of the open society on the assertion that Communists stand for violence, for the institution of a lawless tyranny and the destruction of the democratic rights of individuals.

In making these three charges he makes as many mistakes. Let us consider first the question of *violence*.

Dr. Popper confuses militancy with advocacy of violence. Marxism advocates that mass organisations of working people should not be prepared meekly to abide by instructions issued by authorities not controlled by themselves and victimising working people for the benefit of their exploiters. They should be intransigent in their opposition to any sort of control of power by the exploiting class. And they should be united in their demands for what they immediately want done, and prepared to back their leaders and those in whose hands they entrust power in getting it done. This attitude of opposition to the dictation of an exploiting minority should not be confused with an attitude of violence directed against democratic institutions.

Marxism makes no proposals for the use of violence to destroy legally established democratic institutions, where such exist. And if anyone does try to use violence to destroy democratic institutions (which has often been tried lately, and sometimes succeeded too), the Communist Party joins with other democratic organisations in their defence. For us, the question of violence can arise only as a question, on the one hand, of how to resist violent attacks on democratic institutions, on the activities of democratic organisations, and on the implementation of the decisions of democratic authorities and, on the other hand, of how to overcome violent methods of preventing democratic institutions and democratic rights being won. As Marxists have said again and again, if the ruling class resorts to violence, either to deprive people of existing democratic rights or to prevent their winning them, then violence must if necessary be used to defeat this violence. But without a doubt, the better organised, the more disciplined and the more united the democratic mass movement is, the less opportunity is there likely to be for the ruling class to resort to violence, and the less violence will be required to repel violence if it occurs.

This matter was touched on by Marx as long ago as December 8, 1880, in a letter (which Dr. Popper himself quotes) to Henry Hyndman.

In it Marx discussed the likelihood of "a revolution" in Britain, in a context which makes it clear that by "a revolution" was meant a violent uprising. "If the unavoidable evolution turn into a revolution", wrote Marx, "it would not only be the fault of the ruling classes, but also of the working class. Every pacific concession of the former has been wrung from them by 'pressure from without'. Their action kept pace with that pressure and if the latter has more and more weakened, it is only because the English working class know not how to wield their power and use their liberties, both of which they possess legally." So Marx told Hyndman that if the class struggle in Britain should ever lead to the violence of civil war, that would be the workers' fault, because "they know not how to wield their power and use their liberties". If they learned how to do so, then the "unavoidable evolution" to socialism could be completed without revolutionary violence. The current programme of the British Communist Party takes up and spells out in contemporary political terms these ideas of Marx about knowing how to wield the power of democratic organisation and make good use of democratic rights.

Dr. Popper has taken upon himself to argue that Marxists always adopt "a violent attitude" because we always declare ourselves prepared to use violence to put down violence. He freely admits that Marx himself refrained from predicting that the socialist revolution would inevitably in all circumstances be a violent one. But, he goes on, "the social revolution is an attempt by a largely united proletariat to conquer complete political power, undertaken with the firm resolution not to shrink from violence, should violence be necessary for achieving this aim, and to resist any effort of its opponents to regain political influence". And "if a man is determined to use violence in order to achieve his aims, then we may say that to all intents and purposes he adopts a violent attitude, whether or not violence is actually used in a particular case" (2–OS. 150).

So, according to Dr. Popper, Marxists always adopt "a violent attitude" because we always declare ourselves prepared to use violence to put down violence. According to him, we are men of violence because we not only propose to win and use democratic rights to get a socialist government elected, but also declare ourselves ready to use violence if anyone tries violently to deprive us of the use of democratic rights or to resist the implementation of socialist measures. Yet how could democratic rights be preserved, or any democratically decided policy be implemented, unless we were prepared to repel those who attempted by violence to prevent rights being used and policies being put into effect? Dr. Popper himself agrees that physical force is required for such purposes. We propose not to shrink from violence if it is required to defend a socialist state and the democratic organisations on which it is based, or to prevent a ruling class from prohibiting and crushing democratic organisations. We propose to disarm those who carry arms against the people, and if necessary to carry arms ourselves in order to be able to do so.

In this we assume far less of "a violent attitude" than some of those so-called democratic authorities whom Dr. Popper professes to admire so much. If he wants to condemn "a violent attitude" today (1966–67) he had better turn his attention first of all to that adopted by the President of the United States of America. The fact is that while Dr. Popper, along with other would-be friends of the open society, expresses horror at the idea that Marxists should advocate violence to defend democratic organisations from their opponents, or to get them established, he first of all forgets that it is the opponents and not those who are trying to win and use their democratic rights who necessitate this by taking up a violent attitude, and at the same time forgets to condemn the immense, iniquitous and systematic use of violence, including violence of the most cruel kind imaginable, in military campaigns to defend the rights of capital. Professed advocates of the open society often express their horror at the violence and cruelties sometimes practised by people who have been long deprived of rights and are driven to seek desperate remedies. The violence and cruelty of legally instituted authorities is excused even while it may be regretted.

Dr. Popper's real objection appears to be not against violence as such, which he admits is sometimes necessary, but against *illegal* violence. If he thinks violence should be under legal control, and so controlled as to be used only to the minimum extent necessary to win and protect democratic rights and carry through democratic policies, then we entirely agree with him. We have no wish to let loose armed bands in the streets and let them hang up on the lamp-posts anyone they do not favour. And incidentally, the last time such bands got loose was in Hungary, in 1956, when the "freedom fighters" ran amok. But we want to put down not only the *illegal* violence of fascist bands and groups of military conspirators directed against legal democratic institutions, but also all *legalised* violence for the purpose of defending profit and privilege.

Of all the threats to winning through to an open society the most menacing now is the threat of war. It comes from the fact that control over vast armed forces is vested in military organisations charged with protecting capital and capitalist profits. They are deployed to stop the liberation movements in colonial and former colonial territories from ousting capitalist control over their governments and their economies, and (as was revealed in Greece in 1967) they have plans all ready to operate to overthrow democracy at need anywhere. The chief thing in the fight for the open society is to get democratic control over the military, to combat the hysteria and "totalitarian irresponsibility of the individual" on which militarism thrives and, where the militarists are already waging war, to force them to stop. On the global scale this requires a combination of democratic resistances, the exercise of their democratic rights by those who possess them and, where necessary, the armed resistance of those against whom military violence is directed.

Second, let us consider the question of *lawless tyranny*. Dr. Popper confuses resistance to laws which perpetuate exploitation and unequal rights with wishing to settle everything by arbitrary decree uncontrolled by law.

One of the achievements of the bourgeois revolution was the establishment of "the rule of law". There is instituted a single system of law applying to everyone within the territory of the state, and an elected assembly vested with the final authority to make and change the laws. This means that the executive officers of the state, and all those who command the means of coercion, have to act within the law. They are charged to enforce the law and forbidden to break it. Their functions are defined by law, and they are liable to punishment if they try to use the force at their disposal for their own purposes regardless of law. Thus at a decisive stage of the bourgeois revolution in England, Parliament brought the Monarchy within the law by force of arms. Earlier, the bourgeoisie had supported the Tudor monarchs because they put a stop to the arbitrary violence of the barons and disbanded their private armies.

The underlying economic reason why the bourgeoisie became champions of the rule of law is clear enough. It is because this was an indispensable condition for security in the commercial development of the home market. Without it, they could never have become as prosperous and powerful as they did become. And this necessitated laws to protect the right to exploit and curtail the right to oppose it.

Marxists are opposed to exploitation, and oppose it even when the law steps in to protect it. But that, says Dr. Popper, means we want to break the rule of law and carry on without it, whereas without law there can only be anarchy or tyranny.

The law which Marxism opposes is law in so far as it has been instituted to protect the rights of exploiting classes. We are not in favour of submitting to laws which are designed to protect the security and rights of exploiters and hamper the organisation of the masses. We propose to nullify such laws. But that is not to oppose the reign of law in general. We do not propose that any individuals or any organisations should assume powers to set themselves above the law, but that through democratic institutions the law should be recast to correspond to the work of democratic organisations to recast social relations. Indeed, it is evident that the rule of law is a condition for effective democratic management. Democracy supposes instituted procedures for arriving at decisions and controlling what is done. And that supposes enforcement of law and regulation of the whole business of management by law. Without law there can be no security, no rights and no democracy. Consequently where lawless dictatorships exist, trampling on democratic rights for the benefit of a gang of exploiters, we propose establishing, or re-establishing, in their place the rule of law to protect human rights.

This may lead us to query a forcible statement written by Lenin in 1917, at the beginning of his pamphlet *The Proletarian Revolution and the Renegade Kautsky*: "The revolutionary dictatorship of the proletariat is power . . . unrestricted by any laws." Lenin's subsequent arguments made clear what he had in mind. Kautsky (anticipating Dr. Popper) had condemned the Soviet regime as a lawless tyranny because Russian workers were disregarding the old laws before they sat down to draw up new ones. "He expects us to have a constitution all complete to the very last word in a few months", Lenin wrote. ". . . When reactionary lawyers have for centuries been drawing up rules and regulations to oppress the workers, to bind the poor man hand and foot . . . oh, then bourgeois liberals and Mr. Kautsky see no tyranny. This is law and order: the ways in which the poor are to be kept down have all been thought out and written down . . . But now that the toiling and exploited classes have begun to build up a new proletarian state . . . all the scoundrelly bourgeoisie, the whole gang of bloodsuckers with Kautsky echoing them, howl about tyranny."

Strong words, no doubt. They express the fact that the task of a socialist revolution is to establish effective control of power by popular organisations and use it to suppress capitalism. In this they will not be bound by old laws which circumscribed popular rights, and if necessary will assert those rights in action before defining them in law. But that does not imply that they have not the task of constructing a legal system. On the contrary, the task remains of instituting a system of procedures of management and of law which will protect the rights and personal property of individuals, control and set limits to all powers, and *embody in institutional procedures the practice of free discussion and criticism, of settlement of disputes, of tolerance, of free research and expression, and of working together to produce for all the means and opportunities of a free life.*

This brings us to the final question about *the democratic rights of individuals.* Dr. Popper confuses resolute action in enforcing decisions with stifling democracy in popular organisations.

No one with any sense of political realities can deny that in conditions of struggle measures have to be decided and put into operation quickly and effectively. For this reason measures cannot always wait while committees deliberate and all and sundry voice their objections, but a relatively small number of responsible individuals have to be given powers of command. The word "dictator" originally denoted an officer given temporary command to deal with a situation of national emergency in the democratic Roman Republic. And it was obviously because he foresaw the need for emergency powers in order to effect the transition from capitalism to socialism that Marx (a man well-read in the classics) used the phrase "dictatorship of the proletariat" to describe a workers' government. Some Marxists nowadays try to explain that by "dictatorship" he did not mean what he said; but evidently he did.

Dr. Popper warns us that once individuals are given any dictatorial powers they are apt to hang on to them, increase them, and misuse them, in defiance of democracy. And indeed the experience of many revolutions bears out this warning. It has happened not once but several times that revolutions have thrown up dictators, these dictators have sought to preserve and increase their power by turning it against the popular organisations which gave it to them, others have then risen up to overthrow the dictator, and so on. This process is now regarded by many as an inviolable law of revolution: "the revolution devours its children". What are we to do about it? Are we for this reason to abjure any democratic efforts to force through a fundamental change of the social system? The arguments of Dr. Popper are hardly of recent birth, and had Englishmen listened to them three hundred years ago we would have continued to enjoy the benefits of the divine right of kings—just as had Russians listened to them fifty years ago they would now be labouring for the greater profit of monopoly capital.

The problem is a problem of *the democratic control of power*. For this democratic control of power in the socialist revolution there must exist *popular mass democratic organisations*—well organised, imbued with a voluntary discipline, well managed, clear about their demands and their aims. Such organisations, embracing in their membership the majority of the working people, can break the capitalist control of power and set up their own power, make it as firm and strong as circumstances require, and control it democratically.

The essential condition is that *organisations shall be organised on well-established principles of democracy*—that is to say, of the orderly conduct of discussion of business, of criticism of persons and policies, of carrying out decisions, of the election of leaders and officials, and of the responsibility of these to the organisations for carrying out the policies for which they were elected. Clearly, such democracy of organisation must not be merely inscribed in a rule-book but have become a habit, embedded in the consciousness of the masses, solidified as a result of practical experience, a law of life of all organisations.

This sort of democracy, which governs not merely the methods of appointment and dismissal of officials, but the activity of millions of citizens, is no "mere form". Without it, it is not possible for rulers, even though democratically appointed, to be subject to effective and continuous democratic control. And incidentally, this explains in what sense Marxists do "disparage" the "mere formal" democracy of general elections and representative government. Dr. Popper says these provide "the only known device by which we can try to protect ourselves against the misuse of political power". Experience shows that that is not true, since despite general elections and representative government political power is still misused, thanks to its control by capitalist organisations. The point is that there must be democratic organisation embracing the day-to-day activity of millions; and that and only that can provide effective protection against the misuse of political power, and at the same time invest in individual office-holders all the power necessary to carry through against opposition measures on behalf of the people.

Control has to be exercised through a series of links—and the only way this can be done is by the organisation of individuals in democratic organisations in which the members continually exercise their rights of discussion, criticism, hearing reports from officials and voting on policies. If the executive is controlled from below by such organisations, then the organised individuals do, each of them, exercise a real and not merely an occasional and nominal control over the executive. Rulers are held continually responsible to the organisations that entrusted them with power. Each individual then exercises a real individual control through the rights he possesses as a member of an organisation.

To sum up. Marxism proposes organised mass opposition to ruling-class violence; it proposes opposition to laws which exist to protect the privileges of the ruling class and the institution of a system of law to protect the rights of the common people; and it proposes the firm control of political power by mass organisations so as to eradicate capitalism and advance on the road to communism. These are the practical proposals of the fight for an open society. On the other hand, policies of using violence—military violence and police violence, legalised violence and illegal violence—to enforce the interests of exploiting classes; policies to make laws and enforce them to protect the exploiting classes; and policies to keep political power out of the control of the organised masses—these are the policies of the open society's enemies.

3.   THE RATIONALIST BELIEF IN REASON

But effective action towards the open society is only possible, so Dr. Popper repeatedly informs us, on the basis of reason or reasonableness. In other words, it has to be decided on as the outcome of argument and criticism, of looking for and sifting evidence, of reckoning up consequences and testing opinions by experience.

Reasonableness, he continues, brings people together. For it enables them to test their premises, draw valid conclusions and concert their efforts. Where they disagree it enables them to argue it out, and to reach agreement by assisting each other in discovering mistakes. But this is exactly what Marxists, with their doctrines of class war, refuse to do. They refuse to try to reach agreement with "the class enemy". Hence they decline reasonable discussion about differences, resent criticism, ignore evidence which conflicts with what they have decided must be true, are reckless of consequences, and believe blindly. And this is sheer irrationalism.

Dr. Popper, like many others, finds himself in a contradiction when he reasons about reason and the need for reasonableness. On the one hand he is all for reasonableness and says how unreasonable Marxists are in proposing to do away with capitalism. But on the other hand, he declines to reason about what changes in conditions must be brought about before counsels of reasonableness can prevail. He is caught in the same dilemma as advocates of reasonableness have always been. On the one hand, affairs will never go well until reasonableness prevails over the clamour of competing interests. On the other hand reasonableness cannot prevail unless people are reasonable, which competing interests prevent. The difficulty was brought out long ago by David Hume (that very reasonable philosopher) in his studies "of human nature". Men, he said, are moved by interest and passion, not by reason. And so at the same time as he recommended what he concluded to be a reasonable attitude in life, he concluded from this same reasoning that the majority of men would never adopt it. In the same way Dr. Popper exhorts us to be reasonable. But from the way things go there is no prospect in sight of building a rational society.

However, the feebleness of the encouragement offered by Dr. Popper's rationalism is compensated by the vigour of his denunciation of the irrationalism of Marxists. Rationalism, he tells us, "is an attitude of readiness to listen to critical arguments and to learn from experience" (2-OS. 225). But Marxism discourages the whole attitude of listening and learning. According to "Marx's historical philosophy" the course of social development can be decided only by "the chosen class, the instrument of the creation of a classless society, and at the same time, the class destined to inherit the earth". This, says Dr. Popper, is on a par with "the historical philosophy of racialism or fascism" according to which "the chosen race" is "the instrument of destiny" (1-OS. 9-10). Marx, he concedes, was in spirit and intention "a rationalist . . . But his doctrine that our opinions are determined by class interests hastened the decline of this belief. . . . Marx's doctrine tended to undermine the rationalist belief in reason. Thus threatened both from the right and from the left, a rationalist attitude to social and economic questions could hardly resist when historicist prophecy and oracular irrationalism made a frontal attack on it" (2-OS. 224).

So, it seems, Marxists join with racialists and fascists "to undermine the rationalist belief in reason". And they do this by their "doctrine that our opinions are determined by class interests".

If this "doctrine" is supposed to imply (as Dr. Popper seems to think) that class interests and class interests alone determine all the opinions of every individual, then obviously the doctrine is false, and as obviously it would "tend to undermine the rationalist belief in reason". But Marx never propounded any such doctrine. Indeed, he never propounded any "doctrine" whatever about this matter. He investigated in concrete cases the influence of class interests in processes of opinion-formation, and on the basis of these investigations he concluded that in class-divided societies class interest is a constant determining factor in opinion-formation. His whole approach to the question was scientific.

The way in which class interest determines opinion is to be traced, not in the first place in *individual* processes of opinion-formation, but rather in the *aggregate* of opinion-forming and opinion-expressing interactions of individuals in a society divided into classes. There is (as Marx discovered, but he is not alone in remarking on it) a very close connection, always observable in the aggregate though often not in the case of single individuals, between economic or class interest and mental interest. The ambiguity in the word "interest" is significant here. Class interests have the effect of making people interested in certain themes, certain problems, about which it becomes important, from the point of view of class interest, that opinions should be formed. Simultaneously they have the effect of creating what may be termed blind-spots in opinion-formation: certain ranges of experience are ignored, certain questions are simply not asked, and this kind of opinion-censorship is sustained by the indignation (or in certain instances it may be the indifference) with which any opinions tending to trespass on blind-spots are received. Again, class interests lead to unquestioned assumptions being made both in factual judgments and in value judgments. In general, *whatever class is dominant, or specially active in furtherance of its interests, its interests will receive reflection in major directions of interest and of opinion-formation in society at the time.*

These and many other effects of class interest on aggregate opinion-formation cannot but have a very pronounced influence on the opinions formed by all individuals in society. The starting point for all individual interest (that is to say, mental interest) and opinion is the aggregate of interest and opinion which the individual finds current in society, towards which he has to orient himself. So his interests will take their direction from class interests (but not necessarily exclusively those of the class into which he himself is born), and his opinions will tend to be for or against class-determined opinions, and so inescapably bear a class as well as an individual character. When individuals of exceptional mental ability and originality elaborate opinions, they tend to serve the interests of one or another class. When they question received opinions, their very questioning tends to aid one class interest or another. Or if the individual's opinions break right away from any class interest (in both senses of "interest"), then he becomes an isolated eccentric in his society, and he and his opinions suffer accordingly. And this is to say nothing of the upbringing and education which individuals receive, which cannot but play a determining part in their opinions, and in which all manner of class-determined interests, blind spots and assumptions are put into their heads.

Such being roughly the facts, it follows that Dr. Popper assumes without reason that no opinions determined by class interest can at the same time be reasonable. For there is no reason why class interest should always and necessarily preclude "an attitude of readiness to listen to critical arguments and to learn from experience". On the contrary, on many topics class interest may demand the formation of reasonable opinions—namely, on those topics in which the class interest is better served by truth than by illusions.

So far from Marx's scientific conclusions about the way class interests determine opinions undermining "the rationalist belief in reason", they provide the clue to understanding at long last *the practical means by which an attitude of reasonableness can be made to prevail.* To promote "a rationalist attitude to social and economic questions" does not demand pitting "reason", as some kind of ideal force free from such mundane influences as class interest, against the irrationality of class interest. It does not demand that a few rationalists who have managed to overcome in their thinking every influence of circumstances should somehow manage to get the ear of the swinish multitude and teach them too to think disinterestedly. These are the contradictions of "rationalism" which have caused so many in the past and present to conclude that reasonableness is an ideal incapable of realisation. No, *to work for reasonableness to prevail is to work for the victory of that class interest which is served by reasonableness.*

Recently the French Marxist, Louis Althusser, has presented us with a definition of "ideology" which distinguishes it sharply (as class-determined opinion) from science. "There is no question here of giving a profound definition of ideology," he writes. "It suffices to say very schematically that an ideology is a system (possessing its own logical consistency) of representations (images, myths, ideas or concepts as the case may be) endowed with an existence and an historical role within a given society . . . ideology as a system of representations is distinguished from science in that with it the practical-social function outweighs the theoretical function (or the function of yielding knowledge)" (*Pour Marx*, Paris 1966, 238)

Here is a case of a Marxist engaging in that very habit of setting up abstract antitheses against which the Marxist dialectic is directed (so Althusser is right to call it "very schematic"). Of course, if one contrasts, say, the "system of representations" of the constitution of the material world which was current in medieval society with the conceptions of nature current today, one can contrast the former as "feudal ideology" with the latter as science. However, the reason why scientific conceptions of nature ousted feudal ideology was that the development of capitalism demanded and encouraged a scientific approach to the knowledge of nature. Industry could not use images or myths, and it could not develop without scientific ideas or concepts. So far as nature is concerned, the "representations endowed with an existence and an historical role" within bourgeois society are scientific. This has been forwarded by the interest (in both senses of the word) of the capitalist class. It is not due to the "practical-social function" having ceased to outweigh the "theoretical function", or to demands for winning knowledge having contrived to outweigh the demands of practice. It is due to circumstances in which the practical-social function could only be served by genuine scientific inquiry. So in this department bourgeois ideology is scientific—and reasonable. It is a great mistake to set up *science* in abstract antithesis to *ideology*. *Under definite circumstances ideology can only be developed to satisfy its practical social function by the adoption of the methods of science.* And if that were not so, it would be a kind of miracle that the methods of science, and the attitude of reasonableness in the formation of opinions, should ever begin, let alone come out on top.

So far as class interests are concerned in the circumstances of the present day, it is quite clear that the class interests of the capitalist class, and the sorts of ideologies which its social dominance promotes, do not preclude "an attitude of readiness to listen to critical arguments and to learn from experience" in many matters. In these matters they favour reasonableness and scientific thinking, as a result of which these good things have made some progress in capitalist societies. This applies particularly in the development of science and technology; and it also applies, though with rather definite limitations, in what Dr. Popper calls "social engineering" and, in more theoretical matters, in the discussion of a number of problems of philosophy, morals, aesthetics, and so forth. But when it comes, theoretically to basic questions about human relations and the development of society, and practically, to the management of social production, the conduct of class struggle, the control of state power and the framing of political policies—there the attitude of reasonableness, the readiness to follow through and act on the conclusions of scientific inquiry, the readiness to listen to critical arguments and to learn from experience ceases. What takes over is irrational prejudice, preconceived opinion, refusal of critical questioning, sophistry, blindness, recklessness of conse- quences, refusal to face facts and unreasoning indignation against anyone who draws attention to them.

In all these vital matters it is the working-class interest, and that alone, which demands reasonableness and the aid of science. Not to preserve the exploitation of man by man, but to fight to end it, and to arrive at policies to guide the movement to do this effectively, *demands nothing in ideology except what can be concluded from a scientific view of the human situation tempered and developed by critical argument and the tests of experience.*

Hence if today the voice of reason has a better prospect of ampli- fication and of making itself heard than "the voice of one crying in the wilderness" as of old, this is because it is not, as rationalists have imagined, the accuser against every interest but, on the contrary, the true voice of the interest of the working men. Whether recognised by them or not, the working classes are interested in the cultivation of reasonableness in all ideas, in all dealings, in all practical policies. Anything else injures them. And so reasonableness has the prospect of growth out of the soil of class interest. And intellectuals who are concerned to arrive at a rational outlook find a common language with workers, but can find it with no other class.

Rationalists have posed the question: how can reasonableness be made to prevail in human affairs? To answer it they must themselves cultivate a rational and scientific approach to social questions. And for that they must stop trying to refute Marxism, and join with Marxism in opposition to the ideas of the exploiting classes. Then the answer appears. *It is in the struggle of working people against exploitation that reasonableness can find support, and out of it reasonableness can in the end prevail.* This is where it grows, so help it grow there. And oppose everything that throttles it, whether from outside the movement or from inside.

It follows that reasonableness is not (as Dr. Popper and many others appear to suggest) the same thing as universal tolerance, nor as non-violence, nor as the reconciliation of all interests. *It is not the counsel of reason that where incompatible interests exist a way should always be sought to reconcile them all.* On the contrary, where they conflict one must always in practice be subordinate to another (as those who in capitalist countries counsel reconciliation counsel the subordination of the working-class to the capitalist interest), and *what is reasonable is to subordinate the interest which opposes human progress to that which promotes it.* It is not the counsel of reason to tolerate the blocking of progress by organised vested interests, nor to refuse to use physical force to overcome physical force.

Our century has been called "the century of the common man". This is because of the growth of democratic institutions and democratic organisation. The "common man" has no interest in exploiting his fellows, and still less in fighting with them over economic issues, territorial claims or ideological differences. If contrary to all reason exploitation and enmity continue, this is not because of the inherent unreasonableness of the common man but because of the interested irrationality of administrators, legislators, leaders and rulers. Our trouble is not in the irrationality of the common man but in the institutions which set men at loggerheads and place over us the rulers we have still got. The reasonable ideology we must have in order to end these conditions is one which subjects them to rational criticism so as to show how institutions must be changed by us, and rulers and policies brought under control. Its principles are those of science and reason, its development comes through critical questioning and learning from experience, it unites people in rational opposition to the clamours and incitements of divisive ideologies, it relies on the totality of scientific ways of thinking and promulgates not "doctrines" but a well-tested method of practical thinking.

INDEX

WORKS BY MARX, ENGELS AND LENIN,
CITED IN CORNFORTH,

THE OPEN PHILOSOPHY AND THE OPEN SOCIETY,

AVAILABLE IN INTERNATIONAL PUBLISHERS EDITIONS

MARX. *Capital,* 1967. Volume 1: "The Process of Capitalist Production"; Volume 2: "The Process of Circulation of Capital"; Volume 3: "The Process of Capitalist Production as a Whole".
—— *Critique of the Gotha Programme,* 1938.
—— *The Eighteenth Brumaire of Louis Bonaparte,* 1963.
—— *Pre-Capitalist Economic Formations,* 1965.
—— "Preface to Critique of Political Economy", in Marx and Engels, *Selected Works,* 1 vol., 1968.
—— *Theories of Surplus Value: Selections,* Eds. G. A. Bonner and Emile Burns, 1952.
—— "Theses on Feuerbach", in Engels, *Ludwig Feuerbach,* 1941.
—— *Wage-Labor and Capital,* 1933.

ENGELS. *Anti-Duhring,* 1966.
—— *Dialectics of Nature,* 1940.
—— *Ludwig Feuerbach,* 1941.
—— *The Origin of the Family, Private Property and the State,* 1942.
—— *Socialism: Utopian and Scientific,* 1935.

MARX AND ENGELS. *The German Ideology,* 1947.
—— *Selected Correspondence,* 1846–1895, 1942.

LENIN. "Karl Marx", in Lenin, *The Teachings of Karl Marx,* 1964.
—— *"Left-Wing" Communism, An Infantile Disorder,* 1940.
—— *Materialism and Empirio-Criticism,* 1927.
—— *What Is to be Done?* 1929.
—— *The Proletarian Revolution and Renegade Kautsky,* 1934.